# Children's
# Literature
# Review

# Guide to Gale Literary Criticism Series

| For criticism on | Consult these Gale series |
| --- | --- |
| Authors now living or who died after December 31, 1959 | *CONTEMPORARY LITERARY CRITICISM (CLC)* |
| Authors who died between 1900 and 1959 | *TWENTIETH-CENTURY LITERARY CRITICISM (TCLC)* |
| Authors who died between 1800 and 1899 | *NINETEENTH-CENTURY LITERATURE CRITICISM (NCLC)* |
| Authors who died between 1400 and 1799 | *LITERATURE CRITICISM FROM 1400 TO 1800 (LC)*<br><br>*SHAKESPEAREAN CRITICISM (SC)* |
| Authors who died before 1400 | *CLASSICAL AND MEDIEVAL LITERATURE CRITICISM (CMLC)* |
| Black writers of the past two hundred years | *BLACK LITERATURE CRITICISM (BLC)* |
| Authors of books for children and young adults | *CHILDREN'S LITERATURE REVIEW (CLR)* |
| Dramatists | *DRAMA CRITICISM (DC)* |
| Hispanic writers of the late nineteenth and twentieth centuries | *HISPANIC LITERATURE CRITICISM (HLC)* |
| Native North American writers and orators of the eighteenth, nineteenth, and twentieth centuries | *NATIVE NORTH AMERICAN LITERATURE (NNAL)* |
| Poets | *POETRY CRITICISM (PC)* |
| Short story writers | *SHORT STORY CRITICISM (SSC)* |
| Major authors from the Renaissance to the present | *WORLD LITERATURE CRITICISM, 1500 TO THE PRESENT (WLC)* |

ISSN 0362-4145

volume 42

# Children's Literature Review

Excerpts from Reviews,
Criticism, and Commentary
on Books for Children
and Young People

**Diane Telgen**
**Linda R. Andres**
Editors

GALE

DETROIT · NEW YORK · TORONTO · LONDON

## STAFF

Diane Telgen and Linda R. Andres, *Editors*

Shelly Andrews, Joanna Brod, Sheryl Ciccarelli, Alan Hedblad, Kevin S. Hile, Motoko Huthwaite, Paul Loeber, Sean McCready, Thomas F. McMahon, Gerard J. Senick, Kathleen L. Witman, *Contributing Editors*

Marilyn Allen, *Assistant Editor*

Joyce Nakamura, *Managing Editor*

Marlene S. Hurst, *Permissions Manager*
Margaret A. Chamberlain, Maria Franklin, Kimberly F. Smilay, *Permissions Specialists*
Diane Cooper, Edna Hedblad, Michele Lonoconus, Maureen Puhl, Shalice Shah, *Permissions Associates*
Sarah Chesney, Jeffrey Hermann, *Permissions Assistants*

Victoria B. Cariappa, *Research Manager*
Cheryl L. Warnock, *Project Coordinator*
Jennifer Lund, *Research Specialist*
Alicia Noel Biggers, Laura C. Bissey, Michelle Lee, Tamara C. Nott, Michele Pica, Tracie Richardson, Norma Sawaya, *Research Associates*

Mary Beth Trimper, *Production Director*
Deborah Milliken, *Production Assistant*

Sherrell Hobbs, *Macintosh Artist*
Randy Bassett, *Image Database Supervisor*
Robert Duncan, Mikal Ansari, *Imaging Specialists*
Pamela A. Reed, *Photography Coordinator*

♾™ This book is printed on acid-free paper that meets the minimum requirements of American National Standard for Information Sciences—Permanence Paper for Printed Library Materials, ANSI Z39.48-1984.

Library of Congress Catalog Card Number 76-643301
ISBN 0-8103-9985-7
ISSN 0362-4145
Printed in the United States of America

10 9 8 7 6 5 4 3 2 1

# Contents

Preface   vii
Acknowledgments   xi

# Preface

Literature for children and young adults has evolved into both a respected branch of creative writing and a successful industry. Currently, books for young readers are considered among the most popular segments of publishing. Criticism of juvenile literature is instrumental in recording the literary or artistic development of the creators of children's books as well as the trends and controversies that result from changing values or attitudes about young people and their literature. Designed to provide a permanent, accessible record of this ongoing scholarship, *Children's Literature Review (CLR)* presents parents, teachers, and librarians—those responsible for bringing children and books together—with the opportunity to make informed choices when selecting reading materials for the young. In addition, *CLR* provides researchers of children's literature with easy access to a wide variety of critical information from English-language sources in the field. Users will find balanced overviews of the careers of the authors and illustrators of the books that children and young adults are reading; these entries, which contain excerpts from published criticism in books and periodicals, assist users by sparking ideas for papers and assignments and suggesting supplementary and classroom reading. Ann L. Kalkhoff, president and editor of *Children's Book Review Service Inc.,* writes that "*CLR* has filled a gap in the field of children's books, and it is one series that will never lose its validity or importance."

## Scope of the Series

Each volume of *CLR* profiles the careers of a selection of authors and illustrators of books for children and young adults from preschool through high school. Author lists in each volume reflect:

- an international scope.

- representation of authors of all eras.

- the variety of genres covered by children's and/or YA literature: picture books, fiction, nonfiction, poetry, folklore, and drama.

Although the focus of the series is on authors new to *CLR*, entries will be updated as the need arises.

## Organization of This Book

An entry consists of the following elements: author heading, author portrait, author introduction, excerpts of criticism (each preceded by a bibliographical citation), and illustrations, when available.

- The **Author Heading** consists of the author's name followed by birth and death dates. The portion of the name outside the parentheses denotes the form under which the author is most frequently published. If the majority of the author's works for children were written under a pseudonym, the pseudonym will be listed in the author heading and the real name given on the first line of the author introduction. Also located at the beginning of the introduction are any other pseudonyms used by the author in writing for children and any name variations, including transliterated forms for authors whose languages use nonroman alphabets. Uncertainty as to a birth or death date is indicated by question marks.

- An **Author Portrait** is included when available.

- The **Author Introduction** contains information designed to introduce an author to *CLR* users by presenting an overview of the author's themes and styles, biographical facts that relate to the author's literary career or critical responses to the author's works, and information about major awards and prizes the author has received. The introduction begins by identifying the nationality of the author and by listing the genres in which s/he has written for children and young adults. Introductions also list a group of representative titles for which the author or illustrator being profiled is best known; this section, which begins with the words "major works include," follows the genre line of the introduction. For seminal figures, a listing of major works about the author follows when appropriate, highlighting important biographies about the author or illustrator that are not excerpted in the entry. The centered heading "Introduction" announces the body of the text.

- **Criticism** is located in three sections: **Author's Commentary** (when available), **General Commentary** (when available), and **Title Commentary** (commentary on specific titles).

  - The **Author's Commentary** presents background material written by the author or by an interviewer. This commentary may cover a specific work or several works. Author's commentary on more than one work appears after the author introduction, while commentary on an individual book follows the title entry heading.

  - The **General Commentary** consists of critical excerpts that consider more than one work by the author or illustrator being profiled. General commentary is preceded by the critic's name in boldface type or, in the case of unsigned criticism, by the title of the journal. *CLR* also features entries that emphasize general criticism on the oeuvre of an author or illustrator. When appropriate, a selection of reviews is included to supplement the general commentary.

  - The **Title Commentary** begins with the title entry headings, which precede the criticism on a title and cite publication information on the work being reviewed. Title headings list the title of the work as it appeared in its first English-language edition. The first English-language publication date of each work (unless otherwise noted) is listed in parentheses following the title. Differing U.S. and British titles follow the publication date within the parentheses. When a work is written by an individual other than the one being profiled, as is the case when illustrators are featured, the parenthetical material following the title cites the author of the work before listing its publication date.

    Entries in each title commentary section consist of critical excerpts on the author's individual works, arranged chronologically by publication date. The entries generally contain two to seven reviews per title, depending on the stature of the book and the amount of criticism it has generated. The editors select titles that reflect the entire scope of the author's literary contribution, covering each genre and subject. An effort is made to reprint criticism that represents the full range of each title's reception, from the year of its initial publication to current assessments. Thus, the reader is provided with a record of the author's critical history. Publication information (such as publisher names and book prices) and parenthetical numerical references (such as footnotes or page and line references to specific editions of works) have been deleted at the discretion of the editors to provide smoother reading of the text.

- Centered headings introduce each section, in which criticism is arranged chronologically; beginning with Volume 35, each excerpt is preceded by a boldface source heading for easier access by readers. Within the text, titles by authors being profiled are also highlighted in boldface type.

- Selected excerpts are preceded by **Explanatory Annotations,** which provide information on the critic or work of criticism to enhance the reader's understanding of the excerpt.

- A complete **Bibliographical Citation** designed to facilitate the location of the original book or article precedes each piece of criticism.

- Numerous **Illustrations** are featured in *CLR*. For entries on illustrators, an effort has been made to include illustrations that reflect the characteristics discussed in the criticism. Entries on authors who do not illustrate their own works may also include photographs and other illustrative material pertinent to their careers.

## Special Features: Entries on Illustrators

Entries on authors who are also illustrators will occasionally feature commentary on selected works illustrated but not written by the author being profiled. These works are strongly associated with the illustrator and have received critical acclaim for their art. By including critical comment on works of this type, the editors wish to provide a more complete representation of the artist's career. Criticism on these works has been chosen to stress artistic, rather than literary, contributions. Title entry headings for works illustrated by the author being profiled are arranged chronologically within the entry by date of publication and include notes identifying the author of the illustrated work. In order to provide easier access for users, all titles illustrated by the subject of the entry are boldfaced.

*CLR* also includes entries on prominent illustrators who have contributed to the field of children's literature. These entries are designed to represent the development of the illustrator as an artist rather than as a literary stylist. The illustrator's section is organized like that of an author, with two exceptions: the introduction presents an overview of the illustrator's styles and techniques rather than outlining his or her literary background, and the commentary written by the illustrator on his or her works is called "illustrator's commentary" rather than "author's commentary." All titles of books containing illustrations by the artist being profiled are highlighted in boldface type.

## Other Features: Acknowledgments, Indexes

- The **Acknowledgments** section, which immediately follows the preface, lists the sources from which material has been reprinted in the volume. It does not, however, list every book or periodical consulted for the volume.

- The **Cumulative Index to Authors** lists all of the authors who have appeared in *CLR* with cross-references to the biographical, autobiographical, and literary criticism series published by Gale Research. A full listing of the series titles appears before the first page of the indexes of this volume.

- The **Cumulative Index to Nationalities** lists authors alphabetically under their respective nationalities. Author names are followed by the volume number(s) in which they appear.

- The **Cumulative Index to Titles** lists titles covered in *CLR* followed by the volume and page number where criticism begins.

## A Note to the Reader

*CLR* is one of several critical references sources in the Literature Criticism Series published by Gale Research. When writing papers, students who quote directly from any volume in the Literature Criticism

Series may use the following general forms to footnote reprinted criticism. The first example pertains to material drawn from periodicals, the second to material reprinted from books.

[1]T. S. Eliot, "John Donne," *The Nation and the Athenaeum,* 33 (9 June 1923), 321-32; excerpted and reprinted in *Literature Criticism from 1400 to 1800,* Vol. 10, ed. James E. Person, Jr. (Detroit: Gale Research, 1989), pp. 28-9.

[1]Henry Brooke, *Leslie Brooke and Johnny Crow* (Frederick Warne, 1982); excerpted and reprinted in *Children's Literature Review,* Vol. 20, ed. Gerard J. Senick (Detroit: Gale Research, 1990), p. 47.

# Suggestions Are Welcome

In response to various suggestions, several features have been added to *CLR* since the beginning of the series, including author entries on retellers of traditional literature as well as those who have been the first to record oral tales and other folklore; entries on prominent illustrators featuring commentary on their styles and techniques; entries on authors whose works are considered controversial; occasional entries devoted to criticism on a single work or a series of works; sections in author introductions that list major works by and about the author or illustrator being profiled; explanatory notes that provide information on the critic or work of criticism to enhance the usefulness of the excerpt; more extensive illustrative material, such as holographs of manuscript pages and photographs of people and places pertinent to the careers of the authors and artists; a cumulative nationality index for easy access to authors by nationality; and occasional guest essays written specifically for *CLR* by prominent critics on subjects of their choice.

Readers who wish to suggest authors to appear in future volumes, or who have other suggestions, are cordially invited to contact the editor. By mail: Editor, *Children's Literature Review,* Gale Research, 835 Penobscot Bldg., 645 Griswold St., Detroit, MI 48226-4094; by telephone: (800) 347-GALE; by fax: (313) 961-6599; by E-mail: CYA@Gale.com@Galesmtp.

# Acknowledgments

The editors wish to thank the copyright holders of the excerpted criticism included in this volume and the permissions managers of many book and magazine publishing companies for assisting us in securing reprint rights. We are also grateful to the staffs of the Detroit Public Library, the Library of Congress, the University of Detroit Mercy Library, Wayne State University Purdy/Kresge Library Complex, and the University of Michigan Libraries for making their resources available to us. Following is a list of the copyright holders who have granted us permission to reprint material in this volume of **CLR.** Every effort has been made to trace copyright, but if omissions have been made, please let us know.

**COPYRIGHTED EXCERPTS IN *CLR,* VOLUME 42, WERE REPRINTED FROM THE FOLLOWING PERIODICALS:**

*Appraisal: Science Books for Young People,* v. 20, Fall, 1987. Copyright © 1987 by the Children's Science Book Review Committee. Reproduced by permission.—*The Atlantic Monthly,* v. 190, December, 1952 for a review of "A Hole Is to Dig: A First Book of First Definitions" by Margaret Ford Kieran; v. 102, December, 1953 for a review of "A Very Special House" by Margaret Ford Kieran. Copyright 1952, renewed 1980; copyright 1953, renewed 1981 by The Atlantic Monthly Company, Boston, MA. Both reproduced by permission of the author./ v. 184, December, 1949 for a review of "The Happy Day" by Jane Cobb Berry and Helen Dore Boylston. Copyright 1949, renewed 1977 by The Atlantic Monthly Company, Boston, MA. Reproduced by permission of Jane Cobb Berry and the Literary Estate of Helen Dore Boylston.—*Australian Book Review,* n. 136, November, 1991 for a review of "No Such Country" by Meg Sorensen. Reproduced by permission of the author.—*The Book Report,* v. 12, September-October, 1993. © copyright 1993 by Linworth Publishing, Inc., Worthington, Ohio. Reproduced by permission.—*Booklist,* v. 56, June 15, 1960; v. 65, September 15, 1968; v. 65, April 1, 1969; v. 67, September 1, 1970; v. 70, November 15, 1973; v. 70, May 15, 1974; v. 73, October 15, 1976; v. 74, July 15, 1978; v. 75, May 15, 1979; v. 76, September 1, 1979; v. 76, October 15, 1979; v. 77, September 15, 1980; v. 78, October 15, 1981; v. 79, October 1, 1982; v. 81, April 1, 1985; v. 83, April 15, 1987; v. 84, May 15, 1988; v. 84, July, 1988; v. 85, April 1, 1989; v. 86, March 1, 1990; v. 86, April 15, 1990; v. 87, September 1, 1990; v. 87, January 15, 1991; v. 87, April 1, 1991; v. 87, April 15, 1991; v. 88, October 15, 1991; v. 88, December 15, 1991; v. 88, January 15, 1992; v. 88, May 1, 1992; v. 89, January 1, 1993; v. 89, June 1 & 15, 1993; v. 90, January 15, 1994; v. 90, February 15, 1994; v. 90, May 1, 1994; v. 91, September 15, 1994; v. 91, November 15, 1994; v. 91, December 15, 1994; v. 91, February 1, 1995; v. 91, May 1, 1995; v. 92, September 15, 1995. Copyright © 1960, 1968, 1969, 1970, 1973, 1974, 1976, 1978, 1979, 1980, 1981, 1982, 1985, 1987, 1988, 1990, 1991, 1992, 1993, 1994, 1995 by the American Library Association. All reproduced by permission.—*Books for Keeps,* n. 76, September, 1992; n. 77, November, 1992; n. 84, January, 1994; n. 96, January, 1996. © School Bookshop Association 1992, 1994, 1996. All reproduced by permission.—*Books for Your Children*, v. 17, Summer, 1982. © *Books for your Children* 1982. Reproduced by permission.—*Bulletin from Virginia Kirkus' Service,* v. XXVI, February 15, 1958. Copyright © 1958 The Kirkus Service, Inc. All rights reserved. Reprinted by permission of the publisher, *Bulletin from Virginia Kirkus' Service* and Kirkus Associates, LP./ v. XXXII, July 1, 1964. Copyright © 1964, renewed 1992, The Kirkus Service Inc. All rights reserved. Reproduced by permission.—*Bulletin of the Center for Children's Books,* v. 20, July-August, 1967; v. 21, November, 1967; v. 21, April, 1968; v. 23, December, 1969; v. 24, October, 1970; v. 25, April, 1972; v. 25, February, 1972; v. 27, January, 1974; v. 27, July-August, 1974; v. 29, September, 1975; v. 29, December, 1975; February, 1977; v. 30, March, 1977; v. 31, April, 1978; v. 32, October, 1978; v. 34, October, 1980; v. 34, July-August, 1981; v. 37, December, 1983; v. 40, March, 1987; v. 41, April, 1988; v. 44, September, 1990; v. 47, January, 1994; v. 47, February, 1994; v. 47, July-August, 1994; v. 48, January, 1995; v. 49, November, 1995. Copyright © 1967, 1968, 1969, 1970, 1972, 1974, 1975, 1977, 1978, 1980, 1981, 1983, 1987, 1988, 1990, 1994, 1995 by The University of Chicago. All reproduced by permission of University of Illinois Press./ v. XV, March, 1962; v. XV, April, 1962; v. XVI, January, 1963; v. XVIII, February, 1964; v. XVIII, May, 1965. Copyright © 1962, renewed 1990; copyright © 1963, renewed 1991; copyright © 1964, renewed 1992; copyright © 1965, renewed 1993 by The University of Chicago. All reproduced by permission of University of Illinois Press.—*Canadian*

**COPYRIGHTED EXCERPTS IN *CLR,* VOLUME 42, WERE REPRODUCED FROM THE FOLLOWING BOOKS:**

**PERMISSION TO REPRODUCE ILLUSTRATIONS APPEARING IN *CLR,* VOLUME 42, WAS RECEIVED FROM THE FOLLOWING SOURCES:**

Ingraham. By permission of Morrow Junior Books, a division of William Morrow & Company, Inc.—Krauss, Ruth. Illustration entitled "Portrait of the Author as a Young Star" from *Under Twenty* by Ruth Krauss. Toad Press, 1970. Reproduced by permission of the author.—Pfister, Marcus. Illustration from *Penguin Pete* by Marcus Pfister. North-South Books, 1987. Copyright © 1987 by Nord-Süd Verlag AG, Gossau Zürich, Switzerland. Used by permission of North-South Books Inc., New York.—Pfister, Marcus. Illustration from *The Rainbow Fish* by Marcus Pfister. North-South Books, 1992. Copyright © 1992 by Nord-Süd Verlag AG, Gossau Zürich, Switzerland. Used by permission of North-South Books Inc., New York.

**PERMISSION TO REPRODUCE PHOTOGRAPHS APPEARING IN *CLR*, VOLUME 42, WAS RECEIVED FROM THE FOLLOWING SOURCES:**

Photograph of Mary Calhoun by Portfolio/James Steinberg: **p. 1**/Photograph of Sharon Creech by Matthew Self. Courtesy of HarperCollins Publishers, Inc.: **p. 36**/Photograph of Gary Crew. Courtesy of Gary Crew: **p. 45**/Photograph of Arthur Dorros. Courtesy of Arthur Dorros: **p. 63**/Photograph of Sarah Ellis by Keith Maillard. Courtesy of Sarah Ellis: **p. 74**/Photograph of Nikki Grimes by Joëlle Petit Adkins: **p. 88**/Photograph of Ruth Krauss. Source unknown: **p. 96**/Photograph of Marcus Pfister. Courtesy of North-South Books Inc., New York: **p. 132**/Photograph of Geoffrey Trease by T. Bailey. Courtesy of the Nottingham *Evening Post*. Reproduced by permission of Geoffrey Trease: **p. 142**/Photograph of Geoffrey Trease (with brothers, George and Bill). Courtesy of Geoffrey Trease: **p. 157**/Photograph of Geoffrey Trease (at desk). Courtesy of Geoffrey Trease: **p. 177**.

# Children's
# Literature
# Review

# Mary Calhoun

## 1926-

(Pseudonym of Mary Huiskamp Wilkins) American author of fiction, picture books, and retellings.

Major works include *Wobble, the Witch Cat* (1958), *Katie John* (1960), *The Thieving Dwarfs* (1967), *Ownself* (1975), *Cross-Country Cat* (1979), *High-Wire Henry* (1991).

## INTRODUCTION

A popular and well-known writer of stories for children and young adults, Calhoun is particularly admired for amusing, clever, and entertaining picture books that lend themselves to reading aloud. Engaging a wide variety of subjects, the author has met with the greatest success with her "Katie John" series—realistic tales of youth in rural, 1960s Missouri—and her award-winning stories of the keen-witted, acrobatic cat Henry. Lauded for her inventiveness and skillful narrative style, Calhoun has also been praised for her capacity to create local color, as in the Missouri backdrop of *Katie John,* and to recreate the patterns of colloquial speech in longer works such as *The Horse Comes First* (1974) and *Ownself.* This same skill forms an integral part of her retellings of regional fables and folktales, such as her hillbilly version of a La Fontaine fable in *Old Man Whickutt's Donkey* (1975) or her collections of European fairy-tale books, stories of elves and witches drawn from her love of nineteenth-century folklore. Although her work covers a wide range of audiences and subjects, Calhoun has noted that all her books spring from a common source: "a strong emotion and a desire to tell the story to certain children."

### Biographical Information

Calhoun was born in Keokuk, Iowa, in 1926. Educated in her home state, she graduated from the University of Iowa in 1948 and began her writing career as a journalist in Cedar Rapids, later working in Omaha, Nebraska. Her first children's book, *Making the Mississippi Shout* (1957), was inspired by her childhood love of the river that flows near Keokuk, and was soon followed by *Wobble, the Witch Cat,* a story which she had first told to her two preschool-age sons about a feline familiar frightened of riding on a broom. Memories of her youth spent on the Mississippi were the source of her most enduring series of children's books, which begins with *Katie John.* The work was well received by critics, among them Miriam James, who wrote that "the headstrong lass is as realistically charming as any we've met in many books." In the 1960s Calhoun's growing interest in European folklore provided the impetus for a string of books about fairies, including *The Hungry Leprechaun* (1962), *The Thieving Dwarfs,* and *The Runaway Brownie* (1967). The 1970s saw the au-

thor's first publication of a novel for young teens, *It's Getting Beautiful Now* (1971), followed by other works in the genre, such as *Ownself* (1975), about which Virginia Haviland commented: "Percipient in developing characters and their relationships, the author has written a story both subtle and powerful." In the late seventies Calhoun brought her most well-known creation—the clever Siamese, Henry—before the public in *Cross-Country Cat.* The work spawned several sequels in the following decades, *Hot-Air Henry* (1981), *High-Wire Henry,* and *Henry the Sailor Cat* (1994).

### Major Works

*Wobble, the Witch Cat* was one of Calhoun's first published works, and with its simple, humorous story represents many of the qualities typical of the author's picture books. Its hero is a likable feline who has trouble finding the courage to ride on a flying broomstick, a problem solved when his witch gets a modern vacuum-cleaner instead. The story forms a prelude to a favorite subject of Calhoun's: cats. *Cross-Country Cat* features the somewhat arrogant but decidedly intelligent cat, Henry. Accidentally left behind following a skiing trip, Henry reluctantly uses a pair of cross-country skis, fashioned by "the Kid" as a joke, to reunite himself with his family. He outwits a rabbit, a jay, and a coyote while making his way through the snow, only to cleverly disguise his adventure by shedding his skis and laying in a snowbank near the family's cabin while awaiting "rescue" by "the Man." Further books starring Henry find him flying a hot-air balloon, walking a high-wire, and sailing a boat. Another prominent topic in Calhoun's picture books is folklore, especially that which features elves, goblins, pixies, and other fairyfolk. The first of these tales, *The Hungry Leprechaun,* is based on Celtic lore, and relates the mythic origins of the potato in Ireland. Derived from a German folktale, *The Thieving Dwarfs* is the first of five instructive books about fairies. It tells the story of Karl, a wheat farmer who manages to stop the wee folk from stealing his crops. He befriends the creatures, who are then driven away by angry villagers, but not before the dwarfs leave a pot of gold to pay for what they have stolen. *The Runaway Brownie* is based upon the Scottish tale of Angus, a hard-working half-man/half-beast who flees when his greedy new master tries to bribe him in exchange for riches. Other tales in the series, *The Last Two Elves in Denmark* (1968), *The Goblin under the Stairs* (1968), and *The Pixy and the Lazy Housewife* (1969) teach lessons about conceit, tolerance, and hard work respectively.

The long-lived "Katie John" series opens with *Katie John,* which tells the story of the ten-year-old Katie John Tucker, who reluctantly spends the summer away from her friends at a huge old house in Missouri. But, as she explores the secret nooks of the house with a new friend, Katie John finds surprises and excitement while she grows to love her new home. In the sequel, *Depend on Katie John* (1961), the Tuckers inherit the rambling old building and turn it into a rooming house, providing Katie John with new responsibilities and adventures. These exploits continue in *Honestly, Katie John!* (1963). Calhoun returns to the subject of a young girl growing up in Missouri in *Ownself,* one of her most successful novel-length works. The story blends elements of historical fiction with the realism of the Katie John stories and a dose of fantasy. Set in the early 1900s, *Ownself* follows Laurabelle, who has lost the feeling of closeness she shared with her father since his conversion to a strict brand of Methodism. Fascinated by the legends of her Welsh ancestors, Laurabelle conjures a fairy, thereby incurring the wrath of her father, who immediately summons a preacher to perform an exorcism. The novel ends with Laurabelle realizing that she cannot change even the people she loves, so she must instead learn to accept them and herself.

## Awards

*Cross-Country Cat* received a 1979 Golden Kite Award Fiction Honor citation as well as several state readers' awards; its sequel, *High-Wire Henry,* also earned state readers' awards from California and Maryland in 1994.

## AUTHOR'S COMMENTARY

### Mary Calhoun

SOURCE: "Developing the Picture Book Story," in *The Writer,* July, 1981, pp. 16–8, 46.

There's nothing like a good idea! One of the most glorious moments of a writer's life comes when a good idea flashes. And it had better be good. I've found that editors more often reject picture book scripts because the idea isn't strong enough than because the writing isn't skillful enough.

*Testing: What quality about this idea gives it special appeal for the four- to eight-year-old child?*

Anyone who has learned the craft of writing can take a set of characters—the rabbit, the duck and the horse—and work out a story. But the story must have a largeness of appeal for an editor to want to publish it as a book and for the book *to continue to sell.*

Often that magical quality seems to rise from two things going on in a writer: a strong emotion and a desire to tell the story to certain children. The energy surging in the writer gives the idea a special vitality, and the writer of picture books should be quick to draw from those times of intensity.

Enthusiasm for a subject may carry a book, but not always. Out of a boundless fascination with folklore I've written many picture book stories, including a series about elves in different countries. But not all of my folk tale scripts have sold. Beyond enthusiasm, a strong emotion seems to have impelled my most successful books, though the emotion may be only a buoyancy of well-being and playfulness.

I felt that way when, on the spur of the moment, I told my two preschool sons a story about a witch cat who was afraid to ride on a broom. **Wobble the Witch Cat** was published in 1957 and is still selling well. The emotion may be love. I wrote the first Katie John book for older children out of my love for the big old house in which I grew up, the love brought fresh by a flood of homesickness. What's more, *I wanted to tell the story to children.* My sons and their playmates lived in rows of shoebox houses; many other children lived in city apartments. I thought the children would like to know how it felt to live in a big house that one's great-grandfather had built. Now, twenty years after that idea began, the majority of my fan letters still come from readers of the Katie John books.

More recently a picture book, **The Witch Who Lost Her Shadow,** developed from my grief over my lost cat, Shadow, who never came back. The theme was clear: you can't stop loving; you have to accept a new friend. I think children in today's mobile society of fragmented families can identify with loss (of friend, parent or pet) and the need to love and be loved.

And *Cross-Country Cat* started with a moment of pure happiness. Although I'm not adept at the sport, I love to get out on touring skis. One sunny winter day, when the snow was deep, I came in from an afternoon of skiing, my body and spirits glowing from the fun. My blue-eyed half-Siamese cat was sitting in a clump on the couch. I wished everyone, even the cat, could feel the joy of skiing!

Exuberantly I exclaimed, "Kitty, you ought to get out on skis! With your coloring, you'd look so beautiful against the snow. You'd be a cross-country cat!"

Then I thought, That sounds like a book title.

However, the flash of emotion and discovery did not at once translate into a book idea. I was working on something else at the time, and I tucked the title into the back of my mind. Months later I was visiting a class of third-graders in a Denver school. The children asked if I had ever written about skiing.

I said, "No. I've got a title, *Cross-Country Cat.* But that would be too silly, a cat on skis, wouldn't it?"

"No!" chorused the kids. "Write it! Write it!"

What a stimulus to the imagination, knowing someone *wants* the story! I went home and started thinking, All right, *why* would a cat be on skis? (Writers ask themselves lots of questions.) Maybe he was accidentally left behind at a mountain cabin, and the only way out was to ski out. It was a breezy explanation, so naturally he'd be a breezy skier. His name was Henry—that just came to me. And he'd be a cat with pizzazz. Of course, I didn't know all about Henry at first; I got to know him as I worked on the story. He is nothing like my cat, Dusky, who has the personality of a sofa pillow.

An idea was developing from that initial moment of emotion. As I explored how the story might go, I also was testing the idea.

*Is this subject matter of special interest to children?* I need to know children. I draw deeply from memories of myself as a child, and I spend a lot of time with today's children—both with groups and individuals. I need to observe children, react to them, empathize with them. Certain Colorado third-graders were enthusiastic about the subject matter, but how about other kids? I knew cross-country skiing was America's fastest-growing sport. More and more children are having a chance to ski, downhill and cross-country. Yes, the idea of a cat on skis should appeal to kids—if I can pull it off.

*Would readers like my hero?* Henry was a swagger of self-confidence, yet he was fallible and in some ways as dependent as a child. I saw that readers could admire Henry and his pizzazz but also at times feel fondly superior to him. I soon saw that the character I was imagining could have that effect.

*Has a book like this been published recently?* Of course, I can't know about every picture book published, but I sample books at the libraries, and I scan publication lists in *The Horn Book, Publishers Weekly* and the *Bulletin of the Society of Children's Book Writers.* Librarians and booksellers let me look at their publishers' catalogues. As far as I could learn, there was no picture book fiction about cross-country skiing.

All signs seemed GO, and I gave myself happily to working out the idea. It was a help that from the start I thought of it visually. I don't always *see* my story happening, because basically I'm a word person, and I have no artistic talent. (The editor usually chooses the artist.) Yet these are *picture book* stories; the art is at least as important as the text. While writing, I'm aware that a new picture possibility should occur every hundred words or so; there must be action and some change of scene and characters—or change of emotional intensity.

The idea for *Cross-Country Cat* began with a picture in my mind of a beautiful Siamese cat skiing over the snow. As I wrote, I saw the characters acting in certain mountain settings I know. And I was blessed to have Erick Ingraham as artist, for he has portrayed Henry and his story beautifully, beyond the powers of my visual imagination.

However, Erick's work came later. First, I had to put the idea into story form. That always means playing with the idea, asking myself questions, finding out whether the idea *will* take a story form. Would the cat be on two skis or four? It would have to be two skis for agility! But how could Henry learn to ski? Perhaps by singing, stepping in rhythm to his singing, just as I learned. Mine is the sedate beat of "Prisoner of Love," but Henry is a better skier than I. His song, which he'd heard The Kid sing, is "This Old Man." Makes a much jazzier stride!

So the cat learns to ski. But that doesn't make a story. *What happened next?* For this I turned to a formula I've learned from long study of folk tales, the rhythm of three's. There are three encounters, three attempts to solve a problem. Those events form the main body of action, the middle of the story. (Who doesn't have to try, try again to succeed?) But the attempts don't solve the problem. There is the gloom of seeming defeat or the fear of imminent disaster. Then the hero makes a fourth climactic effort that ends in success.

What might Henry logically meet while he was skiing? An elk, a snowshoe rabbit, a Steller's jay—and a coyote! Once a coyote actually stole one of my cats from the deck of our mountain home. Here enters author's revenge: Henry escapes from the coyote—in a plausible way. And there should be a quick kicker ending that points up the story's theme. In this book I wasn't trying to tell a moral story, and I worried a little about the theme.

With some of the story in mind, I started to write. As I typed, I imagined I was telling the story to my grandson, who lived far away then. I saw Copper wanting the story, reacting to it; and my writing style became matter-of-fact, lively, and humorous. I have learned that the more I concentrate on a story, the more my imagination will help me in unexpected ways. The very heat of writing stimulates ideas. Like the bit about Henry's skiing rhythm: He steps out briskly at first, thinking, "Smart cat! Smart cat!" But by the time Henry is tired and can hear the coyote's teeth snapping behind him, he thinks in a stumbling rhythm, "End-of-the-line, end-of-the-line." Children have told me they particularly like those bits.

The last line of the story just popped out—"Some smart cat!" I usually write the first page many times, trying to get it right. Then I write the rest of the story in one or two long sessions, so the endings usually come after a concentrated burst.

When I had finished the first draft, I studied the shape of the story. I rewrote to balance episodes in length, to build intensity to "all-is-lost." I pared the ending for impact.

Next I worked on sharpening verbs, which are the backbone of action in a children's book and also give the particular style or flavor to the story. In general, I scrutinized the text to say each word and phrase the best way I could. As in a poem, every word counts in a picture book story.

At that point I was cutting. I usually write too long a script; but I'd rather have more story and compress than have a wispy story and pad. Word lengths for picture book stories usually run about 1000 to 1500 words. After 2000 words, it's no longer a *picture book* story. Writing for children's magazines with their set word lengths taught me to pare words—and that leads to writing concisely and vividly.

A final polish . . . off to the editor . . . high hopes! But I seldom get it exactly right the first time out. (Usually I am glad for editorial suggestions on how to make the story better. If I can't see how the suggestions will help, I send the script to another editor.) My Morrow editor spotted some weaknesses in the story, matters of logic. I hadn't established Henry's ability as a hind-leg walker. And it strained credulity that the cat made his own skis (first version). Each brick and bit of mortar that builds a fantasy must be logical and reasonable for the reader to believe the story and live in it. So I rewrote the beginning of my story.

Perhaps the fantasy of this book works, too, because both the text and the art are carefully based on detail. Although I seldom meet the artists of my books, Erick visited me. Together we studied pine boughs to note whether they'd be straight enough to use for ski poles. Erick wanted to see mountain cabins in my part of the country—and the very chinking of the logs shows up in his pictures. I pointed out that our mountain jays (where elk and coyote also live) are the black-masked Steller's jays, not the Eastern Jay that Erick had planned to depict.

Thus, a burst of emotion developed into a viable story

idea. The idea took shape in story form with a likable hero in a provocative situation. Within the form came conflict in three encounters, followed by the climactic event. Resolution came in a quick and plausible ending that satisfies the reader.

However, it isn't quite the end of my play with this jazzy cat. Next, Erick and I are sending Henry up with a hot-air balloon, **Hot-Air Henry**. Because I adore ballooning!

---

# TITLE COMMENTARY

### 📖 *MAKING THE MISSISSIPPI SHOUT* (1957)

*Virginia Kirkus' Service*

SOURCE: A review of *Making the Mississippi Shout,* in *Virginia Kirkus' Service,* Vol. XXIV, No. 22, November 15, 1956, p. 843.

A story in the vernacular, with zip and vigour, takes a sidewheeler of the upper Mississippi for its setting and the ambition of Tad Berry to play its "cally-ope" for the central theme. A musical boy, Tad also wants to make part of the river his own and forms a daring plan to play the calliope of the *River Queen,* an excursion boat. Doing it rouses the captain's extreme ire, but help from a friend, some sensible explanations and an emergency in which Tad's playing averts disaster, bring on a rousing climax. There is a healthy supply of river lore too.

**Margaret Sherwood Libby**

SOURCE: A review of *Making the Mississippi Shout,* in *New York Herald Tribune Book Review,* February 3, 1957, p. 8.

For boys of nine or so (those who enjoy Glen Round's stories like his recent amusing "Whitey Ropes and Rides" with its endearing combination of cowboy interest and little-boy limitations) this is a diverting "period piece" by Mary Calhoun. A small boy, Tad Berry, living about the turn of the century, has a consuming passion to play a steam calliope on a Mississippi River steamer. His story, simply told, moves quickly and is enlivened with black and white sketches by Paul Galdone. The local color is excellent, and there is drama (nearly melodrama) when the "River Queen" is twice nearly wrecked, first because Tad ignored the Captain's orders and then with Tad playing a surprising part in the amazing rescue, his dream working at last with the Captain's dream so that everybody rejoiced that he "could make this old river shout."

***Bulletin of the Children's Book Center***

SOURCE: A review of *Making the Mississippi Shout,* in

*Bulletin of the Children's Book Center,* Vol. X, No. 7, March, 1957, p. 87.

Eleven-year-old Tad Berry could hardly wait for the day when the *River Queen* would arrive in Summitville for its annual visit. Not only did he look forward to the boat ride and picnic, but he also had plans for climbing to the top deck and playing the boat's calliope. He wanted to "make the Mississippi shout." His plans almost brought disaster to himself and the boat, but later, in a storm, he was able to put his talent to good use by playing the calliope to attract attention and bring much needed help. A well-told story, with good pace and suspense to hold the reader's interest.

**Virginia Haviland**

SOURCE: A review of *Making the Mississippi Shout,* in *The Horn Book Magazine,* Vol. XXXIII, No. 2, April, 1957, p. 132.

A great deal happened on the one day of this story when Tad Berry made his annual excursion on the Mississippi steamboat *River Queen.* Most important to him of all the ship's excitements was the steam "cally-ope," which he aimed to play—and did. His conniving to do this brought on the captain's anger at once, but there was gratitude later when Tad could play a blaring tune during a storm and thus summon help for the disabled ship. The author succeeds well in recreating the spirit of carnival and the glamour of the great boat that looked like a "giant birth-day cake." Paul Galdone adds amusement with his sketches of clerk Jubilee Jones, Captain Sterling, prissy Betty, and the girl-hating Tad.

**Miriam James**

SOURCE: "Two Afloat," in *The New York Times Book Review,* July 21, 1957, pp. 21–2.

Mary Calhoun's Tad Berry is one lively, determined river lad with a yen to play the River Queen's cally-ope—to "own" the part of the great Mississippi that he could make shout with his music. Fortune smiles at him when the cally-ope player is disabled, but the smile is mightily overshadowed by Captain Sterling's icy anger. But during the harrowing night in a tornado Tad does get to make the river shout and saves the River Queen to boot. Paul Galdone's line drawings lack the depth of the lad's character and of the danger but are quite as light-hearted as the gala excursion's beginning.

📖 *THE SWEET PATOOTIE DOLL* (1957)

*Virginia Kirkus' Service*

SOURCE: A review of *The Sweet Patootie Doll,* in *Virginia Kirkus' Service,* Vol. XXV, No. 13, July 1, 1957, p. 437.

It was careless of Lucy to leave the tiny doll she had made from a sweet potato on the stump, for it wasn't long before it was found by Old Mr. Coon. But with her irresistible smile focused on him somehow he lost his appetite. Neither he nor Silly Young Fox nor Ole Man B'ar had the heart to eat her. It was Lucy's Hound Dog who brought the doll safely back to the tree stump.

📖 *THE RIVER-MINDED BOY* (1958)

*Virginia Kirkus' Service*

SOURCE: A review of *The River-Minded Boy,* in *Virginia Kirkus' Service,* Vol. XXVI, No. 2, January 15, 1958, p. 34.

Rone anticipated a summer as a real riverman aboard the *Black Hawk,* a Mississippi towboat. But the thirteen year old boy was disgusted when he learned that the only available job was mess boy—working in the kitchen. And Buck, a bigger boy on board, resented Rone bitterly. In a fist fight, when Buck takes a line from Rone's locker without his consent, Rone knocks him by accident into the water. Buck's leg is broken and Rone, in disgrace with his crewmates, is put ashore to take Buck home. But when Rone escorts Buck to his family farm, the boy's father is not at home. A flood threatens the house and the injured boy. Buck foregoes his chance on another tow-boat to look after Buck—with final consolation for Rone in the Captain's offer of another summer aboard the *Black Hawk.* A brief, relatively easy reading action story for boys based upon the author's assumption that a thirteen year old boy could work on a family-owned boat despite restrictive child labor laws.

**Miriam James**

SOURCE: "Messboy on the Mississippi," in *The New York Times Book Review,* March 30, 1958, p. 36.

Rone Tyler, at last, was through watching the boats trail their silver ripples down the Mississippi and go off be-yond the bend. The moment he stepped on board The Black Hawk, the 13-year-old began to learn that having a job on a boat was far from being a riverman. Being neph-ew of the towboat's owner was one strike against him, so far as the crew was concerned. And a messboy's job seemed like woman's work to Rone. Only when his hot-headedness landed him on shore did the boy recognize his own failure to meet serious responsibilities. A Missis-sippi rampage gave him the chance to prove his new maturity and when he stepped on board again his wel-come was well won.

Mrs. Calhoun writes a smooth descriptive narrative of the grand old river and of a boy's step toward self-under-standing. Rone himself being portrayed only in relation to his rather special problem, hasn't the depth to live long in a reader's memory.

## 📖 *WOBBLE, THE WITCH CAT* (1958)

### *Virginia Kirkus' Service*

SOURCE: A review of *Wobble, The Witch Cat*, in *Virginia Kirkus' Service*, Vol. XXVIII, No. 15, August 1, 1958, p. 543.

It's no good being a witch's cat, even a friendly witch like Maggie, if you get mouse scared every time you mount a broom. But Wobble *was* scared and the more scared he got, the more ashamed he got, and the more ashamed he got, the more grumpy he got until . . . The story of how a vacuum cleaner changed Wobble from a land-loving scare cat into a dashing star-chaser, combined with striking illustrations by Roger Duvoisin, make this a thoroughly bewitching bit of cat-tailery.

### Virginia Haviland

SOURCE: A review of *Wobble the Witch Cat*, in *The Horn Book Magazine*, Vol. XXXIV, No. 5, October, 1958, pp. 376–77.

Picture-book listening groups can have good Halloween fun with this new adventure in sky riding. The author relates how Wobble became a crosspatch of a cat when Maggie, his amiable fat witch, got a new broomstick too slippery to offer him a good seat, and how he managed to have her substitute her more comfortable vacuum cleaner (not the first time that this invention has been used for such witchery).

### Pamela Marsh

SOURCE: "Widening Horizons," in *The Christian Science Monitor*, October 23, 1958, p. 15.

There's a lot to be said for the machine age. Now it has come to the aid of witches' cats. Poor Wobble was very uncomfortable riding behind Maggie the witch (a motherly witch with plenty of the right kind of charm) on her new broom with its thin, slippery handle. But when Maggie moved with the times all was well again. Roger Duvoisin does magic things with pictures that sweep the story along over pages that change color with the mood. He lends plenty of character to Maggie and Wobble, spicing a gay tale to be read and reread to the 4–8s.

### Ellen Lewis Buell

SOURCE: "Midnight Riders," in *The New York Times Book Review*, October 26, 1958, p. 50.

Witches have come down in the world considerably since Cotton Mather's day (when they were blamed for everything from pinkeye to a sick cow), but for the young there is still a pleasantly shivery feeling in the shadow of a peaked hat or a broomstick—especially at this time of year. This Halloween young children who are not quite ready for the grimmer examples of the sisterhood have a modern version of old magic in Mary Calhoun's *Wobble, the Witch Cat*. This features Maggie, a good gay witch, who likes to sweep the sky clean so that children can enjoy trick-or-treating. Her cat, Wobble, however, simply can't abide those night-flights because Maggie's broom (soft-brush type) is too thin and shaky. Secretly, he disposes of the broom, but Maggie finds that a witch's magic works even on a vacuum cleaner, and they both ride off in high style. This gentle spoofing is nicely pointed up by Roger Duvoisin's amusing pictures in Halloween colors of black, gray, russet and yellow.

## 📖 *HOUN' DOG* (1959)

### Virginia Haviland

SOURCE: A review of *Houn' Dog*, in *The Horn Book Magazine*, Vol. XXXV, No. 5, October, 1959, p. 377.

A fast-paced, tellable, and humorously illustrated picture story about a southern mountain foxhound with the "sharpest smeller" and "sweetest beller" of all the dogs in his county. Houn' Dog lost these talents in a trial run, due to Slyfoot Fox's strategy, but fortunately got them back (with a mudpack on his nose and wild honey in his throat) so that in the next night's big fox hunt he led the way.

### *Bulletin of the Center for Children's Books*

SOURCE: A review of *Houn' Dog*, in *Bulletin of the Center for Children's Books*, Vol. XIII, No. 7, March, 1960, p. 111.

A picture book with text that has a Southern Mountain flavor. Houn' Dog was distinguished by having, of all the dogs in the hills, the sharpest smeller and the sweetest beller. He was tricked by Slyfoot the Fox into getting stung by a swarm of bees, but recovered in time to outrun the pack in the big fox-hunt. The writing has humor of the tall-tale flavor, and the illustrations [by Roger Duvoisin] are well suited to the text.

## 📖 *KATIE JOHN* (1960)

### *Virginia Kirkus' Service*

SOURCE: A review of *Katie John*, in *Virginia Kirkus' Service*, Vol. XXVIII, No. 2, January 15, 1960, p. 48.

Katie John, an impulsive and enthusiastic child, is at first reluctant to settle down with her family in the old Missouri home of her deceased Aunt Emily. But as the summer progresses, Katie becomes fascinated by the house and its many links with nineteenth century American history. Many adventures, mainly instigated by her facile imagination, bind her to the house, which by Thanksgiving is really home to Katie John. Mary Calhoun, author of *Houn' Dog* and other books, imbues her story with a good feeling of locale, a strong sense of seasonal change, and above all a vigorous portrayal of an appealing and lively heroine.

**Miriam James**

SOURCE: "Old House, New Home," in *The New York Times Book Review,* April 3, 1960, p. 40.

Katie John Tucker ran out of the great red brick house that first morning, turned round and gave a "Yahnnn," complete with the worst face she could make. The Tuckers had come all the way from California to sell this old Missouri house, and Katie had a sizeable grouch against it. But the 11-year-old's resentment was as short as it was sudden. Sue Halsey appeared to announce that the house was haunted. The two whirled off on a series of adventures in and around the sprawling old home—not the least of which was exhuming a (probably) "fine old pioneer bone" right in the backyard!

During an often hilarious summer Katie grew in more than her love for the ancestral home. She thought through—carefully, for once—a plan to keep the house, and found that if you love something, you even *want* to work for it. The headstrong lass is as realistically charming as any we've met in many a book.

**Bulletin of the Center for Children's Books**

SOURCE: A review of *Katie John,* in *Bulletin of the Center for Children's Books,* Vol. XIII, No. 9, May, 1960, pp. 143–4.

A very pleasant and realistic story about a ten year old girl as she adjusts to a new home and new friends. This is the sort of book that will be especially welcomed by those readers who enjoy the details of everyday life. No dramatic events occur in the life of Katie John Tucker, save for the small dramas that happen to any lively youngster. The Tuckers have moved into an old house (newly inherited) so that they can sell it more easily; they grow to love it and decide to stay. Katie John's new friend, Sue, says the house is haunted, but it seems the noise comes from the old system of speaking tubes; Katie John gets stuck in the old dumb-waiter—but is easily rescued by her mother; the two girls have a spat, but they quickly forget their grievances. All very simple, credible, smoothly written; characterization is consistent and the author has written perceptively of the attitudes of pre-adolescent girls toward boys and toward older sisters.

**Silence Buck Bellows**

SOURCE: "With Names Like Liza, Jennie, and Katie John," in *The Christian Science Monitor,* May 12, 1960, Sect. B, p. 2.

Great Aunt Emily's big, ugly, square, red-brick house in Missouri didn't look attractive to Katie John, and she was glad that Father and Mother were going to sell it and go to live in New York. But a house that develops mysterious voices and hides a folded-away satin wedding dress in its attic can't stay uninteresting very long. And any house that is really lived in gets to be a home. The story belongs to Katie John and to the house, and is told with a pace and verve that the 8–12's will find compelling.

**Booklist**

SOURCE: A review of *Katie John,* in *Booklist,* Vol. 56, No. 20, June 15, 1960, p. 632.

Katie John, ten, is far from happy when the family moves to a small Missouri town to live in Great-Aunt Emily's house—which they have just inherited—long enough to sell it. But, as she makes new friends, explores the big, old house, and gets acquainted with the "poky" little town she begins to feel more and more at home and in the end finds a way for the family to live in the house permanently. A well-written, agreeable story with a likable heroine, lively doings, and a credible ending.

## DEPEND ON KATIE JOHN (1961)

**Virginia Kirkus' Service**

SOURCE: A review of *Depend on Katie John,* in *Virginia Kirkus' Service,* Vol. XXIV, No. 4, February 15, 1961, p. 164.

The author of *Katie John,* that irrepressible utterly real eleven year old gamin, now treats us to another delightful dip into her life. When we start out, Katie is facing many problems. Her new home in Missouri is filled with bothersome boarders, and at school she is the "new girl". Adjustment comes gradually and Katie and her new chum, Sue, take us through some heartwarming and humorous adventures, many of which concern Boys, a budding interest of Katie's. Life at home improves as Katie gains new understanding of her roomers and friendships begin to blossom. A thoroughly engaging book with a refreshingly alive heroine.

**Pamela Marsh**

SOURCE: "Fun in Families," in *The Christian Science Monitor,* May 11, 1961, p. 4.

It is hard to keep tomboy Katie John shut up between the covers of Mrs. Calhoun's latest book for the 8–12's. Brimful of affection for the world, bouncing with marvelous ideas, slipping in and out of misadventures, she takes over the book and the reader's attention whether she is filling the house with boarders or using a Tom Sawyer-like device to get the sidewalks shoveled. Mrs. Calhoun is such an able talespinner, such a convincing voice recorder, that we forget she has a hand in the book at all.

## New York Herald Tribune Book Review

SOURCE: "Family Stories," in *New York Herald Tribune Book Review*, May 14, 1961, p. 35.

The lively little fifth-grade tomboy, Katie John, captured the hearts of a good many girls of her age as she struggled to adjust to leaving her friends in California and beginning life in a little town in Missouri. Now, quite at home in the great house and the new town, imaginative, enterprising Katie copes with a series of new problems. How can she stop being the "biggest nobody in fifth grade"? Which is worse—getting no Valentines at all or a great many all begging her to "be my hot potato," a reminder of an unorthodox means she had taken to warm herself on a bitter cold day? How could she have the Camp Fire Girls at the house when old cousin Ben, ill in bed, kept his door open and shouted at everybody who came in the house? Imaginative solutions are Katie's specialty, and some of them proved so entertaining that they gave her author-father an excellent idea that was to bring good luck to the family. As a step between very simple stories and the longer tales of Elizabeth Enright and Eleanor Estes, Katie John's adventures, with the jolly drawings of Paul Frame, are just right.

## Virginia Haviland

SOURCE: A review of *Depend on Katie John*, in *The Horn Book Magazine*, Vol. XXXVII, No. 3, June, 1961, p. 264.

In a sequel to **Katie John,** of last year, the Tuckers' recently inherited home in Missouri is turned into a rooming house. This means a whole new set of problems for likable Katie John and her parents, but also new happiness and some real growing up for her. Going on twelve, she is becoming aware of boys, and there is more fun for her now at school among her new schoolmates. A well-written story, with a wide variety of characters, considerable humor, and the kind of family security that children enjoy in a story.

## Miriam James

SOURCE: "Good Year," in *The New York Times Book Review*, July 9, 1961, p. 18.

"Depend on Katie!" is a double-edged phrase. In **Katie John** the irrepressible, bouncy heroine had heard it with pride when she had convinced her parents that with her help they could make the ancestral home meet expenses until Dad finished his book. In this sequel she thinks about it grimly when she pulls still another boner—such as dropping the dirty curtains down the stairwell onto a stately prospective roomer. Slaving for

"those roomers" and being "almost-eleven" has taken just a mite out of her bounce but that particular Katie John capacity for both charm and scrapes is still potent. Her days are filled with big highs and deep lows, and when Dad's book sells and most of the roomers are going for the summer, Katie—and her readers—can look back on nearly a year in the little Missouri town and say she's "sure lived a lot!"

## THE NINE LIVES OF HOMER C. CAT (1961)

### Zena Sutherland

SOURCE: A review of *The Nine Lives of Homer C. Cat*, in *Bulletin of the Center for Children's Books*, Vol. XV, No. 2, October, 1961, pp. 24–5.

Text and illustrations [by Roger Duvoisin] have vivacity and humor of a mild sort in a read-aloud picture book about a proud cat. Homer, jealous because his owner praised a dog, lost eight of his nine lives in one foolhardy attempt after another to do a brave deed. When he found that his mistress considered him still a fine cat and remembered that no other animal could purr, Homer was content; he was still proud, but not inordinately so. The concept of "losing" some of his lives may be very difficult for some children to grasp, which defeats the twist of the humor.

### George A. Woods

SOURCE: A review of *The Nine Lives of Homer C. Cat*, in *The New York Times Book Review*, November 12, 1961, pp. 54–5.

How pride can lead to a number of falls is shown in Mary Calhoun's **The Nine Lives Of Homer C. Cat,** pleasantly illustrated by Roger Duvoisin. A proud and pampered cat, Homer C. (for Cuddles) was especially proud of his nine lives. Alas, poor Homer gives them up one by one in a series of misadventures until he's down to one and realizes what it is that makes for a contented cat. There's a good lesson to be learned here and good fun to be had in keeping count of Homer's dwindling lives in the illustrations.

### Margaret Sherwood Libby

SOURCE: A review of *The Nine Lives of Homer C. Cat*, in *New York Herald Tribune Books*, December 24, 1961, p. 13.

Pride and jealousy combined to urge Mrs. Twisp's gay, prancing, shining-striped handsome cat (Homer C. Cat by name) to make terrific efforts to prove his uniqueness, and his superiority to all other animals. Disaster after disaster ensued until Homer lost all but one of his nine lives. It was only after the loss of this, the greatest source of his inordinate pride, that Homer discovered to his infinite contentment that he still had a gift possessed by no other animal.

Mary C. Calhoun has written this simple fable in a skillfully humorous way to please the nursery group and be pleasant practice reading for primaries while Roger Duvoisin's pictures show Homer in all his violence and smugness, sometimes in a black and gray world, sometimes in a tan, blue and green one. An added touch in the illustrations which five and six-year-olds, who enjoy counting everything possible, will like, is the picturing of multiple cats to show the number of lives remaining after each catastrophe.

## 📖 *COWBOY CAL AND THE OUTLAW* (1961)

### Zena Sutherland

SOURCE: A review of *Cowboy Cal and the Outlaw*, in *Bulletin of the Center for Children's Books*, Vol. XV, No. 7, March, 1962, p. 108.

A cowboy tall-tale, written in a breezy and colloquial style. Despite the humor, the story seems over-extended as Cowboy Cal suffers one setback after another. Having had a wild horse run off with his prize possession, a cherished saddle, Cal gave chase on an old horse that stepped in a hole and ran off; then he was treed by a steer, so he rode it. Finally he caught the outlaw horse with his lariat, tamed him and rode him back to the corral.

## 📖 *THE HUNGRY LEPRECHAUN* (1962)

### *Virginia Kirkus' Service*

SOURCE: A review of *The Hungry Leprechaun*, in *Virginia Kirkus' Service*, Vol. XXX, No. 12, June 15, 1962, p. 518.

The luck of the Irish apparently eluded young Patrick O'Michael O'Sullivan O'Callahan. The only leprechaun he could catch was as poor and hungry as Patrick. Instead of transforming the dandelion soup to a pot of gold, Tippery comes up with a bowl of frogs. But his next effort is not in vain. Though the rocks in the fields do not become golden nuggets, they wield their own kind of magic on Ireland—for Tippery is responsible for the first batch of spuds ever known in the land. [Illustrator] Roger Duvoisin is as refreshing in the Gaelic as he is in the Gallic and Mary Calhoun's story makes ideal if delayed St. Patrick's Day reading in school and home libraries.

### Zena Sutherland

SOURCE: A review of *The Hungry Leprechaun*, in *Bulletin of the Center for Children's Books*, Vol. XVI, No. 5, January, 1963, p. 75.

A fanciful read-aloud story about a poor Irish boy who caught a leprechaun, sure that he could obtain gold by commanding a creature with magic powers. Tippery was as hungry and poor as Patrick O'Michael O'Sullivan O'Callahan himself—no help at all; Patrick found himself sharing his dandelion soup with Tippery. Tippery tried magic on the soup, but could only turn it into frogs; he tried magic on rocks, but only his own finger turned to gold. They did find some brown things . . . and being so hungry, took them home. Cooked, they were wonderful. They called the things "potatoes" and soon all Ireland had some; today only Patrick's descendants remember that they can thank a hungry leprechaun for potatoes. A mildly entertaining story, first published in a shorter version in a magazine and showing some trace of having been extended in length; the repetition of episodes in which the leprechaun tries his magic makes the ending seem anticlimactic.

## 📖 *HONESTLY, KATIE JOHN!* (1963)

### *Virginia Kirkus' Service*

SOURCE: A review of *Honestly, Katie John!*, in *Virginia Kirkus' Service*, Vol. XXI, No. 7, April, 1963, p. 359.

This third book about the young girl who moved to Missouri (*Katie John,* 1960, and *Depend on Katie John*) is a record of the lass' troubles after she loudly declares that she hates boys, and becomes a leader of the Boy-Haters Club. Her comrade, Edmund, is hurt by her pronouncement, and no longer seeks her friendship. Even when other six graders begin wearing lipstick, learning to dance, and trying to lure the boys back, Katie sticks stubbornly to her stand. Only after learning about the life of a girl who had lived in her house years ago, does Katie John try to enjoy feminine fancies. The story is too drawn out (there is too much of the same), but young confused—or one-time confused—tomboys will enjoy and identify with lively Katie John, and her experiences.

## 📖 *THE WITCH OF HISSING HILL* (1964)

### *Virginia Kirkus' Service*

SOURCE: A review of *The Witch of Hissing Hill*, in *Virginia Kirkus' Service*, Vol. XXXII, No. 13, July 1, 1964, p. 588.

Mary Calhoun returns to the subject of witches and their cats (*Wobble, the Witch Cat,* 1958) in this story of an exceptionally wicked witch who specializes in raising evil, black cats as familiars for her colleagues. By some genetic mishap, one of her cats produces a yellow kitten, which throws Sizzle and her other cats into a tizzy. Yellow cats, it seems, are nice—something no self-respecting witch could be expected to put up with. The yellow kitten, who counteracts all of the spells directed at her, turns Sizzle's fresh pot of hate potion into a love medicine, and ends by turning Sizzle into a good witch. The illustrations [by Janet McCaffery] in big blobs of bright colors, are full of witches with hooked noses and round orange cheeks and of shapeless cats, and are as genially spooky as the text. A refreshing Halloween brew.

**Ethel L. Heins**

SOURCE: A review of *The Witch of Hissing Hill,* in *The Horn Book Magazine,* Vol. XL, No. 5, October, 1964, p. 488.

High on a lonely hill lived old Witch Sizzle, who raised, for sale, "the witchiest, the wickedest, the very worst, wonderful witch cats in the world." Their eyes were the evilest, their coats the blackest, as they hissed and howled, spit and scratched—until the shocking day a sunny yellow kitten was born. Now yellow witch cats, though they have a dash of mustard for spice, are good witch cats; soon the benign yellow magic proved to be so much more potent than the worst of the black that the hate brew was transformed into love medicine and Sizzle's customers changed from malevolent hags to fairy godmothers.

## 📖 *HIGH WIND FOR KANSAS* (1965)

*Virginia Kirkus' Service*

SOURCE: A review of *High Wind for Kansas,* in *Virginia Kirkus' Service,* March 1, 1965, p. 238.

A gusty tall tale told with a yarn spinner's twang about the first and last voyage of a magnificent land ship out of Westport, Missouri and into legend. Windwagon Jones saw no reason to waste the steady prairie wind which he saw as a natural fuel. He rigged out his wagon bed like a ship with a sail and used the tongue for a tiller. He cruised into town to the sound of laughter, but this was "show me" country even then. He showed them and they were willing to speculate. The Overland Navigation Co. was formed and a flagship built. The stockholders piled aboard and they set sail on wind power. Jones couldn't resist showing off. After a great launching, he put over to sail into the wind. The passengers dived for their lives but Jones stuck to his rudder in the best land-going tradition. That's why the prairie states have a phantom ship all their own. Easy to read and fun to tell with excellent illustrations by W.T. Mars who can draw all sorts of boats to perfection.

**Jerome Beatty**

SOURCE: A review of *High Wind for Kansas,* in *The New York Times Book Review,* May 9, 1965, pp. 24, 26.

The truth is hard to beat when you're writing fiction. Getting back to people, no better proof could be offered

than *High Wind For Kansas,* by Mary Calhoun. The author ran into some material on one Windwagon Thomas, a real character who attached a sail to a prairie schooner a century ago and tried to make the "schooner" part literal by tacking across the plains. From this she has constructed a funny and imaginative anecdote. If it didn't happen, it certainly could have.

**Charlotte A. Gallant**

SOURCE: A review of *High Wind for Kansas,* in *School Library Journal,* Vol. 11, No. 9, May 15, 1965, p. 98.

Windwagon Jones thought that nobody had a right to go just "whistling by, not doing nobody a lick of good," so he proposed to harness the wind and revolutionize western migration. His monster-big windwagon comes to an inglorious end and it's the end of the Overland Navigation Company, as well! An extravagant tall tale, based on several authentic incidents, told with sparkle and humor and illustrated [by W. T. Mars] in the same carefree way.

## 📖 *THE HOUSE OF THIRTY CATS* (1965)

*Virginia Kirkus' Service*

SOURCE: A review of *The House of Thirty Cats,* in *Virginia Kirkus' Service,* Vol. XXXIII, No. 18, September 15, 1965, p. 980.

The situation, even the title is similar to last season's *27 Cats Next Door* by Anita Feagles. This is the better written story, but the other offered a more realistic and honest portrayal, and was more thought-provoking. In both there is an elderly, eccentric old lady, solitary except for a super-abundance of cats, and a neighborhood child who makes the effort to offer her friendship. Here it is Sarah Rutledge, who is herself a lonely, almost friendless person. Sarah is very well drawn. Her inability to be at ease with others is painfully evident, so are her imaginings. Her understanding of the varying personalities of each of the thirty cats, and later, as she attempts to match the cats to people she knows, her gradual comprehension and sympathy for humans, leads to a very genuine development and maturation. The trouble with the story is that reader sympathy is entirely directed toward the cats and their mistress, Miss Tabitha. When her next-door neighbor, Colonel Mace, is enfuriated that the cats have destroyed his carefully tended plants and disturb him with their noise, and has them declared a public nuisance, he is shown only as a cold, unfeeling man. Other complaints of yowling and garbage-scrounging are off-handedly directed to one bad alley cat. And it is totally denied that Miss Tabitha's house is anything but spotless and odor-less. It's hard to accept, so is the town council's soft-hearted reversal of the ruling that the cats be removed. Individual characters and descriptions are excellent, but the story fails in its inability to locate the boundaries of social responsibility.

**Patricia H. Allen**

SOURCE: A review of *The House of Thirty Cats*, in *School Library Journal*, Vol. 12, No. 1, September 15, 1965, pp. 3786, 3788.

An unusual story of a little girl whose love of cats and friendship for a little old lady lead her to an understanding of people and give her the courage and resourcefulness to do the right thing. Miss Tabitha Henshaw devotes her house and her energies to providing a home for all kinds of cats. As Sarah gets to know her and each one of her cats she finds she acquires a deeper understanding of people—each one a little bit different from what he seems to be. There is a jarring note in the violent death of the ruthless cat Tarnish, and the town librarians are the all-too-familiar stereotypes. Miss Calhoun tells a good story and constructs a seemingly frail theme which grows subtly stronger as the story progresses.

**Margaret Berkvist**

SOURCE: A review of *The House of Thirty Cats*, in *The New York Times Book Review*, November 7, 1965, pp. 38, 40.

Sarah, a shy and lonely girl, is trying to summon up courage to knock on Miss Tabitha Henshaw's cottage door. Miss Tabitha has 30 cats, and because Sarah so badly wants a kitten she finally conquers her timidity. The two cat lovers immediately take to one another and Sarah is soon spending many happy hours with Miss Tabitha and her charges. Into this gentle world come Tarnish, a vicious nomad cat, and Colonel Mace, an equally vicious new neighbor, who insists the town council order Miss Tabitha to get rid of all but three of her cats. Distraught enough at her friend's plight to forget her own shyness, Sarah resolutely plots a solution.

How she tackles this disheartening situation makes an affecting story. It will appeal especially to cat people, and to shy people, but anyone other than a Colonel Mace is likely to become attached to the attractive characters, human and feline, whom the author so sympathetically portrays.

**Margery Fisher**

SOURCE: A review of *The House of Thirty Cats*, in *Growing Point*, Vol. 5, No. 7, January, 1967, p. 845.

Sarah Rutledge wants a cat: old Miss Tabitha Henshaw has a houseful. Chance acquaintance ripens into unlikely friendship, and Sarah learns to appreciate cat-personality as she champions the crowd against complaining neighbours—and against Tarnish, the sinister stray at the bottom of all the trouble. An attractive tale from America, rejoicing in an illustrator [Mary Chalmers] who knows cats well.

**Publishers Weekly**

SOURCE: A review of *The House of Thirty Cats*, in *Publishers Weekly*, Vol. 220, No. 4, July 24, 1981, p. 149.

With [Mary] Chalmers's endearing, animated drawings, Calhoun's story is a can't-fail offering for cat lovers. Rich in characters and incidents, the book draws readers into the lives of the child Sarah Rutledge and the town eccentric, old Miss Tabitha Henshaw. The small, proud lady insists on being addressed by her full name when necessary and keeps herself isolated in "The House of Thirty Cats," a Victorian mansion that intimidates everyone, including Sarah. But the girl forms a close bond with Miss Tabitha, becoming her ally when irate townspeople try to force the women to "dispose of" the unwanted stray cats she has devoted herself to caring for. The resolution involves tensions, hurts and exhilarating surprises.

📖 *THE THIEVING DWARFS* (1967)

### Kirkus Service

SOURCE: A review of *The Thieving Dwarfs*, in *Kirkus Service*, Vol. XXXV, No. 7, April 1, 1967, pp. 405–6.

Bosch-like faces in grim black and mustard or slightly lighter mint green, mustard and shocking pink settings illustrate a tart Germanic tale, based on Hessian folklore and told in blank verse. Karl, an honest farmer, tries to stop the dwarfs' pilfering of his wheat and ends up making friends with them. One night his wife catches a glimpse of the little ones and immediately the secret is out. The villagers' revenge is to knock off the elves' hats, making them visible and forcing them to emigrate; they leave behind a pot of gold in payment for the stolen goods. First in a projected series about the elvish people—a bittersweet story appropriately in bittersweet colors.

**Eleanor Dienstag**

SOURCE: A review of *The Thieving Dwarfs*, in *The New York Times Book Review*, April 30, 1967, p. 26.

Mary Calhoun's **The Thieving Dwarfs,** based on German legend, is a gay, exuberant tale of dwarfs who, made invisible by their miraculous mist caps, carry on their lives—working, feasting, stealing grain from farmers' fields—without the local population knowing about it. One day farmer Karl catches sight of these little people without their hats on, and a unique friendship ensues. Though this special relationship comes to a not unhappy but definite end, I suspect every child who reads about those enchanted days will devote himself to figuring out how he would have better handled the whole problem of relations between little people and adults. The busy, Breughel-like illustrations by Janet McCaffrey, are a joy, and help make this a charming book that should appeal to that mischievous, spirited imagination.

### Virginia Haviland

SOURCE: A review of *The Thieving Dwarfs,* in *The Horn Book Magazine,* Vol. XLIII, No. 3, June, 1967, p. 339.

This fresh picture book is inspired by German legendary lore from the Harz Mountains. The dwarfs that lived there "lived much as people do. . . . But no one saw them, for they wore mist caps that made them invisible." At one time they had joined in neighborly borrowing and lending, but after being spied on, they had become only thieves. When the villagers seized the dwarfs' caps, a mass departure was the result, for, without their means of invisibility, the dwarfs could not endure a life among people. Most of the broad spreads in browns, green, and fuchsia show panoramas of domestic busyness (full of medieval flavor), as the "stumpy" long-nosed dwarfs, humming at their work, hurry about and become entangled with the villagers.

### Zena Sutherland

SOURCE: A review of *The Thieving Dwarfs,* in *Bulletin of the Center for Children's Books,* Vol. 20, No. 11, July-August, 1967, p. 167.

A read-aloud book with lively, scrawly illustrations in subdued hues, the story based on folklore of Hessian Germany. The writing style has an easy, conversational quality that makes it eminently suitable for story-telling. Long ago there lived a farmer who discovered that the dwarfs had mist caps that made them invisible; by catching some of the thieving dwarfs he was able to strike a bargain: they would not steal from him, and he would tell nobody about them. The dwarfs were seen, however, and the townspeople learned that if they could knock off the mist caps, the dwarfs could be caught. That was the finish; that began the exodus of the dwarfs and that is why a dwarf is no longer seen in Germany—a rather flat ending to the story.

## THE RUNAWAY BROWNIE (1967)

### Kirkus Service

SOURCE: A review of *The Runaway Brownie,* in *Kirkus Service,* Vol. XXXV, No. 14, July 15, 1967, p. 801.

Miss Calhoun has determined to find the wee folk wherever they were, to present them however they were: this is the second in a series that began with *The Thieving Dwarfs.* From Scotland comes the brownie, a hardworking, honest species attached one to a family. This particular brownie, Angus, runs away when his greedy new master, Duncan, tries to give him rich gifts in hopes of rich rewards. Neither Meg, the housekeeper (who finds him in the hollow of a tree) nor Duncan himself (who climbs to seek him in a cave) can persuade Angus to return; only after Duncan's departure does Angus' young

admirer, Rob, get him back. Again (as in *Dwarfs*), the illustrations [by Janet McCaffery] have a floridity and nervousness which will not appeal equally to everyone, this time in tones of heather and mustard and green. The blank verse sometimes seems labored and the pace slow, but authenticity, atmosphere and pictorial animation overbalance.

### Jane Yolen

SOURCE: A review of *The Runaway Brownie,* in *The New York Times Book Review,* September 10, 1967, p. 38.

Mary Calhoun stays in touch with the ways and language of Scotland in *The Runaway Brownie.* But the book seems more forced than flowing. It amounts to a predictable tale of how a family woos its elf back after he has gone off, taking good luck with him. Janet McCaffery's illustrations in the colors of heather are appropriately gruff and full of detail, though her people appear rather toothy.

### Zena Sutherland

SOURCE: A review of *The Runaway Brownie,* in *Bulletin of the Center for Children's Books,* Vol. 21, No. 3, November, 1967, p. 37.

A story that comprises elements of various Scottish fairy tales, tales in which the brownie is a proud creature and belongs to a single family. Here the brownie, Angus, is offended when the old master dies and the avaricious young one tries to bribe the brownie into producing riches. Disgusted, the young master departs and Angus returns to the farm to serve the small nephew, Rob, who really cares for the family brownie. The story is nicely told albeit rather slow-moving; the illustrations [by Janet McCaffery] are quite busy with detail and most of them are suffused with a pinkish-lavender glow that palls.

### Ethel L. Heins

SOURCE: A review of *The Runaway Brownie,* in *The Horn Book Magazine,* Vol. XLIII, December, 1967, p. 741.

An original story "woven from fragmentary tales mostly from the southwest of Scotland" about a brownie called Angus, "a gruff little creature, half-man, half-beastie." Angus belonged to a farm where, like all brownies everywhere, he helped faithfully with the labor, played tricks on the folk "just to make them behave," and brought good fortune to the household. But brownies are creatures of integrity and honor, and when a greedy new master inherited the farm and tried to bribe Angus into bringing more riches, the wee man departed in a rage, plunging the farm and the family into bad luck and evil days. The author's second story about Celtic fairy folk will be as well liked as *The Hungry Leprechaun;* but the artist, [Janet McCaffery,] carried away by her own striving for a misty, heathery look, has unfortunately drenched her well-drawn pictures with too many purplish tones.

## THE LAST TWO ELVES IN DENMARK (1968)

### Kirkus Reviews

SOURCE: A review of *The Last Two Elves in Denmark*, in *Kirkus Service*, Vol. XXXVI, No. 5, March 1, 1968, p. 253.

Quick Fritz of Bol contends Hans of Aasgard is a pampered *nisse*, and Hans counters that Quick Fritz is a slave *nisse*. After all, Helga the farmer's daughter often neglects to feed Fritz—and more than once they come to blows. The elves resolve to fight it out with Peter the stableboy as witness; changing from *nisse* to cat to dog to flaming wheel, Quick Fritz overruns his rival with a strong assist from Peter. With victory comes the realization that he's the only elf in Denmark. "Well, if that be so, I'll be the best one," grins Fritz, and he's off to trick Helga fulltime. Like *The Thieving Dwarfs* and *The Runaway Brownie, The Last Two Elves* lose some of their exuberance to strident (tangerine) coloration, but they're still fun to watch.

### Zena Sutherland

SOURCE: A review of *The Last Two Elves in Denmark*, in *Bulletin of the Center for Children's Books*, Vol. 21, No. 8, April, 1968, pp. 123–24.

Once there had been thousands of nisses in Denmark, little old elves who helped about the farms, "but the magical men moved away when Christianity came to the country." Now only two were left—the nisse at Aasgard, Hans, a spoiled darling; and Quick Fritz, the Bol nisse, neglected and mischievous. Only the stableboy was kind to Quick Fritz; even Hans taunted him. The two elves turned themselves into cats and, fighting fiercely, into dogs, then into huge wheels. Helped by Peter, Quick Fritz ended the life of Hans, and then the stableboy and the only elf in Denmark laid their plans to play new tricks on the family. The illustrations [by Janet McCaffery] are scrawly and lively; the story has verve and pace, but seems anticlimactic at its close.

### Dorothy Gunzenhauser

SOURCE: A review of *The Last Two Elves in Denmark*, in *School Library Journal*, Vol. 93, No. 8, April 15, 1968, p. 1782.

This is a rather sad story about the last two Danish nisses, those helpful, though mischievous little men who at one time could be found on most Danish farms. Instead of living peacefully on their respective farms,

Hans, whose good treatment has made him conceited, and Quick Fritz, who is faithful though ill-treated, fight until only one remains. The slightness of the story makes this book less interesting than the previous two by the same author and illustrator (*The Thieving Dwarfs* and *The Runaway Brownie*), but this book shows a similar attention to detail in text and illustration.

## THE GOBLIN UNDER THE STAIRS (1968)

### Kirkus Service

SOURCE: A review of *The Goblin under the Stairs*, in *Kirkus Service*, Vol. XXXVI, No. 13, July 1, 1968, p. 685.

The Yorkshire boggart—a hairy seen through knotholes who vanishes as doors open—is a wee frisky man to the farmer's son who discovers him, a wild houseplaguing goblin to the farmer, a neat servant elf to the wife who leaves him cream and a honey cake at night. Whether twisty-spinning the house into chaos, hiding in the cart when they try to move, or twisty-spinning the house back into order, he outsmarts the lot with elfin charm.

### Zena Sutherland

SOURCE: "Books are Bridges," in *Saturday Review*, Vol. LI, No. 34, August 24, 1968, pp. 42–3.

One of the small creatures of English folklore is the boggart, a hairy wee thing full of mischief who attaches himself to a family and cannot be pried loose. This rather slight story about a boggart who does just that is nice to read aloud and just right for storytelling. All of the traditional theories about boggarts are included: they can only be seen through a knothole, they look different to different people, and they can be beguiled into permanent cooperation if a succulent snack is left for them each night.

### Ruth P. Bull and Betsy Hearne

SOURCE: A review of *The Goblin under the Stairs*, in *Booklist*, Vol. 65, No. 2, September 15, 1968, p. 112.

A hairy boggart who moves into a closet under the stairs of an English farmhouse is discovered when the farmer's son, attracted by a rustling, peeks through a knothole in the wall. To the boy the boggart is a sprightly playmate, to the farmer's wife he is a good servant elf who will keep her kitchen clean; the farmer, however, looks upon the boggart as a house-plaguing, tormenting goblin and orders him to leave. The diverting picture-book story of the commotion that ensues before boggart and family settle down amicably together is told with humor and spirit in well-matched text and illustrations.

### THE PIXY AND THE LAZY HOUSEWIFE (1969)

#### *Kirkus Reviews*

SOURCE: A review of *The Pixy and the Lazy Housewife,* in *Kirkus Reviews,* Vol. XXXVII, No. 5, March 1, 1969, p. 233.

Slovenly Bess tricks the pixies into cleaning her cottage—but "How to get rid of the plague of pixies" once they've discovered they've been duped? "Work, they said? Then work she must" . . . until the pixies satisfied, leave her in peace. And work she will henceforward, lest they return. Further animated by infusions of Devonshire folklore: Bess sighting the pixies by touching a girl carrying a four-leaf clover, dispelling a sudden pixyish mist by turning her "cloak on the fairy folk"—and drawn with telling detail (and less strident color), this is perhaps the most successful of the series, pert and scrappy.

#### Sidney D. Long

SOURCE: A review of *The Pixy and the Lazy Housewife,* in *The Horn Book Magazine,* Vol. XLV, No. 2, April, 1969, p. 160.

Unknown to the pixies in Devon, England, there lived a slovenly housewife named Bess, a woman too lazy even to turn over in bed. Since pixies in Devonshire could not abide dirty houses, it was only the remote location of Bess's cottage that saved her from their wrath. But being foolish as well as lazy, Bess decided to entice some pixies home—planning to take advantage of their tidy ways. So she tricked pixy Willy Tatters and his mates into her basket and carried them back to her cottage. And although her scheme for pixy labor seemed at first to work, the tables were soon turned and Bess found herself scrubbing her own floor. The story is full of pixy lore, and the illustrations [by Janet McCaffery] suggest the greens, pinks, and golds of Devon summertime.

#### *Booklist*

SOURCE: A review of *The Pixy and the Lazy Housewife,* in *Booklist,* Vol. 65, No. 15, April 1, 1969, p. 884.

Another amusing picture-book story by the author and the illustrator of *The Goblin under the Stairs.* A slovenly Devon housewife, so lazy she thinks twice before turning over in bed, tricks the pixies into working for her and then finds the joke is on her—she is forced to mend her ways before she can get rid of Willy Tatters and the other angry, pesky pixies. The flavorsome illustrations [by Janet McCaffery] match the mood of the tale.

#### Zena Sutherland

SOURCE: A review of *The Pixy and the Lazy Housewife,*
in *Saturday Review,* Vol. LII, No. 19, May 10, 1969, p. 55.

Once upon a time there lived in Devon a slovenly housewife, fat and cheery, and so lazy she thought twice before turning over in bed. Now, the pixies of Devon occasionally cleaned people's homes, but none wanted to tackle the dirt and disorder that Bess made. When some of them were tricked and caught by Bess, they soon turned the tables on her, and tormented the poor woman until she worked harder than she ever had in her life. The message is clear, but it is so cheerfully conveyed that the story is not weighted by a minatory burden. The flyaway pictures of the buxom woman and the darting pixies are in happy accord with the colloquial ease and humor of the writing. Nice for storytelling as well as for reading aloud.

#### Zena Sutherland

SOURCE: A review of *The Pixy and the Lazy Housewife,* in *Bulletin of the Center for Children's Books,* Vol. 23, No. 4, December, 1969, p. 55.

Legend has it that the household pixies of Devon are hard workers but cunning in their teasing. So, at least, Old Bess found them when she trapped some to help her with her work, for Bess was the laziest woman there was, and the most slovenly. Outwitted by the pixies, Bess was tormented and punished until she changed her lazy ways. The tale is gold in folk style, effective for reading aloud and good for storytelling. The writing has gusto and humor; the illustrations [by Janet McCaffery] have an antic note.

### THE TRAVELING BALL OF STRING (1969)

#### *Kirkus Reviews*

SOURCE: A review of *The Traveling Ball of String,* in *Kirkus Reviews,* Vol. XXXVII, No. 12, June 15, 1969, p. 629.

A tongue-in-cheek teaser, American-style, from the collaborators on *The Goblin Under the Stairs, The Runaway Brownie,* etc. The Widow Tuckett, the "savingest woman" around, held onto jar lids, scraps of cloth, combings from her hair, and had a ball of string "that was the seven-days' wonder of the county." It was something of a pet to her—she talked to it and had a special place for it. But when the shed boards gave way, the string went on a downhill rampage—overrunning a wagon, upsetting the church bazaar and strawberry festival, scaring horses, then landing on a runaway's back and thus saving the child in the wagon behind it. "Always knew that string would come in handy some day," says the Widow of her knotty hero. The text has traces of backcountry breeziness and the predominantly red and blue drawings [by Janet McCaffery] have the same easygoing spunk.

## Diane Farrell

SOURCE: A review of *The Traveling Ball of String,* in *The Horn Book Magazine,* Vol. XLV, No. 6, December, 1969, p. 664.

A slaphappy tall tale about "the savingest woman," Widow Tuckett, who saved a ball of string as "Big as a rain barrel, only fatter around." One day the string burst the boards of its shed and rolled downhill, knocking down everything in its path. It tore through "the church ladies' annual open-air bazaar and strawberry festival," scaring a horse hitched to a buggy with a little child inside. The horse bolted, but the string laid the horse flat. "'Always knew that string would come in handy some day!' said Widow Tuckett. . . . Saved a child! Think of that!" The illustrations [by Janet McCaffery] are as bold and funny as the tale.

## 📖 *MAGIC IN THE ALLEY* (1970)

### Kirkus Reviews

SOURCE: A review of *Magic in the Alley,* in *Kirkus Reviews,* Vol. XXXVIII, No. 5, March 1, 1970, p. 242.

Dismayingly arcane beyond the skeletal beginning when characterless Cleery of improbable Cricklewood starts seeking a magical adventure—and just happens to happen on an enchanted boxful in an alley antiquary. She has a thing about alleys anyway and explores Cricklewood's phenomenal number with friend Knobs and the stuffed crow named Crow she revives. They meet a mermaid, an elf, and a witch, among others, while auto-enrapturous verbiage mildews the brew: "They passed through a scarf of fog. . . . Knobs looked up into the cottonwood tree, black sculpture of limbs lifting through the whiteness." And then the whole dreamy fantasy turns into a nightmare of evil as a scarecrow attacks Cleery, forcing her to use up the "Last Magic." An ordinary bag of tricks become alchemy fraught with hallucinations, complications, implications . . . almost malignantly merchandising magic for its own sake in no substantive context whatever.

### Susan M. Budd

SOURCE: A review of *Magic in the Alley,* in *School Library Journal,* Vol. 95, No. 10, May 15, 1970, p. 69.

Cleery thinks alleys are secret, mysterious, magical places, so she is not surprised to find a box of seven magic items in an alley junk shop. The magic changing powder, when sprinkled on a stuffed crow, brings him to life, but he cannot fly; Cleery then uses the "One Wish" stone to wish for something enchanted in each new alley she will explore that summer. She, her friend Knobs, and Crow set out to explore the alleys of Cricklewood to find a magic to make Crow fly. They encounter a goldfish turned mermaid who prophesies Crow will fly

again when he finds his own "weather of magic." In their search, they discover an enchanted garden, a haunted tree house, a lawn statue turned elf, and an old lady turned witch, but no "crow weather." Finally, they find it in a last nightmarish adventure in which Cleery is attacked by an evil, hissing scarecrow and Crow flies to protect her. The characters are flat and the writing is pedestrian. Unfortunately, there is no magic here.

### Ethel L. Heins

SOURCE: A review of *Magic in the Alley,* in *The Horn Book Magazine,* Vol. XLVI, No. 3, June, 1970, p. 295.

Cleery—bred on vigorous tales of witches, elves, trolls, and fairies—was a true believer in magic. "Magic was an unseen power, shimmering just beyond what she could see and touch. Like a wind that hadn't blown yet. Cleery was ready for magic whenever it was ready for her." And in the ordinary, everyday world of Cricklewood, the most likely place for magic to be lurking was in one of the back alleys that crisscrossed the old town. In such a forgotten place Cleery one summer morning discovered The Alley Junk Shop; and in its dim interior she found and purchased an old carved wooden box. In it were seven magic objects, including such obviously useful items as a bottle of powder "for changing things," a twenty-four hour cloak of invisibility, and a green wishing stone. Enthusiastic but somewhat inept, Cleery brought an ancient stuffed crow to life, gave him the power of speech, but failed to restore flying ability to the indignant bird. Cleery, along with her best friend Knobs, a sensible boy "who likes to explore things," and the grounded, often cantankerous, crow became inseparable companions through a long, luxurious summer of enchanted adventures with a mermaid, a ghost, an elderly elf, and "a good, old-fashioned witch." A capable storyteller has written a well-constructed, convincing fantasy, created three highly individualized characters, and infused her writing with delightful bits of practical, down-to-earth, unmagical wisdom.

### Booklist

SOURCE: A review of *Magic in the Alley,* in *Booklist,* Vol. 67, No. 1, September 1, 1970, p. 55.

Cleery, a firm believer in magic who is always exploring alleys in search of unusual treasure and uncommon adventures, has her fondest wish come true the day she discovers a carved wooden box with a trick lock in a junk shop. Inside the box are seven magic items one of which she tries out on an old stuffed crow that comes to life and can talk but, much to its annoyance, cannot fly. With the aid of the other six items, Cleery, her friend Knobs, and the crow share some extraordinary magical experiences while trying to find a special magic to make the crow fly. A light, engaging story. . . .

Then he wobbled. Batting his paws didn't help, so he waved his tail to catch his balance and stretched his whiskers wide. In the dark, he could feel the fence rail guiding his feet.

*From* High-Wire Henry, *written by Mary Calhoun. Illustrated by Erick Ingraham.*

### WHITE WITCH OF KYNANCE (1970)

**Andrea Brooks**

SOURCE: A review of *White Witch of Kynance,* in *School Library Journal,* Vol. 95, No. 10, May 15, 1970, p. 81.

A light novel about the conflict between reason and superstition in 16th-Century Cornwall. Hoping to learn the spells which will drive away her demons, Jennet Trevail becomes an apprentice to the local white witch. A belief in God and the science of healing gradually replace her fear of the devil and awe of witchcraft. Though the plot is slight, the characters are engaging and unpretentious; the atmosphere reeks of pentacles, spells, and brews and will appeal to the astrologically hooked.

**Kirkus Reviews**

SOURCE: A review of *White Witch of Kynance,* in *Kirkus Reviews,* Vol. XXXVIII, No. 13, July 1, 1970, p. 687.

God vs. demons in 16th-century Cornwall, and in frustratingly slow-to-catch-on Jennet Trevail who thinks white magic can exorcise the dark powers of her medieval mind. The story proceeds in hyperbolic platitudes through Jennet's ESP—she can presage death somehow

and share other people's pain—to her apprenticeship to wise good-witch An Marget, above superstition . . . except in regard to a long-dead phantom lover. Indeed Jennet's mistress almost comes unhinged when (beset by a demon called desire) she nearly believes the unbelievable; but there's a warning in the form of a colic woman's need for her treatment—it was God reminding An Marget "which power He had given her and which power was His alone." Now, only at the end, does Jennet find her own self exultantly in this manifestation: "She'd be no priestess of magic—and was An Marget really?—but she could heal. And she could be a wife." To Robin Bender, who long since had said "I'm just God's fool, I guess. I trust Him," whenever Jennet in her private terror asked how he could laugh away the things that plagued her. The metaphor itself is obvious, like the cliches: the hollow parson "Piggy" Thomas, the kettles of herbs, the talking bird, the village vixens quick to slander; but then there are those long expository passages and the problem of the Church alluded to, never laid bare. So much inflated form, so little content—phantasmagoria with no finesse.

**Jean Fritz**

SOURCE: A review of *White Witch of Kynance,* in *The New York Times Book Review,* October 4, 1970, p. 30.

It may be better for a girl in Elizabethan England who is afraid of demons to find herself a green-eyed husband than to flirt with magic. But Jennet won't believe it. Instead she apprentices herself to An Marget, a white witch who lives in a stone cottage that has her shadow built into its walls. Jennet reasons if she could only learn the proper words, the right charms, she would always be safe. But even in An Marget's cottage there are no such words—no words strong enough to keep a white witch from being tempted by black magic, no words strong enough to persuade a green-eyed young man from trying to raise the dead.

It all makes a grand story and if it turns out that magic is supposed to be less powerful than everyday goodness, the spell has already been cast. What is *really* important is being with Mary Calhoun in West Cornwall: running across the moors, top-toeing in midnight graveyards, climbing grassy cliffs, listening to a meadow pipit, smelling gorse and tasting salt air. This is the perfect place for anyone who, like Jennet, needs at times to be out of sight of the smoke of her own chimney.

### MERMAID OF STORMS (1970)

**Kirkus Reviews**

SOURCE: A review of *Mermaid of Storms,* in *Kirkus Reviews,* Vol. XXXVIII, No. 13, July 1, 1970, p. 677.

Screaming red and yellow and yet, surprisingly, supple: the first impression of fauve flashiness dissolves as Carita, the smallest mermaid, is borne in . . . "Laughing and swishing, she swirled up a stormy sea, then riffled it smooth again with her tail." But the special storm she has promised her sisters is stayed by Pedro's shell music; his "father is a fisherman and he and his friends are out in their boats on the water. If you make a storm, they might drown." "What is that to me?" retorts Carita until, lured by the boy's flattery, lulled by the fun of playing with him, she's divested of her magic comb and can't persuade him to return it but might, with her sister-sirens, sing him to the bottom of the sea; then, understanding what drowning means, she repents and promises safety for him and his family in return for her comb. At the last the boats are in and the mermaids dance on the billows in joyful abandon—by which time the nubile water-nymphs green and pink, the red and blue ribbon waves, the flying red tresses of the one, the transfixed white peaks of the other, have come to seem integral with the story. Pedro fares less well by this treatment but what chance has a boy against a minx of a mermaid?

**Margaret Riddell**

SOURCE: A review of *Mermaid of Storms*, in *School Library Journal*, Vol. 96, No. 22, December, 1970, p. 32.

In no way comparable to the exquisite *Little Mermaid* of Andersen, lacking even the gaiety of Slobodkin's now out of print *Little Mermaid Who Could Not Sing*, this features pseudo-poetic prose and wildly colored illustrations which together constitute a cheap-looking, unbeautiful book. The little mermaid here frolics with a human playmate and then finds she cannot sing up a storm because the boy, son of a fisherman, has stolen her magic comb. Only when she promises that none of his family shall ever drown is her comb returned to her. The two now go their separate ways amicably, making plans for future play. Nothing imaginative or exciting relates this story to the classic lore of the sea people as it is evidenced in, for example, the charming tales in *A Book of Mermaids* (1968), collected by Ruth Manning-Sanders, any one of which evokes more interest than the *Mermaid of Storms*.

### 📖 *DAISY, TELL ME!* (1971)

#### *Kirkus Reviews*

SOURCE: A review of *Daisy, Tell Me!*, in *Kirkus Reviews*, Vol. XXXIX, No. 11, June 1, 1971, p. 587.

"Two little girls named Sarah and Carrie,/Each picked a daisy, asked,/'Does he love me?'/Each plucked off petals, chanting together,/He loves me, he loves me not./He loves me, pluck,/He loves me not, pluck." Janet McCaffery colors them spring in lemon and lime, jelly-bean pinks, blues, and oranges, and she tones them old-fashioned in all their disporting while below she records each process of elimination (one can play along): who shall I marry? what dress shall I wear? on my feet? ("'Boots,' said Sa-

rah. /'Roller skates,' said Carrie"); how shall I ride? ("'Coach!' said Sarah/'Wheelbarrow!' said Carrie"); the bouquets? the bridesmaids—"Princess, fairy, washerwoman, gypsy?" . . . "And we'll be beautiful. . . . And live happily ever after . . . With our ever-loving beggar man/And our ever-loving Indian chief!" Whimsy to take (or to leave) for the gossamer spirit and not for the letter (the jacket copy, asking for trouble, suggests it for "all little girls with fun in their hearts and marriage on their minds"); it lilts (if unevenly) away from here and now as though resisting any stabs at making a mountain out of a meadow lark.

#### *Publishers Weekly*

SOURCE: A review of *Daisy, Tell Me!*, in *Publishers Weekly*, Vol. 200, No. 9, August 30, 1971, p. 274.

Here are nonsense chants for fun with flowers. The first chant is the most familiar: the daisy game of plucking the petals to determine if he does or doesn't love the player. The rest are less familiar, or were before this book, for its illustrations, bright as a May morning, will go far to making them all equally favored by small girls, eager to read their future in the flowers.

#### **Susanne Gilles**

SOURCE: A review of *Daisy, Tell Me!*, in *School Library Journal*, Vol. 96, No. 22, December 15, 1971, p. 51.

Both story and watercolor paintings [by Janet McCaffery] are bland here. Two little girls in a flowery meadow pick petals off flowers to see who they will marry, what flowers they will carry, where they will live, etc.; their findings are related in eight short chants, all connected with weddings (e.g., "'And what shall we wear/ On our feet at our weddings?' They asked a devil's paintbrush./ Slippers, sandals,/ Roller skates, boots?/ 'Boots,' said Sarah. 'Roller skates!' said Carrie."). The book ends with each little girl tripping off with her flower-chosen bridegroom—a beggar man and an Indian chief, respectively. The jacket blurb says: "This glimpse into the future will enthrall all little girls with fun in their hearts and marriage on their minds." It's doubtful—and anyway, why should little girls have marriage on their minds?

### 📖 *IT'S GETTING BEAUTIFUL NOW* (1971)

#### *Kirkus Reviews*

SOURCE: A review of *It's Getting Beautiful Now*, in *Kirkus Reviews*, Vol. XXXIX, No. 18, September 15, 1971, p. 1020.

The standard teen-age novel updated and generally improved, with a realistic treatment of marijuana use, a hopeful but far from euphoric ending, and a snappy montage form. A series of present-tense, first-person sketches, from a few lines to a few pages in length, presents the senior (high school) year in the life of one Bert Tomlinson, a decent but troubled boy whose moderately rebellious acts are motivated by the need for his father's acceptance. Caught buying grass, Bert is taken from his frequently absent truck driver father and placed, pending his hearing, in the middle-class home of his friend Howard Fredrichs. The Fredrichs are good to Bert and offer to keep him indefinitely, but "it just isn't my home," and at the final disposal hearing both Bert and his father request and are granted another chance to make a home together. Beneath the jazzy surface the characters are stereotyped and the motivation is mechanical; but Bert assumes some dimension as the story progresses, and it's a relief to read a junior novel in which the only ill effects of pot smoking are the legal consequences.

**Jack Forman**

SOURCE: A review of *It's Getting Beautiful Now,* in *School Library Journal,* Vol. 96, No. 22, December 15, 1971, p. 62.

Everything turns out predictably well in this story of Bert Tomlinson, a confused boy who is on the outs with his father Nick (his mother had long ago abandoned the family) and in trouble with the law. In the process of straightening himself out and reconciling his differences with Nick, he is arrested for shoplifting and smoking marijuana. Throughout the story, Bert stays with a friend's more close-knit family, which constantly prompts thought of the mutual lack of respect and, seemingly, of love between himself and his own father. What's unusual about this story is its deliberately fragmented format: it alternates between effective sections of Bert's often introspective first-person narrative and frequently confusing chunks of text which are either Bert's conversations with other people or other people's conversations about Bert. Despite the different format and the inclusion of references to *Crime and Punishment* and some rock lyrics for relevance, this remains little more than a typical teenage-boy-in-trouble adventure.

**Dorothy M. Broderick**

SOURCE: "Growing Time," in *The New York Times Book Review,* January 16, 1972, p. 8.

The cast of characters reminds one of an Agatha Christie mystery and serves to forewarn that identification will replace characterization of the participants. Alternately told in various voices, this novel (with a big dose of psychology) shows the many sides of 17-year-old Bert Tomlinson's problems, particularly his finding himself and still being acceptable to his truck driver father.

**Zena Sutherland**

SOURCE: A review of *It's Getting Beautiful Now,* in *Bulletin of the Center for Children's Books,* Vol. 25, No. 6, February, 1972, p. 88.

Bert has been living with his father in a trailer, but they can't get along. Tough and contemptuous, Bert's father has little sense of responsibility—only anger. When Bert is caught buying marijuana, he is taken in by a friend's family. The story is told in short segments, either commentary by Bert or brief passages of dialogue. Although choppy, the device serves both to clarify the characters' viewpoints and to establish their personalities. Bert is faced with the decision: a year on probation with the friend's family or a year in a reformatory, but he begins to feel that there is hope: his father has shown up unexpectedly and asks if he may have a chance at making a better home for his son. Although there are eventful incidents, the story line is not strong; the book is an often-vivid depiction of a situation, realistic and candid, but it has little impetus.

## CAMELS ARE MEANER THAN MULES (1971)

**Nan Pavey Kurtz**

SOURCE: A review of *Camels Are Meaner than Mules,* in *School Library Journal,* Vol. 97, No. 12, June 15, 1972, p. 2236.

Young readers who enjoy tales of Pecos Bill, Paul Bunyan, Stormalong, et. al. will find entertaining reading with a fresh touch here. The Southwest in pre-Civil War days is the stage for an experiment in using camels to move the Army instead of mules. "Humpbacked trouble compounded of meanness and smell" is how former mule skinner Pete defines a camel, but readers will chuckle at the dour dilemmas into which Gertie the galooty camel maneuvers her keeper. From Val Verde, Texas to California, Gertie and Pete become involved in midnight capers, races, camel concerts, and even a love affair. Though certainly not a first purchase, this brief, cheerful title makes good bait for slow readers in the upper elementary grades and junior high.

## THE FLOWER MOTHER (1972)

**Kirkus Reviews**

SOURCE: A review of *The Flower Mother,* in *Kirkus Reviews,* Vol. XL, No. 3, February 1, 1972, p. 129.

An art nouveau Flower Mother with "fronds of forsythias for hair" showers the earth successively with poppies, daisies and hollyhocks, but each rain of flowers is destroyed by the onslaughts of Dry Wind until at last (laughing "my time has come . . . the first of May") she touches the weeds sown by Dry Wind and they bloom into a field of dandelions, bringing spring to the Land of Sticks and Stones. Wintry bluster might have been a more appropriate adversary than the hot blasts of Dry Wind, and, though this para-mythological explanation of the origin of May Day is cleverly contrived, it founders under the combined weight of excessive ambition and lush overdecoration.

## Publishers Weekly

SOURCE: A review of *The Flower Mother,* in *Publishers Weekly,* Vol. 201, No. 10, March 6, 1972, p. 63.

Wherever the Flower Mother walks, flowers appear; but when Dry Wind blows, the flowers become weeds. Their struggle for control of the Land of Sticks and Stones remains at a standstill until the arrival of May Day when the weeds are converted into golden dandelions. In this version of the events leading up to the first May Day, Mary Calhoun and Janet McCaffery make a sharp division in both text and illustrations: Flower Mother, who has fronds of forsythia for hair and a cloak woven of lilacs and apple blossoms, is pictured in bright colors; while Dry Wind, shaped of dust and snagged with tumbleweed, is illustrated in browns and gray. The writing is skillful, the content imaginative; but illustrations in art nouveau style overburden the text to the point of confusion.

## Zena Sutherland

SOURCE: A review of *The Flower Mother,* in *Bulletin of the Center for Children's Books,* Vol. 25, No. 8, April, 1972, p. 118.

Long ago, when the Flower Mother walked in the land, her cloak woven of lilacs and apple blossoms and her hair made of fronds of forsythia, flowers sprang up wherever she walked. Only in the arid Land of Sticks and Stones did Dry Wind defeat her. But Flower Mother knew her time would come, the month of May, and she covered the land with dandelions. Sturdy and golden, they resisted Dry Wind (unlike the poppies, hollyhocks, and daisies that had come before) and then Flower Mother covered the land with spring flowers. It may confuse children who are familiar with gardens to find spring flowers coming after daisies and poppies, but the verdant theme has appeal. The illustrations are interesting in design, but florally heavy-handed: the poetic cloak of lilacs and apple blossoms appears as purple berry-like blobs and pink circles.

## 📖 MRS. DOG'S OWN HOUSE (1972)

### Kirkus Reviews

SOURCE: A review of *Mrs. Dog's Own House,* in *Kirkus Reviews,* Vol. XXXIX, No. 4, August 1, 1972, p. 856.

Mrs. Dog is happy with her plain and simple house until on the successive advice of her friends—a rooster, a squirrel, a pig, etc.—she gradually turns it into a mansion by adding a tower, an elaborate staircase, a parlor, a kitchen,

and finally an oak-beamed banquet hall in which she gives a magnificent party. But when the butler appears with a tray of raspberries, Mrs. Dog comes to her senses ("Dogs don't eat raspberries"), demolishing all the grand additions before her guests can grab a bite. McCaffery accentuates the ludicrous in Mrs. Dog's flowery extravagance, adding a sort of fiesta flourish to Ms. Calhoun's commonplace object lesson.

## Publishers Weekly

SOURCE: A review of *Mrs. Dog's Own House,* in *Publishers Weekly,* Vol. 202, No. 9, August 28, 1972, p. 264.

Mrs. Dog is perfectly happy in her simple house until friends—Mr. Rooster, Mrs. Sheep, Mr. Squirrel and others—point out its lacks. Mrs. Dog then adds a tower, a kitchen, a marble fireplace, soft divans and cushions, and other amenities. She gives a house-warming party to which all her friends are invited. When the cook serves raspberries, which dogs don't eat, Mrs. Dog realizes she has been foolish, trying to please everyone but herself. She sweeps away all the fancy additions and winds up with her original comfortable house, just right for a dog. A lively little fantasy, with appropriate pictures.

## 📖 THREE KINDS OF STUBBORN (1972)

### Carol Chatfield

SOURCE: A review of *Three Kinds of Stubborn,* in *School Library Journal,* Vol. 96, No. 22, December 15, 1972, pp. 4085–86.

Three tales define Missouri stubbornness in Mary Calhoun's **Three Kinds of Stubborn.** In the first, Cousin Emmett learns to handle his mules by being more stubborn than they are; next, Little Ida, determined to prove she is right, shakes up a setting hen, outpicks a bear in a blackberry patch, and her umbrella is struck by lightning; last, Blue-Louisey puts a hex on the house in which she works: "'Nothin' come outta that house 'til it be something good.'" Each episode is introduced by a storyteller which unnecessarily slows down the action. And Cousin Emmett's slang expressions and casual speech patterns—"Git up now, honey, dad-gum it," and "Move, you zingle-tailed varmint! Ding blast the luck!"—will limit the book's usefulness to more advanced readers. However, Calhoun's style lends itself to reading aloud and Edward Malsberg's drawings add an appropriate touch of humor.

## 📖 THE BATTLE OF REUBEN ROBIN AND KITE UNCLE JOHN (1973)

### Kirkus Reviews

SOURCE: A review of *The Battle of Reuben Robin and Kite Uncle John,* in *Kirkus Reviews,* Vol. XLI, No. 13, July, 1973, p. 680.

The battle for a length of string, between an old man with a kite (called, reasonably enough, Kite Uncle John) and a bound-determined robin who wants the kite string for his nest, ends when Kite Uncle John manages to reel in the kite with bird attached ("still flapping, feet braced against nothing, Reuben Robin came skidding down the sky"), then tosses the robin a tuft of his own beard as material for the nest. After that, as Kite Uncle John is a patient man, "he gave his beard and he flew his kite every March for the rest of his life." Mary Calhoun's easy colloquial lilt and Janet McCaffery's breezy pictures keep this light-weight contrivance aloft.

## Booklist

SOURCE: A review of *The Battle of Reuben Robin & Kite Uncle John,* in *Booklist,* Vol. 70, No. 6, November 15, 1973, p. 336.

The struggle between a determined bird and an old man over a piece of string that one wants for building his nest and the other needs for flying his kite carries a tallish tale high up into the air. The Missouri dialect and folktale tone are not always convincing, but [Janet] McCaffery's earth-hued, fuzzy-edged illustrations lift the story above the ordinary.

## Zena Sutherland

SOURCE: A review of *The Battle of Reuben Robin & Kite Uncle John,* in *Bulletin of the Center for Children's Books,* Vol. 27, No. 5, January, 1974, p. 75.

Vigorous illustrations add humor to a tallish tale that is written with the cadence of speech, nice for reading aloud and for storytelling. A lively, elderly man, called "Kite Uncle John" because he taught all the children how to fly kites, had found a superlative string for kite flying—but when his kite was made, he saw that Reuben Robin had also discovered the string, in fact was using it for nest-building. John took the string, the robin fussed; John flew the kite, the robin followed, scolding. Kite Uncle John ran himself breathless trying to outwit the competitive bird, who rode the kite, pecked at the string, and finally just took it in his beak and hung on. The problem is solved to the satisfaction of both parties in a rollicking, light-weight, pleasant story.

## THE HORSE COMES FIRST (1974)

### Kirkus Reviews

SOURCE: A review of *The Horse Comes First,* in *Kirkus Reviews,* Vol. XLII, No. 6, March 15, 1974, p. 297.

Despite the instant rapport that springs up between Randy and the two-year-old gelding Charlie Stride, the immature, high-strung Randy has trouble remembering Grandad's basic law of horse training—the horse comes first. Randy's first weeks caring for Grandad and Aunt Connie's three trotters are marked by the kind of head-strong carelessness only a relative (and then only a fictional one) would tolerate, and when he does begin to develop a sense of responsibility his concern is for Pen, the meek stable girl who is his rival for Charlie's affections. But though stable work seems to have a therapeutic effect on Randy, it's obvious that readers will lean toward Grandad's sense of values—and give the lore of training harness winners (glossary appended) first place in their attention.

### Betsy Hearne

SOURCE: A review of *The Horse Comes First,* in *Booklist,* Vol. 70, No. 18, May 15, 1974, p. 1054.

Throughout the summer Randy Meister spends with his grandfather and Aunt Connie, he struggles to adjust to their reserved ways and complete dedication to the horses they own and train for harness racing. At first, fatherless Randy imagines that his city-boy ignorance is the dampening factor in his persistent attempts to relate to his grandfather. When the reticence continues even after he learns enough to help with routine work, he wonders if in fact his grandfather loves him at all. Calhoun's resolution is neither tidy nor pat. As Randy's colloquial narrative unfolds readers will see him accept his grandfather's ways and realize that while the horses will always come first, he has gained a quiet approval from the old man. A helpful glossary of harness racing terms is appended.

### Mary M. Burns

SOURCE: A review of *The Horse Comes First,* in *The Horn Book Magazine,* Vol. L, No. 5, October, 1974, p. 136.

City-raised Randy had anticipated an exciting summer on his grandfather Hartshaw's farm, where horses and harness racing were the family's principal concerns. But from the moment of his arrival in Olden, Iowa, his uncontrolled enthusiasm tended to create problems for his less loquacious, disciplined relatives, who firmly believed that "'the horse always comes first.'" Because of his difficulty in adjusting to this alien concept and because of his envy of the girl Pen, whose horse sense had earned her a special place in the Hartshaw ménage, Randy was ready to forfeit his vacation and return home. Only his intense interest in the two-year-old trotter Charlie Stride prevented this admission of defeat. As the summer progressed, Randy learned as much about self-control as he did about horses. Although the characters are more predictable than distinctive, Randy's first-person account of his memorable summer is a fast-moving blend of horse lore and local color. A helpful glossary of harness-racing terms is appended.

# *OWNSELF* (1975)

## Barbara Whitaker

SOURCE: A review of *Ownself,* in *School Library Journal,* Vol. 21, No. 8, April, 1975, p. 50.

Twelve-year-old Laurabelle Morgan half-believes in fayries—or at least in one particular fayry named Elabegathen whom she summons one sunny afternoon in the meadow of her family's Missouri farm. She wants the fayry to help her win back the love of her Welsh-born father James, lost to her since he became a "shouting Methodist." A realistic story—touched only incidentally by fantasy—of a girl growing up in a small town at the turn of the century, this could be about any child overcoming shyness and finding her own uniqueness. The plot moves briskly, and the characterizations are well-executed, particularly the troubled father, caught between his superstitious beliefs and his desire to embrace fundamentalist faith. Laurabelle grows from a shy child to a mischievous, confident girl with whom most 12-year-olds can identify.

## *Kirkus Reviews*

SOURCE: A review of *Ownself,* in *Kirkus Reviews,* Vol. XLIII, No. 7, April 1, 1975, pp. 371–72.

There is a great difference between possession and enchantment; Laurabelle, living near the Mississippi River in the early 1900's, raised with a background of Welsh story-telling until her unpredictable and irascible father got religion, discovers a spell in a book lent by a teacher and conjures up a fairy ("Elabegathen A. Fayrie") in defense against and defiance of her father, whose love and interest she covets (and probably in reaction to her insipid mother, prudish older sister and bloodthirsty twin brothers). Laurabelle is then "entered" by the fairy, who says she comes from "ainsel," Laurabelle's "own self," and indeed it seems her own mischievous nature which comes to the fore in her subsequent escapades. These culminate in the filling of the church with stuffed valentine hearts and flowers by Laurabelle and the son of the town store-keeper just in time for the visit of the minister, come to exorcise whatever spirit is in possession of Laurabelle (or whatever spirit she possesses). It is James, Laurabelle's father, who becomes disenchanted, however, with the minister (though only partially); Laurabelle clings to the nature of Elabegathen as her own and refuses to give up as evil what she believes to be good and joyful. The story is somewhat limited, and yet Laurabelle's desire for recognition from her father and her determination cling to her "ownself" invites response.

## *Publishers Weekly*

SOURCE: A review of *Ownself,* in *Publishers Weekly,* Vol. 207, No. 14, April 7, 1975, p. 81.

The time is the beginning of the 1900s; the place is an insular town in Missouri and the heroine of Ms. Calhoun's bright, ebullient novel is Laurabelle Morgan. She is odd girl out in her big family, picked on when she's noticed at all, especially by her father, who has become a religious fanatic. Laurabelle is reminded of her Welsh ancestry when she gets hold of a book about the "fayrie" folk. Using an ancient spell, the girl conjures up a fairy, Elabegathen A. Fayrie. This being appears and, before Laurabelle can stop her, becomes part of the human girl. When she tries to talk to the spirit, all she hears is a word which seems magic, "Ainsel." The action is explosive and often very humorous as the girl's father tries to get a hell-fire preacher to conjure "the devil" out of Laurabelle.

## Virginia Haviland

SOURCE: A review of *Ownself,* in *The Horn Book Magazine* Vol. LI, No. 3, June, 1975, pp. 265–66.

Into the ordinary background of a country story set in horse-and-buggy days, the author has injected charm, urgency, and poignancy. Laurabelle, the bright young heroine, had shared with her father a love of Welsh fairy lore and songs until his conversion to shouting Methodism ("'devil's talk,'" says Preacher Jenkins of this fairy business). Laurabelle's passionate acceptance of fairies leads her to use a spell to call up Elabegathen A. Fayrie—a spirit the girl believes enters her body after it has exhorted her never to be afraid. A gathering at the church is planned for the preacher's exorcism of the fairy devil, but Laurabelle and a young friend stuff the pews with flowers and straw-filled bags painted with red hearts—with a sensational outcome. Percipient in developing characters and their relationships, the author has written a story both subtle and powerful.

## Zena Sutherland

SOURCE: A review of *Ownself,* in *Bulletin of the Center for Children's Books,* Vol. 29, No. 4, December, 1975, p. 59.

Ever since her father had become a "shouting Methodist" convert, he'd scoffed at the folk and fairy lore he'd once loved and shared with Laurabelle. When she had truly summoned a fairy, a laughing girl who had told her "Never be afraid. Take joy," Laurabelle defied her stern father and even admitted that the fairy had entered into her. So Dad sent for the Preacher to exorcise the spirit. The story ends with Laurabelle aware that her father will not change but equally convinced that she must be her own self. The setting is a small Missouri town at the turn of the century, the flavor of period and locale giving color to a story that has convincing characters but a slow-moving plot; the blend of realism and fantasy is smooth, but seems not quite in balance, since there is so little of the latter.

## 📖 *OLD MAN WHICKUTT'S DONKEY* (1975)

### Mary M. Burns

SOURCE: A review of *Old Man Whickutt's Donkey,* in *The Horn Book Magazine,* Vol. LI, No. 4, August, 1975, pp. 367–68.

"One day Old Man Whickutt set off down the mountain with his donkey and his boy, going to the mill. Donkey, he carried a sack of corn; boy, he carried a stick; and Old Man Whickutt, he carried the boss words to keep them both going straight." Transplanted into a rural American mountain setting, La Fontaine's durable fable of the redoubtable trio who tried to please everybody and consequently pleased nobody is zestfully told in a rhythmic, folksy style, well-suited to storytelling or reading aloud. Unlike their anonymous French counterparts, the characters are given names suggestive of the locale. The comic mood is extended in the four-color illustrations which delineate the cartoon-like figures; the end papers are reminiscent of folk motifs found in antique samplers and quilts.

### Zena Sutherland

SOURCE: A review of *Old Man Whickutt's Donkey,* in *Bulletin of the Center for Children's Books,* Vol. 29, No. 1, September, 1975, p. 4.

Engagingly funny pictures [by Tomie dePaola] complement the rustic flavor of a sort of hillbilly version of the La Fontaine fable about the man who ends a journey carrying his beast of burden. Here it's Old Man Whickutt and his boy (grandson) and his donkey who go off to the mill with a sack of corn. The sack slides, the donkey rears, and the old man says, "Derned fool donkey! Acts as addled as a hen with its head off," and he slings the sack under the donkey's belly. Comments of passersby elicit various other methods, and the ending has a bit of new embroidery. The colloquial conversation, the regional idiom, and the humor of the pictures make this as much fun for the readers as for their audience.

### Esther Manes

SOURCE: A review of *Old Man Whickutt's Donkey,* in *School Library Journal,* Vol. 22, No. 1, September, 1975, p. 77.

A fresh and funny retelling of La Fontaine's fable about a man, a boy, and a donkey on their way to the miller with a sack of corn. In this version, the setting and style are purely American rural: crusty Old Man Whickutt can't figure out who should carry what on their journey. The sack's too heavy for the donkey, the donkey's too heavy for Whickutt and the boy, etc. Finally, there is a surprise conclusion, when the old man learns, "I'm derned if I do, derned if I don't." Throughout [Tomie] dePaola's colorful drawings, smiling cats, dogs, and other small animals

wryly observe the gentle farce. A good choice for picture book collections.

## 📖 *EUPHONIA AND THE FLOOD* (1976)

### Kirkus Reviews

SOURCE: A review of *Euphonia and the Flood,* in *Kirkus Reviews,* Vol. XLIV, No. 15, August 1, 1976, p. 841.

"One time there was an old woman named Euphonia who had a broom, a pig and a boat"—and when a flood comes up, with water "sashaying out of the creek banks," they all float downstream to see where it's a-rushing to. Picking up some stranded animals along the way (because—though we're not sure it follows—"If a thing is worth doing, it's worth doing well"), they end up in Farmer Stump's millpond and a picnic on his (dry) land. Hardly seems worth all the ruckus, even though Calhoun trots out all the tricks of oral narration and [Simms] Taback splashes his primitivish pages with TV-style sight gags.

### Joan E. Bezrudczyk

SOURCE: A review of *Euphonia and the Flood,* in *School Library Journal,* Vol. 23, No. 3, November, 1976, p. 43.

Euphonia, her pig Fatly, and her broom Briskly decide to follow the floodwater in this cumulative tale based on the familiar theme that "If a thing is worth doing, it's worth doing well." Written in dialect with a downhome quality (e.g., "all kinds of water sashaying out of the creek banks"), the story readily lends itself to reading aloud, but the busy full-color folk primitive illustrations [by Simms Taback], which show a variety of articles being swept along by the flood, will be best appreciated by independent readers.

### Zena Sutherland

SOURCE: A review of *Euphonia and the Flood,* in *Bulletin of the Center for Children's Books,* February, 1977, pp. 87–8.

A breezy tall tale has humor, action, and some word play to appeal to the read-aloud audience; it is illustrated [by Simms Taback] with busy drawings, awkward but vigorous. Euphonia, a brisk maiden lady in leg-of-mutton sleeves and sunbonnet, has a motto: "If a thing is worth doing, it's worth doing well," and this recurs throughout the story, as Euphonia, her broom Briskly, and her pig Fatly careen along in a flooded creek, rescuing animals whether they want rescuing or not. Just before the waterfall, they turn in to shore (they've been riding just to see where the flood was going) and join Farmer Stump at the picnic tables he's set up. Calhoun is a capable and experienced storyteller, and her writing has a cadence that makes her stories useful for telling as well as for reading aloud.

## 📖 MEDICINE SHOW: CONNING PEOPLE AND MAKING THEM LIKE IT (1976)

### Kirkus Reviews

SOURCE: A review of *Medicine Show: Conning People and Making Them Like It,* in *Kirkus Reviews,* Vol. XLIV, No. 17, September 1, 1976, p. 983.

The razzle-dazzle of the pitch doctor selling Kickapoo Indian Sagwa or Hamlin Wizard Oil has been replaced by the TV aspirin commercial, and Calhoun—along with Cliff Mann, a survivor of one of the last, motorized shows of the Thirties, whom she quotes extensively—makes you positively nostalgic for their return. Some of the patent medicines contained cocaine, opium and/or as much as 40% alcohol and there are reported cases of widows bilked of thousands of dollars and whole towns tricked by one pitchman, The Diamond King, who "died" at every stop leaving a heartrendingly penniless widow. But Calhoun shows that most practitioners regarded conning as an art, gave good value in entertainment and excitement, and considered their products harmless. Princess Lotus Blossom, later Madame V. Pasteur, made and lost fortunes selling "Tiger Fat" which she manufactured in hotel bathrooms, and the doctors' exotic pitches for such "remedies" were almost always accompanied by musicians, comic vaudeville routines, buck and wing dances, acrobats and magic tricks—the only entertainment some small towns ever saw. Perhaps it's only in retrospect that the ballyhoo takes on a glittering innocence; McNamara's *Step Right Up* (adult, 1975) struck the same chord. This simpler, more personalized saga duplicates much of McNamara's spiel, but with a charm of its own.

### Denise M. Wilms

SOURCE: A review of *Medicine Show: Conning People and Making Them Like It,* in *Booklist,* Vol. 73, No. 4, October 15, 1976, p. 321.

It's clear that medicine shows fascinate Calhoun, just as they fascinated their audience of years ago. Her curiosity has spawned an easygoing, indulgent narrative that explains the setup and speculates on the motives of the enterprising individuals who put it on the road. Calhoun finds something appealing about an artful con; the best medicine shows left their audiences a dollar poorer, perhaps, but happy. The products they pushed might possibly have been helpful (many were laxatives) and were at least harmless—this in contrast to the seamier side of the business, where dubious concoctions might cause illness, and charlatan doctors "consulted" with patients before pushing their cure-all for suspected ills. Medicine-showman Cliff Mann provides Calhoun with firsthand recollections of what it was like working for Doc McDonald's Indian Medicine Show; his regret at the passing of these enterprises in the wake of slicker TV and movie "cons" won't be lost on readers.

### Zena Sutherland

SOURCE: A review of *Medicine Show: Conning People and Making Them Like It,* in *Bulletin of the Center for Children's Books,* Vol. 30, No. 7, March, 1977, p. 102.

A conversational, breezy, but well-researched survey of the quacks and confidence men—and some women—who toured the United States from the mid-19th century to the 1940's. Much of Calhoun's story is based on the reminiscences of her son's father-in-law, Cliff Mann, who was part of a touring family from the age of eight. This is both a history of the medicine show and some of its most illustrious or infamous stars, and an explanation of the way in which the confidence man operates; it is rife with color, with the jargon of the trade, and with dramatic and humorous anecdotes about the "doctors," the fake royalty, and the musicians and other performers who amused the crowds until the serious business of the pitch came along.

### Cynthia Richey

SOURCE: A review of *Medicine Show: Conning People and Making Them Like It,* in *School Library Journal,* Vol. 23, No. 8, April, 1977, pp. 62–3.

A history of the medicine shows which traveled through the United States from the 1850's to the 1940's. Calhoun describes the medicines they sold (miracle tonics were simply flavored epsom salts, Princess Lotus Blossom's "Tiger Fat" was mostly petroleum jelly), explaining that, while customers wanted to believe in sure cures, constipation and calluses were practically the only ailments alleviated. Although people were conned by the pitch doctors, the author still feels the shows had some redeeming value as an early form of vaudeville and that medicine showmen were a step above hit-and-run swindlers. The behind-the-scenes look at the shows, the performers, and potions is interesting and unusual, and Calhoun rounds out the coverage by tracing the gradual development of federal controls on patent medicines.

## 📖 THE WITCH'S PIG: A CORNISH FOLKTALE (1977)

### Kirkus Reviews

SOURCE: A review of *The Witch's Pig: A Cornish Folktale,* in *Kirkus Reviews,* Vol. XLV, No. 4, February 15, 1977, p. 160.

In her usual calculated rhythms, Mary Calhoun tells how Tom, believing his cousin Betty to be just a noddy old woman and not a witch as gossip would have it, slyly outbids her for a pig at market and then gets nothing but trouble out of his purchase. At last, with Tom on his way to sell the now skinny sow, a hare leads it on a wild chase and into a tight-fitting drainpipe, from which Betty appears to extricate it, after buying it from Tom for a pittance. Tom's left with a new respect for "she who could take the shape of a hare"; readers are left with a passable tale, slightly overflavored in the telling, but oddly enough not vivified in the particulars—or in [Lady] McCrady's higgledy-piggledy scenes.

### Dana Whitney

SOURCE: A review of *The Witch's Pig: A Cornish Folktale,* in *School Library Journal,* Vol. 23, No. 9, May, 1977, p. 49.

"Betty Trenowith . . . was known for a witch. But her cousin Tom said she was nought but a noddy old woman." When Tom buys the pig Betty wants, he gets more than he bargained for. The pig digs up gardens, eats voraciously yet grows thinner, and causes Tom endless problems. When he believes the pig hopelessly stuck in a hole, Tom allows Betty to purchase the troublesome animal. She calls "Chee-ah, chee-ah!" and the pig docilely follows her home. Lady McCrady's pencil-on-board illustrations (full-color spreads alternate with ones that are aqua-green and black) are themselves appropriately noddy: bats hover around the margins; the sun hangs from a string; the pig looks unabashedly devilish; and Tom appears increasingly more frazzled and bedraggled. This adaptation of a Cornish tale is lilting and bursting with sly humor and a must for folklore collections.

### Ann A. Flowers

SOURCE: A review of *The Witch's Pig: A Cornish Folktale,* in *The Horn Book Magazine,* Vol. LIII, No. 4, August, 1977, p. 433.

Cousin Tom refused to believe that Betty Trenoweth was a witch—"'She's naught but a noddy old woman,'" he said—so when he slyly underbid her for a fine pig, he had no fear of retribution. The pig, however, caused no end of trouble. She ran away, rooted in the neighbor's fields, and simply would not fatten up. So Tom decided to sell her at the Penzance fair. Now Betty turned herself into a hare and lured the pig into a drain. When Tom saw she was completely stuck, he sold her to Betty for a pittance. Out she came from the drain like a cork and "many a fat piglet grew up, child to the witch's pig." The folk tale, taken from one volume of William Bottrell's *Traditions and Hearthside Stories of West Cornwall,* is fetchingly illustrated. In the illustrations [by Lady McCrady] the pig has a cheerful, vastly knowing expression, as does Betty in her tall black Cornish hat, something like a witch's hat; and the countryside of Cornwall is shown replete with sly cats, sheep, bats, and mysterious standing stones.

### 📖 *JACK THE WISE AND THE CORNISH CUCKOOS* (1978)

### Laura Geringer

SOURCE: A review of *Jack the Wise and the Cornish Cuckoos,* in *School Library Journal,* Vol. 24, No. 8, April, 1978, p. 67.

Three loosely woven episodes in the do-gooding career of a wise fool named Jack (Cornish cousin to Sholom Aleichem's rabbi of Chelm) who flies over hill and dale on the airborne heels of his godmother, Gracey Goosey. Rejoicing in the discovery of a flock of dead sheep floating in a bay, Jack advises his neighbors to haul in the "strange new kind of fish," a deed that earns him a meal of mutton, a bag of coins, and a blessing. Next, he settles a tiff between Tom the tailor and his mulish wife who prepares to go to her grave (a coffin is bought, the "corpse" dressed, etc.) rather than admit she's wrong. Finally, summoned to the town of Towednack by a "runner" (the narrative glue wears thin here), Jack finds the people lamenting their lack of an end-of-winter holiday. In lieu of a patron saint, he makes the cuckoo bird the theme of a celebration and builds a pen out of stones to keep the elusive herald of summer at the villagers' beck and call. A merry procession ends the book, with church bells ringing "in the squatty tower" and Jack, crowned with feathers, prancing off to yet another non-adventure. This is more diffuse and not as droll as the author's *Witch's Pig* (1977), but Calhoun's light, rhythmic prose trips along, and [Lady] McCrady's graceful sepia and wash illustrations evoke magic while capturing the homely stances of a portly, aging, sly and gap-toothed group of silly revellers.

### *Kirkus Reviews*

SOURCE: A review of *Jack the Wise and the Cornish Cuckoos,* in *Kirkus Reviews,* Vol. XLVI, No. 7, April 1, 1978, p. 366.

Jack the Wise, with his unruffled confidence that all that happens is for the best, is Calhoun's own invention within the simpleton tradition, and she uses him to string together three episodes based on Cornish folklore. Jack sets one town fishing for "sheep fish" when a wind blows a band of sheep into the water; he almost causes a stubborn woman to be buried alive, but saves her life at the last minute with a lie that saves her face; and he solves two problems with one stroke by dreaming up a Cuckoo Feast for a community wishing for both the end of winter and a special festival. It's fluently told and [Lady] McCrady strikes the proper daft note; but the "all is for the best" philosophy applies to only the first of the three episodes, and Jack never comes through as a clear enough character to give the story any zip or direction.

### *Publishers Weekly*

SOURCE: A review of *Jack the Wise and the Cornish Cuckoos,* in *Publishers Weekly,* Vol. 213, No. 21, May 22, 1978, p. 232.

Suggested by folklore from West Cornwall in England, Calhoun's tale is rich in ludicrous appeal. It is immeasurably helped by [Lady] McCrady's skilled paintings of country bumpkins in their old-timey clothes, men and women either grinning inanely or glowering stupidly. In this company, stupid Jack is a logical leader. At his christening, he opts for a feather out of the three gifts offered by his godmother—the others are a golden ball and a currant cake. Since a ball can roll away and a cake is soon eaten, his choice is deemed wise. And so it goes, throughout his life. His silly choices enhance his reputation for wisdom, especially when his idea of fencing in cuckoos gives the community a valid reason for an early "feasten."

## Charlotte W. Draper

SOURCE: A review of *Jack the Wise and the Cornish Cuckoos,* in *The Horn Book Magazine,* Vol. LIV, No. 4 August, 1978, p. 384.

Drawing together fragments of Cornish dialect and folk belief, the author has invented the buoyant character of Jack the Wise, whose good sense justifies his name. Jack is turned out of his cottage after his parents die but finds good fortune among the fishing folk of Saint Ives Bay when he urges them to fish for sheep blown into the water. After ten days of feasting on mutton, the grateful townsfolk reward Jack with a bag of coins, and he goes off to Tom the Tailor for new clothes. Jack resolves a domestic quarrel between Tom and his wife, and his fame spreads; he is then summoned by neighboring villagers to make spring come early.

## CROSS-COUNTRY CAT (1979; published in England as *Snow-Cat,* 1980)

### Publishers Weekly

SOURCE: A review of *Cross-Country Cat,* in *Publishers Weekly,* Vol. 215, No. 15, April 9, 1979, p. 110.

Calhoun's story races as swiftly as the cocky hero's downhill skis and keeps one in hair-curling suspense, to say nothing of laughs. With his family—The Kid, The Woman and The Man—Henry is at a ski lodge but yowls his Siamese cat's disdain at using the tiny skis and pole The Kid makes for him. Then the pet leaps unnoticed from the family car when they leave for home, to retrieve a prized possession. Now the smart cat is deserted. The only way to catch up with the humans is to dare the skis. His adventures multiply on the slope and come to an abrupt but gratifying stop when Henry is reunited with his people after escaping from a pursuing coyote. Competing with the author's tale in verve and artistry are [Erick] Ingraham's snowy scenes in exactly the right shades of blue, sepia and gray, set off by glaring white.

### Booklist

SOURCE: A review of *Cross-Country Cat,* in *Booklist,* Vol. 75, No. 18, May 15, 1979, pp. 1436–37.

As Calhoun's story opens to scenes of a hind-leg-walking Siamese named Henry snapping after flies or otherwise reaching about, there's no reason to think this is fantasy. But there's no reason to think it isn't, either, so when the cat inadvertently gets left behind at the family cabin and starts out for home with the cross-country skis "The Kid" fashioned for him as a joke, the fantasy falls into place surprisingly well. What's special, though, is the art. [Erick] Ingraham's earthy blue and tan tones provide some beautiful lighting effects for the soft-focus drawings. They interpret the story well, summoning up absolute involvement with both the desolate setting and the drama of Henry's ordeal. Fresh in both concept and execution.

## Ann A. Flowers

SOURCE: A review of *Cross-Country Cat,* in *The Horn Book Magazine,* Vol. LV, No. 4, August, 1979, pp. 404–5.

Henry was a cat—"a hind-leg walker"—who enjoyed prancing about on his back legs so much that he was given his own pair of cross-country skis. Accidentally left behind at a mountain cabin, Henry gathered some provisions—in the form of mice—put on his skis, and departed. He met with difficulties along the way; there was a sassy rabbit, a blue jay, and an evil-minded coyote—but he managed to get quite far before his people came back for him. Prudently jettisoning all his equipment, Henry kindly let his escape look like a rescue. Henry in all his Siamese glory as well as the snowy mountain and forest backgrounds are magnificently depicted in tones of blue and brown. Fully meriting the illustrations is the unusually strong narrative, told in a straight-faced, realistic, way.

## Carol Chatfield

SOURCE: A review of *Cross-Country Cat,* in *School Library Journal,* Vol. 26, No. 2, October, 1979, p. 134.

Cats on cross country skis don't come along every day, but that's Calhoun's latest flight of fancy. Henry is a Siamese who likes to walk on his hind legs. When the rest of the family tries a weekend on skis, The Kid fashions a pair for Henry too. The sport is not Henry's bag, however, and the skis are put away. A favorite cat toy is not packed at the close of the weekend, and Henry is inadvertently left behind as he goes off to retrieve it. The only way down from the snowed-in mountain cabin seems to be the skis, so Henry dons them, matches the skiing rhythm to the tune of "This Old Man," and having safely gotten out to the road, finds that the family has come back. To preserve the myth that The Man saves Henry's life, the wily cat sheds the skis and flounders in the snowbank howling. While everyone knows it's all impossible, a smart cat on skis, other wild creatures, a snowstorm, and an outdoorsy family make a good storyline.

## THE WITCH WHO LOST HER SHADOW (1979)

**Blair Christolon**

SOURCE: A review of *The Witch Who Lost Her Shadow,* in *School Library Journal,* Vol. 26, No. 1, September, 1979, p. 104.

Falinda the healing witch loses her pet cat, Shadow, and feels she can find no other to take his place. Faced with loneliness, Falinda accepts the friendship of a new cat only after she copes with the problem of loyalty to Shadow. Once again Calhoun has written a moving tale based on a strong theme. Children will relate to Falinda's hurt as they visualize the story with the aid of Calhoun's descriptive poetic phrasing—"Shadow was a black cat, a proud cat, a silent-slipping wisp of a cat." Illustrations in three colors set the bucolic scene. [Trinka Hakes] Noble expresses sadness, anger, tenderness, and joy by using simple uncluttered lines for facial features. School and public librarians will find many story-telling possibilities in this simple but meaningful text.

*Booklist*

SOURCE: A review of *The Witch Who Lost Her Shadow,* in *Booklist,* Vol. 76, No. 1, September 1, 1979, p. 38.

Falinda, a good witch, has a haughty, sleek black cat she calls Shadow because it follows her everywhere. When the cat disappears, Falinda is inconsolable and wants nothing to do with the gray striped kitten that appears at her doorstep. The kitten persistently brings her gifts of mice, but though Falinda feeds it milk and lets it warm by the fire, she resists the animal's devotion. The day the kitten is late returning, Falinda finally realizes it has captured her heart and she claims it with the name Homebody. This gentle good-witch story has a folktale quality that works, and the small cat's determination is commendable. [Trinka Hakes] Noble, whose clean lines and subtle tones bring to mind the work of Margot Tomes, deftly shades the yellows, reds, and browns into a multicolored effect.

**Ethel L. Heins**

SOURCE: A review of *The Witch Who Lost Her Shadow,* in *The Horn Book Magazine,* Vol. LV, No. 5, October, 1979, pp. 523–24.

The genial witches who populate children's fiction are surely a sentimentality—for, of course, they are not witches at all. The author says that Falinda "was a white witch, and she did only good"; actually she was nothing more than a kindly woman skilled in the art of healing with herbs. Shadow was her proud black cat, who shrank from affection but accompanied her faithfully wherever she went. When Shadow disappeared one night, Falinda was inconsolable and refused all manner of proffered gifts—

cats of every description. Then a timid, homeless kitten turned up, and Falinda learned to recognize an entirely different kind of faithfulness. A pleasant but rather thin story is considerably enriched by attractive, carefully made watercolor illustrations, [by Trinka Hakes Noble] but some of the pictures are badly placed and thus detract from the book's overall design.

*Kirkus Reviews*

SOURCE: A review of *The Witch Who Lost Her Shadow,* in *Kirkus Reviews,* Vol. XLVII, No. 19, October 1, 1979, p. 1139.

First, Falinda the witch is not a broomstick-riding hag but a white witch, which is to say a folk healer. And Shadow is the name of her black-cat companion, who follows her everywhere but suddenly disappears. Disconsolate, the witch apologetically turns down the village children's offer of substitute cats, and when she takes in a striped stray kitten who won't go away it's with the understanding that "no one could take the place of her Shadow." This is not, then, what you might expect from the title, but rather—with Falinda finally adopting the kitten after a moment of fear that he too might have run off—a relatively pawky specific for a child still recovering from the loss of a pet. [Trinka Hakes] Noble's sedate, old-timey pictures in muted tones nicely suit the story's real business.

## KATIE JOHN AND HEATHCLIFF (1980)

*Booklist*

SOURCE: A review of *Katie John and Heathcliff,* in *Booklist,* Vol. 77, No. 2, September 15, 1980, p. 112.

The summer before seventh grade, Katie John reads *Wuthering Heights* and discovers Heathcliff, the most romantic of heroes. When she meets Jason, who shares her table in cooking class, she finds the boy's shaggy dark hair and half-smile to have a startlingly similar effect. For the first time, Katie John is aware of boys and feels lost and confused over how to react to them. Her thoughts and actions turn more and more toward pierced earrings, perfume, and Jason, especially when her old friend Edwin seems interested only in collecting geodes in the creek bed. Sharing a balloon flight with Jason, worrying over a school dance, trying out for cheerleader, and playing a game at rival Trish's party prove perplexing to Katie John, but it isn't until her own highly anticipated Halloween party that she sees Edwin and Jason in their true lights. Fans of Katie John's will be pleased to see the return of this high-spirited heroine, and Calhoun doesn't let them down—giving a warm, sensitive, and humorous portrayal of these trying years.

**Zena Sutherland**

SOURCE: A review of *Katie John and Heathcliff,* in

*Bulletin of the Center for Children's Books,* Vol. 34, No. 2, October, 1980, pp. 27–8.

In a fourth book about Katie John, she's in seventh grade and, as the founder of the Boy-Haters' Club, is shocked to find she's now finding boys very attractive. In fact, after reading *Wuthering Heights,* she's seeing Heathcliff in several of the boys she meets in junior high—but it doesn't change her relationship with her old buddy Edwin. The story is filled with small, if not close, encounters; few readers will be surprised that when Katie John gives a Hallowe'en party it turns out to be steady old Edwin who's the most satisfactory male friend Katie John has. This has little drama and lacks a strong story line, but it's written in a lightly humorous style, it's believable and pleasant, and it accurately depicts the concerns and behavior of younger adolescents.

### Kirkus Reviews

SOURCE: A review of *Katie John and Heathcliff,* in *Kirkus Reviews,* Vol. XLVIII, No. 20, October 15, 1980, p. 1357.

Twenty years after her first appearance at age ten, Calhoun's **Katie John** is entering seventh grade and finding herself suddenly conscious of boys. ("Honestly! What was the matter with her?") Having read *Wuthering Heights* during the summer, she is looking for a Heathcliff, and settles on new boy Jason, who gives her long deep looks in cooking class but seems to spend more attention on rich, pretty, cool Trish—one of the first girls at school to sport the KC badge. (It stands for "Kissed Club," to Katie's disgust.) Katie frets over Jason and Trish till Halloween, when she gives a party they consider kiddish. Then she realizes on the spot that there is nothing under Jason's cool looks, and that her unromantic old friend Edwin is the companion for her. The time period of the story is a puzzle: It has the Fifties sensibility (and the even older slang word "swell") of the earlier Katie John stories, but references to skateboards and Pizza Huts and hanging out in shopping malls suggest, inappropriately, a more recent background. It's also a little corny for today, but readers who don't mind that will empathize with Katie John in her innocent scrapes—as when she wins a carpet sweeper and is stuck lugging it along the one time Jason walks her home from the movies. In other words, more of the old Katie John, less dimmed by the time lapse than bruised by the update.

### C. Nordhielm Woolbridge

SOURCE: A review of *Katie John and Heathcliff,* in *School Library Journal,* Vol. 27, No. 3, November, 1980, pp. 70–1.

Katie John Tucker is about to cross one of the thresholds of adolescence: leaving the security of elementary school for junior high. Reading and rereading *Wuthering Heights* has left her smitten by Heathcliff and determined to find a reasonable facsimile for herself. The boys from her elementary school are too childish so she settles on Jason Schreiber and winds up vying with a rich, conceited classmate for his attention. She loses before the battle has even begun but not before Jason's dull personality and old friend Edwin's fierce loyalty have been exposed. The preoccupations of this vulnerable time of life are all included: the cheerleading tryouts, the pierced ears, the humiliations suffered at parties that were supposed to be "fun." The naiveté of both plot and writing style will seem just right to elementary-aged girls but a bit shallow to those already in junior high.

### AUDUBON CAT (1981)

### Publishers Weekly

SOURCE: A review of *Audubon Cat,* in *Publishers Weekly,* Vol. 219, No. 10, March 6, 1981, p. 95.

Left alone in her family's Rocky Mountain home, Hilda the cat takes charge with all the wit and wisdom of her proud one year of age. Today, she will be Hilda the Huntress, disdaining her bowl of Audubon-approved cat food and feasting on a plump chipmunk or bird. Hours of frustration and the barbs of claw and beak send Hilda limping off, easy prey for the big owl that flies away with her. Yowling against the indignity of being eaten by a bird, Hilda startles the owl and he drops her, luckily into a tree that breaks the fall. Back home, she finds her own food all gone and a ferocious pack rat ready to finish what the owl has started. Readers will keep the pages flying as Hilda learns basic lessons in Calhoun's amusing, informative story of wildlife, mightily enhanced by [Susan] Bonners's luminous portraits of Hilda and many kinds of birds and animals.

### Kirkus Reviews

SOURCE: A review of *Audubon Cat,* in *Kirkus Reviews,* Vol. XLIX, No. 8, April 15, 1981, pp. 497–98.

Audubon *cat?* Yes, so Hilda is called by The Girl in her life because she's such an avid bird-watcher (and the family's an Audubon-Society family). Now, with The Girl away for two days, Hilda decides to make up for the loss of her cat food—to chipmunks and a pack rat—by catching herself some birds (while "The Girl wasn't there to scold her for endangering the species"). And so the jests go—the instincts of cats rubbing against the interests of birders. The various birds that Hilda spots but doesn't succeed in catching are identified (though the two-color illustrations don't really enable us to recognize them); and after she's escaped from a predatory owl—but, she feels, proved herself a faithful bird-watcher—she's ready to settle for "her fish-flavored, Audubon-approved dry cat food." The problem with *that* resolution, however, is that we were originally told that the chipmunks and pack rat had made off with all the cat food put out for Hilda, "and The Girl would be gone until the next day." Maybe kids won't notice, since it's all so contrived—but certainly contrived to elicit recognition from young birders with a cat on the prowl.

**Zena Sutherland**

SOURCE: A review of *Audubon Cat,* in *Bulletin of the Center for Children's Books,* Vol. 34, No. 11, July-August, 1981, p. 209.

Soft, almost fuzzy, and highly textured drawings of Hilda, called the Audubon cat because she's such a devoted bird-watcher, and of the many birds she sees and tries to catch, are one of the stronger aspects of this picture book. Left alone for two days while her family is on a trip, Hilda is hungry because a rat and some chipmunks have taken all the cat food left out for her. Save for the heightened action of one encounter (Hilda is picked up, then dropped by an owl) this is basically a tepid account of Hilda's spotting of some grouse, some chickadees, juncoes, redpoll finches, pine siskins, etc. References to such things as Hilda's "life list" of birds will mean little to those not initiated into the practice of bird watching, the plot is slight, and the book is further weakened by attribution of human thought processes to the cat.

**Margaret L. Chatham**

SOURCE: A review of *Audubon Cat,* in *School Library Journal,* Vol. 27, No. 10, August, 1981, p. 53.

Hilda, called the audubon cat because of her devotion to bird watching, is left "in charge" while her family goes off overnight to see the Rocky Mountain fall colors and birds. When chipmunks and a pack rat steal her supply of cat food, Hilda fancies herself a mighty huntress and sets out to catch something, *any*thing, for dinner. Her efforts are all in vain, and she narrowly escapes becoming the great horned owl's dinner herself. But her problems are solved when she finds where the pack rat hid her food and the owl carries off the rat. Whether you prefer cats or birds, Hilda is attractive and true-to-life in both pictures and text. And it's a real prize for birders, humorously adapting birding terms to Hilda's activities. The realistic airbrush illustrations [by Susan Bonners] detail all the species Hilda encounters and glow with autumnal aspen gold.

### HOT-AIR HENRY (1981)

*Publishers Weekly*

SOURCE: A review of *Hot-Air Henry,* in *Publishers Weekly,* Vol. 220, No. 4, July 24, 1981, p. 148.

Calhoun's resourceful Siamese cat Henry is literally up in the air when he defies his human family (The Man, The Woman, The Kid) and sneaks into the basket of a hot-air balloon. The Man is furious, for this is their first flight and no cats are allowed. It happens, though, that the balloon takes off with only Henry on board as pilot, navigator and passenger. The unflappable cat flaps, for the first time in his arrogant life, but uses his head and comes safely through a series of near disasters. Back on the ground, Henry remembers to put on his smarmy, humble and seductive act with The Man to ensure forgiveness and keep his happy home.

**Margaret Chatham**

SOURCE: A review of *Hot-Air Henry,* in *School Library Journal,* Vol. 28, No. 3, November, 1981, p. 72.

Henry, the *Cross-Country Cat* (1979), is back. This time he tries to stow away on The Man's first hot-air balloon, accidently fires the burner and takes his own solo flight instead. By trial and error, he learns how to control the balloon and makes the most of his chance to invade the realm of birds. It's a great adventure, but doesn't quite measure up to *Cross-Country Cat.* [Erick] Ingraham now has full color to work with, but the size disparity between balloon and cat shrinks Henry into impersonality a fair part of the time. Calhoun expects readers to be already acquainted with Henry and his family and lets Henry slip farther toward being a person in fur instead of a believable smart cat. But set that exciting balloon against these small faults, and you still come up with a winner.

*Kirkus Reviews*

SOURCE: A review of *Hot-Air Henry,* in *Kirkus Reviews,* Vol. XLIX, No. 21, November 1, 1981, p. 1337.

The same cat who skied to meet his human family in *Cross-Country Cat* (1979) is put through a less winning repeat performance in this story about his solo balloon ride. Scooting into the empty basket when its beginning pilot, "The Man" of the family, jumps out for his camera, Henry accidentally pulls the cord that fires the burner, and so takes off. His further progress does not rely on accident, though, for Henry now knows how to go up and soon figures out how to pull the air-spilling cord to go down. Humming to "a tune of the Kid's about 'Sailing, sailing, over the bounding main'"— just as he had skied along to "This Old Man"—Henry glories in his flight and manipulates the cords to land and then to rise again in pursuit of a flock of blackbirds. Aloft once more, he scares an eagle with a roar from the burner, and at last, after a little run-in with a perching goose, lands for good near the family's truck. [Erick] Ingraham supplies some spanking realistic visuals with his colorful balloon and his winter landscapes. But where *Cross-Country Cat* had the take-it-or-leave-it charm and conviction of an odd little wonder tale, this seems clearly contrived and a shade too cute—except, perhaps, for the sizable cat cult.

## 📖 THE NIGHT THE MONSTER CAME (1982)

### Publishers Weekly

SOURCE: A review of *The Night the Monster Came,* in *Publishers Weekly,* Vol. 221, No. 17, April 23, 1982, p. 93.

The author of award-winning picture books and novels for children of all ages, Calhoun presents a dandy adventure here, expertly illustrated by [Leslie] Morrill's drawings. They reflect the tensions affecting nine-year-old Andy O'Reilly while he's alone evenings, in his home at the edge of the North Woods. Andy is ashamed of his fears; he insists he'll be fine on his own as his father leaves to work the night shift in the sheriff's department and his mother goes to her class. But Andy is terrified of the legendary Bigfoot, reported to roam the woods near his house. When he hears loud noises and sees huge paw-prints in the snow, he's convinced that the 10-foot-tall man-beast is just outside. There really is a formidable beast out there, and the boy's handling of the problem makes a heartening story about how compassion can overcome fright.

### W. A. Handley

SOURCE: A review of *The Night the Monster Came,* in *School Library Journal,* Vol. 28, No. 10, August, 1982, p. 94.

For children the worst fears of all are the imagined ones. The nine year old of this story is especially frightened of Bigfoot. When he is at home alone during a snowstorm he is frightened by the creaks, moans and other noises that are constantly given out by houses. But later in the story the boy handles a real threat (both to himself and, potentially, to his parents) from a wounded bear. The book captures readers immediately and moves very quickly through the plot. The full-page illustrations that appear in each of the nine chapters don't overpower readers; the format with its large, readable type is just right for younger readers. Good for nine or ten year olds who want a mystery.

### Denise M. Wilms

SOURCE: A review of *The Night the Monster Came,* in *Booklist,* Vol. 79, No. 3, October 1, 1982, p. 201.

Andy's active imagination makes it easy for him to believe that the giant footprints he discovers around the garbage can on a snowy night when he's alone in the house belong to Bigfoot. After all, his house isn't at all far from a stand of trees he thinks is part of the Great North Woods—and he knows that Bigfoot lives in the North Woods. Later in the week Andy sees "a huge beast" jumping the fence to the field and is concerned enough to call his mother home from her real estate class. She's skeptical of his Bigfoot ideas but realizes he must have

seen something—and indeed he has. Canny readers won't be surprised when the object turns out to be a scavenging bear. Andy devises a way to lure it into the garage until his policeman father can arrange to have the animal tranquilized and transported to a remote area. Andy is a likable protagonist whose fears and courage will bring out kindred responses in readers. An on-target piece of storytelling for this age group.

## 📖 BIG SIXTEEN (1983)

### Hazel Rochman

SOURCE: A review of *Big Sixteen,* in *The New York Times Book Review,* November 20, 1983, p. 39.

"Now, Big Sixteen was his name, 'cause that was the size of his shoe! This was back in slavery times, when Big Sixteen worked for The Old Man. And Big Sixteen was so big and so strong that The Old Man thought he could do anything, fetch anything."

In this exuberant retelling of a black tall tale (based on versions anthologized by Langston Hughes and Arna Bontemps), Big Sixteen performs stupendous tasks. He even goes down to hell and kills the Devil. When Big Sixteen dies, heaven is too scared of his power to let him in. The Devil's wife won't let him into hell either, but she gives him a flaming coal to start a hell of his own. And that is the light you see in the swamp or the woods at night, Big Sixteen looking for a home.

The cheerful play of the master-slave relationship will be offensive to some readers. But Big Sixteen transcends the setting. He is part of a long tradition of heroes forced to perform impossible tasks, from Hercules to John Henry.

True to the tale, Trina Schart Hyman's black-and-white illustrations depict hell as a wildly macabre domestic scene, with the Devil's wife preparing to slam the door on the striding giant as she grabs her half-monster children from their mischief among the skulls, bones and snakes in the flaming yard. Then, after all the dramatic movement and comic exaggeration, the last page shows a still, compelling, dark giant carrying fire on a bare mountain peak. The story's final impression is of a force so powerful and enduring that it cannot be contained.

### Zena Sutherland

SOURCE: A review of *Big Sixteen,* in *Bulletin of the Center for Children's Books,* Vol. 37, No. 4, December, 1983, p. 63.

Bold, dramatic black and white drawings of a black folk hero of slavery times and of the horned and hairy devil (and his wife and children) illustrate a folktale that is close to the version (same title) in the Moritz Jagendorf collection *Folk Stories of the South.* Storytellers may also be familiar with the variant called "Wicked John and the

Devil," in *Grandfather Tales* by Richard Chase, in which John is a blacksmith; the unifying facet is that all these tales explain what the flickering fire is that is called will-o'-the-wisp. Here Big Sixteen is a handsome black man, very tall and strong, who fulfills every request of the Old Man (shown as a small white plantation owner); when he says "I b'lieve you could fetch me the Devil himself!" Big Sixteen brings the Devil's corpse back up to Earth. After a long and virtuous life, Big Sixteen is turned away by a black Saint Peter, then tries the Devil's wife; she won't admit him either, but gives him a hot coal, tells him to start a hell of his own, and leaves poor Big Sixteen to wander forever, the story ends, carrying his coal and "a-lookin' for a place to go." The illustrations [by Trina Schart Hyman] make this a handsome picture book, but the story—although capably retold—seems one that would be more appealing to older children.

**Marion Hawkins Parker**

SOURCE: A review of *Big Sixteen,* in *School Library Journal,* Vol. 30, No. 4, December, 1983, p. 64.

Big Sixteen (his shoe size), a strong, gentle slave who has superhuman strength, is told by his owner to "fetch me the Devil himself." With a pick and shovel, he steps into Hell 30 days later and tricks the Devil, hammers him on the head and returns with him under his arm. Told that the Devil is too ugly to keep, Big Sixteen drops him back into the hole. Years later when he dies, he tries to gain entry into Heaven, but is told by St. Peter that he can't come in because he is so big and strong that no one could control him if he got out of hand. With no place left to go, he tries to gain entry into Hell. The Devil's wife and children refuse to let him in, but give him a hot flaming coal to go "start a Hell of your own." This is a retelling of a Southern motif which the author credits on the copyright page. . . .

Written in the storyteller's style, the writing is simple though local expressions and dialect are used. The illustrations, line drawings with gray shadings, give positive impressions of black American slaves but the Devil and his family are portrayed as horned black characters with wings, hooved or clawed feet and neatly cropped Afros. The Devil himself is black and pictured with hooves, wings, tail, goatee and an earring in one ear (both of which are pointed). Some children expecting the traditional red devil will be disappointed; others will be offended. Unfortunately, the retelling itself is not strong enough to carry the book above the objections of the caricatures of the Devil's family.

**Elizabeth Fitzgerald Howard**

SOURCE: A review of *Big Sixteen,* in *The Horn Book Magazine,* Vol. LX, No. 1, February, 1984, pp. 41–2.

Big Sixteen, a brawny black fellow in slavery times, wore size sixteen shoes and would fetch anything for the Old Man. Yassuh! When Big Sixteen thought the Old Man wanted him to fetch the Devil, he dug down, killed the Devil, and brought him up. Years later, when Big Sixteen died, Saint Peter wouldn't let him through the Pearly Gates. So Big Sixteen went down below. But the Devil's wife wouldn't let him in, either. She handed him a hot coal, saying, "'Now you go start a hell of your own!'" The black American folk tale, like the familiar Appalachian variant, may be acceptable for storytelling to older children and adults, depending on the audience and the storyteller. But the picture book version is an unbelievable combination of stereotyping, violence, and blasphemy: The black-and-white illustrations [by Trina Schart Hyman] are unfunny, crude, ugly, and offensive. Big Sixteen is powerfully built but of very little brain, obsequious in manner and speech. Yassuh! The Devil's wife seems to be the prototype of the prostitute; the Devil's children, with their horns, tails, and bulging eyes, are the most grotesque little varmints in picture books. Aside from its gross depiction of black people, the book is also reprehensible for the violence shown when witless Big Sixteen viciously killed the Devil. And although the sin of blasphemy is not a popular concern these days, to show heaven and hell in such pseudocomical fashion denigrates the traditional importance of religion to black people. There is hidden wealth in black folk tales, which needs to be uncovered for young readers in order to awaken their awareness and appreciation of black culture. The questions are which tales to retell and, more important, how to retell and illustrate them with sensitivity and taste.

## JACK AND THE WHOOPEE WIND (1987)

**Publishers Weekly**

SOURCE: A review of *Jack and the Whoopee Wind,* in *Publishers Weekly,* Vol. 231, No. 8, February 27, 1987, p. 162.

Calhoun and [illustrator Dick] Gackenbach have captured perfectly the flavor of the Old West in this uproarious tall tale. Jack lives in Whoopee, Wyoming, where he's just about lost his patience with the wild wind that has blown away everything Jack holds near and dear. But when the wind tampers with Jack's faithful old dog, Mose, it's the last straw. Jack vows to stop the wind and he and the town hatch some clever schemes, but nothing works. Finally, Jack realizes he can't stop the wind, but he can harness it, and put it to good use to boot. This rollicking story is ideal for reading aloud, with high comedy in the pictures of the wind-blown town.

**Kirkus Reviews**

SOURCE: A review of *Jack and the Whoopee Wind,* in *Kirkus Reviews,* Vol. LV, No. 6, March 15, 1987, p. 468.

Such is the wind in Whoopee, Wyoming, that cats have to be tied down and the chickens are all bald.

Jack doesn't mind a breeze now and then, but he gets riled at a wind that can snatch his dog up into the air—he's not going to let it get away with *that*. Evenly matched in craft and stubbornness, the two do battle. Jack, with the help of the whole town, tries a giant fan, a huge windsock, a curtain, a drive-in movie screen, even a U-shaped tunnel. The wind defeats every plan until Jack comes to the conclusion that, if it can't be stopped, it can be used. He collects all the state's scrap metal and builds a forest of electricity-generating windmills that not only keep the wind too busy to get into mischief, but make everyone in town rich as well. Like Steven Kellogg in Purdy's *Iva Dunnit and the Big Wind,* [Dick] Gackenbach uses dramatic, swirling lines and plenty of windswept hair, beards, manes and grass. The wind seems more playful then threatening, and the pictures are crowded with airborne livestock, furniture and less identifiable objects.

An entertaining tale, slightly taller than average.

### Ilene Cooper

SOURCE: A review of *Jack of the Whoopee Wind,* in *Booklist,* Vol. 83, No. 16, April 15, 1987, pp. 1282–83.

Cowboy Jack lives in Whoopee, Wyoming, where the wind is so strong it blows the feathers right off the chickens. Jack and his dog, Mose, try every trick they can think of to stop that darn wind, from quilting a huge windsock to trying to plug the gap between the mountains where the wind originates. But the gusty breeze is too strong. Jack and his friends decide if they can't beat the wind, they're going to use it. They construct a number of windmills and hook them up to generate electricity for the whole area. Calhoun tells her story in true tall-tale fashion with plenty of tongue-in-cheek humor, and [Dick] Gackenbach's pictures are inspired wackiness. The fluid two-page spreads are full of exaggerated fun—abounding in plucked chickens and townsfolk holding on to their hats (and their children). The tans and golds of the prairie are set off by the bright colors in people's clothes and in the decorative blankets used to beat back the wind. Fun for individuals or groups and a nice companion to the Carol Purdy/Steven Kellogg creation *Iva Dunnit and the Big Wind.*

### Blair Christolon

SOURCE: A review of *Jack and the Whoopee Wind,* in *School Library Journal,* Vol. 33, No. 8, May, 1987, p. 82.

This tongue-in-cheek tall tale relates Jack's great battle with the Whoopee wind in Wyoming. The wind blew away most of Jack's farm, took the feathers right off his chickens, and sprinkled his fence posts over the prairie. But when it starts tormenting his dog Mose, Jack becomes determined to come up with a clever scheme. And clever is the word for Calhoun's text. After several of Jack's plans fail, the story comes to a satisfying conclusion that will please readers. The pages are filled to the edge with Gackenbach's colorful drawings. His humorous illustra-

tions show red-nosed, red-cheeked cowboys and bald chickens. The wind heartily swirls through nearly every page adding action to an already fast-paced plot. School and public libraries alike will want to add this selection as an easy picture book example of a tall tale.

## JULIE'S TREE (1988)

### Kirkus Reviews

SOURCE: A review of *Julie's Tree,* in *Kirkus Reviews,* Vol. LVI, No. 12, June 15, 1988, p. 897.

Tree-climber Julie and her dad are getting over her mother's death; both are seeking friendships in the town to which they have just moved. Her dad's new interest in women worries Julie; her inability to make friends—except with a strange younger boy and an old, crusty woman—frustrates her. In this vacuum, she befriends an ancient mulberry tree.

After a slow start, Calhoun's story gains momentum with the impending destruction of the tree—to make way for a parking lot—as focus. Although set in the present, some of the dialogue seems to belong more to the nostalgic past, and Julie doesn't have the zip and humor of the author's popular Katie John. Still, she matures convincingly as she rallies the talents of a disparate group to save her tree. Tree-climbers and tree-lovers will overlook the stilted passages and cursory sketching of minor characters to enjoy Julie's step-by-step ascent of the mulberry.

### Publishers Weekly

SOURCE: A review of *Julie's Tree,* in *Publishers Weekly,* Vol. 234, No. 2, July 8, 1988, p. 56.

From the author of the Katie John books comes a story about Julie, who discovers a gigantic mulberry tree and centers her imagination and time on it as she adjusts both to her mother's death and her new life in Sutterville. She has difficulty making friends until she meets Ned, a fourth grader who also loves to climb Julie's tree and embraces her fantasy world, and Miss Fogarty, an elderly retiree whose property abuts the tree. This slow and not very involving story rallies around a proposed tree-razing, which Julie and her new coterie (Sandy and Becca come into the picture, as well as a tentative girlfriend for Julie's father) protest with signs and a sit-in. The ending is too pat and unbelievable, and the characters simply are not true-to-life.

### Ilene Cooper

SOURCE: A review of *Julie's Tree,* in *Booklist,* Vol. 84, No. 21, July, 1988, p. 1832.

Julie, who has lived with her grandmother since her

mother's death, now joins her father in a new town. Making friends is difficult, but Julie finds solace in the branches of a sturdy old tree, where she spends many happy hours. Slowly, Julie meets others who are interested in the tree as well: Ned, Becca, Sandy (all of whom become friends); Miss Fogarty, who lives next to the tree and pretends not to like the children; and the owner and a worker at a nearby factory. When it appears the tree is going to be chopped down to make room for a parking lot, Julie rallies this coterie to make sure the tree is saved. Even the woman her father has been dating (much to Julie's dismay) makes a valuable contribution to the effort. Though there is much activity throughout, the story has a quiet, almost old-fashioned feel to it. Julie's coming to terms with her new situation is successfully handled, and while this does not have the spark of the author's Katie John stories, its mood and message will appeal to many.

### Katherine Bruner

SOURCE: A review of *Julie's Tree*, in *School Library Journal*, Vol. 34, No. 11, August, 1988, p. 92.

Lonely in the new town where she and her father have moved following the death of her mother, and shy of making friends, Julie settles her affection on an open-armed mulberry tree. As she explores its leafy spaciousness, she draws other children there also. Julie realizes they have become her friends when they join in her efforts to prevent the city from cutting down the old tree to make room for a parking lot. Concerned adults help the thin plot reach a satisfactory, albeit implausible, conclusion. Julie's concern for the old mulberry tree is understandable and her determination to save it is commendable, but readers will find characterizations weak and, at times, disturbingly inconsistent. Hints of a ghost and the prospect that the strange neighbor, Miss Fogarty, is a witch are not developed adequately. Most of the action is limited to tree climbing. Dialogue seldom climbs above the trite. Calhoun's "Katie John" series continues to offer more solid enjoyment.

### 📖 *HIGH-WIRE HENRY* (1991)

#### Kirkus Reviews

SOURCE: A review of *High-Wire Henry*, in *Kirkus Reviews*, Vol. LIX, No. 6, March 15, 1991, p. 402.

The popular Siamese who appeared in *Cross-Country Cat* (1979), etc., copes with competition: a new puppy with whom his family is wholly smitten. Striving for attention, Henry practices balancing on the clothesline, becoming so adept that he's able to run along the telephone wire to rescue the puppy when it climbs out onto the roof. The tried-but-true formula, told with practiced skill, is endearingly extended in the soft, precisely detailed pencil-and-watercolor illustrations [by Erick Ingraham].

### Danita Nichols

SOURCE: A review of *High-Wire Henry*, in *School Library Journal*, Vol. 37, No. 4, April, 1991, p. 90.

A new story about the proud, adventurous, and accomplished Siamese cat featured in *Hot-Air Henry* (1981) and *Cross-Country Cat* (1979). Here, Henry feels his position in the family is threatened by a new puppy. Anxious to prove himself more clever than the dog, he decides to become a high-wire walker, but an embarrassing fall almost makes him abandon the scheme. When the puppy foolishly climbs out on a window ledge, however, only Henry can reach him by walking the telephone line, and he accepts his praise with total satisfaction. The animals in the realistic pictures are especially well drawn, and Henry's every emotion is aptly captured. The full-color illustrations are large enough to use with groups, and upper primary-grade reluctant readers will welcome this as an easy-reading picture book with illustrations [by Erick Ingraham] that have an adult appearance. This is a laugh-out-loud book that will have young listeners and readers in total sympathy with Henry, for his anger, hurt, frustration, and attention-getting antics mirror the emotions of any new sibling.

### Leone McDermott

SOURCE: A review of *High-Wire Henry*, in *Booklist*, Vol. 87, No. 15, April 1, 1991, p. 1574.

Henry the Siamese cat previously demonstrated his amazing talent for hind-leg walking in *Cross-Country Cat* and *Hot-Air Henry.* Now he is spurred on to literally new heights by the arrival of Buttons the puppy. Like any self-respecting cat, Henry insists on being the center of attention, so he stalks off in a huff when the family fusses over Buttons instead of Henry. He decides that a spectacular feat of high-wire walking is just the ticket to remind everyone of how special he is. Unfortunately, Henry's first try ends with an embarrassing fall, followed by lots of sulking in the apple tree. Then one day Buttons chases a squirrel out onto the second-story ledge, and it's Henry to the rescue over the telephone wire. This is a tale of sibling rivalry in the guise of a cat-and-dog story, and children will instinctively empathize with Henry's misery as well as his flamboyant attempts to get attention. [Erick] Ingraham's pencil and watercolor illustrations, in summery greens and beiges, have a lovely light-touched glow. Their textured realism renders even Henry's most improbable actions believable, while the dramatic use of perspective heightens the suspense.

#### Publishers Weekly

SOURCE: A review of *High-Wire Henry*, in *Publishers Weekly*, Vol. 238, No. 17, April 12, 1991, p. 57.

Sibling rivalry is not restricted to humans, or even siblings, as Calhoun tells her story about the cat who is displaced when a puppy is introduced to the family. ("When The Man brought a puppy in, Henry went out . . . and stayed out.") Through the window, the aggrieved Siamese watches as The Kid and The Woman join The Man playing with the tiny newcomer. [Erick] Ingraham's muted illustrations are soft and clear, and fill the borderless pages with tender scenes of summer. His appealing, expressive animals are the real stars, however, and they are amusingly aided by Calhoun's acute sounds ("Yeef," "Warf," "Yow yowie meowl"). Henry is so desperate to regain the attention of his family that he becomes a high-wire performer, first on the fence and then on the clothesline and telephone wire. But it is not until he saves the pup from a high ledge that he feels like part of the family again.

**Mary M. Burns**

SOURCE: A review of *High-Wire Henry,* in *The Horn Book Magazine,* Vol. LXVII, No. 4, July/August, 1991, p. 445.

That smart, high-flying Siamese from **Cross-Country Cat** and **Hot-Air Henry** is back and as spunky as ever in a story of pet-style rivalry. This time, Henry must contend with a new puppy who is playful, cute, and, worst of all, ingratiating. Poor old Henry tries to imitate the pup's every move, which leaves him looking ridiculous. In desperation, he decides to become a high-wire acrobat and, despite a number of false starts, succeeds. His accomplishment goes largely unnoticed until the pup leaps through an open window in pursuit of a squirrel and is trapped on a narrow ledge. Having mastered his art, Henry turns rescuer, earning kudos in his new role as resourceful hero. The story is skillfully narrated with just enough suspense and humor to engage the interest of its intended audience. Erick Ingraham's watercolors offer an elegant and thoughtful visual accompaniment to the narrative. Luminous background impressions of lawn and meadow offer an effective contrast to the softly sculptured, palpably textured forms of the animal protagonists, with the clean-edged architectural details of fence and house suggesting proportion and grounding the story in realistic, everyday life. The combination of two such obviously sympathetic talents produces a seamless and joyous experience.

## WHILE I SLEEP (1992)

### Publishers Weekly

SOURCE: A review of *While I Sleep,* in *Publishers Weekly,* Vol. 239, No. 17, April 6, 1992, p. 63.

Although both text and art of this quiet picture book have much to commend them individually, they seem to strain against each other for different effects. Calhoun's somewhat awkward text begins abruptly: "Time for bed, dear. / *Mama, does everything go to sleep at night?*" What follows is a predictable series: "*Where does the dog sleep, Mama? /* While you sleep / the dog sleeps / flopped by

the fire." Even boats, trains and planes sleep, the child is told, but "the moon stays up all night to watch over you." Each spread consists of a dreamlike scumbled pastel illustration surrounding a dark square. The square containing the text and sleeping dog, e.g., is circumscribed by a yellow-and-green page where the dream dog is pictured running with an animal in its mouth. Even though Ed Young's illustrations are visionary and striking, they seem too abstract for the prosaic text and for the intended preschool audience.

### Kirkus Reviews

SOURCE: A review of *While I Sleep,* in *Kirkus Reviews,* Vol. LX, No. 8, April 15, 1992, p. 534.

Like Ginsburg's *Asleep, Asleep,* another bedtime survey of sleepers, inspired by a child's questions. The repetitive, more pedestrian text here ("Does a boat sleep at night, Mama? Yes, dear. Boats sleep at their docks") is also broader-ranging, going from domestic to wild animals to kinds of transportation and concluding with the sun and the curious child. [Ed] Young sets his night-darkened images of the sleepers in four-inch squares that he imposes on sunny double spreads of the corresponding animals, train, etc. engaged in daytime activities, their evanescent forms distilled to impressionistic simplicity against serene, dreamlike clouds of glorious color. The idea here is trite, but Young's imaginative visualization is a pleasure.

### Deborah Abbott

SOURCE: A review of *While I Sleep,* in *Booklist,* Vol. 88, No. 17, May 1, 1992, pp. 1605–06.

With an author-illustrator combination like this, one expects a strong story line and exceptional art. The story, however, is slight and flawed. When a young child asks if everything sleeps at night, the parents reply, "Yes." Each double-page spread shows a dramatic daytime scene and a small, boxed nighttime sleeping image. For instance, an eagle soars through the air by day but at night is curled in its nest. The author's inclusion of several inanimate objects—a boat, a train, a plane, and the sun—succeeds in showing children that everything must rest, but to call this sleeping may be taking poetic license a bit too far. [Ed] Young's full-page pastel drawings, smudgy yet distinctive in shades of blues, greens, and yellows, are very attractive, but the boxed insets of sleeping figures in grays, blacks, and whites are hard to distinguish at times. There is a quiet, dreamy feeling here that does have appeal for the close-your-eyes crowd, but with so many bedtime stories published, this one will be a choice only for larger collections.

### Heidi Piehler

SOURCE: A review of *While I Sleep,* in *School Library Journal,* Vol. 38, No. 6, June, 1992, p. 89.

Calhoun and [Ed] Young combine their many talents in a bedtime picture book that is ultimately less than successful. An unidentified child asks where animals and vehicles sleep at night; Mama and Papa's answers comprise the narrative. Small framed square illustrations show the slumbering objects or animals superimposed on double-page spreads depicting them in action—a galloping horse, pouncing cat, soaring airplane, etc. These dream sequences feature Young's luminous pastel watercolors and swirling lines. In contrast, the sleep worlds are dark, contained, and have more linear patterns. While all of the illustrations are visually striking, they vary in drama and effectiveness. However, the problem with the book lies neither in the quiet meditative text nor the impressive paintings, but with audience compatibility. Children who are young enough to enjoy the simple bedtime theme may lack the sophistication to understand and appreciate the artwork. Without an explanation or introduction, they may not distinguish between the contrasting sleep and dream states. Older childen will appreciate the book's artistic merit but will be bored by the simple narrative. A literary lullaby that doesn't quite strike the right chord.

## HENRY THE SAILOR CAT (1994)

### Publishers Weekly

SOURCE: A review of *Henry the Sailor Cat,* in *Publishers Weekly,* Vol. 241, No. 14, April 4, 1994, p. 80.

In his fourth adventure, Henry the Siamese cat, star of **High-Wire Henry,** takes to sailing like a duck to water. After the first moments of queasiness have passed, he is scampering up the mast, marveling at dolphins and enjoying the feel of the breeze in his fur. And when one of his human sailing companions tumbles overboard, he proves himself handy with a slipknot and endowed with razor-sharp vision. This unlikely but enjoyable tale is brightly told, with the world viewed through Henry's eyes; it seems that cats and children share similar enthusiasms when it comes to sailing. Henry happily occupies center stage; other characters are reduced to The Man, The Woman and The Kid, friendly peripheral figures. Light-splashed watercolors [by Erick Ingraham] capture the varying blue tones of sky and sea, and, as in other Henry outings, the realistic artwork lends a touch of authenticity to far-fetched feline antics.

### Caroline Ward

SOURCE: A review of *Henry the Sailor Cat,* in *School Library Journal,* Vol. 40, No. 5, May, 1994, p. 89.

That intrepid Siamese cat, Henry, is back in another satisfying adventure. This time he is a stowaway on a small sloop that two members of his family are taking out for a sail. Once discovered, Henry proves that cats are natural sailors. He climbs the mast for a full view, spots cavorting dolphins, and watches carefully while The Man gives The Kid a lesson on coming about and stopping the

boat. When the adult accidently slips overboard, it is quick-thinking Henry who leads the rescue. [Erick] Ingraham's finely detailed, realistic watercolor illustrations are full of expression, and interesting perspectives make the feline's daring escapades totally believable. Seamlessly complementing the art is a text that captures the lure of sailing ("The water lapped gently, as if it was stroking the boat.") The practices portrayed are authentic, and the exciting rescue makes this an on-the-edge-of-your-seat read-aloud.

### Carolyn Phelan

SOURCE: A review of *Henry the Sailor Cat,* in *Booklist,* Vol. 90, No. 17, May 1, 1994, p. 1606.

Children who have followed this cat's adventures as a cross-country skier, a high-wire walker, and a hot-air balloonist will surely want to be in on the adventure when he stows away on a sailboat. The Man (as Henry calls him) takes the Kid out on the ocean for a day of sailing. Initially annoyed to find Henry aboard, the Man changes his mind when Henry saves him from drowning. A storm breaks, the Man falls overboard, and the Kid (who was in the cabin at the time) must find his dad in the rough waters and steer the sailboat toward him with only Henry as his guide. Yes, the story *is* a bit unlikely, but the cat's point of view is utterly convincing, and Henry's fans will be pleased to find this smart Siamese playing the hero once again. With its realistic approach, fine lines, and delicate shades of color, [Erick] Ingraham's artwork is a riveting part of the storytelling. A satisfying read-aloud.

### Kirkus Reviews

SOURCE: A review of *Henry the Sailor Cat,* in *Kirkus Reviews,* Vol. LXII, No. 9, May 1, 1994, p. 627.

The popular Siamese returns as a stowaway on a jaunt with "The Man" and "The Kid." When hiding below makes Henry queasy, he comes on deck to enjoy the sights (including dolphins and a whale), ascend the mast, note how the small craft is sailed, and play a crucial role in rescuing The Man when he falls overboard. The story is slight and predictable, but it's smoothly told by this old pro, while the carefully crafted realistic illustrations (remarkably precise for watercolors) [by Erick Ingraham] are sure to appeal to Henry's fans and other cat lovers.

### Ann A. Flowers

SOURCE: A review of *Henry the Sailor Cat,* in *The Horn Book Magazine,* Vol. LXX, No. 4, September-October, 1994, p. 573.

The intrepid Siamese cat Henry of **Cross-Country Cat** has returned in a new adventure, this time on a sailboat. Henry's family—the Man, the Woman, and the Kid—are in agreement that Henry won't like sailing because cats don't like water. But Henry, determined not to be left behind, slips away and gets on board unobserved at the fuel dock. Uncomfortable below, he goes on deck to be greeted by the horrified Man and the amused Kid. Insouciantly, he climbs to the top of the mast and uses it as an observation post; he calls out to dolphins and watches as the Man teaches the Kid to steer. Only our hero Henry sees the Man fall overboard and alerts the Kid, pointing in the right direction and yowling. With Henry's guidance, the Kid rescues the Man, and they race home before the oncoming storm. An exciting, happy tale with a remarkably clever hero, illustrated [by Erick Ingraham] with handsome, realistic sailing scenes and lively portraits of Henry that reveal his distinctive personality.

---

**Additional coverage of Calhoun's life and career is contained in the following sources published by Gale Research:** *Contemporary Authors New Revision Series,* **Vol. 18, and** *Something about the Author,* **Vols. 2, 84.**

---

# Sharon Creech
## 1945-

(Also writes as Sharon Rigg) American author of fiction.

Major works include *Absolutely Normal Chaos* (1990), *Walk Two Moons* (1994).

## INTRODUCTION

A respected author of fiction for young people, Creech is praised for her multilayered stories involving young adults struggling to survive adolescence. Filling her novels with scenes from her own life while creating memorable, true-to-life characters and plots, the author examines such topics as death, self-realization, love, and separation. A writer who "fashions characters with humor and sensitivity," according to *Kirkus Reviews,* she is also noted for her smooth and imaginative writing style. In her works, Creech attempts to give her readers an understanding of others' lives. As she noted in her Newbery Medal acceptance for *Walk Two Moons,* through her stories and characters she invites people to "come along and walk with us awhile, slip into our moccasins so that you might see what we think and feel, and so that you might understand why we do what we do, and so that you might glimpse the larger world outside your own."

### Biographical Information

Born and raised in Cleveland, Ohio, Creech often fantasized about being Native American, sometimes telling people she "was a full-blooded Indian." After receiving a Bachelor of Arts degree from Hiram College, Creech moved to Washington, D.C., to attend George Mason University, where she earned a Master of Arts degree. She stayed in Washington for a number of years before moving to England with her two children in 1979. Since 1984, she has been teaching American and British literature at the TASIS England American school in Thorpe, England. Her husband, Lyle D. Rigg, is headmaster of the same school.

### Major Works

In her first book, *Absolutely Normal Chaos,* which was published in the United States after the Newbery Medal-winning *Walk Two Moons,* Creech uses the device of a journal to unravel the story of Mary Lou Finney, a thirteen-year-old girl on the edge of adulthood. Mary Lou writes about her friends, crushes, and "normally strange" family with plenty of emotion and humor. She also writes about her cousin Carl Ray from West Vir-

ginia, who is somewhat of a mystery to her. By summer's end, however, Mary Lou learns more about Carl and more about herself. In *Walk Two Moons,* Creech revolves the story around a car trip, inspired by a trip taken with her parents in 1957 from Ohio to Idaho. Thirteen-year-old Salamanca Tree Hiddle (Sal) travels with her grandparents in search of her mother, who left home suddenly for Idaho and has not return as promised. During the six-day journey, both literal and metaphorical, Sal tells her grandparents about her friend Phoebe, whose mother is also missing. By the end of the trip, Sal learns what happened to her mother and to Phoebe's mother, and, like Mary Lou, learns more about herself.

### Awards

*Walk Two Moons,* winner of the 1995 Newbery Medal, was also a School Library Journal Best Book selection in 1994 and an American Library Association Notable Children's Book selection in 1995.

## AUTHOR'S COMMENTARY

**Sharon Creech**

SOURCE: "Newbery Medal Acceptance," in *The Horn Book Magazine,* Vol. LXXI, No. 4, July-August, 1995, pp. 418–25.

Most of you are probably familiar with the Newbery traditions: the secret choice, the phone call, the "Today" show summons, and the frenzy which follows. I have lived overseas for sixteen years and was not aware of these traditions. All I knew was that the Newbery Medal was the most honored of blessings.

On February 6th, I was home alone in England and had been wrestling all morning with a manuscript. Feeling ornery and frustrated, I fled to our back yard to vent one of my muffled screams (muffled because I am a headmaster's wife and it isn't seemly for me to scream too loudly). In the midst of that scream, the phone rang.

A ringing phone in a headmaster's house often signals a crisis, and when it rings, I'm well-trained: I grab pen and paper, ready to record the name of the student with appendicitis or the name of the dormitory whose pipes have burst. That afternoon, I scribbled: *American Library Association and Newbery Med . . .*

The writing trails off there.

I still go weak when I think of that call coming so unexpectedly, jolting my world so intensely. My first reaction was disbelief, followed by overwhelming gratitude. I felt as if the eye of God had beamed down on me, and I'd better do everything I was told. In the days that followed, whenever the phone rang (and it rang constantly—constantly), I stared at it suspiciously, expecting that this caller would say, "Oops, sorry! We made a mistake. It wasn't *your* book . . ."

I had a lot of difficulty coming to grips with why I was receiving such good fortune, and why *my* book was receiving such an honor. I'll be honest: I never dreamed a dream this big.

When I first read articles referring to me as an "unknown," I was amused. It made me feel peculiar, as if I'd previously been invisible. But the articles were accurate: I *was* virtually unknown in the field of children's books in the States. An unknown has simple prayers: please let my books be published; please let readers know these books exist; please let me keep writing. What the Newbery does is answer all of these prayers. It calls attention not only to my books, but to other new books as well. It celebrates children's literature. What a grand thing this Newbery is!

Several days after the Newbery call, I returned to the manuscript I'd been working on that extraordinary day, and I reread this opening paragraph:

"Life is like bowl of spaghetti . . ." That's what my grandmother used to say, and I'd imagine myself rummaging among twisted strands of pasta. But there was more to her saying. "Life is like a bowl of spaghetti—every now and then you get a meatball." It seemed to me that the meatball was a tremendous bonus you might unearth in all those convoluted spaghetti turns of your life. It was something to look forward to, a reward for all that slogging through your pasta.

On February 6th, I received news of one glorious meatball in my plate of spaghetti, and no one on this earth could be more grateful than I am to receive it tonight. Thank you.

I'm grateful to many people for the birth of **Walk Two Moons,** and some of these include:

My husband, children, and larger family, who provided inspiration for many of the characters in this book.

Five editors, each of whom left his mark, as they came and went during the three years it took to polish **Walk Two Moons:** in England, Marion Lloyd, Lynette Wilson, and Isabel Barrett; and in the States, David Gale and Nancy Siscoe.

I would also like to thank Bill Morris, Virginia Anagnos, Alicia Mikles, Lisa Desimini, George Nicholson, and everyone at HarperCollins who contributed to **Walk Two Moons** or who aided me these past months.

My agents, Carol Smith and Jonathan Dolger.

My gratitude also extends to that wild and crazy Highlights group at Chautauqua in 1988, who convinced me that writing for children was a most worthy and noble pursuit.

As for the American Library Association and the Newbery Committee, I don't know if I'll ever be able to convey to you how much this award means to me. With one phone call from Philadelphia to London on February 6th, you dramatically altered my plate of spaghetti.

And now to writing and the evolution of this book. I have to begin on a serious note, because it was a serious jolt that led me to all these words.

In 1980, when my children and I had been in England for nine months, my father had a stroke. Although he lived for six more years, the stroke left him paralyzed and unable to speak. Think of all the words we wanted to say to him, and all the words he must have wanted to say to us. Think of all those words locked up for six years, because his mind could neither accept nor deliver words.

A month after he died in 1986, I started my first novel, and when I finished it, I wrote another, and another, and another. The words rushed out. The connection between my father's death and my flood of writing might be that I had been confronted with the dark wall of mortality: we don't have endless time to follow our dreams; but it might also be that I felt obligated to use the words that my father could not.

How does a book begin? Here I would like to tell you something that my mother related to me in a phone call last year. She'd awakened suddenly in the night, to a voice commanding her to dash something to the floor. She grabbed the nearest thing at hand—the television's remote control—which she dutifully dashed to the floor. But no, that did not satisfy the voice. Next she grabbed the lamp and dashed it to the floor. There. That was it. The voice was quiet.

"Mom," I said. "Did the lamp break?"

"Yes," she said. "It did." She did not seem troubled by the broken lamp, nor did she wonder why it was a lamp that needed to be dashed to the floor in the first place. Instead, she seemed relieved that she had accommodated the voice.

This is similar to how I begin a book—with a voice commanding me to dash something not to the floor, but onto paper, and I dutifully snatch any words or characters which appear. Only after the book is completed can I begin to identify some of the seeds from which these seemingly arbitrary characters and situations come, but I am reluctant to dig too deeply, and to explain why, I need to tell you about the talcum powder.

I once owned a bottle of Chanel talcum powder which I used daily. Oddly, the contents never seemed to diminish. Would the container never be empty? Did it refill and replenish itself? It was a mystery which I enjoyed. But I also feared that someone would come along and explain exactly why it was that it never seemed to empty, just as someone once explained—to my horror—that dreams are merely little chemicals sloshing around randomly in your brain at night. The truth is: I don't want to know the explanations for the mysteries of dreams or of a replenishing bottle of talcum. Like Salamanca, who needs to believe a tree is singing or that the spirit of someone she loves inhabits that tree, it is the mystery I need. And although I can, and will, tell you some of the sources for *Walk Two Moons,* I hope to leave some of it a mystery —even to myself.

Four yours ago, after I'd already written two very different versions of this book—versions which did not include Salamanca or the Hiddles—I received this message in a fortune cookie at a Chinese restaurant in Surrey: Don't judge a man until you've walked two moons in his moccasins. Beneath this saying was the note: American Indian proverb.

This seemed a curious thing to receive in a Chinese restaurant in England. At the time, I would have preferred a more traditional fortune—perhaps one like Patricia MacLachlan once received that proclaimed, "Your talents will soon be recognized," or the one Lois Lowry received, forecasting that she would become rich and famous in a far-out profession. Still, I was intrigued by the American Indian proverb with its suggestion of a journey and the resonance of that single word *moccasins.*

My cousins maintain that one of our ancestors was an American Indian. As a child, I loved that notion, and often exaggerated it by telling people that I was a full-blooded Indian. I inhaled Indian myths, and among my favorites were those which involved stories of reincarnation. How magnificent and mysterious to be Estsanatlehi, the "woman who never dies. She grows from baby to mother to old woman and then turns into a baby again, and on and on she goes, living a thousand, thousand lives." I wanted to be that Navajo woman. I wanted to live a thousand, thousand lives. I crept through the woods near our house, reenacting these myths, and wishing, wishing, for a pair of soft leather moccasins. (I admit—but without apology that my view of American Indians was a romantic one.)

I also climbed trees. I think I spent half my childhood up a tree, for I had somehow got it in my mind that Indians climbed trees. And there in those trees—oh! You could climb and climb, and you could reach a place where there was only you and the tree and the birds and the sky. It was a place where the sky was wide, and something in you—which was larger than you—was alive. And maybe the appeal of trees also lay in the sense that they live "a thousand, thousand lives," appearing to die each autumn, and then—miraculously—be reborn in all their glory each spring.

During the summer of my twelfth birthday, my family took a car trip from Ohio to Lewiston, Idaho. What a journey! What a country! What spectacular and unexpected sights reared up around each bend! Midway through this journey—and because it was my birthday, I can tell you the exact date: July 29, 1957—we stopped at an Indian reservation, and there I was able to choose a precious gift: a pair of leather moccasins.

On the final day of our outward-bound journey, we crested Lewiston Hill and stared down at the road which switchbacked all the long way down into Lewiston, nestled at the bottom alongside the Snake River. And all the way down that hill, I prayed, for I feared that we would never make it to our destination alive.

Those of you who have read *Walk Two Moons* will recognize similarities between Sal's journey and my own. The significance of my journey in 1957 is that I remember it not only as a literal and physical journey across America, but also as a metaphorical journey: it was a time when I was enriched and inspired by our vast country and all the various people who populate it. There was a larger, lush, and complex world outside my own.

The proverb in my fortune cookie revived that trip for me and restored the girl who wanted to be an Indian. I don't see Salamanca as a Native American; I see her as an American, who, like me, has inherited several cultures, and who tries to sort out who she is by embracing the mystery of one strand of that heritage. Salamanca needs those stories of reincarnation; they give her hope.

The portion of the proverb which became the title appealed to me on another level as well. In **Walk Two Moons,** I saw an invitation, from characters to writer, and from writer to reader: come along and walk with us awhile, slip into our moccasins so that you might see what we think and feel, and so that you might understand why we do what we do, and so that you might glimpse the larger world outside your own. You could live a thousand, thousand lives! Every book implicitly offers this invitation, and every book offers a journey, whether it is a literal one, a metaphorical one, or both.

Mysteries appeared as I wrote—the singing tree, the marriage bed, the characters themselves. In the afternoons, when I reread what I'd written in the morning, I didn't have the vaguest idea how some of these things got on the page.

It is nearly three years since **Walk Two Moons** was completed, and now I look at it with a different eye. I can see that Salamanca is me and my daughter. I can see that Gramps and the goodman-father combine elements of all the good men in my family, and that Gram is what you might get if you took all the women in my family and rolled them into a ball. I'd better add that we are not perfect people. If you spent some time with us, you'd see that sometimes we drive each other crazy, and we would probably drive you crazy, too. As one of my brothers once said, referring to our annual family reunion at Chautauqua, "It's a zoo, but it feels good in the heart."

And I know where the singing tree came from. On our school campus, bordering the playing fields, is a magnificent bank of trees. Overhead, clouds drift across a wide expanse of sky. While I was writing **Walk Two Moons,** I'd often escape to this place, where, increasingly, I felt that my father was inhabiting those clouds. It was comforting to think that he was always nearby (for there are always clouds in an English sky); he was watching over me. One day I heard a magnificent birdsong coming from the top of a tree, and it seemed that the tree itself was singing. Instantly, I had the further sense that my father had leaped from the clouds to the tree.

A few years ago, when my youngest brother and I were sitting on the porch at Chautauqua Lake, I told him about this incident and asked him, "Do *you* ever have the feeling that Dad is—in the clouds—or in the trees?"

My brother glanced at the clouds and the trees. "Nope," he said. "Can't say that I do."

Ah, well. Still: maybe the talcum powder, the clouds, and the singing tree which surfaces in **Walk Two Moons** are related, for they all represent beautiful mysteries, and they all offer hopes of *life never-ending.*

I can also, I think, retrace the evolution of Gram's spontaneous eruptions of joy *(huzza, huzza!),* though I do so with a bit of worry about the talcum powder—for I'd hate to empty all the mystery. But here's one speculation I can offer.

In my study are dozens of pictures of my family, so that everywhere I look, someone is looking back at me. On the bulletin board nearest my desk are two quotes and two of my favorite pictures; these things have something in common. In one photo, my son is standing on an alpine peak, silhouetted against the sky; in a similar one, my daughter is reclining on a different mountain peak. There they are at the top of the world, like me in my trees, where the sky is wide and something in them is *alive.* You should see the expressions on my children's faces. Each has been caught in a moment of supreme joy, and there is something else, too, less definable. I think it might be hope.

One quote tacked nearby is from Ernie Pyle's Second World War correspondence. It reads simply: "The human spirit is just like a cork." I love that line. The second quote is from an autobiographical essay my mother wrote in 1933. She was fifteen years old; it was the middle of the Depression; her life was not an easy one. But she says, in the middle of this essay, "Whenever I feel especially happy, I tap dance." And I love that line, too.

It is hard to picture my mother tap-dancing, but I like to think that she has had many moments in her life when she felt so happy that she tap-danced, when her spirits rose like a cork bobbing to the surface.

Perhaps Gram's *huzza, huzzas* in **Walk Two Moons** grew out of those pictures on my wall, the notion of a spirit rising like a cork, and the image of my mother tap-dancing.

When I was writing **Walk Two Moons** the newspapers and the BBC were filled with images of war and disaster: of bombings, riots, floods, earthquakes, famine, torture. Every day my students stared into Pandora's box, rifled with all the evils of the world. Every day there was something difficult to face. Maybe I wrote this book because my students and I, like Salamanca, had stared those horrors in the eye as best we could, and then needed, for a time, to clutch the hope that was down in the bottom of Pandora's box, and with that hope turn to the other box, the one with the mysteries and "smoothbeautiful folds" inside. Salamanca and I need to face the evils, but we also need mystery, and we need hope. Maybe you do, too.

When I read Salamanca's story now, with some distance, I hear such longing in her voice—for her mother, for her father, for the land—and I know that her longing is also my longing. I know this book was also written because I was living an ocean away, longing for my children, my larger family, and for my own country.

I'm going to close soon, before I empty all the talcum powder out of this book, but I'd like to give it just a few more brief shakes.

Recently I received another meatball in the mail. It was not a Newbery-medal-sort-of-meatball. It was a packet of letters written by my father to my aunt during the Second World War, and they, too, are filled with longing—for his wife, for his first child (who was born while he was overseas), and for his country. The miracle of this gift! There is his voice; there are his words! The last line in each of his letters is identical. He says, "Write me often." Fifty years later, maybe that's also part of what I'm doing: writing him often.

The final letter in the stack was not written by him—it was from my mother, telling my aunt that she'd just heard from my father, and that he was on his way home from the war. My mother wrote, "I'm so tickled and happy that I can hardly work. I jumped and squealed for joy last night." Do you hear that cork rising? Do you think she tap-danced?

People have asked me how I feel now, four months after the Newbery call. I'm very emotional about it: I still feel overwhelming gratitude; I still have bouts of disbelief, and I still fear that someone is going to come along and take this meatball away.

Thank you for honoring this book and for making it possible for me to be in *these* moccasins tonight. If I could sprinkle some hopes over all of you, they would include these: I hope you each find a meatball in the spaghetti of your life; I hope your talcum powder never empties, that your spirit is like a cork, and that you all live a thousand, thousand lives.

And finally:

At the end of the Newbery call, K. T. Horning, the committee chairperson, said, "We have one last thing we'd like to say to you." What she said is also the last thing I'd like to say to you tonight, and it is the last thing Salamanca Tree Hiddle says in *Walk Two Moons:*

"Huzza, Huzza!"

---

# TITLE COMMENTARY

## ABSOLUTELY NORMAL CHAOS (1990)

### Joan Zahnleiter

SOURCE: A review of *Absolutely Normal Chaos,* in *Magpies,* Vol. 6, No. 4, September, 1991, p. 32.

The summer journal of Mary Lou Finney, aged 13, of 4059 Buxton Road, Easton, Ohio, begins with a letter beseeching her new English teacher not to read it because, as she says, "How was I to know all this stuff was going to happen this summer?" The summer certainly is eventful, not only for Mary Lou but also for what she terms her "normally-strange family". Her life is disrupted in more ways than one by the arrival of a gangling, uncommunicative cousin, Carl Ray, from West Virginia, by his curious relationship with Charlie Furtz, the genial neighbour from across the road, who subsequently dies of a heart attack, and by her own budding romance with Alex Cheevy. With typical teenage theatrics, Mary Lou rattles off her perceptions of the mysterious events unfolding around her as she records them in her journal. Her mother's injunction against her continual use of "God", "Lord" and "stuff" sends her to the thesaurus with colourful results, e.g. "stuff" becomes "sum and substance" and "God" becomes "Deity". The flip humour implicit in Mary Lou's ingenuous analyses of the situations in which she finds herself (do kisses taste like chicken?) keep the story romping along. Despite her stormy outbursts and sometimes extravagant emotionalism, she comes across as a warmly caring person, swinging between bafflement, embarrassment and elation as she weathers the stormy process of growing up. The new English teacher will not be bored by her journal, nor will readers aged 11+.

### Roger Sutton

SOURCE: A review of *Absolutely Normal Chaos,* in *Bulletin of the Center for Children's Books,* Vol. 49, No. 3, November, 1995, p. 87.

Mary Lou Finney is finding her thirteenth summer complicated by the arrival of her cousin, Carl Ray, from West Virginia. Carl Ray, slovenly and monosyllabic, is just something else to deal with along with the romantic travails of Mary Lou's best friend, the continuing importunations of Mary Lou's family, and Mary Lou's own gently developing romance with Alex. Published in England prior to Creech's Newbery-winning *Walk Two Moons* . . . (in which Mary Lou plays a small part), this novel shares some of that book's over-the-top plotting, but where *Walk Two Moons* was ultimately convincing in its exhilarating, almost-magical realism, *Absolutely Normal Chaos* seems weakly contrived. The story is told through Mary Lou's summer journal entries, a school assignment, and while her voice is authentically that of a thirteen-year-old, her life is that of a thirteen-year-old of an earlier, gentler era. While lacking the contemporary swing of, say, Rachel Vail's books, the trials of Mary Lou's first date, first kiss, etc. will speak to younger girls dreaming about what's in store for them. However, Carl Ray's circumstances, which give the novel its narrative core, are well-nigh unbelievable, involving a secret adoption, a fortuitous death, a legacy from an anonymous benefactor, and, later, a car crash. Where *Walk Two Moons* understood and played with its own implausibility, this book seems as oblivious as Mary Lou herself to its hokey devices. Still, Mary Lou is entertaining (if occasionally longwinded) and readers hooked on happy endings will be pleased to see that everything works out perfectly.

## Cindy Darling Codell

SOURCE: A review of *Absolutely Normal Chaos,* in *School Library Journal,* Vol. 41, No. 11, November, 1995, p. 119.

Creech's newest story is told as a summer journal begrudgingly started as an English assignment. Mary Lou, 13, wonders if kisses with boys really taste like chicken; if her best friend will ever shut up about her new boyfriend; and how her visiting cousin, Carl Ray, can be such a silent clod, especially when someone has anonymously given him $5000. Later, when he is in a coma following a car accident, she rereads her journal and wonders how she could have been so unseeing. Mary Lou is a typical teen whose acquaintance with the sadder parts of life is cushioned by a warm and energetic family. Her entertaining musings on Homer, Shakespeare, and Robert Frost are drawn in nifty parallels to what is happening in her own life. When forbidden by her mother to say "God," "stupid," and "stuff," she makes a trek to the thesaurus to create some innovative interjections. Creech's dialogue is right on target. Her characterization is nicely done also. By comparison, this book is differently voiced than *Walk Two Moons,* lacks that book's masterful imagery, and is more superficial in theme; but appropriately so. Creech has remained true to Mary Lou, who is a different narrator, and one who will win many fans of her own. Those in search of a light, humorous read will find it; those in search of something a little deeper will also be rewarded.

## Nancy Vasilakis

SOURCE: A review of *Absolutely Normal Chaos,* in *The Horn Book Magazine,* Vol. LXXII, No. 2, March-April, 1996, pp. 204–05.

The Finneys, as described by thirteen-year-old Mary Lou in this funny first-person narrative, are a perfect example of that elusive reality, the typical middle-class family. Readers will immediately feel comfortable with Mary Lou and her siblings, friends, and neighbors. Sharon Creech, whose previous novel for young adults, *Walk Two Moons,* received the Newbery Medal, employs a commonplace narrative framework here by having her main character write the events of the past summer into her journal. Gossipy revelations about her best friend, Beth Ann; daydreamy notes about her fledgling romance with cute Alex Cheevey; and artless interpretations of the *Odyssey* ("The only thing I don't like about Odysseus is that he brags so much about how clever he is and how many cities he sacked and how many people he killed. I think he'd be put in jail if he were alive today") fill the pages of Mary Lou's journal. These are soon overshadowed by the unexpected visit of cousin Carl Ray from West Virginia. This lanky, taciturn houseguest and his strange country ways take some getting used to, and a bit of a mystery takes shape around the real reason for his long-term stay. Although its resolution—which involves Carl Ray's real father and the Finneys' next-door neighbor—demands a suspension of disbelief, Mary Lou's inimitable way of spin-

ning the tale makes it all worthwhile. Her own hilarious brush with culture shock occurs when she accompanies Carl Ray on a trip to his home. This visit also provides Mary Lou with some insights into what her cousin has had to endure at her house. Mary Lou grows in a number of important ways throughout the summer, and the metaphors she now recognizes in the *Odyssey* could, she realizes, very well apply to her own life.

## WALK TWO MOONS (1994)

### Kirkus Reviews

SOURCE: A review of *Walk Two Moons,* in *Kirkus Reviews,* Vol. LXII, No. 12, June 15, 1994, p. 842.

During the six days it takes Sal's paternal grandparents to drive her west to Idaho in time for her mother's birthday, she tells them about her friend Phoebe—a story that, the 13-year-old comes to realize, in many ways parallels her own: Each girl had a mother who left home without warning. The mystery of Phoebe's more conventional mother's disappearance and its effects on her family and eventual explanation unfold as the journey, with its own offbeat incidents, proceeds; meanwhile, in Sal's intricate narrative, the tragic events surrounding *her* mother's flight are also gradually revealed. After Sal fell from a tree, her mother carried her back to the house; soon after, she bore a stillborn child. Slowly, the love between Sal's parents, her mother's inconsolable grief, and Sal's life since her departure emerge; last to surface are the painful facts that Sal has been most reluctant to face. Creech, an American who has published novels in Britain, fashions characters with humor and sensitivity, but Sal's poignant story would have been stronger without quite so many remarkable coincidences or such a tidy sum of epiphanies at the end. Still, its revelations make a fine yarn.

### Connie Tyrrell Burns

SOURCE: A review of *Walk Two Moons,* in *School Library Journal,* Vol. 40, No. 10, October, 1994, p. 142.

An engaging story of love and loss, told with humor and suspense. Thirteen-year-old Salamanca Tree Hiddle's mother leaves home suddenly on a spiritual quest, vowing to return, but can't keep her promise. The girl and her father leave their farm in Kentucky and move to Ohio, where Sal meets Phoebe Winterbottom, also 13. While Sal accompanies her eccentric grandparents on a six-day drive to Idaho to retrace her mother's route, she entertains them with the tale of Phoebe, whose mother has also left home. While this story-within-a-story is a potentially difficult device, in the hands of this capable author it works well to create suspense, keep readers' interest, and draw parallels between the situations and reactions of the two girls. Sal's emotional journey through the grieving process—from denial to anger and finally to acceptance—is depicted realistically and with feeling. Indeed, her initial confusion and repression of the truth are mirrored in the book; even readers are unaware until near the end, that Sal's mother has died. Phoebe's mother does return home, bringing with her a son previously unknown to her family, who is accepted with alacrity. Overall, a richly layered novel about real and metaphorical journeys.

## Ilene Cooper

SOURCE: A review of *Walk Two Moons,* in *Booklist,* Vol. 91, No. 6, November 15, 1994, p. 590.

Thirteen-year-old Sal Hiddle can't deal with all the upheaval in her life. Her mother, Sugar, is in Idaho, and although Sugar promised to return before the tulips bloomed, she hasn't come back. Instead, Mr. Hiddle has moved Sal from the farm she loves so much and has even taken up company with the unpleasantly named Mrs. Cadaver. Multilayered, the book tells the story of Sal's trip to Idaho with her grandparents; and as the car clatters along, Sal tells her grandparents the story of her friend Phoebe, who receives messages from a "lunatic" and who must cope with the disappearance of her mother. The novel is ambitious and successful on many fronts: the characters, even the adults, are fully realized; the story certainly keeps readers' interest; and the pacing is good throughout. But Creech's surprises—that Phoebe's mother has an illegitimate son and that Sugar is buried in Idaho, where she died after a bus accident—are obvious in the first case and contrived in the second. Sal knows her mother is dead; that Creech makes readers think otherwise seems a cheat, though one, it must be admitted, that may bother adults more than kids. Still, when Sal's on the road with her grandparents, spinning Phoebe's yarn and trying to untangle her own, this story sings.

## Deborah Stevenson

SOURCE: A review of *Walk Two Moons,* in *Bulletin of the Center for Children's Books,* Vol. 48, No. 5, January, 1995, p. 162.

Salamanca—Sal—grew up in Kentucky, but she and her father moved to Ohio after her mother's death; she and her grandparents are currently taking a road trip to Idaho, where her mother is buried. As they travel, Sal relates to her grandparents the story of her friend Phoebe, whose unhappy mother left Phoebe's family; Sal finds that recounting Phoebe's story helps her understand the desertion of her own mother, who was later killed when the bus taking her away from her family crashed. Creech skillfully keeps these layers separate but makes their interrelationship clear, and the plot moves along amid all this contemplation with the aid of a mysterious note-leaver, a local "lunatic," an eccentric English teacher, and Sal's budding romance, not to mention Mount Rushmore, Old Faithful, and a poisonous snakebite along the road of Sal's trip with her grandparents. The style is smooth and imaginative but cheerfully plain-spoken ("I wanted to jump up and say, 'Phoebe's mother has disappeared and that is why Phoebe is acting like a complete donkey,' but I

didn't"), and the folksiness of Sal's grandparents (Sal's grandfather calls Sal his "chickabiddy" and his wife "gooseberry") is warm and uncontrived. Readers who enjoyed Barbara Hall's *Dixie Storms* will appreciate this strong and tender novel about all kinds of gain and loss.

## Hazel Rochman

SOURCE: "Salamanca's Journey," in *The New York Times Book Review,* May 21, 1995, p. 24.

We keep hearing that books for young people are doomed, mowed down by the traffic on the information superhighway. Yet a controversy now rages about a coming-of-age novel, **Walk Two Moons,** the surprise winner of the 1995 Newbery Medal as "the most distinguished contribution to American literature for children" published last year. The fight is about literary criticism and popular taste, about multiculturalism and markets and about our view of childhood. What's wonderful is that everyone is so het up about, of all things, a work of fiction. A book.

The author, Sharon Creech, is an American who teaches in England. She was unknown in this country, though she's published three books in Britain. **Walk Two Moons** is about 13-year-old Salamanca Tree Hiddle, proud of the "Indianness in her blood." She's driving west with her grandparents on a 2,000-mile journey from Ohio to Idaho to find the mother who left her. The book got mixed attention from critics; it was generally praised for its storytelling, panned for its plot contrivances. Without the Newbery, it might have faded within a few years.

Should it have won? Who's to say? All of us who have been on the Newbery committee know that the choice is as much the outcome of group dynamics as of literary quality. The committee is made up of 15 members of the American Library Association's children's division. The members are mostly school and public librarians, and there are a few critics and academics from around the country. Most know about books. Most know the audience.

As with any committee, a few members have already made up their minds before the meetings begin. Some are quietly authoritative. Some are obsessed. Some bully or cajole. Power groups form. Men and women (most of the members are women) argue differently. Compromises are made. One thing is certain: When you talk about books, you get close to people fast, especially when the choice matters so much. Though it was years ago, I can still remember where each member of my committee sat around the long table as we talked, argued, sneered, sulked, schemed and listened through the long days and nights of discussion. I loved being on that committee, even though my first choice didn't win.

The proceedings are secret, which adds to their intensity.

Also, no one except those present really knows what happens. Leaks and rumors aren't reliable; everyone has a different version of the fray. Sometimes a split between two strong favorites allows an outside choice to win, just as with the Academy Awards. I have heard publishers with a hot contender agonize about timing: Will the book crest too early? If they bring it out in the spring and it gets lots of critical acclaim, will that create a backlash before the winter meeting? Lois Lowry's novel *The Giver* (1994) was a popular choice. So was Patricia MacLachlan's *Sarah, Plain and Tall* (1986). But everyone has a comforting example of a great book that didn't win—from E. B. White's *Charlotte's Web* to Paula Fox's exquisite contemporary story *One-Eyed Cat* (which, incidentally, is also about a mother who leaves).

Whenever there's an unpopular choice, people say that the Newbery Medal will lose its authority. On the contrary, 73 years after the first winner (Hendrik Willem van Loon's book *The Story of Mankind*) the Newbery is more important than ever. It is much more visible and influential than any other children's—or adult—book award. The stakes are considerable. It brings instant celebrity for the author, an invitation to appear on the *Today* show and sales of around 100,000 copies in hard cover in the first year as the book joins the canon of children's literature. Speeches and appearances everywhere. A receiving line at the A.L.A.'s glittering Newbery banquet in June, the acceptance speech recorded and distributed on cassettes. A gold Newbery medallion sticker on the cover of every copy of the book . . . forever.

My two favorites this year weren't even chosen as Honor Books (runners-up). Jacqueline Woodson's *I Hadn't Meant to Tell You This* is also about a girl whose mother has gone away to find herself. It's a stark, beautiful story in which the friendship between the black, middle-class narrator and her poor, white classmate helps them escape the sorrow in their homes and the bigotry in their schools. Was it too honest? Too open-ended? Avi's novel *The Barn,* like the award winner, is set in the West. It's a gripping survival story about a white boy who finds manhood on the frontier, not by fighting, and not by a quest through the wilderness, but by staying home. Now let's face it, no story about a pioneer boy in the West has a hope of winning a prize today, especially if he doesn't have a 1990's consciousness about how his home was taken from the Indians.

I hadn't read **Walk Two Moons** until last month and I didn't expect to like it. A girl into her Indianness on a quest to find herself? I dreaded what Michael Dorris calls the "basket weaving and mysticism" kind of stereotype. I had heard the gratuitous insult that the book only won because it was P.C. Then there were the arguments from the authenticity watchdogs: How dare a white outsider write about the sacred Indian experience? Creech is stealing, they said, and she gets it all wrong.

In fact, the Indianness is one of the best things about this book, casual, contemporary and mythic, not an exotic thing apart. Sal is only a small part Indian, and she knows her parents gave her what they thought was the tribe's name but got it wrong. Still, the heritage is a part of her identity. She loves the Indian stories her mother told her, and they get mixed in with Genesis and Pandora's box and Longfellow and with family stories and, above all, with a celebration of the sweeping natural world and our connectedness with it. For once in a children's book Indians are people, not reverential figures in a museum diorama. Sal's Indian heritage is a natural part of her finding herself in America.

It's great that the hero on the archetypal quest here is a young woman in search of courage and identity. In the old days, it was always a boy like Theseus who went to find his father, and, as Joseph Campbell pointed out, when the hero found his father he found himself. As Sal retraces her mother's steps through the Badlands and the Black Hills, she tells stories about her friend's mother, who also left, and we learn Sal's mother's story and her grandparents' story and her own. The storytelling is comic and affectionate, each chapter building to its own dramatic climax. Sal's voice is sometimes lost and lonely, expressing her grief and also her awe for the great country she's traveling through. We recognize that she's been stuck physically and emotionally. She learns that "a person couldn't stay all locked up in the house. . . . A person had to go out and do things and see things."

What goes wrong with the story is that the perilous journey in all its surprise and beauty and danger and discovery is blockaded by the contrivances and messages. Everything is reduced to therapy. "You can't keep the birds of sadness from flying over your head, but you can keep them from nesting in your hair." There's actually a blind, eccentric old lady who talks funny but can "see," and she leaves portentous messages on doorsteps. And, just in case we don't get the heavy plot parallels with Sal's friend's mother, it's spelled out many times: "Don't judge a man until you've walked two moons in his moccasins." All the women characters turn out sweet and good and a bit peculiar. All the men too—the fathers, the teacher, the boyfriend, the police, even the thief. By the end of the novel this noble 13-year-old decides that maybe her mother left to set her daughter free. Everything is pat; hope is shining. We have what John Leonard calls the formula of "good will, coincidence and pluck."

Even so, some have attacked the book as too realistic. One wonders what the family-values crowd makes of *Hansel and Gretel.* The problem is that we don't trust kids to read for themselves. We hover and harangue, and we expect each book to carry the whole coming-of-age experience, to be fair to everyone, to leave nothing out. Forget pity and terror: the prize goes to the right role model.

Enthralling stories help us imagine the lives of others in all their passionate conflict. Save the messages for the Internet.

## David Bennett

SOURCE: A review of *Walk Two Moons,* in *Books for Keeps,* No. 96, January, 1996, p. 12.

This multiple award winner sees a 13-year-old girl journeying across America, telling her grandparents the story of her friend, Phoebe, whose mother once left home. As layer builds on layer the story takes on more and more significance for the travellers until the final, very moving denouement.

Here's a novel about growing up, love, separation, grief and, most importantly, about not judging a man until you've walked two moons in his moccasins.

I can't recommend it highly enough for youngsters who relish a read which challenges them to reflect.

## Joanna Brod

SOURCE: "Storytelling Sorcery," in *Metro Times,* Vol. XVI, No. 14, January 3, 1996, p. 44.

"Don't judge a man until you've walked two moons in his moccasins." In 1991 Sharon Creech, an American who lives and teaches in England, received this Native American proverb inside a fortune cookie. It inspired an inventive young adult novel of mystery and surprises.

Creech's *Walk Two Moons,* her first U.S. novel following three books published abroad, received the 1995 Newbery Medal for the most distinguished contribution to American literature for children.

At the center of the action is 13-year-old Salamanca Tree Hiddle's six-day road trip from Ohio to Idaho with her grandparents. It has been more than a year since Sal's mother announced that she was going away for a while, and now Sal is hoping to find her and convince her to come back. Along the way she shares a true story with her grandparents.

The story begins less than a year before. Sal and her dad have just learned that her mother will not be returning home, and have relocated from their Kentucky farm to Ohio. There Sal befriends a girl named Phoebe Winterbottom.

Strange things begin happening to Phoebe. She finds a series of cryptic notes on her porch, she is visited by a mysterious young man and then her mother disappears. Desperate for answers, Phoebe decides that her mother has been kidnapped or possibly murdered by the young man, and that the notes are meant to be clues.

As she tells Phoebe's story, Sal discovers that her own story is buried beneath it. With her grandparents, she is following the same route her mother took to Idaho, encountering the same landmarks she visited, exploring the Native American bloodline that links them, and in the process beginning to define herself as a separate individual.

The three plotlines (the car trip, Phoebe's mystery and the period leading up to Sal's mother's departure) come together as Sal comes to grips with the truth about her mother. The main character's candid, perceptive narration is especially effective at moments when her grief gives way to sudden elation.

Creech's storytelling sorcery is matched only by her quirky yet down-to-earth characters. In particular, Sal's unpredictable, warmhearted grandparents are a breath of fresh air.

Some have found the plot of *Walk Two Moons* too contrived, while others have called it overly realistic. There's a grain of truth in both accusations, but in each case Creech reveals a keen understanding of the age group for which she writes.

Young adult readers will likely appreciate the exotic flavor of Phoebe's mysterious messages and not be turned off by their overt symbolism. And although it's realistically portrayed, Sal's struggle is a safe read in part because it's buffered by the support and nurturance of the adults around her.

For the child approaching adulthood and for the seeker in all of us, *Walk Two Moons* is a journey well worth taking. Slip into its moccasins and come along for the ride.

# Gary Crew
## 1947-

Australian author of fiction.

Major works include *Strange Objects* (1990), *No Such Country* (1991), *Lucy's Bay* (1992), *Angel's Gate* (1993), *The Lost Diamonds of Killiecrankie* (1995).

## INTRODUCTION

Lauded for his ability to write novels that are often literary and experimental in style yet still accessible to young readers, Gary Crew is best known for young adult works that impart little-known information about Australian history. Using literary and biblical allusions, symbolism, and a variety of narrative techniques, Crew's stories challenge the values of contemporary urban Australian society and encourage coexistence with, and an embracing of, Aboriginal culture. While Crew's work often explores the history of Australia, critics observe that the exploitation and prejudice he discusses have occurred in every country's history, and readers of all nationalities will benefit from learning about the mistakes of the past. Reviewers also note that the universal themes of alienation and the search for identity experienced by Crew's characters reveal his empathy for young readers.

### Biographical Information

Born in Brisbane, Australia, on September 23, 1947, Crew was often ill as a child, which allowed him time to read and develop an extensive literary background. He was often sent to recuperate at his great-grandmother's house in Ipswich. The letters home that the young Crew wrote to his mother were his first attempts at writing, and his great-grandmother's house would later inspire his second novel, *The House of Tomorrow* (1988). Crew had to leave school at sixteen because of his family's financial situation, and he became a draftsman for an engineering firm. He found this job unsatisfying and decided to become an English teacher instead, as a way of sharing his great love of literature. He went back to school and earned his bachelor's and master's degrees at the University of Queensland. Crew taught English at Everton Park State High School and Mitchelton State High School, both in Brisbane. After entering a short story contest on a lark and placing, Crew decided to seriously consider writing as a career. His students inspired him to write novels for young adults, and his exploration of Australian history soon affected his novels too. In addition, Crew has written story books for young children. "My main objective in writing is to open the minds of my readers," he said, "to say 'the world can be a wonderful place—its possibilities are open to you and your imagination.'" Crew continues to write, as well as lecture on creative writing at Queensland

University of Technology, and works as a series editor for Heinemann Octopus publishers.

### Major Works

*Strange Objects,* Crew's third novel for young adults and recipient of the Australian Book of the Year Award, was based on Crew's interest in Australia's past and garnered much attention worldwide. In the novel, he uses a variety of narrative forms—diary entries, newspaper clippings, text from library and history books, psychological studies, and footnotes—to document what occurs when sixteen-year-old Stephen Messenger finds a journal, a ring, and some other objects in a cave. These objects are believed to have come from the two survivors of a shipwreck off the coast of Australia in the early 1600s. When Messenger puts on the ring, he has visions of the cabin boy who wore it, allowing readers to experience some of the wrongs perpetrated by the European colonization of Australia. Australia's history is also the focus of *No Such Country,* Crew's next young adult novel, which contains literary and biblical allusions. Sam, whose mother was an

Aborigine, comes to the isolated fishing village of New Canaan to learn the identity of his father and family, but the all-white locals are suspicious rather than cooperative. He befriends Sarah and Rachel, two teenagers who live there, and together they find a mass grave and learn that twenty years ago the local townsmen had trapped all the village's Aborigines in a huge net and drowned them. Sam also learns the identity of his father, the same Father who has blackmailed the town with its terrible secret. *Angel's Gate* likewise explores a crime and is set in an isolated town. A gold prospector is murdered in the small town of Jericho, and his two children, who witnessed the event, flee and live in the wild. After several months, the oldest child, Leena, is found and put into the care of the town's only doctor and nurse. The story is told in the first person through the eyes of the doctor's sixth-grade son, Kimmy Marriott. He has led a sheltered life up to this point and, at first, he is afraid of Leena, who is locked up in a room at his house to protect her from the murderer, who is still at large. He eventually befriends Leena and becomes a stronger person for it, rescuing her brother Micky from the murderer. A subplot involves Kimmy's older sister, Julia, who is just as spirited as Leena and Micky and whose "prison" is Jericho. When the murderer is caught, Leena and Micky are released into the care of welfare officers, and Julia flees Jericho. While some critics believe that readers will be confused by the symbolism and diverse narrative techniques in Crew's young adult novels, other critics say that the author's writing style challenges readers to judge evidence and question the status quo, thus encouraging them to interact with his books.

Crew also writes story books for children. *Lucy's Bay,* his second picture book, is about Sam, whose sister drowned while he was supposed to be watching her. In this story, he returns to where the tragedy happened and tries to come to terms with it. Crew parallels Sam's struggle to overcome his guilt with the cyclical patterns of nature on the beach where the story is set. *The Lost Diamonds of Killiecrankie* blends an adventure story with a history of the Tasmanian Aboriginals' fate. The story is told by the fictitious 53-year-old Geoff Middleton, who is writing to the real Crew and illustrator Peter Gouldthorpe via their equally real publisher. Middleton's story is fiction, based on facts extensively researched by Crew and illustrated with Gouldthorpe's photographs, sketches, and paintings of the actual island and its inhabitants.

**Awards**

*Strange Objects* received a Book of the Year Award from the Children's Book Council of Australia and an Alan Marshall Prize for children's literature in 1991. *Lucy's Bay* was shortlisted for the Children's Book Council of Australia's picture book of the year award in 1993. *Angel's Gate* was a 1994 Australian Children's Book of the Year honour book, and Peter Gouldthorpe and Steven Woolman each earned the Australian Children's Picture Book of the Year Award for their illustrations for *First Light* and *The Watertower,* respectively.

# AUTHOR'S COMMENTARY

## Gary Crew

SOURCE: "New Directions in Fiction," in *Magpies,* Vol. 7, No. 3, July, 1992, pp. 5–8.

Perhaps, more than other mortals, it is the writer of children's fiction who suffers most from the desire to return to the past; to that long lost world of childhood, where, according to Hesse in *Demian,* "very many are caught forever" and "cling painfully to an irrevocable past, the dream of the lost paradise, which is the worst and most ruthless of dreams."

No writer can entirely eliminate the events of the past from a work—no matter how ugly, how traumatic or how utterly worthy of being forgotten those events may have been, they will ultimately, emerge and, curiously, undergo that metamorphosis which, in the writer's art, transforms all experience—from the banal to the bizarre—into that illusion of life which is fiction.

I know that I cannot entirely abandon my own past. Once I would have longed to; I would have given anything to at least redress, at best forget, the forces that shaped me—but, as I grow older, and more confident in my art, I am not so certain.

I wonder if the whole idea of putting the past behind is such good advice.

I wonder if it is remembering not forgetting that engenders growth.

A writer who cannot remember must produce lean fare.

And surely, a children's writer who cannot remember is no writer at all.

So, as a writer of children's literature, before I consider *New Directions* in my art, I am obliged to return to those that shaped my past.

I was a Queensland kid, born and bred. I was brought up in what was called a "worker's dwelling" and spent most of my childhood with the local kids racing around the neighbourhood at a time of day I now recall as fixed in perpetual twilight.

As an adult, I find it impossible to comprehend such wild, yet innocent happiness—unless I glimpse it in my son.

My parents were working class; my father shovelled the coal that fired the power station so faithfully described in **The Inner Circle.** My mother was a milliner, though she never worked at her trade for profit in my lifetime. Both my parents were very religious, and I now appreciate (though I never would have ever believed it possible at the time) that the many hours spent in church have contributed so much to my love of literature. I have no clear memory of listening to what went on at these services, but I am convinced that certain language patterns, certain rhythms must have been psychically subsumed. In re-reading *No Such Country* when it arrived fresh from the publishers, I noticed that one sentence, of over 250 words, uses the word "and" twenty-three times. Now that's what I call a Biblical legacy.

It was at these church meetings that my sister and I drew pictures and coloured in, and of course, read. Curiously, with such an upbringing, neither our creativity nor our reading was ever censored.

What did we read? Anything. *National Geographic,* comics . . . tonnes of comics, both English and American.

> With left hand stretching the *singai* and the right twisting the head, Beizam pulled strongly but evenly upwards. There was a pronounced "click" and a sob, the head parted, and as Beizam raised it on high, a tapering streak of marrow was drawn out with it. Beizam clenched his teeth on the grisly neck and sucked and chewed. Thus was the courage and strength of the dying man being drawn into himself.

And there were ghost stories. Shipwreck stories. Encyclopedia. We had a set of Arthur Mee encyclopedia at home, and my sister and I would sit at the dining room table and turn the pages, looking and reading, pushing the books across to each other to share the good bits. There was *The Life and Work of Millet* (pronounced as the grain, sounding the "t") and *Great Steam Engines of the World,* and *A Day in the Orkneys* and *Joan of Arc,* thin cross in hand, her eyes raised to heaven as the green faggots smouldered.

And *Coles Funny Picture Book.*

I can't say for sure what other kids did during the 50s but that's what *we* did.

But my son Joel, who is twelve, and a child of the present, lives in a different world.

Although we live near the most wonderful Australian creek, complete with eels, and a bridge—which Joel calls *The Secret Valley Bridge,* since it stands in the lee of a hill dense with bush—we will not let him play there. We have seen who else hangs around the place. Fearful people. We are teaching our boy the limits of freedom. We are teaching him to distrust. We say, "Get into the car with nobody—unless they're blood. Not even a neighbour."

And although Joel reads, he has no print icons as we did, no Professor Challenger, no Alan Quartermain, not even a Biggles. Certainly he knows Bilbo Baggins. And Willy Wonka. He enjoyed *The White Mountains.* But his heroes are not in print. His heroes are visual constructs—Schwarzenegger and Stallone. Through them he has a somewhat warped notion of adventure and excitement that seems, so often, to emanate from the horrors of Vietnam—a war he knows nothing about politically, nor historically, being unable to separate it from WW II and

the Korean War—which has something to do with *M.A.S.H. . . . doesn't it?*

Yet, in spite of television and videos, our Joel has read more books than I ever had, when I was his age. And what books he reads. Where was the Science Fiction in my day? Not quite safe enough, nor in sufficient supply, to have made it to the school library shelves. And where was Fantasy? By comparison, Joel is well catered for. Thirty minutes of sustained silent reading a day. A wealth of picture books. Novels to suit his every whim—and the non-fiction—he could keep me broke with his coffee table cricket books and his golf magazines.

No, Joel has no trouble with reading, nor finding books to read. He knows his Dahl, his Kelleher, his Klein, his Rubinstein, his Thiele. The best book he ever read? Le Guin's *A Wizard of Earthsea.* Then, Joel is only twelve.

But what will Joel read when he's fifteen?

*Taronga* has already touched on post-holocaust issues; *Beyond the Labyrinth* made him ask about the bomb; *Came Back to Show You I Could Fly* was about drugs; *Peter* made him re-think the gay thing . . . So, what's next? What happens when kids of thirteen say, "We read this in primary school"? It could well be. No doubt they have either read the novels mentioned above, or had them read to them by some well meaning primary teacher. And why not? Weren't they written for kids? Don't be fooled by back cover recommendations like the one on *Peter,* that says: "For readers fifteen and over." What does that mean? Does the publisher believe that a kid who turns fifteen next month is going to put it down and say, "Geez I can hardly wait. Twenty-eight more days and I will be old enough to read *Peter?*" Of course not. Nobody could have stopped me reading *The Drums of Mer.* And in the reading agenda of every kid, from the advanced to the barely literate, there will always be "the allure of the taboo".

In *Books For Keeps* (March 1988) Margaret Clarke, Editorial Director of the Bodley Head, commented:

> The argument of the '70s was that good kids would move naturally from C.S. Lewis to Kafka, while the slow might progress from Enid Blyton to Hammond Innes . . . This has given way under a cold blooded study of demographics . . . a wickedly accurate assessment of the current publishing scene is that if you publish books for 10–14 year olds, you're on a good thing.

Who can argue with that? But what happens to the kid that I call the true older reader—I mean the kid of (say) 14 plus, who has read everything on the Children's Book Council Short List, and a lot more—but, in all honesty, is not ready to plunge into the world of Peter Carey?

Several options present themselves.

Depending on sexuality, the popular teen or adult pulp market in what is called "Romance" can come to their aid. In 1989 there were 34 million Sweet Valley High books in print in the USA. The notion is, just as an American girl of 10 or 11 grows out of Barbie, the Wakefields step in to take her place. Some would argue that the books are worthwhile, no more than modern myths, a ritual of hope in which the same events occur again and again. They argue that the books are read as "understood fantasy", as soap operas are intended, for the sophisticated viewer, taken with a grain of salt.

The flaw in the argument is that no sophisticated reader reads them.

Others would argue that: "If Janie is reading paperback romances *ad nauseum* she has recognised that [reading] is a pleasurable activity, and she might even expand her vocabulary." (*Journal of Reading,* vol. 26, no. 7, 1983)

Again, we are faced with a flawed argument: are we to believe that the teenage girl who reads Teen Romances comes away from that experience with no more than an improved vocabulary? While that possibility is dubious in the extreme, it is incredible to me that any educated person, writing in this day and age, could take the stance that reading is a culturally neutral activity; that any teenage girl could digest a sustained diet of Teen Romances and remain unaffected by the issues, themes and negative female stereotypes represented in them?

Having brought an entirely new meaning to the term "ghost-writer" through her marvellous literary innovation, "the pre-quel", the newly-deceased-but-unfortunately-undead Virginia Andrews now offers the world the modern interpretation of the Victorian Parlour Maid's novel. In a survey conducted, *USA Today,* March, 1991, Andrews' *Flowers in the Attic* was voted America's most popular teenage novel.

As the parent of two daughters, one twenty, one eighteen, I am less concerned about the forbidden eroticism of incest which drives Andrews' novels, than the author's representation of the scheming sexuality of her female characters:

> How I missed my optimistic mother. I was sixteen when she died—just when I most needed to have those woman-to-woman talks with her that would tell me how to win a man's heart.
>
> (*Garden of Shadows*)

Who said death could be unfortunate?

As for the young "read-out" male in search of a good book, a likely option is that he will turn to the delights of Stephen King. And why not? In King's own words he is the novelist of "The Post-Literate Age":

> . . . Most of them [his novels] have been plain fiction for plain folks, the literary equivalent of a Big Mac and a large fries from McDonalds. I am able to recognise elegant prose and respond to it but have found it difficult or impossible to write it myself . . .
>
> (*Different Seasons*)

In many ways, it is difficult to deny King's reasoning; his honesty is, to say the least, disarming. Now and then, everyone likes a peek into bedlam, a bit of a look at a public execution; he argues:

> And I think most people do, or the bookstores wouldn't still be filled with biographies of Adolf Hitler . . . The fascination of the abomination as Conrad would call it.
>
> (*Playboy,* 1983, Interview)

What can I say? The genius of King, and his attraction to kids, especially boys, is evident in one single text, *The Cycle of the Werewolf.* This short story, stage-dressed as a novel of 128 pages, is divided into 12 chapters, one for each month of the year. The story focuses on that time, each month, when the werewolf will make its transformation and subsequently, attack. The novel is fully illustrated, both in black and white, and lurid colour. The story centres on a disabled boy, confined to a wheelchair, who ultimately destroys the wolf as it attacks him. Triumph of the underdog. It's a Stephen King marketing phenomenon: it's short, it's illustrated, it's violent, it's fast, it's folksy . . . it's a designer remedial reader.

So, where does all this leave me, and my intentions as a writer? I believe now that I can answer that question.

I do not attempt to deny the obvious delights of writers such as Andrews and King. In remembering my past, which a writer must do, I admit to reading trash as a kid, and confess that I still vary my adult literary diet with a fair sprinkling of junk-reading. Most of us do. Let's be honest—at least pulp fiction has a plot. So, while my reading of Idriess did not turn me into a cannibal, I doubt that your teenage daughter will seek out sex with your spouse after reading Virginia Andrews' work (despite my warnings of its more insidious danger) nor will your son sprout fangs after reading Stephen King.

But for me, when I am writing, I can't entirely leave behind those richer elements of literature that I experienced as a child. When I am writing, I think, will these words reach out and take hold of my reader and not let go? I think, will these words show the world as a better place, will they open up new worlds and possibilities?

That's what I think, that's what I hope for, when I am writing.

---

## GENERAL COMMENTARY

### Joan Zahnleiter

SOURCE: "Know the Author: Gray Crew," in *Magpies,* Vol. 6, No. 4, September, 1991, pp. 17-9.

On a balmy Sunday afternoon at the end of Children's

Book Week, Gary Crew and I sat on a verandah overlooking the beautiful rainforest garden which he and his wife Christine have created. It was a time to mull over an exciting week in which *Strange Objects* had won the Book of the Year: Older Readers, and to admire the handsome medal. A firm contract had been signed for film rights to *Strange Objects,* though whether it was to be a documentary, a TV or feature length film was yet to be decided. It had been one of four offers, and now an offer for film rights for *No Such Country* had been received.

Characteristically of Gary Crew, it was also a time to look to the future and to talk about his next book, due to be released by Heinemann on 16 October, 1991. In *No Such Country: a Book of Antipodean Hours* his ambition has been realised of writing another "big" novel, a literary work rather than a book for teenagers about kids' problems. He feels that if there is a gap in the genre of adolescent literature, it is here. *No Such Country*'s subtitle *a Book of Antipodean Hours* gives some indication of its nature. On the broader canvas there is a continuation of the issues explored in *Strange Objects*—the search for identity at the national level, and contact with the Aboriginal presence, though not in the tribalised state. This is a modern book whose central characters are young adults, Sam, Rachel and Sarah. They influence the course of the story, having the drive and wit to recognise the evil implicit in the activities of the mysterious Father and to stand against his threats in order to shape their own destinies.

As always with Crew's work, the genesis of the book is underpinned by a considerable depth of research. Stimulated by John Pilger's work in *The Secret Country,* he began by investigating the issue of massacres of Aborigines, but as the book began to take on a life of its own, it became apparent that it was better, in Crew's words, "to redress this hideousness, not to forget it, but to represent it in a way that allowed us as a nation to grow out of disaster rather than wallow in it." Consequently the motif of massacre, though still important, became less dominant, as the character of Sam, a black, science-oriented anthropology student, assumed the role of a level-headed progressive young man very appropriately determined to discover the country of his past but, having discovered it, growing on through it and looking to the future.

There was also the urge, for survival as a writer, to produce a book with a strong female presence. (This is not contrary of Gary Crew's nature at all. He acknowledges willingly that he lives with "three wonderful strong women"—his wife and daughters, Rachel and Sarah.) He pondered the possible murder of one of the female characters. However he felt strongly that he didn't want to write another sombre book but rather one that emphasised hope and human worth. So, in his words, "I put down the past and brought up the future."

His mind was also exercised by the notion of Fate and what places people in certain situations at certain times. This led to exploration of Fortune's wheel and eventually

to the *Book of Hours of the Virgin* which traces a Messianic theme. This concept, personified by the white clad figure of the Father, the priest of the fishing village of New Canaan, Crew has turned on its head. It has become an antipodean structure in which it is the black youth who is resurrected and comes through Armageddon. He says "the idea was to turn upside down those absolutes of colonialism and religion" that had cast the people of New Canaan into bondage under the manipulative Father. Locked into the traditions of the past, the Father uses his knowledge of a particularly evil event in the past of New Canaan to blackmail the superstitious fisherfolk into accepting him as the Messiah who controls their lives with his great book. There is an irony in the name of the village since Canaan, in Biblical terms, is the Promised Land, but New Canaan is quite the reverse. The book has deeply religious concepts embedded in it so that a working knowledge of the Bible enriches the reading of it. However it is a story which works well for the reader without that knowledge.

The foreboding symbol of the fishing net which catches sinners and which is developed as a sustained metaphor throughout the story, focuses attention on the idea that "sooner or later, the net will be drawn, for the individual or the epoch". For the black people today the time has come when they are saying "We move on. We take our Dreaming but we move on".

For Gary Crew, *No Such Country* has been a pleasure to write. He says with feeling, "I never ever, ever, ever want to go back to that narrative form that has me being seventeen, though I may write another first person narrative. The seventeen-year-old voice, even with Messenger, I found very hard." With *No Such Country* he enjoyed the ease of using his own language patterns and vocabulary to extend sentences and develop the imagery which enriches the story. It is a very "visual" story which evokes a strong sense of place and of the characters living and moving in it.

The three young people, Rachel, Sarah and Sam act and interact convincingly. The reader becomes involved with them as their relationships with one another develop. This is an important part of the plot structure as they draw strength from one another, particularly the two girls, though their own unique identities are preserved. Their reactions to the Father and to his henchman, the Angel (Angelo Rossellini) are true to their own natures but mesh together to provide strength in withstanding the threat of evil.

Placing the setting is tantalising. Given the title, the author has been freed to create a place that may or may not exist on the east coast of Australia but could also be on a Pacific island off the coast. The interpolation of a long dormant volcano suddenly becoming active (as with Mount Pinetubo) provides a somewhat apocalyptic climax. It gave the ending what Crew describes as "Armageddon without the drum rolls".

The key to the book lies in the denouement when Sam

mourns the passing of his people in terms of the symbolism of black and white, and then turns to the future.

The splendid book jacket by Greg Rogers picks up the motif of the *Book of Hours* in its design, as does the book itself in the chapter headings and illuminated initial letters. The pilgrimage of characters extends across the whole jacket in front of a pictorial map of New Canaan. It promises all that the book delivers and forms a guide to the action of the story.

The close collaboration between Gary Crew and Greg Rogers has not only produced a well-crafted book in *No Such Country* but also a picture story book and a picture book, thus widening the scope of their activities for both of them. Of their team work, Crew says "It is exciting to see how the artist interprets the print text. We each have our own integrity but I feel that Greg and I are perfectly complementary to one another. We are amazed at our good fortune." Needless to say, extensive conferencing goes into their cooperative effort in order to produce such pleasing results.

The picture story book *Lucy's Bay* is a moving and visually beautiful book full of unusual perspectives. It concerns Sam, aged about twelve, his summer holidays by the sea with his grandfather, and one summer holiday in particular when his little sister Lucy was taken by the sea while in Sam's care. He has never been back to the scene of the tragedy since. On this visit though, Sam faces his fears and his sorrow and returns to the bay where Lucy vanished. For him this journey is a rite of passage from childhood into maturity, to scale the dreaded red cliffs, to go over into the bay, to find Lucy's memorial plaque and to go on into the next bay, to carry on with his life. The text is rich in images of the sea and its creatures and Rogers has incorporated them into his sensitive illustrations. This is a gentle book to share with older children. It is being published by the new Queensland company, Jam Roll Press in April 1992.

*Tracks* the picture book, describes the night time explorations of a small boy of about six. Named Joel after Crew's son, he sets out with his dog, from his little tent, to explore the rainforest and then the jungly garden with a torch, examining all the tracks he finds. The one that captivates him is a meandering silver track which he discovers, finally, is made by a humble slug. Amazed and delighted, Joel has discovered that there is beauty in everything. His activities are those which appeal to children in this age group who are interested in camping out and in finding creatures in the environment. Again the illustrations are by Rogers who has played up the effect of torchlight to produce a nicely eerie atmosphere for the young hunter. The text is presented in matching thought units and eye spans, catering to the reading abilities of its intended audience. Repetition of phonic patterns also supports the beginning reader. There is also a filmic quality to it as one sharp image after another flashes down the short lines. *Tracks,* to be released internationally by Lothian, February-March, 1992, is likely to cause a lot of flat torch batteries once children discover it.

The project which has Gary Crew fully engaged at present is his next book *Homo Ferus/Wild People* [published as ***Angel's Gate*** (1993)], involving two feral girls. The planning journal is well under way. The map of the setting and the story plan are complete and the research has all been done thoroughly. The key idea comes from Clifford Geertz's *The Interpretation of Cultures,* and is quoted thus in the frontispiece: *We are, in sum, incomplete or unfinished animals who complete or finish ourselves through culture.*

This has been the focus of his research. Crew feels strongly that the key idea should be kept on the back burner as long as possible to sharpen that focus. In this story, concerning what he terms "the domestication of the fantastic", the inclusion of the reality of the research detail underpins the fantastic to give it a logic of its own.

There is also a question inherent in the working out of this theme. By what right is a person deprived of her liberty? There are issues of the limits of freedom and of civilising forces here. Something for the reader to chew on.

The story concerns two girls, aged seven and thirteen, daughters of a hobo who fossicks around mine shafts. The father is murdered and the girls disappear. The mine site is flooded for a dam, which flushes these feral girls out. They raid local farm houses for food and, on being caught, are put in the care of the local doctor who has a daughter who is something of a wild girl herself, though in a different way. The story maps the process of civilising the girls and how the girls themselves come to terms with the civilising forces. It is narrated by an adult voice, that of the doctor's son, who, as a small boy, had the two girls brought into his room. Thus there is a male voice relating a female experience, or perhaps a universal one, which happens to have female protagonists in this instance.

These complexities are exercising Gary Crew's mind at present. He plans to take long service leave in February and March 1992 to extend the Christmas holidays in order to put in intensive work on the book. Keeping up production as an author on top of a full teaching load is no mean task. He is a highly organised person, utilising skills acquired over long years of study.

The path to success has not been an easy one for Gary Crew, though perhaps it has been a case of "Out of evil cometh good". Prolonged serious illness in childhood meant that he read extensively, even precociously, and started drawing and writing. Obliged to leave school, much against his wishes, at age fifteen, he became a cadet engineering draftsman, completing his qualifications as a mechanical and engineering draftsman at Queensland Institute of Technology in 1969. Successful but not satisfied, he studied for matriculation and then his teaching qualifications at Kelvin Grove Teachers College, graduating in 1973. Next came a Bachelor of Arts degree with a double major in literature in 1979 and Gary Crew had found his homeland. A Master of Arts specialising in

Commonwealth Literature followed in 1984. His Ph.D. studies in Commonwealth Literature are on hold pending the completion of the book. Since 1974, he has taught at Everton Park and Mitchelton State High Schools. Later he became subject master in English at Aspley High School and presently at Albany Creek High School, in Brisbane. He also teaches creative writing at Queensland University of Technology in the Communications and Journalism course.

Gary Crew looks forward to the day, perhaps five years or so from now, when he can afford to teach part time or even opt out of the classroom to write full time. Meanwhile he is keenly aware of his family responsibilities and that his children's ambitions cannot be sacrificed to his own. His dearest wish is to become a mature writer who can be fully engaged in the creative act. For now, the accolade of the Book of the Year Award and its medal, glowing in its blue velvet lined case in the afternoon sun, are encouragement to hope that these ambitions may be realised in time.

## Maurice Saxby

SOURCE: "The Young Adult: Gary Crew," in *The Proof of the Puddin': Australian Children's Literature,* Ashton Scholastic, 1993, pp. 698–700.

Gary Crew, a young Queensland writer and academic, whose first novel *The Inner Circle* (1986) was published in the same year as Gillian Rubinstein's *Space Demons,* works not through direct statement, but through symbolism and implication to share disturbingly potent insights with his readers.

Crew's first published novels were slow to receive popular applause—his publishers seem not to have entered the first two in the Children's Book of the Year Awards—but they have excited both his fellow academics and the young people who have been given them to read. Only in 1990—*Papers* Vol 1 No 2—did a highly perceptive critical article in praise of Crew appear: 'Identity in Australia; Gary Crew's Adolescent Novels' by Sharyn Pearce. But by this time Crew had been discovered by the readers themselves. More than most other current writers, Crew has the ability to rivet his readers with his plots, raise serious social and personal issues, speak with the voice of today's young people and also to write serious literature. His novels epitomise young adult literature in Australia, to date.

Crew's novels are structurally, thematically and linguistically diverse and grow successively more complex. The plot of *The Inner Circle* unfolds as two first-person confessional narratives are interwoven; that of Tony, an indulged white teenager alienated because of his parents' marriage break-up, and Joe, the Aborigine, who is supported emotionally by the family and culture from whom he is physically removed, but because of his race, alienated socially in the city where he has come to work. *The House of Tomorrow* (1988) is the case-study, journal-like narrative of an ageing English master, in which he includes the personal folio of a deeply disturbed pupil, Danny Coley. *Strange Objects* (1990) is ostensibly a documentary drama made up of 'Notes on the Disappearance of Steven Messenger, Aged 16 years by Dr Hope Michaels, Director Western Australian Institute of Maritime Archaeology'. It is a compilation of news items, Steven's personal journal, transcripts of audiotaped press conferences, an interim report about the contents of a leather-bound manuscript located in a cliff cave in the Murchison River district of Western Australia. In addition, letters, sketches, extracts from publications, real and fictional, are included to provide an illusion of verisimilitude.

Each of Crew's novels deals with the now-familiar concerns of young adult fiction: a search for identity, alienation and displacement, the need for harmony and wholeness. In addition, *The Inner Circle* and *The House of Tomorrow* explore the concept of a personal freedom which can help promote growth and regeneration. *The House of Tomorrow* and *Strange Objects* also raise questions about death and disintegration, suggesting, however, that death itself could be regenerative. For example, the suicide of another teenage outsider, Jules Kerwin, in *The House of Tomorrow* and the death of the narrator's wife and child are precursors to Danny's symbolic rebirth (when he becomes a star performer at school), but then to his ultimate destruction in a fire at his grandfather's house. As in *The Inner Circle,* events are cyclic—a bicycle wheel features on the cover of the first book. And in *Strange Objects,* Pelgrom, Pelsart's cabin boy marooned on Australia in 1629, brings death and destruction in the Aboriginal community, but 'lives on' in the person of Steven Messenger in 1986, who finds and wears Pelgrom's cursed ring. Other themes in Crew's novels are race relations, environmental and cultural pollution by evil human intrusion, authoritarianism, fundamentalist charismatic religious fervour, rebirth and reincarnation and 'Life's longing for itself'—the latter being from Kahlil Gibran's *The Prophet* quoted in *The House of Tomorrow.*

These themes emerge unselfconsciously and naturally from the interaction of plot and character and through a multiplicity of symbols, all of which are integral to the structure of the novels.

In *The Inner Circle,* a Binkar cabbage palm is the focal mandalic symbol which, along with a hen's egg, Angie's ring and the bicycle wheel itself, speaks of wholeness, harmony and continuity. Symbolic baptism signifies rebirth and metamorphosis in *The House of Tomorrow,* while in *Strange Objects,* the ring which had belonged to Pelgrom and which Steven Messenger steals, is a kind of inverted mandala, bringing disharmony and disintegration.

In addition to using symbols, Crew also introduces literary allusions—for example, references to Gibran, Poe, the Brontes, Swift, even echoes of 'The Ancient Mariner'—and the repetition of motifs: the BMX bike, colour and vegetation, for example, in *The Inner Circle;* voices, dreams (literary and metaphorical as in the reference to

*The Rocky Horror Picture Show*), photographs, even musical airs in *The House of Tomorrow;* a sled, a beached whale and a lizard carcass, among others, in *Strange Objects.*

Although *The House of Tomorrow* and *Strange Objects* are highly complex and richly textured novels, even ambitious (almost every page reveals some example of cross-referencing), the prose is never dense or inaccessible. Crew is one of the few writers who are able to assume an intelligent, articulate teenage voice which is highly literate without being intimidating. Tony, Joe, Danny and Steven always speak—or write—in character. Their narratives are vital, dramatic, yet idiomatic enough to involve even the most reluctant reader. They also contain enough mysticism—even aspects of the supernatural—to titillate teenage sensibilities, yet are so structurally and linguistically complex that even experienced readers find them challenging. Crew exemplifies the best in young adult fiction. While truly 'bridging the chasm between classic and cult', without being 'heavy', they are in no way lightweight. They successfully combine popular appeal with intellectual, emotional, psychological and spiritual substance.

When *Strange Objects* was awarded the 1990–91 Children's Book of the Year Award for Older Readers—'primarily on literary merit'—there was general acclaim.

From so much that is trivial, trite and ephemeral in young adult fiction, Gary Crew, with Gillian Rubinstein, Victor Kelleher, Nadia Wheatley and their kind demonstrate the enduring nature of and value of literature written from the heart.

## Shelda Debowski

SOURCE: "The Varied Talents of Gary Crew," in *Reading Time,* Vol. 40, No. 2, May, 1996, p. 40.

Gary Crew has distinguished himself in a number of ways, not the least of which is his constantly evolving approach to his craft. Each new tale shows a new dimension to his talent and vision. These three stories are no exception.

*Barn* is the simplest of the three works, and explores a city-bred boy's disgust at leaving his familiar territory to live on a ramshackle farm and attend a backward school. It is only the barn which redeems the move. Mysteries deepen each time the building is revisited, until some answers emerge offering even more interesting possibilities for the future. The tale is a simple one, but it reflects many of the features of which Crew is becoming renowned. The quirky twists to the storyline and the strong development of the character's point of view are evident in this and the other two titles. Tom Jellett's illustrations complement the ironic tone and focus of the story quite effectively.

*Caleb* evidences another style of writing. This narrator is a university student with a very strange room mate named Caleb. He recounts the strange tendencies of Caleb, leaving much to the interpretation of the reader—assisted greatly by [Steven] Woolman's marvellous intricate illustrations. We know Caleb is strange, but the differences only become fully apparent as we reach the end of the picture book—when Caleb is depicted flying away. The analytical nature of the account adds veracity and a feeling of reality to a very unusual tale.

But the third work, *The Lost Diamonds of Killiecrankie* is the jewel in the crown. The tale derives from a young artist's experience in a remote Tasmanian settlement off Flinders Island, where he discovered a compelling legend of a lost green diamond which matched that worn by Queen Victoria. Obsessed by the thought of finding the gem, he befriended a young boy, Aaron, and set out to solve the mystery. He does so, but with tragic consequences.

The tragedy remained hidden until the artist, Geoff Middleton contacted Crew and [illustrator Peter] Gouldthorpe after they had spoken of their craft at the local primary school. The resultant picture book is a rich, complex amalgamation of a personal story and history, combining Middleton's own archival records with the Crew version of his tale. The characterisation of Middleton is a strong central pivot of the work, but the inclusion of photographs, maps, sketches, watercolours, letters and other documents also adds strong veracity and enhancements.

In reviewing these works I was particularly impressed by the strong presence of the narrator in each tale. Crew has a particular strength in his evocation of personalities: the reader can see every nuance of the narrator's emotions and responses. A further talent Crew has honed is sense of timing. All three stories are beautifully structured and sequenced, ensuring there is a natural rhythm and progression which leads the reader through the work. A further strength lies in the use of the element of surprise. Crew hints but makes us wait, building up the tension as we work through the story line. All three tales use this suspense element throughout. The other characteristic which was strongly evident was the strong rapport between writer and illustrator. All three artists offer extension to the text in different ways, but help to set a strong atmosphere and add to the incremental tension.

Crew has a strong niche in Australian children's literature, and seems to have identified a number of ways in which he can extend the boundaries of presenting tales. These three works offer older readers some rich and multifaceted visions of other realities or times. Of the three, I preferred *The Lost Diamonds of Killiecrankie,* as it worked strongly on several levels and was enriched by the historic element. All three tales demonstrate the rich and imaginative talent which emanates from Crew, and which ensures we are always offered new visions of the world in each new title.

## TITLE COMMENTARY

📖 *STRANGE OBJECTS* (1990)

### Gary Crew

SOURCE: A review of *Strange Objects,* in *Reading Time,* Vol. 35, No. 3, 1991, pp. 11–12.

Agnes Niewenhuizen, the children's literature critic, has recently said of *Strange objects* that "it examines how information is sought, gathered and interpreted: how stories are told: and consequently how history is assembled and read . . . the novel calls into question how 'history' and 'truth' might be and are established . . ." (Editions Jan 1991).

Kathryn Hope says "Gary Crew's *Strange objects* . . . exercises his imagination more in the manner of Poe. The tale has all the time honoured elements of a good frightener: long-lost documents, human remains, hints of cannibalism . . ." (*Australian Book Review* Dec 1990).

The reviewer in *Reading Time* (Vol. 35 No 1 Feb 1991) believed: "Gary Crew has created a new approach to the novel".

As the author of *Strange objects,* I suppose there is no harm in saying what I thought I had written . . . and the answer is: all of the above.

*Strange objects* was first conceived from my interest in Commonwealth Literature, that is, writing from countries which had borne the burden of British Colonialism. This area of fiction and history had formed the basis of my Master's Degree and I became fascinated by the notion of history as an ever changing discourse, rather than some fixed and absolute body of fact . . . as history (so called) texts would often lead the reader to believe.

Secondly, I had a long term interest in the more macabre elements of our Colonial past—stories of cannibalism, shipwreck, castaway children—an interest I attribute directly to the old Queensland Museum and its amazing collection of artifacts from the Torres Strait region (not like the present Queensland Museum, which may be more up to date and scientific, with lots of buttons to push for electric shocks and pre-taped lectures, but utterly lacking in romance!).

As a child I had often visited the old museum with my parents, and one particular exhibit—now unfortunately removed—particularly haunted me: this was a tank of badly corroded iron, possibly three metres square and a metre deep, in which a certain Mrs Watson, wife of a beche-de-mer fisherman, had made her escape from Lizard Island off the Great Barrier Reef. Mrs Watson had evidently upset or disturbed the local aboriginal population and had cast herself away in the iron tank—taking her baby and a Chinese servant with her. All three died of exposure.

I never forgot that story, and the displayed remains of Mrs Watson's tattered journal, handwritten with the stub of a pencil, are very clear in my memory.

To complete the list of motivations, I was also interested in Teenage Fiction, since I had a long associations with teenagers from my years as a teacher, and having previously published two novels, *The inner circle* and *The house of tomorrow,* for the young adult audience.

Furthermore, William Heinemann had appointed me as Series Editor for their new up-and-coming teenage series.

Out of this combination of ideas and influences, *Strange objects* emerged. It was, to attempt to define it, to be a really fast moving adventure plot with a central teenage character (with identity problems), set against the earliest known historical evidence of the white invasion of Australia—but I also wanted to be true to my historical method: not to pin down, or close off, historical possibilities. To begin, I used the concepts of *The other.* This concept figures in both colonial discourse and popular writing of the macabre—albeit with vastly different interpretations—which I set about uniting. *The other* in colonial discourse usually refers to the indigene being feared as a cannibal. I had long been fascinated by Hakluyt's *Virginia voyages* and other early imperial views of 'pre-colonial' idigenes. I was also strongly influenced by the works of Todorov, both *The fantastic* (a study of the fantastic literary genre) and also *The conquest of America,* a fascinating analysis of the rape of the Americans. These 'views' of 'the other' I now linked to the Australian Colonial context.

I read as widely as possible in the genres of the first contact personal journal, with particular attention being given to Eyre, and later the Western Australian explorer, George Grey, both of whom I admired, as men and writers. Certainly, their eye for the fantastic amazed me. I especially drew on Eyre's description of the Mount Deception ranges (*The journals of Edward John Eyre* Vol. 1), where he notes: " . . . The whole scene partook more of enchantment than reality . . . as the eye wandered over the smooth and unbroken crust of pure white salt . . .".

This description bore remarkable similarities to American Colonial texts where the Mountains of the fabled El Dorado were reportedly too dazzling with mineral wealth to be viewed by daylight. I was also happy to locate so many well documented child 'castaway' stories, and these are re-represented in *Strange objects* as Item 25. The 'other' view of these stories is presented as Item 26—I had no intention of investing in absolutes. From my knowledge of contemporary teenage reading habits, I had read widely in the work of Stephen King. The macabre or horror discourse is very well analysed in *Danse macabre,* King's treatise on the horror genre in print and film. Here, the 'other', is the thing we fear most—from the bogey man to our inner selves. With this in mind, and my adolescent readership, I set about finding a likely issue to unite these ideas, and in my research, as noted in Item 7 of *Strange objects,* I happened upon the character of Jan Pelgrom, the 17 year old mass murderer from the vessel

"Batavia", which had been wrecked off the Australian coast in 1629. Pelgrom and his companion, Wouter Loos, were the first authenticated white inhabitants of this country, but interestingly enough, both were murderers and rapists. Pelgrom was no doubt a psychopath, delighting in the murder of children.

While various novels and plays had been written on the "Batavia" wreck, to my knowledge, none had picked up the case of Loos and Pelgrom, and the fact that instead of being hung for their crimes they were cast away. The contemporary character, Steven Messenger, is really only a literary construct to allow me, the author, and you, the reader, to gain access to both the text and the past. Messenger is also used, in HG Wells' terms to 'domesticate' the fantastic; that is, as a means of contact with the everyday. The character Nigel Kratsman also is used in this way. He is the so-called 'normal' character ( . . . or is he?). The novel is not based on a 'time-slip' structure, but the possible mental aberrations of our contemporary narrator, Messenger, while the parallelism of the text arises from recurring motifs (the 'strange objects', both animate and inanimate) which suggest that:

Messenger = Pelgrom
and
Kratzman = Loos.

Could it be that history, which lives, is simply repeating itself? Could it be that once the 'cannibal pot' of the past is opened—or dare we say, the Pandora's Box of the past—frightful things are released? And what part does Hope play in all this? It is, ironically, Hope Michaels who 're-mains' to tell the story.

*Strange objects* is, therefore, as any historical text, able to be interrogated as a combination of genre. It is at once:

* an epistolary novel, being made up of letters and documents;

* a non-fiction/historical novel, being based on re-searched evidence—yet equally, utilising the comparative method of historical research;

* a fantasy novel, as it arises out of the fantasies of a teenage boy and the Quest of Loos to find the Shining Hills . . . the El Dorado;

* a horror novel in that it deals with the dark forces of human evil;

* an adventure novel in that action comes thick and fast;

* a novel of social realism. If Steven Messenger is schizophrenic, as he was believed to be by Dr Hope Michaels, this would be a reasonable solution to the otherwise fantastical events described. Using this theory, there would have been no 'literary' hitchhiker standing beneath the Roadhouse sign. At night, with his bed light on, Messenger would have seen no more than his own reflection staring back from the darkened glass. Of course, we should also ask who gave the archaeologist Hope Michaels the authority to comment on the boy's mental condition? And mightn't there be just a dash of wishful thinking in the Hollywood eyes of the truck driver, Meryl McAlpine?

But for me, most of all, it is a novel of colonial discourse intended to challenge the reader to examine what has happened in our past, to re-assess what forces shaped this nation—and the effect the white invasion has had on the original inhabitants of this country. After all, at the conclusion of the novel, the Murchison Aboriginal Council is re-empowered to deny, or approve, white access to what little remains of their land—even although the request is to view the bones of a whiteman.

**Alice Casey Smith**

SOURCE: A review of *Strange Objects,* in *School Library Journal,* Vol. 39, No. 5, May, 1993, p. 124.

A bizarre, mystical, and very Australian novel. On a school field trip to the outback, 16-year-old Steven Messenger discovers a 17th-century iron pot containing a leather-bound diary and a mummified human hand. These artifacts are turned over to the authorities, but an antique ring from the hand becomes Steven's prized possession and results in out-of-body experiences and dabblings in aboriginal religion. Told through the reports of archaeologists, historians, newspaper accounts, Steven's personal writings, and the diary of Wouter Loos, a 17th-century murderer, the story both intrigues and confuses. For readers well versed in the area's history, geography, lore, and ethnicity, it may be compelling. However, the violence and mysticism create a strong, skewed, negative vision of Australian human relations both past and present. The main characters, historical Wouter Loos and contemporary Steven Messenger, echo racial misunderstandings and prejudice. Loos recounts in his diary the prevailing European stereotypes of "natives," while Messenger describes Aborigines as "all looking alike," dirty, and "drinking cheap wine." His comments and physical attack on an elderly Aborigine are disturbing, to say the least. Couple these sentiments and events with the effect that possessing the magical ring has on Messenger, and you have one complicated ball of wax. *Strange Objects* is a strange book that will most likely baffle American young adults.

*Kirkus Reviews*

SOURCE: A review of *Strange Objects,* in *Kirkus Reviews,* Vol. LXI, No. 10, May 15, 1993, p. 658.

A supernatural mystery of a high order—named Australia's "Best Children's Book for Older Readers" in 1991—looks into that country's sometimes brutal relations with its indigenous people, challenging readers to interpret the past anew. The hero (or antihero—interpreting Steven Messenger is one of the intriguing tasks Crew sets) stumbles upon sacred, perhaps magical objects belonging to local aborigines: an ancient human hand and a curious gold ring in an iron pot. To whom these really belong becomes a matter of national debate—and focus of a struggle between Steven and his conscience, and between him and a tribal leader. The book is skillfully framed as a collection of documents, alternating with Steven's experiences—police accounts, letters, news stories, historical records, psychological testimony, translations, commentaries—amassed by a researcher; most compelling is the 350-year-old journal of a survivor of the ill-fated ship *Batavia,* whose account eventually explains the source of the objects and whose strangely possessed companion is, in many ways, Steven's diabolical double. A demanding book that forces readers to judge the evidence (it would be fascinating to analyze with a high-school English class). Whether or not its lack of resolution is stimulating may be a personal matter—some will find the inconclusive ending more annoying than provocative. Still, for anyone who's interested in literature or history, there's much here to ponder.

**Chris Sherman**

SOURCE: A review of *Strange Objects,* in *Booklist,* Vol. 89, No. 19–20, June 1 & 15, 1993, p. 1812.

When 16-year-old Stephen Messenger finds an old iron pot containing a mummified hand and a 300-year-old journal on a school biology field trip, he sets off a chain of events that ends in the death of an old aborigine and in his own disappearance. The story unfolds through a series of documents released by anthropologists studying the artifacts, the serial publication of a journal (which tells the strange and hopeless story of two castaway murderers, one of whom is psychopathic—or possibly evil personified), newspaper accounts, and a notebook Stephen sends to an anthropologist in which he tells of finding the pot and the experiences that followed. The academic bickering of specialists interpreting the journal and artifacts provides a wonderful contrast to Stephen's matter-of-fact account of his visions and increasingly bizarre behavior. Crew's fantasy-mystery won the 1991 prize for Children's Book of the Year: Older Readers in Australia. It is challenging fiction, but it is so engrossing that readers won't want to put it down. Easy to booktalk, it is sure to generate a lot of discussion.

**Kathleen Krahnke**

SOURCE: A review of *Strange Objects,* in *Voice of Youth Advocates,* Vol. 16, No. 3, August, 1993, p. 162.

*Strange Objects* is a wonderfully complex story by Crew, a new Australian author. Using a crisp journalist style of writing, Crew propels the reader deeper and deeper into Steve Messenger's life. Starting with page one, the reader is captivated by this unusual tale.

Steve Messenger is sixteen when he disappears from his mother's trailer on the side of a desert highway in the outback of Australia. His story unfolds through his journals, newspaper accounts, and police records. It begins

when he finds an old pot which contains a journal of a seventeenth century convicted murderer who was castaway on the shores of Australia and a mummified hand of a white girl. The hand has a ring on it which Messenger is compelled to keep in his possession after he turns the other artifacts over to authorities. It is not long after this that his nightmares begin and he starts thinking of blood and death. The diary which he found reveals that an earlier owner of the ring was prone to violence. Does the ring have powers to influence the bearer or is it just coincidence that the two people to own the ring became murderers? This is a question for the reader to answer.

*Strange Objects* is a very exciting book with a double story line that will keep the reader eager for the next chapter. It would have been helpful to include a glossary of Australian terms and a map of the area. Even with this slight oversight the book is highly recommended and will be very easily booktalked.

**Andrea L. Mills**

SOURCE: A review of *Strange Objects,* in *The Book Report,* Vol. 12, No. 2, September-October, 1993, p. 41.

Award-winning Australian author Crew appears on the United States adolescent book market for the first time with a story that not only deals with strange objects but also with strange events. On a high school marine biology field trip, 16-year-old Steven, the story's protagonist, finds an ancient pot, which everyone dubs "a cannibal pot" because it contains a mummified hand and a 17th century diary. In the excitement, Steven does not notice that a gold ring with a glowing red stone that had been originally waxed onto the hand has fallen into his sleeping bag. What surprises the reader is that Steven does not give the ring to the police or to the archaeologists who are studying the artifacts. The ring and his obsession with it take Steven out of his world in the barren isolation of the Australian roadside station where his only companion is another teen who devotes himself totally to his greasy mechanic work and his "girlie magazines." Spellbound by the ring, Steven finds himself in a world of nightmares and hallucinations. His story is alternated with a translation of the old diary from the cannibal pot. The diary is by Wouter Loos, a 17th century Dutch sailor and convicted murderer, who was castaway on the coast of Australia with 17-year-old Jan, the original owner of the ring. Jan was an unstable psychopath, and his personality traits begin to appear in Steven. By the end of the story, Steven has disappeared after having attacked and possibly killed an old aborigine who was trying to help him understand some of the supernatural powers with which he was dealing. The story line might be difficult for some readers to follow because of the alternating pattern in which it is told, because of the constant shifts in time, and also because the translation of the diary is heavily footnoted to make it appear scholarly. Steven's black tale is suspenseful, but the suspense is often broken due to the weaving of Jan's horrific experiences into his own.

## NO SUCH COUNTRY (1991)

### Meg Sorensen

SOURCE: A review of *No Such Country,* in *Australian Book Review,* No. 136, November, 1991, pp. 53–5.

[*No Such Country* is] the new Young Adult novel from this year's winner of the Children's Book of the Year for Older Readers. Gary Crew took off this award and a string of others for his *Strange Objects,* a shrewdly constructed quasi-postmodern mystery/fantasy comprising historical fact, newspaper articles, narrative and hocus pocus. Following in this tradition, *No Such Country* borrows historical consequence with an opening passage from *A Complete Collection of Voyages and Travels,* John Cambell (Ed.), London, 1744–48. Apart from the fact that the words 'no such country' appear therein, I can't work out its relevance. (I anticipate with trepidation a whole new subsection of Young Adult Fiction comprised of tram tickets, letters from Great Uncles, labels of historically pertinent jam jars—interspersed with crystal gazing narrative.) Anyway, after another quote ('Dark night time, night time Bethliem / All sleep wake and get up / Mother likes him child christ clean white baby'), we arrive at the prologue. 'There were those who believed that the Father had existed from the beginning . . .' and we're launched into the world of New Canaan.

Omens and signs start forming in the sky, a viper takes a woman's life and the air is steaming with mystery and foreboding. Two young girls seem destined to be the initiators of the downfall of the old order in this strange town, where a deep dark secret from the past has made its gloomy inhabitants somewhat inhospitable. The town is presided over by a sort of anorexic priest who drapes around in long white robes with a sub-normal muscle-bound youth in attendance. This boy is in love with one of the girls and this girl falls for another boy who comes into the mysterious town on a motor bike to do a 'dig' for his university Anthropology course. Anyway, it turns out that this boy is an orphan and the deep dark secret of the town was that his aboriginal mother's people were murdered and buried in a mass grave. The white priest who witnessed all this and, from that day, had a dreadful power over the town, lay with the black woman and the boy was produced. Then it was written that boy would come back and all would be vindicated and it is. And he and the girl ride off on the motorbike.

Gary Crew is no slouch in juggling all the elements of this busy book and only a few times when the text turns into a geology lesson is he ever in danger of losing his reader's attention. For me the moment of reckoning came when the writer found no other way out of an impasse in the plot than to reach into his hat and start pulling out rabbits. The earth is moving, the end is nigh and we are still to solve the problem of the young boy's origins—although anyone who hasn't guessed it by now is simply not paying attention. There is a book in which the Father has been recording the town's events forever. It is a powerful book, perhaps with the ability to change the future as much as to uncover the past. The two girls and the boy ransack the church and find the book and before their very eyes the past plays out its dastardly events—they see the fate the tribe of aborigines met and they see the boy's true parentage:

> 'Show me,' he shouted, 'Show me who I am. Tell me!' And in his own shadow appears a dim room and in it two persons, one, the girl, dark and slender, his mother, whom he knows by heart, and the other, the Father, touching her, stroking her, too close, too close. . . .

I suspect that Gary Crew wrote this book FOR Young Adults and I wonder if that is not the reason he has taken liberties he may not take if he was writing an adult book. There are too many threads left hanging or untackled— the weird behaviour of the town's residents is only scantily sketched in, (and implausibly they are never really made accountable) like a one dimensional backdrop in front of which the theatre unfolds—although Crew's evocation of place via detailed topographical descriptions is painstaking and there are enough clever ideas and mysteries unfolding to keep a young reader's mind alert throughout.

Crew certainly understands all the elements a writer has at their disposal to keep a reader hooked to the text— dishing out a little here, just enough there, enticing you towards the treat at the end of the maze. Trouble is all you are left with at the end is a hollow feeling in your belly along with the disquieting sensation that you have been elegantly conned.

### Kirkus Reviews

SOURCE: A review of *No Such Country,* in *Kirkus Reviews,* Vol. LXII, No. 12, June 15, 1994, p. 842.

The title may be a literal translation of "utopia," but the isolated Australian fishing village of New Canaan is anything but—as Rachel and Sarah, two teenaged residents, and Sam, a visiting student, discover. Following a clue uttered by his mother (an aborigine) on her deathbed, Sam has come to track down his father and family; but his inquiries are met with silent suspicion by the twisted, disturbed locals, all white. Crew gradually builds a charged atmosphere lit by signs and portents of what's to come. Led by Sarah's half-deranged mother, Sam and his young friends uncover a mass grave concealed in a thicket of lantana and later find the town's awful secret laid out pictorially in an eerie codex; 20 years ago, in a drunken frenzy, the men captured the last local aborigines in a huge net and drowned them. After this revelation, Crew creates an apocalyptic climax in which a nearby volcano erupts, destroying grave, book, and an enigmatic, white-robed religious leader known only as The Father—a literal title, it turns out, in Sam's case. Crew also explored the effects of racial violence in *Strange Objects* (1993); here, he develops that theme on a more obviously symbolic level.

**Mary Jo Drungil**

SOURCE: A review of *No Such Country,* in *School Library Journal,* Vol. 40, No. 7, July, 1994, p. 116.

Set in a small Australian fishing village, this thought-provoking tale probes religious fascism and genocide. A priest (known as the Father) generally controls the behavior of the inhabitants of New Canaan, but Rachel and Sarah, both 15, are suspicious of him. Rachel is also dismayed by the unwanted attention of a boy known as the Angel. He insists in a bullying manner that she belongs to him, an idea perpetuated by the Father. Enter Sam Shadows, a university student doing anthropological work at an aboriginal site nearby. His interest in the place is more than intellectual; raised in a home for boys, he is searching for clues about his mother, an aboriginal girl who came from New Canaan. He is aided by Rachel and Sarah, who have their own reasons for wanting to solve the mystery behind the power the Father wields over their village. The novel is compelling, though the Angel's malevolent character is underdeveloped. The text's overall freedom from Aussie slang increases its appeal, for this is a story that could take place in other settings, including the United States. A good candidate for discussion.

**Elizabeth Bush**

SOURCE: A review of *No Such Country,* in *Bulletin of the Center for Children's Books,* Vol. 47, No. 11, July-August, 1994, p. 353.

The small Australian fishing village of New Canaan is clearly in the Father's thrall. Adults are reluctant to discuss him, and children (very few, and now in their teens) have grown to regard his meddling and intimidation as the natural order. But when Eva Burgess dies of a seasnake bite while tending her husband's nets, and her dearest friend slips into a trance, the townsfolk begin to speak openly of "signs and wonders." Eva's daughter Rachel and her close friend Sarah dig—literally—for the truth with the help of Sam, a geology student who has chosen New Canaan's fossilized oyster beds as a good project site and a likely place to uncover his own half-Aboriginal roots. The visionary ravings of Sarah's mother, Sam's suspicions about his parentage, the discovery of ropes beneath a shell mound, and mystical revelations from the Father's hidden book finally disclose the town's guilty secret: years ago the village men had drowned the Aboriginal population of the town and buried them under the shell bed. In an apocalyptic climax, the Father is swallowed up in a volcanic eruption. Because the Father's sin of omission (he knew of the slaughter but failed to bring the offenders to justice) and spiritual blackmail pale beside the crime of his congregation, and the townsfolk are portrayed as more relieved than repentant, this resolution may strike readers as unsatisfying. A secondary theme concerning the fragile relationship between Rachel and Sarah, as Sam's attentions to Rachel divide them, is handled with greater success, and Sarah's painful acceptance of her friend's inevitable departure is bittersweet and believable. But Crew's emphasis on the town-with-a-secret never quite blends the natural and supernatural elements into a convincing whole.

**Maeve Visser Knoth**

SOURCE: A review of *No Such Country,* in *The Horn Book Magazine,* Vol. LXX, No. 5, September-October, 1994, pp. 596–97.

The author of **Strange Objects** has written a compelling, sinister story of a small isolated village in Australia. As Rachel approaches her sixteenth birthday, she dreams of leaving the stifling, cult-like community of New Cannan; but when her mother dies, she must take over the tasks of the woman of the family and relinquish her dreams of escape. New Canaan is dominated by the Father, a priest who not only is the spiritual leader but reigns as a god in the eyes of the villagers. He makes all rules—separating the women and men into traditional roles, deciding how they will dress, even naming each of the villagers—and keeps the records of the community. No one remembers a village before his arrival. When anthropology student Sam Shadows comes to research the area, he is clearly unwelcome, and only Rachel befriends him. But as Sam searches for the history of the local indigenous peoples, as well as for links to his own parentage, he and Rachel gradually discover the horrible secret which the villagers are hiding. They uncover the bodies of the last Aborigines of the area, murdered by drunken villagers and buried in a mass grave. Their knowledge breaks the deception at last, transforming the village and dissolving the Father's power. Bizarre details and fantastic happenings are carefully woven in with the realistic setting and events that make New Canaan seem possible. The Father appears to possess supernatural powers through his great book of records, and when the villagers stand at the place where they buried the Aborigines to face up to their crime, the volcano above them erupts, giving them a physical as well as spiritual new beginning. Throughout the fantastic drama, Rachel and Sam both struggle with universal adolescent issues of identity and separation. Crew explores the nature of evil and the power of adolescents to use the truth to transform themselves and their surroundings.

*LUCY'S BAY* (1992)

**Francis Kelly**

SOURCE: "Down Under Australiana," in *Emergency Librarian,* Vol. 20, No. 4, March-April, 1993, p. 17.

Two picturebooks which must be included in this year's list [of best Australian books of 1992] are **Lucy's bay** from Jam Roll Press, and *Space travellers,* from Ashton Scholastic. Gary Crew, the hard hitting, multi-award winning Queensland writer, best known for challenging readers to question history, and giving very sound reasons for doing so (**Strange objects, No such country,** 1990, 1991), has combined with fellow Queenslander, Gregory Rogers, to produce the deeply moving **Lucy's bay.** If I said that the underlying theme is about dealing with guilt, this would discount the myriad other responses the title will produce in readers of all ages.

**Mandy Cheetham**

SOURCE: A review of *Lucy's Bay,* in *Magpies,* Vol. 8, No. 3, July, 1993, p. 31.

This remarkable picture book demands considerable emotional response from the reader. It is a story about bereavement, the passage of guilt and the process of expiation. Told with harmony and illustrated with a masterly degree of sensitivity, the book has a poetic quality which clarifies and expands the complex theme.

Each year Sam spends the summer holidays at his grandfather's hut by the sea. Always, he avoids one small bay, the scene of a childhood tragedy for which he carries an agonising burden of responsibility. Eventually his decision to make the painful journey back to the scene is the catharsis he needs in order to confront and finally let go of his guilt.

Placed on the page like photographs in an album, the illustrations are a compelling evocation of the text. A combination of artistic media has been used to enhance the haunting and almost menacing nature of the beach, scenes which mirror the turmoil in the boy's mind. The mood changes in the final double page spread to show a calm expanse of beachline washed clean by the tide, a symbolic representation of the final stage of Sam's liberation.

While this is not a picture book for young children, it should not be categorised by age level. It is not a book for a quick read or read aloud. Rather, it is an invitation for contemplation and quiet reflection.

## TRACKS (1992)

**Nola Allen**

SOURCE: A review of *Tracks,* in *Magpies,* Vol. 8, No. 2, May, 1993, p. 27.

"Night. Joel is hunting." A short prose poem by a Children's Book Council Award-winning author, forms the text of this picture book story about the nocturnal discoveries of a young boy and his dog in a rainforest and in his own backyard.

The spare text makes use of repetition and questioning to create a pensive tone. While the words echo Joel's view of his explorations, the grainy illustrations add an eeriness to the story through the perspective of the night creatures watching the boy's movements. Even though the majority of the double-page illustrations are set at

night, entailing the use of dark, muted colours, a luminous quality is also present. A superb final close-up view of Joel and the creator of the mysterious silver track aptly captures our human wonderment at nature's offerings.

When read aloud, the text's hypnotic quality along with the evocative illustrations provides an opportunity for young readers to reflect on the simple pleasures to be derived from our environment.

## ANGEL'S GATE (1993)

**Kevin Steinberger**

SOURCE: A review of *Angel's Gate,* in *Magpies,* Vol. 8, No. 4, September, 1993, p. 4.

The notion of "feral man" (Homo ferus) has been around for a long time, from the legendary Romulus and Remus to the more recent, albeit dubious, cases of the Wild Boy of Aveyron and the Wolf Children of Midnapore. From my own childhood in far north Queensland in the 1950–60s I remember a reclusive young man dubbed "Tarzan" who subsisted in the bush like his namesake and strongly resisted attempts to "rehabilitate" him.

This notion of "feral man" and the fundamental questions it raises about limits on personal freedom and the new civilisation of the individual are at the core of this first-person narrative, a more conventionally structured, less complex novel than Crew's previous works. It remains, however, in Crew's particular style, rich in symbolism and metaphor as he pursues familiar themes of alienation, disharmony and a search for identity. For less searching readers it is a thoroughly compulsive story of a murder in a small rural community.

Central to the story is "The Laurels", the large sandstone surgery-residence of Doctor Marriott and his family. In the old gold rush days it was a military barracks, later it was a lunatic asylum. Vestiges of its dark past remain in barred cells in the cellar, a high stone wall around the property and unfounded stories of murder and suicide in the house. Now, it offers a privileged, insular position from which young Kimmy Marriott observes the curious events in the little dairying-timber town of Jericho that follow the murder of a vagrant fossicker.

The man was known to have had two children. They have fled from their bush camp and taken to prowling among farms by night for food. After many months sixteen year old Leena is captured and brought to "The Laurels" where she is locked up in one of the old cells, her presence there kept secret the murderer try to silence her as a witness. Much later her brother Micky is captured in a remote cave and brought to join her. When the circumstances of the murder and the identity of the perpetrator are revealed, the children are released into the care of welfare services officers.

Interwoven with the principal story is a sub-plot that

expands on the themes inherent in the children's circumstances and illustrates the universality of their predicament. Just as feisty as Leena and Micky but struggling in a different context is sixteen year old Julia Marriott whose rebellious streak and desire for independence away from Jericho has earned her "a bad reputation".

*Angel's Gate* is a thoroughly absorbing novel in the best tradition of crime fiction although to call it a crime novel would be to grossly undervalue it. An undercurrent of suspicion prevails throughout, encouraging the reader to consider each character closely, mindful of the children's fear of a certain "Mister". The urge to reach for the resolution of the murderer's identity is relentless and when it is revealed it quite surprises. A wide, varied cast of minor but roundly developed characters and a setting that includes forested mountains, valleys, a dam construction site and distant farms does not allow for facile resolutions.

No readers, however quickly they read this novel, will fail to light upon the contrast the author draws between the children's life before and after capture and the similarities between Julia and Leena. The author does not labour these thematic devices but the symbolism, perhaps a trifle overdone, is occasionally glaring in its intent. The doctor's taxidermy is a case in point. Displayed in the surgery is an eagle, its wings "spread wide as it swooped on a pop-eyed field mouse trapped forever in its talons". His proudest specimen is a ghost bat but it is kept in the cellar, "'Exactly where it belongs,' my mother said. 'In the dark and out of sight.'" Later, the children, labelled ghosts after their first confused sightings, are to suffer the same fate.

The themes are best served by a dialogue that captures well the true voices and perceptions of the many different characters in Kim's world, and also by incongruities in their behaviour. The children are captured ostensibly for their protection but are then virtually imprisoned by the doctor. While he spares them the trauma of appearing in court he readily hands them over to the welfare people. The "last sight of them was through the rear window of the station wagon. They didn't wave. Their fingers gripped the bars of the metal grille that was fitted there."

But for Julia there is hope. She recognises the forces and conventions that threaten the individuality she cherishes. She fights against them but only succeeds when she takes flight from Jericho, aptly named, where she fears she'd "die of claustrophobia".

*Angel's Gate* is an exceptional work that further consolidates Gary Crew's reputation as a writer of considerable artistic merit, well attuned to the adolescent psyche and with that rare talent of being able to bring together popular appeal and literary depth.

### Publishers Weekly

SOURCE: A review of *Angel's Gate,* in *Publishers Weekly,* Vol. 242, No. 32, August 7, 1995, p. 461.

In the weird rural Australia of Crew's fiction (*Strange Objects; No Such Country*) it's not surprising to encounter characters out of *The Road Warrior:* feral children, a brutish prospector scratching around in the bush. Such types people the author's suspenseful new yarn. Kim, a boy in sixth grade, relates how gold hunter Paddy Flannagan is found murdered, prompting an all-out search for his two wild children, teenage Leena and eight-year-old Micky. Leena is captured and put into the care of Kim's father and mother, the town's only doctor and nurse. Under the assumption that Paddy's killer is still at large, Leena's whereabouts are kept secret—until Kimmy, as usual, spills the beans. Then he and his older sister's boyfriend find seemingly autistic Micky, who is likewise hidden. But as someone named "Mister" stalks the two Flannagan children, it falls to Kim to protect them. The mounting tension will keep readers glued to their seats. Teens used to the horrifying climaxes of adult suspense films or fiction may feel let down by the relatively innocuous resolution, but younger readers will probably be relieved.

### Nancy Vasilakis

SOURCE: A review of *Angel's Gate,* in *The Horn Book Magazine,* Vol. LXXII, No. 2, March-April, 1996, p. 205.

Winner of two major children's book awards in Australia, this exciting novel explores the mystery surrounding the murder of a poor gold miner and the disappearance of his two children. The story is told from the point of view of eleven-year-old Kimmy, the son of the local doctor and his nurse wife. Kim and his older sister, Julia, have lived a relatively sheltered life. Julia is a rebellious spirit, constantly striking out against her parents' restrictions, but Kim is quiet and dreamy. The dead miner's children are almost feral, having lived in the hills and away from civilization all their lives. When one of them is caught and brought under the care of Kim's parents, Kim is at first frightened and fascinated by the girl, but eventually he befriends her. As their relationship evolves, Kim discovers hidden strengths in himself, and he eventually musters the courage to rescue Leena's brother from the man who killed their father. This complex novel is rich in nuance and color. The Australian setting and the description of the two wild children will fascinate young readers, and the carefully developed plot will keep them reading until the end.

### 📖 THE WATERTOWER (1994)

### David Lewis

SOURCE: A review *The Watertower,* in *The School Librarian,* Vol. 43, No. 2, May, 1995, p. 63.

At the heart of this picture book is an image so discomfiting that it may well repel many adult readers. Two boys escape the blistering heat of their small town in the Australian outback by going swimming inside the dome of an abandoned watertower. The claustrophobia that emanates from the interior scenes is palpable. But Crew and Woolman have ways of twisting further this simple but chilling plot-line. To begin with, the watertower itself may not be quite what it seems—the cover illustration shows the tower at night with a ghostly green light emanating from underneath, Its influence seems malign for the townsfolk look like zombies and one of the boys is visibly transformed by his sojourn inside the tank. One twist is quite literal: the first two-thirds of the book are so arranged that it must be read on its side. Part way through, however, the printing swivels around so that the book must be completed upside down. *The watertower* is an ingenious book that adults may find crude and clumsy but older primary, and secondary, children will spend time on it and not be quite so hasty.

## THE LOST DIAMONDS OF KILLIECRANKIE (1995)

### Ray Turton

SOURCE: A review of *The Lost Diamonds of Killiecrankie*, in *Magpies*, Vol. 10, No. 5, November, 1995, pp. 4–6.

It has long been held as a truism that fiction contains much truth. Equally interesting is David Macaulay's interpretation of nonfiction. Delivering the Zena Sutherland Lecture for 1989, Macaulay worked his way towards a definition of nonfiction ending with:

> Fiction is the opposite of non-fiction. Nonfiction is based on facts. Facts are anybody's guess. Be not dismayed, however. There is one very simple avenue we have not yet travelled. In England, the kind of books I make are not referred to as either fiction or non-fiction, but rather as information books. I looked up information and discovered it is the communication of knowledge. With my fingers crossed, I then looked up knowledge. The word fact was nowhere to be seen.

> (Hearne, Betsy, editor, *The Zena Sutherland Lectures 1983–1992*, Clarion, 1993, pp 149–150)

So what has this to do with Gary Crew and Peter Gouldthorpe's new book *The Lost Diamonds of Killiecrankie?* It is a work of fiction, the opposite of nonfiction, which provides information and communicates knowledge. By its very nature this book is going to create a great deal of discussion. It looks like a picture story book. It reads somewhere between an adventure story and a nonfiction book. It is, in fact, a mixture of fact and make-believe in a narrative which so skilfully blends the two that it is difficult to work out where one begins and the other ends. Back to David Macaulay (and remember that he is talking about nonfiction, not fiction):

> The fact is that nothing in print or, for that matter, in any other form of communication, is accidental. Everything produced by people is biased. It's unavoidable, natural, and desirable. Whether it's the way a story is told, the mood created, what is emphasised and what isn't, the question we must always ask ourselves is what was the writer's or photographer's or illustrator's

point of view? Where are they standing both literally and metaphorically? What were they trying to say and why?

> (Hearne: 1993, p 152)

What are Peter Gouldthorpe and Gary Crew doing with *The Lost Diamonds of Killiecrankie*? The book itself is a clever manipulation of facts, both visually and textually, and presents on one level a straightforward adventure, on another a carefully presented history of the fate of the Tasmanian Aboriginal, and at yet another level a political statement of the exploitative nature of the British Empire under Queen Victoria.

And where are Gouldthorpe and Crew standing? Literally, in a maze of intermingled fact and fiction; metaphorically, in an historical exploration of the purported demise of the Tasmanian Aborigines: the history of which is an example of the phenomenon of regeneration and regrowth, a philosophical belief in which both writer and illustrator share. For although the Tasmanian Aborigines were officially deemed to have died out with the death of Truganini, in fact, the race survived through the actions of the worst kind of men—those sealers and whalers who abducted, for sexual purposes, the native Tasmanian girls and took them to the Furneaux group of Islands. There were conceived the offspring which kept alive the Tasmanian Aboriginal race.

The idea for *The Lost Diamonds of Killiecrankie* came out of an odd mix of factors beginning with a call from Margo Welsh, the teacher/librarian of the Flinders Island School, asking Gary Crew if he could spend a couple of weeks on the island working with the children. Then other factors began to come into play. Crew's work on his Master's thesis on Post Colonial Fiction relating to the effects of white invasion on indigenous peoples meant that he had a working background knowledge of the fate of the Tasmanian Aboriginal. As he puts it, 'The tectonic plates of my head started to slip' and the idea of something more than a school visit began to gel.

Crew phoned Peter Gouldthorpe. They had formed a strong friendship whilst working on *First Light* and Gouldthorpe had expressed an interest in working with Crew on a book 'from the ground up'. The two had started to call the concept their 'Ayers Rock Novel'. When Crew mooted the idea that Flinders Island could become their Ayers Rock—Gouldthorpe replied that he was 'listening'. As a result both Crew and Gouldthorpe went to Flinders Island where they were joined later by their editor, Helen Chamberlin.

Before leaving they focussed on research, leaving the planning of the form until they were on Flinders Island but keeping in mind certain objectives:

They wanted to re-interpret the picture book and create a format that would entice older more visually oriented readers. Boys in particular, they feel, read often in short bursts and sometimes read captions only, therefore they wanted a book which would cater for such readers. This is not to say that the book won't appeal to girls. One of the central characters is a very powerful female with whom most girls will empathise.

They were conscious of a lack of stories that were 'good ripping yarns' in the style of Ballantyne's *Coral Island* and *The Lost World* of Conan Doyle. At the same time they recognised that these stories are sexist, racist and completely anti-environmental and any modern equivalent must avoid these failings.

They had a perception that Australian children still know very little about many aspects of their country's history.

Summed-up what they wanted to produce was a picture story book that was visually strong with the illustrations totally meshed with the narrative; that had a strong adventure quest as its central theme, and at the same time, without any overt didacticism, narrated a period of Australian history not commonly known. Both were keen but couldn't find the catalyst they needed so they began reading. A varied and exhaustive research which is mirrored in the book as the research undertaken by the narrator of the book as if he were Crew and Gouldthorpe rolled into one: [they] 'researched in libraries . . . sketched in galleries and museums . . . sought out private collections of tattered musty letters'.

Among the many references used by Gouldthorpe and Crew was Plomley's *Weep in Silence* (a massive 1000 page tome which reproduces Robinson's journals for the period of the settlement on Wybalenna). It chronicles the terrible history of the Tasmanian Aboriginals who as James Morris in the first volume of his trilogy *Pax Britannia* says were doomed *"From the moment [they] first set eyes upon an Englishman"*. (Morris: 1973, p 377)

Robinson's journals tell of the terrible years of the settlement at Wybalenna on Flinders Island and how, out of the approximately 200 Aboriginal people who were taken there, at the time when the settlement was closed, only 45 were still alive and were returned to the mainland to eventually die at Oyster Bay. Also in Plomley's book Gouldthorpe and Crew found a footnote reference to the existence of quality topaz on Flinders Island. Further research uncovered the fact that Milligan, the last Superintendent at Oyster Bay, had been approached by the government to find and send some of these topaz gems to Prince Albert's Great Exhibition at the Crystal Palace in London in 1851. No further details were recorded other than that he had returned to the island taking with him an Aboriginal. Working from the lists of deaths of the people at Oyster Bay Gouldthorpe and Crew came to believe that the Aboriginal Milligan took back with him to Flinders Island could be William Lanney. There were no other references, but on checking the catalogue of The Great Exhibition they found listed on display from Tasmania, 200 topaz gems of various colours.

They had found their Conan Doyle quest plot but they still needed a mystery. That they were to create in what Gary Crew refers to as 'the hiatus, which is the domain of the fiction writer, between truth and the unknown—between what is unknown and what may have been'.

On Flinders Island they explored the terrain and ecology of the island, the site of Wybalenna and mapped the island and its habitations. Peter photographed, sketched and painted. They walked the area fitting their story around the landscape and the history. The form began to take shape: characters were delineated (some based on Islanders, some on historical figures). A fictitious world was imposed over the existing with the added *frisson* of the essence of the real world being maintained. The story together with the illustrations of maps, letters, diaries, bulletins, paintings, photographs which are an intrinsic part of the narrative was plotted, changed, reworked.

They chose to have the story told by 53-year-old Geoff Middleton, a sometime art teacher, recounting events that occurred when he was in his twenties. The catalyst for his confession/reminiscence was a public talk he had attended given by Crew and Gouldthorpe during a visit to the island. He sent his story (told in a voice that is very similar to that of the ripping yarn of the colonial period) to them via their publisher. So we have a fictitious person writing to a very real fourth generation Australian publisher who in turn passes the fictitious letter onto a factual author and illustrator. Although the narrator is fictitious and some of his story is fictitious much of the story is fact. I don't want to spoil your enjoyment of the book by saying anymore.

It is not uncommon for works of fiction to have meticulous research behind them. The originality of the presentation of this book makes it different. From the end papers of actual photographs, through the visual form of the discourse encompassing, as it does, letters, broadsheets, photographs, sketches and narrative, to the end statement (an enigmatic portrait of a self-satisfied Queen Victoria), the seamless whole of the book is a fascinating mixture of fact and imagination.

## THE BENT-BACK BRIDGE (1995)

### Sophie Masson

SOURCE: A review of *The Bent-Back Bridge*, in *Reading Time*, Vol. 40, No. 1, February, 1996, p. 29.

This story first appeared as *"Sleeping over at Lola's,"* in the Omnibus anthology *Hair-Raising* and I thought then what an utterly chilling story it was. In this form, as a book on its own, and with Greg Rogers' atmospheric, subtle illustrations, it again packs a powerful punch. Janet is fat, friendless, and when strange, wild Lola befriends her and then invites her to her place to sleep over, she is overcome with joy. But when she arrives at the designated spot, there is nothing, no-one . . . or is there? There is a terrifying coldness at the centre of this story, which recreates the menace of the troll in an entirely distinctive way. It is poor friendless Janet's terrible need for a friend that creates the monster. The horror of this story is in the lack of pity, the black hole represented by the troll. Does poor Janet deserve such a terrible fate? But as we all know, the heart of this kind of myth, the nightmares of humanity, is never compassionate. This is the darkness lurking not only under bridges, but in us all.

Truly macabre, yet never overdone, the text is beautifully complemented and expanded through Greg Rogers' black and white illustrations to convey that tangible sense of menace and utter terror despite the rather lovely and seemingly innocent things they portray: a moth, a dog, a phone booth, the bridge. And the shadows, and the thing waiting under the bridge . . .

## CALEB (1996)

### Michael Gregg

SOURCE: A review of *Caleb,* in *Magpies,* Vol. 11, No. 1, March, 1996, p. 12.

According to the Old Testament, Caleb was sent forth as a precursor to discover a new land and, for his steadfastness, was rewarded with its inheritance. With Caleb it seems that Gary Crew, like the eponymous hero and his Biblical namesake, has again ventured forth beyond the accepted boundaries of the picture book and claimed this new territory as his own. The second of a proposed trilogy of collaborative works between Crew and illustrator Steven Woolman, *Caleb,* like *The Watertower* before it, seeks to redefine our notion of the picture book and in so doing raises some interesting questions about the role and perceived readership of the genre.

This is a dramatic book, from its 'Escher-ish' front cover to its final creepy etching, and definitely not one for anyone with an insect phobia. Told in the first person, the story is a recounting by Stuart, a young university student, of his strange dealings with his flatmate, the child prodigy Caleb. In a style very typical of Crew, the first page sets up an aura of mystery and dread, which carries the reader through to the final page in curiosity and anticipation.

Caleb is odd—oddly dressed, incommunicative, solitary and obsessed with insects. The butt of student incomprehension, he seems unmoved by human contact. Only his meeting with Miss Emily, a noted entomologist, brings some kind of animation to his human relations. . . .

With *The Watertower* the authors created a book with no answer, which kept the reader guessing beyond the last page. In *Caleb* they have put a different twist in the tail, turning predictability on its head. The reader is invited to guess from the very start, and clues abound. Just as the reader is expecting another greater mystery all is revealed. The expected, rejected by the reader suspicious of a trap, becomes a surprising ending.

The authors have set out to intrigue, and have succeeded although perhaps not always in ways they had planned. Having read through it once, the reader is encouraged to return to the text with a critical eye, looking for the detail and piecing together the embedded clues. There is much to entice the mind—although some elements may be rejected by the critical reader. The owl motif which appears at significant moments in the plot is described by Steven Woolman as a red herring, designed to create questions in the reader's mind. Ultimately it is intended to symbolise Stuart, eternally observing. However, as the owl is most identified as either a night hunter or a symbol of wisdom, neither of which describes Stuart, it is perhaps a little too diverting. There are other inconsistencies one could pick on—however, the measure of the author's, and in this context, the illustrator's, art, is that these needn't matter as the reader is swept along immersed in the detective hunt for clues.

For me, the two most appealing aspects of *The Watertower* and *Caleb* are the way readers are encouraged to critically interpret the book in all its aspects; and the reintroduction of the picture book (and the other genres) to the secondary school audience.

Ultimately this is a book that, I suspect, will be remembered not for its unexpected though effective text, redolent of Edgar Allan Poe, H. Rider Haggard and Edgar Rice Burroughs, but for the clever artifice of its authors and for the questions it leaves in the readers' minds—will it be, not the meek, but rather the cockroaches that inherit the earth? And will we be able to tell the difference?

Additional coverage of Crew's life and career is contained in the following sources published by Gale Research: *Authors and Artists for Young Adults,* Vol. 17, *Contemporary Authors,* Vol. 142, and *Something about the Author,* Vol. 75.

# Arthur Dorros

## 1950-

American author and illustrator of fiction and nonfiction.

Major works include *Pretzels* (1981), *Ant Cities* (1987), *Tonight Is Carnaval* (1991), *Abuela* (1991), *Radio Man/ Don Radio* (1993).

## INTRODUCTION

Admired for his beginning-to-read books, Dorros has created a variety of children's works that range from make-believe stories to nonfiction science books to bilingual picture books. Beginning with clever, original tales about silly sailors and shoe-seeking alligators, the author-illustrator quickly branched out into different genres of children's literature. In his entries for the "Let's Find Out and Read" series about nature, Dorros combines simple, colorful illustrations with clear, easy to understand text, answering questions children have about the environment. The artist is perhaps best known, however, for his multicultural stories introducing bits of Spanish to the vocabulary of young readers. In these award-winning books, he explores the lives of Hispanic children living in North and South America and shares their experiences with early readers, teaching them respect, appreciation, and admiration for children of different cultures. Reviewers praise Dorros for his thoughtful works which enlighten children about the diverse world in which they live, while at the same time providing genuinely entertaining books.

### Biographical Information

Born and raised in Washington, D.C., Dorros showed an early interest in art as a young child, supported by a family who encouraged his early talent. As he grew older, however, the author set aside thoughts of becoming an artist and instead worked variously as a draftsman, builder, photographer, and longshoreman after graduating from the University of Wisconsin in 1972. When he discovered at the age of twenty-nine that he could keep a group of children entertained by making up stories, Dorros decided that he would combine these storytelling skills with his artistic ability and create a book for young readers. His first work, *Pretzels*, began a successful career in children's literature and was followed by more funny, offbeat stories and nonfiction science books. After living for a year in South America, he realized that American children suffered from a lack of exposure to other cultures and languages. Back in the United States, Dorros set to work creating several books celebrating the lives of Latino youths. He would compose lively stories which Sandra, his South American-born ex-wife, would then translate into Spanish. His early multicultural works are written mainly in English, interspersed with simple Spanish

words; in his later texts, as children's linguistic skills increase, so does the amount of Spanish. In addition to writing and illustrating children's books, Dorros gives workshops, teaching youngsters how to create their own books. He says, "I enjoy visiting schools and working with children on their own writing and illustration. Everyone has stories to tell."

### Major Works

Dorros's first book, *Pretzels,* established his reputation as a writer of humorous and original easy-to-read books, self-illustrated with light, cartoon-like pictures. Made up of four stories about a ship of bungling sailors, *Pretzels* amuses children with clever nonsense stories. Critics appreciated his fresh approach to books for beginning readers and remarked about his feel for the genre. In 1987, the artist tried a different type of children's book, writing *Ant Cities,* the first of his many nonfiction picture books. In this self-illustrated work, Dorros explains what goes on inside of a large ant hill, showing readers how harvester ants reproduce, carry heavy objects, and build their own immense housing structure. At the end of the book, he includes detailed instructions for children on how to build their own ant farm and observe how ants live and work together. Other nonfiction works explore the wind, rain forests, water, and animals. While some reviewers criticize the author for not providing enough detailed scientific information about his subjects, others appreciate his simple approach to teaching young children about nature using language well within the grasp of new readers.

*Tonight Is Carnaval,* the author's 1991 picture book, gives children a unique view of the Andean mountain culture. A little boy looks forward to celebrating the yearly *carnaval* and playing in the festival band. Excited by the chance to go to town, the boy hurriedly helps his family around the farm, allowing readers to see life on a farm in Peru. Instead of typical picture-book illustrations, the story is told through *arpilleras*—Peruvian wall hangings made from cloth in cheery, primary colors—and at the end of the book, Dorros shows how they are made. The writer returns to the United States in *Abuela,* when a fanciful young Hispanic girl flies with her grandmother all around New York City. In the text, he integrates Spanish words with the English text; some of the vocabulary can be understood by context, but a glossary is provided for challenging phrases. Dorros focuses on the life of migrant workers in his fourth bilingual book. Written at the top of the page in English and translated into Spanish at the bottom, *Radio Man/Don Radio* tells the story of two young boys, Diego and David, who meet while their families are picking cabbages in Texas. However, as the children of migrant workers, both families soon move on to different jobs, but through a special radio program, Diego is able to send a message to his far-away friend. Critics applaud the author's ability to incorporate Spanish words and phrases seamlessly into the English text, allowing children to easily expand their vocabulary.

## Awards

*Ant Cities, Feel the Wind,* and *Rain Forest Secrets* were selected as Outstanding Science Books by the National Science Teachers Association Children's Book Council in 1987, 1989, and 1990 respectively. *Abuela* and *Isla* were named Notable Books in the Field of Social Studies in 1991 and 1996 respectively. Dorros has also won a variety of notable book citations and other honors from several children's literature organizations.

---

# TITLE COMMENTARY

## 📖 *PRETZELS* (1981)

### Judith Goldberger

SOURCE: A review of *Pretzels,* in *Booklist,* Vol. 78, No. 4, October 15, 1981, p. 314.

A mild-mannered kind of humor pervades three episodes in the lives of crew members aboard the sailing ship *Bungle.* With a grossly absentminded captain and a prideful but rotten cook (named "I Fryem Fine" by the crew), a ship is bound to bungle. But nice things happen anyway: First Mate Pretzel inadvertently invents the food named after him when he substitutes I Fryem Fine's biscuit dough for an anchor chain. The *Bungle* crew benefits from its captain's forgetting to take maps along; they're lost in a storm, find land, and discover that it's home port. New juvenile author Dorros has a good feel for the beginning-to-read genre and knows how to draw out the child in his characters. Though reading level is uneven, the fresh appeal of the stories should carry most beginners. And the author's own illustrations—literal, welcoming, and funny—add style and cheer. A seaworthy book.

### Kirkus Reviews

SOURCE: A review of *Pretzels,* in *Kirkus Reviews,* Vol. XLIX, No. 21, November 1, 1981, p. 1342.

A new comic talent, a tub of a sailing ship and its properly eccentric crew—but of the three adventures aboard the *Bungle* here, only the first is distinctive in kind. That's **"How Pretzels Were Invented."** How? Well, when part of the *Bungle*'s anchor chain rusted away (with no replacement—thanks to Captain Fast's fuzzy-headedness), the crew commandeered some of cook I-Fryem-Fine's hard-as-rock biscuit dough and improvised a chain; and he, reusing the twisted dough the next day, shaped it into a new, twisted kind of biscuit, flecked with salt crystals from the sea—which First mate Pretzel devoured so avidly "that the crew named them after him." The second tale, **"The Jungle,"** is conventional—a floating log mistaken for a crocodile, a piranha, and a snake—and the third, **"A New Land,"** is a fairly routine mixup (mapless, the *Bungle*'s crew bungles back home, unbeknownst) that, however, has considerable amusement value just on the basis of Dorros' knack for writing straight-faced nonsense. The pictures are droll in the same simple, offhand fashion—with the result that, even when the story isn't much, the book is mighty companionable.

### Nancy Palmer

SOURCE: A review of *Pretzels,* in *School Library Journal,* Vol. 28, No. 4, December, 1981, p. 74.

*Pretzels* are invented in the course of this tall tale by Arthur Dorros. At sea, aboard the (aptly named) sailing ship *Bungle,* the cook, I Fryem Fine, makes biscuit dough so tough that it can be used as anchor chain, the captain can barely remember where the ship is headed, and the mate thinks he's been attacked by a crocodile when he grabs a log after being dumped in the Amazon River. The three episodes about these bunglers have a refreshing, slightly off-the-wall feel; it is as if they exist in their own little bungled-up cosmos, a feeling enhanced by the loose line and two-color wash illustrations. Kids will enjoy the absurdities, the action ("Piranhas!") and the minor change of pace from other beginner fare.

## 📖 *ALLIGATOR SHOES* (1982)

### Kirkus Reviews

SOURCE: A review of *Alligator Shoes*, in *Kirkus Reviews*, Vol. L, No. 26, August 15, 1982, p. 935.

Dorros is a newcomer (**Pretzels**, 1981) with a genuine, offhand comic talent—but this little pleasantry is a 22-page wind-up to a hoary gag. Alligator Alvin, in search of shoes (because—the book's best line: "He liked watching people. Mostly he saw feet"), gets locked in the shoe store overnight. There he tries on all sorts of shoes—running shoes, dancing shoes, hiking shoes—until, wearying, he falls asleep in the heap of footgear. Says a shopper the next morning: "I like these alligator shoes." And Alvin decamps: better alligator feet than alligator shoes. Since today's exercise-culture has spawned an interest in footgear, kids might enjoy seeing Alvin running, hiking, dancing, etc., appropriately shod; otherwise, next to nothing.

### Mary B. Nickerson

SOURCE: A review of *Alligator Shoes*, in *School Library Journal*, Vol. 29, No. 2, October, 1982, p. 140.

Alvin the alligator resolves to buy some shoes, is mistakenly locked in the store and amuses himself by trying on all the footwear. He falls asleep and is awakened by a woman tugging his foot because she wants alligator shoes. Alvin goes home, deciding that he likes alligator feet better than alligator shoes. This small (4¾" x 5¾"), slight book seems to be an excuse for some fairly nice illustrations featuring the very toothy alligator in various settings; each time Alvin tries on another pair of shoes, the setting and accessories change in keeping with the intended use. Children are expected to understand that this is purely Alvin's imagination at work, but a connecting clue is missing. Pedestrian.

## 📖 *ANT CITIES* (1987)

### Betsy Hearne

SOURCE: A review of *Ant Cities*, in *Bulletin of the Center for Children's Books*, Vol. 40, No. 7, March, 1987, pp. 124–25.

Using harvester ants as a basic example, Dorros shows how the insects build tunnels with rooms for different functions and how workers, queens, and males have distinct roles in the ant hill. Along the way, [he] works in details of food and reproduction, ending with descriptions of other kinds of ants and suggestions for ways to ob-

serve them (including instructions for making an ant farm). The text is simple without becoming choppy, the full-color illustrations are inviting as well as informative. Another successful addition to a series that is varied in scope and authorship but consistent in quality.

### Ellen Loughran

SOURCE: A review of *Ant Cities*, in *School Library Journal*, Vol. 33, No. 1, August, 1987, pp. 66–7.

Dorros introduces ant communities by examining the harvester ant. The book includes information on the organization of the ant community, the specialization of ant roles within the community, and some of the physical characteristics of ant life. The pages on the harvester ant are followed by brief descriptions of several different types of ants, all chosen to catch a child's interest. The book ends with instructions for making a simple ant farm. The material is presented in simple language and large print. The illustrations, which are cartoon-like, colorful, and amusing, make the text more comprehensible and add interest to the book. One problem is that some terms, like *larvae* and *pupae,* are never defined, and there are limited contextual clues to their meaning. Still, this is an adequate introduction to a subject that fascinates the bug-minded, and it will be a useful addition to the science section.

### Martha B. Mahoney

SOURCE: A review of *Ant Cities*, in *Appraisal: Science Books for Young People*, Vol. 20, No. 4, Fall, 1987, pp. 20–1.

*Ant Cities* is part of the "Let's-Read-and-Find-Out Science Book" series. It presents the subject of ants in a way that allows a young child to understand and appreciate them.

The book begins with a question inviting the reader to think about these animals. In his illustrations, the author/illustrator has included four children who seem to be learning as the reader learns. They also help give a perspective on the size of the ants in relation to the children. The ant hill is compared to a small city in which each member has a specific function. The work that each ant does is written about clearly. One diagram shows a cross section of the hill, indicating all of the different work that ants perform, and, thus giving the reader an excellent idea of the intricacies of work in an ant hill.

The diagram on pages eight and nine is clear. The author/illustrator has pictures of weather conditions over the ant hill and then describes what effect each may have had on the hill. The labels in darker print on the diagram seem too small for a young child to read easily.

The functions of the antennae are described and depicted. An ant is very strong. The workers use this characteristic to help carry food to the ant cities. The author describes several of the 10,000 kinds of ants and the types of homes each has.

The last page explains how the reader might make or purchase an "ant farm."

This book is a good introduction to ants. I think it would be a good addition to a children's library

**James Minstrell**

SOURCE: A review of *Ant Cities*, in *Appraisal: Science Books for Young People*, Vol. 20, No. 4, Fall, 1987, pp. 20–1.

Not only does the youngster "read-and-find-out" in this little book, but I suspect that after reading *Ant Cities,* she will be found sitting cross-legged on a sidewalk watching ants at work. This is a delightful book, a clear text with fine illustrations. It captures the busyness of ants and the way in which they cooperate to keep their city alive. Whether it be thief ants, army ants, cornfield ants or janitor ants, Dorros conveys the fascination of these amazing insects. Moreover, he shows how one can set up an ant farm in one's own bedroom! Join in with this exciting adventure, parents!

## 📖   *YUM, YUM* (1987); *SPLASH, SPLASH* (1987)

### *Publishers Weekly*

SOURCE: A review of *Yum, Yum* and *Splash, Splash,* in *Publishers Weekly,* Vol. 232, No. 7, August 14, 1987, p. 100.

A small, curious girl feeds the animals on a farm; a reluctant boy eases himself into his bath routine and finds that scrubbing up isn't so bad after all. Those are the modest storylines of Dorros's two board books, which have sweet watercolors, mostly in pastel hues, but with some bright jolts thrown in: the girl's red overalls, her cat's streaks of orange, the boy's yellow duck and polka-dot curtains in the bathroom. An engaging duo.

### Gale W. Sherman

SOURCE: A review of *Splash, Splash* and *Yum, Yum,* in *School Library Journal,* Vol. 34, No. 7, March, 1988, p. 165.

These two titles are painfully simple even for board books. The illustrations are flat, and the humorless texts are boring. Children are sure to enjoy the fun of Rosemary Wells' *Max's Bath* a lot more than *Splash, Splash.* Likewise, *Max's Breakfast* is a more exciting book experience than *Yum, Yum.* The task of equaling the quality of Wells' text and illustrations on similar themes is formidable. Dorros' books don't pass the test.

## 📖   *FEEL THE WIND* (1989)

### Phillis Wilson

SOURCE: A review of *Feel the Wind,* in *Booklist,* Vol. 85, No. 15, April 1, 1989, p. 1382.

A comprehensible definition of what causes the wind to blow is followed by sensory examples of feeling, hearing, and seeing the effects of wind, which are easy for youngsters to grasp. Dorros notes the wind's varying forces and its applications to kites and boats, as well as the types of work accomplished by such machines as windmills. The relationship of wind to weather forecasting is explained, and directions for making a weather vane are included. While Dorros' line-and-wash illustrations are bland in their depiction of children, they convincingly convey wind-bent trees, storm-darkened skies, and rippled waters in this useful addition to the Let's-Read-and-Find-Out Science Book series.

### William Capie

SOURCE: A review of *Feel the Wind,* in *Science Books & Films,* Vol. 25, No. 2, November-December, 1989, p. 81.

*Feel the Wind* is an attractive and potentially interesting little book that addresses a topic that can seem abstract to youngsters. While the book seems easy to read with two to three sentences per page and supporting pictures, some of the ideas discussed are difficult ones. The notion of invisible air, or feeling moving air and that moving air helps to move things and do work, are quite relevant even to young readers, but "What makes air move?" is a sophisticated question. Movement of cool polar air to replace warming equatorial air is abstract even with colorful diagrams. Finally, the discussion of local variations in winds is not complete. A pretty book, but it needs some work to help kids develop a better understanding of air.

## 📖   *ME AND MY SHADOW* (1990)

### Kay Weisman

SOURCE: A review of *Me and My Shadow,* in *Booklist,* Vol. 86, No. 16, April 15, 1990, p. 1628.

Dorros offers simple explanations of shadows and how they are made in this brief nonfiction picture book. He discusses how the position of a light source affects the length of an object's umbra and explains how shading in art can help define the shape of an object. Day and night, the phases of the moon, and eclipses are detailed, and shadow puppets, X rays, and sonograms are mentioned as well. Colorful illustrations extend the text by detailing many hands-on activities (playing shadow tag, creating shadow puppets, and drawing shadows) that children will want to try for themselves. Most projects do not require adult help. This offering will be useful for classes studying light and is a fine addition to the parent-child activity shelf.

## Kay McPherson

SOURCE: A review of *Me and My Shadow,* in *School Library Journal,* Vol. 36, No. 5, May, 1990, p. 96.

A look at shadows and how they are created. Readers learn how the sun makes shadows and how x-rays and sonograms, which use the same principles, are made. Integrated throughout the book are simple activities for children to do. The text is clear, specific, and to the point. Brightly hued watercolor and pencil illustrations have a breezy style much like that found in Aliki's books; they are presented in an attractive and eye-catching layout. There is scant recent material on this topic for preschool and primary-age children; this book should be well received by teachers looking for useful materials for science activities as well as by parents who are looking for answers to their young children's eternal "Why?"

## *RAIN FOREST SECRETS* (1990)

### *Kirkus Children's and Young-Adult Edition*

SOURCE: A review of *Rain Forest Secrets,* in *Kirkus Children's and Young-Adult Edition,* Vol. LVIII, No. 16, August 15, 1990, p. 1167.

Though the text here is enthusiastic and the watercolors pleasant, this adds little to understanding of its subject. Animals, plants, and people are all stiffly drawn, lacking the fine detail of Powzyk's *Tracking Wild Chimpanzees* (1988); the world map provided to locate rain forests is so dark that it is impossible to distinguish between temperate and tropical forests; and the Amazonian forest is discussed in detail, but Dorros never mentions its location. Elsewhere, abbreviation hampers clarity: "Some scientists think that destroying the rain forests will make the whole earth's climate warmer. The warming is called the *greenhouse effect.*" What have trees to do with climate? Dorros doesn't say. He does include, however, a useful address list of Rain Forest Organizations.

### Zena Sutherland

SOURCE: A review of *Rain Forest Secrets,* in *Bulletin of the Center for Children's Books,* Vol. 44, No. 1, September, 1990, p. 6.

A continuous text is adequately organized, competently written, accurate in providing facts, and fairly broad in its scope. The details, alas, are weak in the many representations of fauna in this threatened type of ecosystem. Some of the animal forms are awkwardly drawn, and the accuracy of comparative sizes seems dubious. The bright colors of jungle flora are attractive; save for one formal border, plants are not identified. Dorros describes the layers

of growth, refrains from rhapsodizing about tropical beauty, and discusses—with a restraint that gives the text dignity for readers in the primary grades—life cycles within the ecosystem, the current rate of rain forest destruction, the greenhouse effect, and other damage to the environment when forests go.

### Denise Wilms

SOURCE: A review of *Rain Forest Secrets,* in *Booklist,* Vol. 87, No. 1, September 1, 1990, p. 49.

Dorros presents a picture book introduction to rain forests, describing their special features and importance to the environment. "From the air, a lowland tropical rain forest looks like a green ocean," writes Dorros, who has visited such areas himself. He describes the forest's zones—the canopy, the understory, and the floor—each with its characteristic flora and fauna meshed in a delicate balance. Interesting facts stud the general descriptions (most of the plants and animals in the rain forest have not even been discovered by scientists yet; one fourth of all medicines come from rain-forest plants), and Dorros is careful to call attention to temperate rain forests, such as those on the Pacific coast of the U.S. The accompanying pen-and-wash drawings are extensive and effective in suggesting the lush greenery, though one map of rain-forest areas is very poorly reproduced. The format and conversational tone will make this accessible to a wide audience, including older reluctant readers. Useful and timely.

### Ellen Fader

SOURCE: A review of *Rain Forest Secrets,* in *School Library Journal,* Vol. 37, No. 2, February, 1991, p. 78.

A serviceable and somewhat engaging look at the ecology of rain forests, describing the animals and plants found there and exploring reasons why these places must be protected. Unfortunately, the text is occasionally weak. The word "canopy" is used twice before it is defined; some words are italicized but never defined or are merely labelled on nearby illustrations; and there is no glossary. The watercolor illustrations are more cartoonlike than realistic, which suits the informal tone of the text. The book's one map uses two such similar shades of green that it nearly negates its purpose: to differentiate between the locations of tropical and temperate rain forests. In addition, only continents are labelled, so the statement "Temperate rain forests grow along the west coast of North America, from northern California to British Columbia, Canada, and Alaska" is valuable only to readers with a good grasp of geography. Also, the text is at times vague; for example, many children will not know what country or continent the following refers to: "The Amazon river, flowing through the biggest rain forest in the world, carries one-sixth of all the earth's water that flows into oceans." Included is a well-balanced list of organizations to contact for further information. Adequate as a starting place for discussion since there is little available on the subject, especially for this age group; complete the picture with books about specific animals and places, and an atlas.

## 📖 *TONIGHT IS CARNAVAL* (1991)

### Leone McDermott

SOURCE: A review of *Tonight Is Carnaval,* in *Booklist,* Vol. 87, No. 10, January 15, 1991, p. 1062.

Life in the Andes Mountains might be hard work most of the time, but for three days every year there is Carnaval. In a book as gay as confetti, Dorros presents daily Andean farm life from the point of view of a boy awaiting this joyous festival. The young narrator is eager to play his flute with the Carnaval band, but before the big day comes, there is much work to be done. Firewood must be gathered, fields plowed, llamas sheared and their wool spun into yarn, and potatoes harvested and taken to market. Everyone in the family participates, even little sister Teresa, as well as nearby friends. Finally, it is Carnaval, when work is forgotten in a whirl of music and dance. Dorros' text is appealing and informative, emphasizing the strong communal life of the village. However, the real star of this book is its illustration. The action is shown in *arpilleras,* the distinctive South American wall hangings made from cut-and-sewn pieces of cloth. The Club de Madres Virgen del Carmen of Lima, Peru, has created about a dozen of these cheerful fabric pictures in bright primary colors. One charming page shows six white llamas cavorting above a blue mountain pool amid children and ducks. The sweet, naïf character of the art and the festive tone of the text are bound to please. Appended are a short glossary of foreign-language terms and an illustrated explanation of how *arpilleras* are made.

### Susan Patron

SOURCE: A review of *Tonight Is Carnival,* in *The Five Owls,* Vol. V, No. 3, February, 1991, pp. 52–3.

A young Peruvian boy excitedly awaits Carnival night in "the big village down the valley"; this year he will play songs ("the songs of our mountains days and nights") on his *quena* (flute) with the others in the band. Meanwhile, he tells us of his family and of his busy working days: collecting firewood, planting and harvesting potatoes, herding llamas and alpacas. The prospect of Carnival Night makes the boy eager to do his work quickly, to hurry the day along toward that grand annual event.

The first-person telling offers a good deal of information about a unique Andean mountain culture; that didactic intent is bostered by a narrative thread about the excitement and anticipation of a great festival with which readers will relate. If the text is in fact overly purposeful in its worthy aim of cultural sharing, this is mitigated by the charming *arpilleras* (quilted wall hangings) used as illustrations. Great care has been taken by the women of the

Club de Madres Virgen del Carmen of Lima, Peru, to picture exactly the words of the text with brightly colored fabric and yarns. Tiny dolls representing the characters and other three-dimensional objects are sewn onto a background which shows what the mountains and land and houses look like; we also see plants and trees and animals. Perspective and composition are childlike and entirely delightful, so that some people in a picture are seen from in front, while others are seen from above. The *arpilleras* amplify and inform the text. Those photographed for the endpapers, showing rows of vegetables, have a stunning artless beauty.

This handsomely designed picture book includes a two-page explanation of how *arpilleras* are made (with snapshots of the *arpillera*-makers) and a glossary of Spanish words that appear in the text. *Tonight Is Carnival* would be useful for teachers who want to convey to young children something of what it may be like to grow up in the mountains of Peru. It is one of only a handful of books in which children can see aspects of South American cultures proudly depicted.

### Eleanor K. MacDonald

SOURCE: A review of *Tonight Is Carnaval,* in *School Library Journal,* Vol. 37, No. 5, May, 1991, p. 77.

The text, illustrated with photographs of *arpilleras* (three-dimensional fabric wall hangings), covers three days in the life of a Peruvian boy as he and his family prepare for a *carnaval* celebration in the nearby village. The boy describes the everyday work that must be finished as he anticipates the festivities and practices the music he will play with his band. The information about the daily life of the people of the Andes is reinforced by the brilliantly colored folk art, made by a cooperative of women. The problem is that the boy exists only as a voice to convey information—which he does in an earnest, but unconvincing, monologue. The folk art, while appealing, does little to convince readers that this is a particular child with emotions. Although the book is a bit of a throw-back (it is primarily an informational book clothed as fiction), it packs in a lot of detail and would be a useful introduction to the culture. The photographs of the *arpilleras* give an additional dimension, and the two pages of photos showing the women making them are among the most interesting in the book. The sale of the *arpilleras* and a percentage of the royalties will go to support relief efforts. Would that such obvious sincerity had produced more inspired fiction and a deeper view of a rich culture.

## 📖 *FOLLOW THE WATER FROM BROOK TO OCEAN* (1991)

### Carolyn Phelan

SOURCE: A review of *Follow the Water from Brook to Ocean,* in *Booklist,* Vol. 87, No. 16, April 15, 1991, p. 1643.

From the dependable Let's-Read-and-Find-Out science series, this picture book describes the earthbound segment of the water cycle, beginning with melting snow on a mountain and following the resulting brook as it flows into a stream, a river, and finally the ocean. Along the way, Dorros introduces concepts such as erosion and water pollution and briefly discusses waterfalls, canyons, reservoirs, dams, and deltas. Cheerful, informal line-and-water-color artwork competently illustrates the text. Children and animals lend interest to the scenes. Primary grade teachers may find this a useful book.

## Rosie Peasley

SOURCE: A review of *Follow the Water from Brook to Ocean*, in *School Library Journal*, Vol. 37, No. 9, September, 1991, p. 245.

An excellent presentation of introductory material about water. Addressing readers in the second-person "you," it clearly explains such terms as "brook," "stream," "river," and "delta," and illustrates such basic concepts as where water comes from, how it travels, and where it goes. The illustrations are simple, almost childlike, in soft colors. In a few cases, however, it is difficult to distinguish between water and land because the contrast in tone is subtle; otherwise the artwork is pleasant and effective.

## *ABUELA* (1991)

### Kate McClelland

SOURCE: A review of *Abuela*, in *School Library Journal*, Vol. 37, No. 10, October, 1991, pp. 90, 94.

An innovative fantasy narrated by a Hispanic-American child who imagines she's rising into the air over the park and flying away with her loving, rosy-cheeked *abuela* (grandmother). From the air, they see Manhattan streets, docks, an airport, tourist attractions, and Rosalba's father's office. The simple text could be enjoyed as a read-aloud or as a read-alone for newly independent readers. What makes the book so interesting is Dorros's integration of Spanish words and phrases via Abuela's dialogue within the English text. While some phrases are translated by the child, others will be understood in context. As insurance, a glossary, which provides definitions and pronunciations, is appended. The illustrations sing out a celebration of the love and joy that underlies the brief, straightforward narrative. Combining vibrant watercolor and pastel images with interesting snippets of collage in an exuberant folk-art style, [Elisa] Kleven depicts the adventurous, warm-hearted Abuela and the jazzy, colorful topography of an energetic, multiethnic city. Thoughtful design extends to the endpapers featuring cloud formations that cleverly echo many images from the story. While not bilingual in the strictest sense, this book is a less self-conscious, more artfully natural approach to multicultural material.

### Deborah Abbott

SOURCE: A review of *Abuela*, in *Booklist*, Vol. 88, No. 4, October 15, 1991, p. 436.

While in the park feeding the birds, with her *abuela* (grandmother), Rosalba wonders what it would be like to fly—and in her imagination—fly they do! Together, the young girl and her grandmother see New York City from above—the neighborhoods, the coastal area, and the docks. At the Statue of Liberty, Abuela says, "Me gusta," remembering her first trip to the U.S. After a brief flight over the airport, they land to visit Tio Pablo and Tia Elisa's store for a *limonada* ("Flying is hot work"). Off they soar again, viewing the skyscrapers before landing back at the park. As they walk around the path at the lake, Rosalba begs Abuela for another adventure. The paddle boats are waiting. Exquisite color collages convey the special relationship between white-haired Abuela and her granddaughter. Each painting is a tableau of details. The animated tableux features a rainbow of ethnic characters, pets, flowers, and bright curtains with the general excitement of a city street. Each illustration is a masterpiece of color, line, and form that will mesmerize youngsters. These are pages to be studied again and again. The smooth text, interspersed with Spanish words and phrases, provides ample context clues, so the glossary, while helpful, is not absolutely necessary. This is similar in some ways to Faith Ringgold's *Tar Beach* and used together, these "wish" books would make a powerful foundation for a multicultural unit for children of all ages. Even if used alone, this book is a jewel.

### Mary M. Burns

SOURCE: A review of *Abuela*, in *The Horn Book Magazine*, Vol. LXVII, No. 6, November-December, 1991, p. 726.

Although one could find many descriptors—multicultural, intergenerational—for this book, any label, no matter how useful, would seem limiting for something that is so unselfconsciously and exuberantly liberating in concept and design. Beginning with a small girl and her grandmother boarding the bus for the park, the story quickly expands in scope as the child imagines the two of them flying high above Manhattan. Wheeling and soaring, they pass over buildings and harbor, past landmarks such as the Statue of Liberty, before returning to the lake in the park—and possibly another adventure. The text is a series of straightforward declarative sentences with Spanish words, carefully integrated into the context, adding piquant syncopation. It is the perfect accompaniment for the energetic, well-composed collage illustrations, a marvelous balancing of narrative simplicity with visual intricacy. Spread out beneath the adventures, the city is transformed into a treasure trove of jewels, dazzling the eyes, uplifting the spirits. Monotony is avoided by changes in focus—mingling long-distance perspectives with close-ups, intimate vignettes with larger compositions. As in Faith Ringgold's *Tar Beach*, allusions to times past are incorporated into the text. Inevitably, comparisons will be made between the two. Yet, despite similarities in the underlying concept—that of flying above the city—each book is an individual creation, with the transition between fantasy and reality more clearly defined in *Abuela*. A handsome book with appeal for a broad range of audiences.

## Molly Ivins

SOURCE: A review of *Abuela*, in *The New York Times Book Review*, December 8, 1991, p. 26.

The chief charms of this flight of the imagination within hard covers lie in the illustrations by Elisa Kleven. Anyone familiar with Mexican and Latin American folk art will recognize the vivid green, turquoise blue, hot pink and bright yellow so characteristic of Latin art. Here's dingy old New York City, certainly a gray enough sight on any gloomy day, suddenly alive with tropical color, whimsically turned into a festival of vividness. It's enough to make one wonder why we stodgy *norteamericanos* don't paint our houses pink and green and red and turquoise as the Latins do. Think of the fun.

The story of *Abuela* is about a little girl named Rosalba who goes with her grandmother (*abuela* in Spanish) to feed the birds in Central Park and wonders, as all children do, "What if I could fly?" And so she does, taking Abuela with her on a tour of the city. They visit the Statue of Liberty, the airport, the sailboats on the Hudson and even do a fly-by of Rosalba's daddy's office, turning a flip as they go by for fun. They zip about the city with the loopy freedom of Matisse's angels, making even adults think again about how super it would be to be able to swoop around in the sky like a bird.

Perhaps children cannot be taught to be imaginative—it's more likely we train it out of them—but this is a book to set any young child dreaming. In a few years, when the computer experts perfect Virtual Reality so that any experience that can be filmed can be perfectly replicated, the faculty of imagination may die out entirely. Until that dreary day comes, books like the charming *Abuela* can still make children dream.

The book has the additional advantage of incorporating elementary Spanish vocabulary on almost every page in the most natural, easy manner. Since Spanish is an exceptionally simple language to pronounce, any reader can handle it, whether familiar with Spanish or not.

I suppose there is some degree to which *Abuela* is "good for children," in the same sense that cod liver oil and spinach are. Non-Spanish-speaking children can pick up a little Spanish and get some sense of the lives of Hispanic children. And Hispanic children presumably will have their self-esteem, which the educators solemnly assure us is all-important, reinforced by seeing someone besides Dick and Jane in a book. But it seems a shame to load down the exuberant charm of *Abuela* with didactic nonsense. It's just joyful. I wish I could fly.

## ANIMAL TRACKS (1991)

### Publishers Weekly

SOURCE: A review of *Animal Tracks*, in *Publishers Weekly*, Vol. 238, No. 50, November 15, 1991, p. 71.

In this interactive parent-child book, Dorros brings hidden woodland animals up close by depicting their tracks—sure evidence of the presence of other creatures in our midst. Readers follow these tracks across watercolor landscapes, turn each page and find the culprit—a turtle dragging itself to a sunny rock, a porcupine heading for a bark breakfast. Although Dorros's approach admirably enlivens his subject, freeing it from frequently dry field-guide literature, his bland palette and somewhat listless text fail to convey the excitement children can feel on encountering tracks. The book is, however, instructive as an introduction to woodland-stream fauna, relative size of tracks and other signs of animal presence. Youngsters may be most intrigued by Dorros's demonstration of how to "trap" tracks by luring nocturnal animals to a flour-covered area.

## Sheilamae O'Hara

SOURCE: A review of *Animal Tracks*, in *Booklist*, Vol. 88, No. 8, December 15, 1991, p. 766.

Dorros shows the marks left by a variety of animals as they go about their daily business. Providing endpaper displays of full or half life-size drawings of the tracks of 22 animals, his text invites the reader to identify the tracks shown in the full-color illustrations with those the animals made in their various habitats. However, to use the endpapers for reference, one must cover the page showing the tracks to be identified. This is an unfortunate drawback in a book that otherwise has much to recommend it. The pictures are realistic and varied, showing the trails animals leave on flora as well as on the ground. There are suggestions for discovering tracks in the city and for preserving tracks for later study. The book is attractive enough to catch the attention of budding naturalists and interesting enough to hold it.

## THIS IS MY HOUSE (1992)

### Publishers Weekly

SOURCE: A review of *This Is My House*, in *Publishers Weekly*, Vol. 239, No. 35, August 3, 1992, p. 70.

In his familiar, child-like style of naïve watercolor and pencil illustration, Dorros attempts a picture-book overview of houses worldwide. More scattershot and larger in scope than last season's *The House I Live In* by Isadore Seltzer which focused only on America, Dorros's work includes 22 dwellings in such diverse locales as Turkey, Norway and Samoa. Unfortunately, the small type identifying each location is frequently difficult to make out, and the short paragraph paired with each drawing offers very little factual information. Bolivia, for example, merits only two brief sentences: "I live in the high mountains, where there are few trees. We built our house out of stone." On each page the phrase "This is my house" appears in that region's language (though it is never identified) and is both translated and transliterated into English. Teachers embracing whole language may find this an effective trade surrogate for traditional sources on shelter, or a useful starting point for children's own explorations of their communities. However, it's hard to predict much recreational use for this essentially curriculum-driven survey.

**Mary Lou Budd**

SOURCE: A review of *This Is My House,* in *School Library Journal,* Vol. 38, No. 9, September, 1992, pp. 215–16.

Readers and young listeners take a worldwide trip to see and learn about people's houses of all descriptions. The spectrum is broad, and the treatment provides historical and sociological backgrounds in a most enlightening manner. There is unlimited value in the succinct, interesting text and pictures that "show and tell" just how and why these shelters are built. Varied lifestyles, climates, and available materials for construction are basic considerations wherever one lives, and young readers with access to this engaging book will readily grasp the concept. With few exceptions, each house is shown on a single page, accompanied by brief explanatory text. The bright, pleasing watercolors have enough detail to catch and hold attention, and children get a real feel for the locale by scanning these scenes for the landscape, people, and, in some cases, their occupations. In addition to providing engaging illustrations and narrative, Dorros includes the phrase for "This is my house" in its appropriate language as well as its phonetic pronunciation. The name of each country appears with the pictures. Attractive endpapers repeat the main illustrations, labeled by country. This is just waiting

SAUDI ARABIA

*From* This Is My House, *written and illustrated by Arthur Dorros.*

for a good browsing session, or for use as a supplement in a social-studies unit.

## RADIO MAN/DON RADIO (1993)

### Kirkus Reviews

SOURCE: A review of *Radio Man/Don Radio: A Story in English and Spanish,* in *Kirkus Reviews,* Vol. LXI, No. 17, September 1, 1993, p. 1142.

As Diego travels with his family looking for work—picking melons near Phoenix, cherries in California, apples in the Northwest—he tunes in to local stations, Spanish, English, or both; that's why his friend David, whom he hasn't seen since they picked cabbages on the Texas border, calls him "Radio Man." When Diego relays a message through a call-in show in Washington, David hears it and they meet again. Dorros's colorful, simply drawn illustrations have a pleasing naiveté and include some nice details—Mama, glimpsed in the rearview mirror, dozing on an all-night drive; an owl nesting in a saguaro cactus while the family listens to "the Night Owl" on "KKTS, *Cactus* radio." Both the Spanish and English texts here incorporate context-defined words from the other language, in the natural manner of those becoming more fluent. An upbeat but largely realistic picture of migrant life—and an entertaining boost to bilingualism.

### Carol Fox

SOURCE: A review of *Radio Man/Don Radio: A Story in English and Spanish,* in *Bulletin of the Center for Children's Books,* Vol. 47, No. 5, January, 1994, p. 151.

A young boy, Diego, travels with his family, itinerant farm workers following the western harvests from Texas to Washington state. His friend David calls him "Radio Man" because he is always listening to the radio. Time and again, Diego leaves and meets his friends and relatives (David and he part the day after the story begins) as his family takes a job, completes it, and then moves on to look for other work. Diego's family's life is hard, but they share their fortune. For the whole family in the field, the radio provides music for pleasure and diversion in the truck at the end of the day, and for celebrating the end of a season. The radio supplies continuity and constancy for Diego, for his relatives, and for the story, and it unites Diego and his friend David at the end. Written in English at the top of the page and translated into Spanish at the bottom, the story has a short concluding Spanish-to-English glossary. The illustrations, done in brilliant acrylics on alternate pages to the text, are deceptively simple; at first glance they look primitive, with childlike drafting and stiff, flat characters fixed in mid-movement, but more careful observation reveals that composition, expression, and color are all chosen to create an authentic atmosphere. The bright colors warm the story as the radio warms the lives of the characters.

### Janice Del Negro

SOURCE: A review of *Radio Man/Don Radio: A Story in English and Spanish,* in *Booklist,* Vol. 90, No. 10, January 15, 1994, p. 924.

Diego and David are good friends. Their families are migrant farm workers who travel all the time—from crop to crop, season to season. The consistent, connecting thread in their lives is the sound of the radio—in the field to ease the picking and in the truck during long night rides. It's also there when the families part, as Diego's family sets out for Washington to pick apples. Once at the orchards, Diego hears KMPO, farm worker's radio and, longing to find David again, calls the radio "bulletin board" with a message: "Hello, David! This is Diego. Are you here?" The typeface is large and clear, with the English and Spanish texts (both handled well) separated by thumbnail watercolors that effectively coordinate with the full-page art on the facing page. The plentiful, naive-style paintings contribute a solid sense of place and reflect the strong family ties and efforts at community Dorros conveys in his story. The final illustration is a smiling David hearing Diego's message on the radio.

### Mary Bahr Fritts

SOURCE: A review of *Radio Man/Don Radio: A Story in English and Spanish,* in *The Five Owls,* Vol. VIII, No. 3, January/February, 1994, p. 61.

Diego works the fields under the hot of a red sun and travels the roads by the cool of a white moon. He belongs to a community of migrant workers, families who uproot themselves as often as the fruits and vegetables they pick. Even so, his migration from farm to farm picking Texas cabbages, Arizona melons, California cherries, and Washington apples, is told and painted by Dorros in warm, cheerful colors.

As Diego waves goodbye to his best friend David in one state ("We won't see each other for a while") and reunites with cousins Sophy and Ernesto in another, we see how it is Diego's radio (besides his family) that remains the constant in his life. It is his radio with English and Spanish voices and music that draws out memories (Grandfather recalls his Mexican village), that reduces Diego's apprehension of the "new" voices ("voices grow louder as we near the next town"), that initiates sing-alongs during the drive and dances after long days in the field. And in the end, it is fitting that Diego's radio reunites him with his best friend.

The reader might suspect the author has traveled this same road, as his acrylic horizons of warm red skies, tall purple mountains, and cool blue nights frame characters on every page but two. Pictures as well as text alternate between the sadness of driving away and the excitement of moving toward. Dorros's art illustrates not merely the obvious (the adventure of driving through a redwood tree, the excitement of dancing under a piñata) but also the subtle (the exhaustion of Grandpa sleeping in the car, Diego's pride in knowing how to choose ripe fruit while the lady in the market does not).

Words in Spanish and English, separated by spot art, offer a learning experience for both cultures; however, the short glossary translates only Spanish phrases. Perhaps a Spanish-speaking child might wish a glossary with English phrases. A colorful map at the end, though a bit small, traces Diego's journey from field to field. An introduction describing a typical day or season in the life of a migrant child would have worked well here, because the story raises many questions: How do migrant children attend school on the move? Do they ever return to a home? What happens to the very old who cannot work? To the very young, born on the journey?

Diego is a happy and adventurous young man who adapts well to his ever-changing world. Dorros offers the reader a look at this world, illustrating not only the hardships but also the strong sense of community and tradition. A distraction is the truck's license plate that reads PIC4U2. Picture-book readers will surely notice. But with Dorros's convincing text, by story's end the reader will realize that vanity plates do not belong in Diego's world.

## ELEPHANT FAMILIES (1994)

**Lesley McKinstry**

SOURCE: A review of *Elephant Families*, in *School Library Journal*, Vol. 40, No. 7, July, 1994, p. 93.

This entry in the popular, easy-to-read series offers an excellent overview of the elephant's habits and life cycle. The concise yet informative text focuses on African elephant families, but mentions Asian species. Accurate watercolors (many of which are full page) supplement the information. Brief captions clarify some of the illustrations. L. Martin's *Elephants* and Elsa Posell's *Elephants* provide similar information in slightly different formats. A list of addresses for organizations dedicated to protecting this endangered species is provided.

**Carolyn Phelan**

SOURCE: A review of *Elephant Families*, in *Booklist*, Vol. 91, No. 2, September 15, 1994, p. 138.

From the Let's-Read-and-Find-Out series, this compact book introduces African elephants, emphasizing their family structure and individual and group behavior, including how they care for their young. Dorros also points out the differences between African and Asian elephants and briefly examines the endangerment of elephants because of the ivory trade. While the drawing sometimes seems awkward, the full-color, line-and-wash illustrations effec-

tively illustrate the text. A useful addition to school and public library collections.

## ISLA (1995)

**Vanessa Elder**

SOURCE: A review of *Isla*, in *School Library Journal*, Vol. 41, No. 9, September, 1995, p. 168.

"When Abuela, my grandma, tells me stories, we can fly anywhere." And so, in this sequel to *Abuela*, Rosalba takes a trip to the Caribbean island where her grandmother, mother, and uncle grew up. They visit Abuela's house and yard, the rain forest, an old city, a country marketplace, and the beach. In everything they do, Rosalba and her Abuela are like " . . . big birds playing." After an evening meal with *tío* Fernando, *tía* Isabel, and cousin Elena, they return to New York City, glowing with happy memories of the experiences they've shared. Dorros's language is rich and magical—readers fly to *la isla*, too. Elisa Kleven's art is whimsical and quiltlike, crowded with sweet things and surprises. There is so much to look at in each picture—fruits and fish and animals and warm people, all rendered in candy colors. Lines of text are placed like poetry on white pages and accented with decorative drawings, or placed below double-page illustrations. Spanish words and phrases are peppered liberally throughout; a good glossary with pronunciations is included at the book's end. An enchanting journey through the imagination that is delightful for sharing again and again.

**Hanna B. Zieger**

SOURCE: A review of *Isla*, in *The Horn Book Magazine*, Vol. LXXII, No. 2, March/April, 1996, pp. 230–31.

In a second book about Abuela, she and her granddaughter use their imaginations to soar through the skies to Abuela's beloved island home—*la isla*—"sparkling like a green jewel in the sea." There they visit relatives, fly over a rain forest, look at the busy harbor and the new buildings in the city, and go *al viejo mercado*—to the old market—before returning to the sparkling lights of New York City. Vivid illustrations [by Elisa Kleven] with myriad details bring the tropical scenes to life, and the well-chosen Spanish words and phrases are easily understood.

Additional coverage of Dorros's life and career is contained in the following sources published by Gale Research: *Contemporary Authors*, Vol. 146, *Something about the Author*, Vol. 78, and *Something about the Author Autobiography Series*, Vol. 20.

# Sarah Ellis
## 1952-

Canadian author of fiction.

Major works include *The Baby Project* (1986; published in the U.S. as *A Family Project,* 1988), *Next-Door Neighbours* (1989; published in the U.S. as *Next-Door Neighbors,* 1990), *Pick-Up Sticks* (1991), *Out of the Blue* (1995).

## INTRODUCTION

Lauded for her deft handling of serious themes, Ellis has received much attention for her preteen and young adult stories about the ups and downs in the lives of ordinary people. Tackling difficult subjects such as crib death, adoption, and single-parenthood, the author creates compelling books featuring believable, well-developed characters. Critics recognize Ellis for her realistic treatment of family problems and for her ability to create a careful balance between lighthearted comedy and thought-provoking tragedy. Her honest approach to the problems children face wins her respect from young readers and reviewers alike. Noted for her books about families with traditional values, the writer firmly grounds her protagonists in stable, loving homes which often reflect trends surfacing in society—parents returning to school, stay-at-home fathers, and professional mothers. Throughout her books, Ellis gives a sympathetic portrayal of adolescents encountering the problems of an adult world; in working through these obstacles, the characters begin their own transition into adulthood. As Judith Saltman observes: "Ellis's stories of growth and change offer both the child and adult reader engrossing experiences of complex personal epiphanies, simply and beautifully told."

### Biographical Information

Ellis was born and raised in Vancouver, British Columbia, the third child of a clergyman and a nurse. Earning her degree at the University of British Columbia in 1973, the writer began her career as a librarian. After taking a year off to study children's literature at Simmons College in Boston, she returned to Vancouver intent on writing her own books for children. Admitting she had a rather uneventful childhood, Ellis turns to her own imagination for story material, saying, "my inspiration for writing comes, obviously, not from a desire to record an event-filled life, but from the pleasures of making things up." Out of this desire to create interesting characters who experience things she never did, the author wrote her first book, *The Baby Project,* in 1986. Since then, she has continued to create books featuring strong heroines who gradually learn that life is much more complex than they ever imagined. While writing new works, Ellis continues

to work as a librarian in Vancouver in addition to contributing a regular column, "News from the North," to *Horn Book.*

### Major Works

Ellis's first novel, *The Baby Project,* received widespread praise from critics throughout North America. When her mother learns she is expecting, eleven-year-old Jessica decides to monitor the progress of the pregnancy as a school project. Soon Jessica has a new baby sister and the entire family actively and happily participates in her development. When the baby suddenly dies of crib death, the family struggles to cope with the unexpected loss. Like its predecessor, *Next-Door Neighbours* received acclaim from reviewers for its perceptive, well-rounded characterization and thoroughly child-centered perspective. Set in 1956, the novel focuses on a rural minister's daughter who must adjust to a new life after moving to Vancouver. After her new schoolmates learn she has lied trying to win their approval, Peggy finds herself without friends for the summer and must settle for the company of George, a young Russian immigrant, and Sing, her neighbor's Chinese gardener and "houseboy." These new friends prove far more important for Peggy than the girls at school, as she comes face-to-face with the unfairness of intolerance, prejudice, and bigotry displayed by her closed-minded neighbors.

Winner of a 1991 Governor General Award for Children's Literature, *Pick-Up Sticks,* Ellis's first young adult novel, deals with the anger Polly feels over her mother's decision to raise a child alone. Polly and her mother, a socially conscious stained-glass artist, have a warm relationship until they must leave their low-rent apartment. Without a stable income, Polly's mother finds adequate housing difficult to afford, so Polly stays with her wealthy aunt and uncle for a while. At the posh residence, Polly discovers that despite the luxuries, the cold and sterile home lacks the warmth and comfort of her mother's small apartment. Missing the close family bond she had with her mother, Peggy begins to respect her mother's decision and alternative lifestyle. In *Out of the Blue,* Ellis once again deals with a family gaining a new member, but this time the new child is a young woman looking for the mother who gave her up for adoption twenty-four years ago. Already the oldest in the family, Megan feels displaced by her new half-sister and is resentful of all the attention Natalie receives. Not until her own parents demonstrate that they have more than enough love for another child in the family does Megan finally accept Natalie. Critics admire Ellis for her superb ability to realistically show how happy, secure families work through difficult and unexpected situations.

## Awards

*The Baby Project* was awarded the 1987 Sheila A. Egoff Children's Prize and *Pick-Up Sticks* won a 1991 Governor General Award for Children's Literature.

---

# GENERAL COMMENTARY

## Judith Saltman

SOURCE: "An Appreciation of Sarah Ellis," in *Canadian Children's Literature,* No. 67, 1992, pp. 6–18.

Sarah Ellis wears a dizzying array of professional hats. She is a critic and teacher of children's literature, a columnist for the prestigious American children's book review journal The *Horn book magazine* and a children's librarian, a professional storyteller and a writer of award-winning children's books. In 1987 Ellis became the first recipient of the B.C. Book Prizes Sheila A. Egoff Prize for Children's Literature for *The baby project,* her first published book [published in the U.S. as *A Family Project*]. And Ellis's *Pick-up sticks* won the 1991 Governor General's Award for Children's Literature in English. . . .

The writing of children's books is a more recent undertaking for Ellis and has had an impact on her column, making her a more appreciative reader, more aware of the structure of books and the effects achieved, and more easily delighted with the original, successful work, recognizing the amount of work in even a lacklustre book. But, adds Ellis in a recent interview, "I still hate to be disappointed. I want people to do better—not to get away with cheap effects and clichéd thinking". . . .

*The baby project* is a modern child and family life story with a contemporary cast of believable, well-rounded characters: a working professional engineer mother, taxi-driver and house-husband father, two older sons, and the protagonist, eleven-year-old Jessica. The family scenes, natural dialogue, and engagement of characters recall the warmth and humour found in the traditional family stories of the 1930s to 1950s. Ellis creates a fully realized world, a family home the reader can walk into and inhabit.

The book is divided into two separate parts. The first half of the book revels in quirky humour and sharpness of characterization that at times veer towards Helen Cresswell's British Bagthorpe saga with such details as the eccentric tenant who writes unforgettable parodies of country-and-western songs.

The first half also explores the new social realism in children's literature with the impact on the family of a late baby (Mom is 42), and the adjustment to the baby by the entire family. After Jessica is surprised by the news that her mother is pregnant, she and a school friend enthusiastically adjust by monitoring her mother's "baby project" as a school science project. This section of the book has unforgettable scenes, from the stormy adolescent brother quietly reading *Motor trends* to the new baby, to Jessica and her friend taping the ocean waves for a baby lullaby.

But this is not just an episodic family story, secure and ordinary. *The baby project* combines humour and pathos, comedy and tragedy. The second half of the book moves unexpectedly into an entirely different dimension. With a twist of direction and tone the narrative shifts into devastating tragedy. The baby dies of crib death and the chaos of the family's reactions, from withdrawal and numbness to rage and isolation, is dealt with honestly. The author does not show any quick, easy, lushly emotional resolution but the tentative beginnings by each family member of finding balance and solace in a cruelly changed world. The tensions and frictions in a family under stress are explored as they are in Jean Little's *Mama's going to buy you a mockingbird.* "I intended on writing a wholly sunny book like Lois Lowry," says Ellis, "a funny, warm family story. It kept getting serious on me. I knew the children were unhappy but I didn't know about what. I picked the baby's death because it didn't involve blame; it was a bolt from the blue."

There is a rare tonal quality in this book—a balance of tragedy and comedy—that recalls the work of Brian Doyle. The notion that life can be cruel and that humour and love are needed to balance its tragedies is handled sensitively. Part of Jessica's healing comes from her friend Margaret, who has already suffered through her parents' divorce and abandonment by her father and has survived. When Jessica questions Margaret on the future sadnesses life may provide, she answers: "I don't think it gets worse and worse. I think it just gets to be more of a . . . sort of mixture, with different kinds of happy and sad" (*The baby project* 112).

The necessity of continuing the emotional celebration of life itself, despite its blows, is portrayed in a magical night bike-ride of Jessica and her brother through Vancouver in a cleansing odyssey that leads them beyond their pain to the threshold of healing, to a renewal of their family intimacy.

Jessica is an intriguing protagonist. We experience her inner psychological life. She is a whole, rounded character on the edge of puberty. Like that of a William Mayne or Jane Gardam character, her mind is constantly turning over ideas and exploring perceptions of self, others, society and the adult world.

Ellis's style is extremely polished and controlled for a first novelist. Much of the wry wit is implied through seemingly artless, very natural and colloquial dialogue balanced with Jessica's inner soliloquies. About the reception of *The baby project* Ellis comments she is amused by the reviews describing the family as hypermodern. "I don't feel like a very modern person," she says with a laugh. "I have no interest in deconstructionism. I'm not very fond of four-letter-word children. I really like the family in *The baby project*", she continues, "I was writing about a 1950s-style stable family. In fact, the initial scene of the book is one parent (the father) baking cookies."

Ellis's memories of childhood are of a family closeness and security closer to the atmosphere found in classic child and family life novels such as Eleanor Estes's secure *The Moffats* than that of the modern dangerous world of Brock Cole's *The goats* where danger comes from the dysfunctionalism of contemporary society. "My worlds aren't really dangerous worlds," she explains, "I am building stable families with traditional, old-fashioned values—even with the stresses of the single-parent family, as in *Pick-up sticks.*"

As in *The baby project,* a Vancouver setting is subtly evoked in Ellis's second novel, *Next-door neighbours* (1989). Set in 1956, it is basically a traditional family story as well as one of friendship. "I feel like it's my warmest book," comments Ellis, "and maybe the most accessible to child readers. It's quite a naïve book, full of real child play."

The balance of humour and pathos found in *The baby project* is here rendered in an examination of the love and kindness of family and friends as opposed to the social cruelties of prejudice and bigotry. Poignant, episodic vignettes and Ellis's low-key, offbeat sense of humour pro-

pel this quietly-paced story of twelve-year-old Peggy who has just moved from the country to Vancouver. Overwhelmed by shyness and feeling alienated at her new school, Peggy tells a lie to gain attention and is ostracized by her schoolmates when it is discovered. Over the summer she finds solace in unlikely friendships with her two "next-door neighbours." Both are unusual friends who extend her limited vision of social acceptance, self-esteem, and humanity. One is Sing, an adult Chinese gardener and house-boy for a wealthy woman who uses him as a kind of slave. The other is George, a young Russian refugee her own age. Both Sing and George have lived through experiences of cruelty and pain. George has harsh memories of the Second World War; Sing's daily treatment by Mrs. Manning is a grotesque humiliation. Yet Sing and George have such a level of self-esteem and acceptance of themselves that they are not destroyed by their roles as "outsiders" in society.

Their summer of friendship involves a satisfying project, the truly child-like creation of a puppet show, with tension caused by Sing's dismissal (he has taken half an hour from work to attend the puppet show which he had helped to create). The children are stricken with a sense of injustice and guilt over this unexpected consequence of their actions. They search for clues to Sing's whereabouts and discover the reality of his life. Their examination of the empty shell of his bare, lonely room extends their understanding of human suffering and courage. However, the love and sensibility of Peggy's family and the wisdom she has shared with Sing and George ameliorate her pain and she faces the new school term with assurance.

The story is quietly told, and as in *The baby project,* the final scene has a celebratory, exuberant fullness restoring order and meaning to Peggy's world as she celebrates her Christmas with a fire-works display sent to her by Sing. It is a celebration of the human spirit's triumph over cruelty and limitations. It is also a rejoicing in the Canadian tradition of multiculturalism.

Ellis says of *The baby project* that writing of the crib death required research; it had not happened to any family that she knew. Peggy's shyness in *Next-door neighbours,* however, has its genesis in Ellis's childhood. "When I was a kid I had no idea that others felt shyness. I thought it was unique to me and I wanted to give Peggy that feeling." To Ellis, "As anger and guilt are reversals, so shyness has to do with shame; it is shame writ small." The source of the protagonist, Peggy's, shame is her constant state of embarrassment, her sense of potential humiliation, and the oppressive struggle with ambivalent feelings about who she is. Ellis explains that *Next-door neighbours* has a more formal story-telling quality than her other novels. There are more stories within stories: Sing's childhood story of jumping into a ditch to avoid embarrassment and the puppet show story of "The fox and the hare." This stronger narrative quality, Ellis feels, makes the novel "an easier book to read. The style is more straightforward, younger and the humour different, more naïve."

The assertion of self within the folktale of "The fox and the hare" becomes the assertion of Peggy and George's sense of unique selfhood and their recognition of the wrongness of intolerance and racial prejudice in the pain of Sing's life.

Ellis says that child-readers respond to this book more openly than to the others. "I've been to schools," she says, "where teachers have gone into it with children. The children want to talk about racial prejudice, moving, shyness. Kids have these experiences."

Also in 1989, Ellis ventured into picture-book territory with the publication of *Putting up with Mitchell: My Vancouver scrapbook,* a witty tour of Vancouver full of charming details in concert with the exuberant and whimsical illustrations of Barbara Wood. While visiting their grandmother in Vancouver, Elizabeth and her obstreperous younger brother Mitchell are taken on day-trips to Vancouver landmarks such as the UBC Anthropology Museum, the aquarium, and the Bloedel Conservatory. The lively book was partly inspired by Vancouver bookseller Phyllis Simon who noted there wasn't a children's book specifically about Vancouver. As an admirer of Barbara Wood's pictures of Vancouver buildings, publisher Terri Werschler subsequently approached Sarah Ellis to create an appropriate storyline and characters to match Wood's style.

With the publication of *Pick-up sticks* in 1991, Ellis crossed the threshold into the genre of young adult fiction. Thirteen-year-old Polly, the protagonist, is older than Jessica or Peggy and her life, as Ellis says, "is more out there in the world. She's not at home in the same way as Jessica and Peggy." Whereas the younger girls' stories are rooted in home and community, family and friendship, Polly's story is one of homelessness: losing roots and community as well as losing closeness to her mother. Polly struggles with the spectre of homelessness and instability in her life with her single mother, a stained-glass artist who decided to have a child without a partner.

The dynamics of *Pick-up sticks* are more complex than those in the earlier novels. The book is thorny with difficult contemporary social issues and public concerns, in subtle juxtaposition with, and straining, the intimacy of Polly's relationships with friends and especially her mother. Vancouver's social and political atmosphere, with its strong alternative life-style community and numbers of the disadvantaged and dispossessed in conflict with the developers and politicians, is even more a concrete figure here than Vancouver's physical presence, pervasive in the earlier novels. "I write about Vancouver and set my books here," says Ellis, "because I live here. It's what I know."

After Polly and her mother lose their home, they go on a quest to find a new one, a depressing search that reveals to Polly the economic disparities and social injustices of her city. Polly also ventures into a different quest: the young adolescent journey of self-discovery, an exploration of personal, familial, and social values. Her struggle with conflicting beliefs and values is set against the dramatic urban headlines which emerge as subtexts: the lack of affordable housing and homelessness; the inclusion of the mentally disabled in society; the increase in disaffected youth and vandalism; the threat of urban violence; the dynamics within non-traditional families and dysfunctional families; the power of social activism in opposition to greed and exploitation.

The weight of such a litany of urban pain could be crushing to a lesser writer, but Ellis's concentration on the personal story of Polly's conflict with her mother provides a concrete focus. The strain of near-homelessness leads Polly to leave her mother and stay with her affluent Uncle Roger's family. The contrast between their life of material privilege and cold, emotionless alienation and Polly's warm life with her free-thinking mother and friends is aptly drawn in Ellis's depiction of Uncle Roger's home:

> Life at Uncle Roger's was so easy. No lugging her horn to school in the rain. Uncle Roger drove her. No busing home from the library. Aunt Barbie came to pick her up. No dishes. Just stow them in the dishwasher. No cleaning out the bathtub. Mrs. Clemens came in on Fridays. If you phoned somebody and the line was busy, you didn't even need to dial again; you just pressed the redial button.
>
> You hardly even needed to talk. The family didn't eat together unless Uncle Roger and Aunt Barbie had a dinner party. When Uncle Roger drove Polly to school he listened to sales motivation tapes. The house was often empty, the only life the little blinking lights of machines—microwave oven, VCR, telephone answering machine, CD player.

(Pick-up sticks 69–70)

Once again, Ellis writes of outsiders in society. In *Pick-up sticks* the portrayals of George and Sing from *Next-door neighbours* are joined by the character of Ernie, middle-aged, mentally disabled, and one of Polly's closest friends. The humour, dignity, and warmth marking the special closeness between the two friends is shaped by Ellis's compassionate acceptance and celebration of human differences and her strong social conscience, as also seen in the depiction of racism and tolerance in *Next-door neighbours.*

The growth and development of Polly's character through the story into a deeper understanding of human nature and need is paralleled by Jessica and Peggy's personal growth and change in the earlier books. Touched by the cruelties and complexities of life, each girl voices within herself an awareness of inner transformation, of slow maturing, however simple or fleeting. In *Next-door neighbours,* Peggy lies in bed at night:

> Beside her curtains, in her mind's eye, hung the plastic ones in Sing's room, the cold linoleum, the stained sink. She looked at her ornament shelf of lovely ceramic ladies, at her desk, her books, her framed paint-by-numbers, and she thought of people in small, mean places—Sing in his scene-decorated basement, and

George in his railway car. The Peggy who had sneaked into Mrs. Manning's basement suddenly seemed like a child years younger than herself, a child she could barely remember being. She punched a hollow in her cool pillow and gave in to sleep.

(107)

Of the thematic links among her three novels, Ellis says, "I have only one major idea and I have it to death— a preadolescent girl discovers that life is more complicated than she had previously thought." Admitting to a somewhat medieval world view of capitalized humours and large emotions, Ellis explains, "In each book I've dealt with one big emotion: grief in *The baby project;* shame in *Next-door neighbours;* anger in *Pick-up sticks.*"

All three of her novels reflect what Ellis calls her "old-fashioned values: love, loyalty, humour, warmth, imagination, kindness, honesty, integrity, tolerance, and compassion." Ellis recognizes, however, that *Pick-up sticks* is different from her two earlier novels. Speaking of her three protagonists, she says, "Polly of *Pick-up sticks* is more out in the world than Jess or Peggy. A lot of the scenes take place not in the home but in a laundromat, running on the street, with an awareness of strangers and the urban threat." She goes on, "With the other children, someone is always at home when they come home; they don't think about money. Jess in *The baby project* thinks about death and cruelty; Peggy in *Next-door neighbours* thinks about tolerance and cruelty; Polly thinks about money, finding a home and a father, the clash of values with her mother."

Ellis does not subscribe to the school of thought that children need lots of plot. "I am trying to work out for myself how to write a compelling book without relying on major events." Ellis's novels are usually episodic in structure. "I tend to write a book in scenes, little set pieces (I can't think of any other way to do it.)"

*Pick-up sticks,* however, has a real plot. Ellis is satisfied with the suspense of the narrative, how the pieces fit together, the shape of the book. "In my other novels," she says, "the interrelationships were the focus and problem. Here, there appears to be a tangible problem: finding a secure home. But that turns out not to be the problem after all. In an earlier draft, I had Polly find a home. Then I realized it was unnecessary since the conflict is actually the clash of values between Polly and her Mom."

Although the genesis of *Pick-up sticks* was a specific CBC *Morningside* interview with a homeless woman which mentioned her daughter's pain and tears, most of Ellis's novels are based on her own childhood memories of family and friends rather than on ideas or on past or present events. "I definitely explore feelings more than ideas. I really admire idea writers: Jill Paton Walsh begins with ideas—the great idea of sending a contemporary child back to Victorian England in *A chance child.* Kit Pearson finds inspiration in history in *The sky is falling.* But I don't. I start with a character. I'm really interested in

trying to get people right, in capturing the subtext and the feeling between people in dialogue."

And, like many writers, Ellis continues her characters' stories beyond the confines of the books, linking the life of the 1950s in *Next-door neighbours* with the 1980s in *The baby project.* "This is all in my head, of course," she comments, "but, when Sing goes to Dawson Creek at the end of *Next-door neighbours* he marries a much younger woman. They have a son and that son is Jessica's friend Margaret's father, the disappeared dad in *The baby project.*"

It is true that Ellis pays meticulous attention to human emotions and life's details. Her writing successfully evokes a vivid quality of livingness: subtle feelings and thoughts explored from within characters' minds; the complexities of human interaction; the clarity and awareness of living in the moment. She says, "I like to notice how things are and try to capture that: the details that build a world, the relationships between characters, the surface of life—how you eat an ice cream cone."

Critics and readers often comment that Ellis is a natural storyteller. But the professional storyteller disagrees. She says of her writing process, "I don't like being a storyteller, always saying what happened. I like saying what is happening, being right in the moment. I tend to think this is what is happening and I'm going to tell it to you in the truest way I can: the crispest, most real, most recognizable way. That level of vividness is what I am trying to give to children in my writing."

This degree of clarity and intensity gives Ellis's narrative voice a freshness and vitality matched by her superb use of language. Her love of language and obsessive search for the exact word and phrase result, she explains, in a difficult writing process. "A recurring problem is my internalized loud-mouth editor's voice which paralyzes me. It doesn't allow me to blurt out and tidy up later. Because I want to get it perfect as I go along, I write slow and tight. And so I am a short writer. I edit too soon. The first draft of *Pick-up sticks* was only 80 pages along. My editor, Shelley Tanaka, said 'Where is the rest?' I said 'I cut it out'. I think I should take a writing course that loosens you up. But I'm superstitious that if I become too analytical about writing I wouldn't do it anymore."

Ellis writes simply, but evocatively. Her use of imagery is restrained: often recurring metaphors convey a sub-text throughout or illumine the changing state of the characters' consciousness. In *Pick-up sticks* the image of the title recurs through the text at climactic moments of pain and resolution. Upon alienating Vanessa, her best friend, Polly poignantly observes a scene from a younger and simpler childhood:

> Polly turned and leaned her head against the small back window. She looked into the yard below. Tony was lying on his stomach playing with a set of pick-up sticks. He arranged them carefully in his fist and then gently released them. They fell into a rainbow-colored pattern on the grass. Polly remembered doing

that when she was little, making patterns, arranging the sticks into families. Sometimes she had even played the real pick-up sticks game. She had played it with Vanessa. The stick flower blurred.

(***Pick-up sticks*** 76)

The gentle pathos in this image of the tentative, beginning realization of life's mutability and changefulness is completed in the novel's conclusion. Here the metaphor reflects Polly's growth, self-discovery, and awareness of life's complexities:

Polly made a see-saw with her two plastic straws. She thought of pick-up sticks. You pull out one stick and the balance shifts and the whole pattern changes.

(***Pick-up sticks*** 122)

Ellis creates a sense of contemporaneity in ***The baby project*** and ***Pick-up sticks*** by building a patina of surface detail; the paraphernalia and pathos of modern life litter the pages, from the bundles of rags in downtown malls that are human beings and the walkman-wired adolescent to the blinking, lonely lights of CD players and microwave ovens. The contemporary colouration goes beyond social atmosphere or satire to become part of internalized metaphor; the contemporary image of the VCR defines Jessica's grief in ***The baby project:***

Later on it seemed as though the week that followed Lucie's death was a video movie played on a machine with only two controls, fast forward and pause. Fast forward and pause, but no play, no record and, most of all, no rewind. In bed at night, scared of giving in to sleep, Jessica tried to rewind the tape to just before Lucie's death and then to make Lucie grow up. . . . But it didn't work. The pictures wouldn't come alive.

(106)

In the denouements of her novels, Ellis offers a vision of discovery, completion, wholeness, and a celebration of family, friendship and the human community. The serious thoughtfulness leavened by wit characterizing Ellis's writing is brought to a rich fulfillment in the rounded conclusions of her books. In each, the circle of quest and self-discovery is closed with a simple, subtle form of ritual, laminating the protagonist into the family and community. Also, in each conclusion, the realism slips for a moment into a kind of magic realism; whether a bicycle ride in the middle of the night, a fireworks display in the snow, or a group of people in a cafe transformed by beauty—the ordinary becomes charged with an extraordinary poetic significance.

In ***The baby project,*** the children's bike ride through the night-time city is bitter-sweet, touched by thoughts of mortality, gentle humour, and exhilarating adventure. Imbued with a softly surreal quality, this final scene evokes an awakening to life's mysterious balance and hope for the future: "All night, every night as she [Polly] lay sleeping and dreaming, there was this same and different world and she had never seen it before" (***The baby project*** 140).

***Next-door neighbours*** ends with a bang—Chinese New Year fireworks (a gift from Sing) set off in the Christmas snow while neighbours gather in amazement and celebration. The inner nucleus of family and friends is extended to include the whole neighbourhood in an embracing vision. All of the community can be the next-door neighbours of the title:

The first explosion made the across-the-alley dog begin to bark, and soon people started appearing. Heads poked out windows, frontdoors opened and porches started to fill up. A line of people formed at the front fence. Mum poured cocoa from thermoses, and Old Billy from the rooming house three doors down started circulating his bottle of rye. . . .

The sky filled with flowers of light. The Murphys, who hadn't gotten around to taking down their Christmas lights, switched them on again and the tiny spots of colour reflected the grand explosions in the sky above. Colin and George began to set off two things at once, and the colours mingled and fell together. In the moment of the fireworks heading whooshing into the sky everyone held their breath and let it all out in an 'ahhh' together. The display ended with the sinuous writhings of the extra-long python snake, and then George went around with sparklers for everyone, even throwing them up to people at windows. The Murphy kids twirled theirs in hoola hoops of light until they fell over in the snow. The grownups stuck theirs in the window boxes and in the fences.

(***Next-door neighbours*** 122–3)

***Pick-up sticks*** ends with a subtle beatific blessing, a vision of Polly's mother as a young woman, at the moment when she sat in a neighbourhood cafe eating blueberry pie and decided to have a baby. As she looks at the people in the cafe, she is struck by the absolute mystery of another human life: "They all looked so beautiful. Human beings seemed like the most wonderful invention" (123). This perception contrasts, like opening and closing parentheses to the text of the book, with the opening scene of Polly's vision on a city bus:

Suddenly, in the cold fluorescent light, *everyone* looked distinctly odd, like Martians or Venusians who had missed one essential lesson on how to pass for Earthlings. She had noticed this before—how one day everyone looks normal, and the next day everyone on the bus and in the school halls and in the library looks like someone in a cult movie.

(***Pick-up sticks*** 4)

The progression of plot between the two scenes echoes the resolution of the mother-daughter conflict and the shared acceptance of each other's choices and needs. The movement from alienation to affirmation in the novel and in these two mirror scenes is complete as Polly thinks of her mother, "finding the world suddenly beautiful" (123), and choosing to have a child. Ellis, as she does in all her novels, closes the story with a measure of solace, certitude, and faith in the changing patterns of human life.

For all the simplicity and understated grace of her writing

style, Ellis returns again and again to complex themes. And although her novels are not dense with theme and subtext, they are serious, and demand a concentrated thoughtfulness from the reader. Although the three novels' denouements are satisfying, the fact that Ellis does, as she says, "write short" leaves, at points, a wish for a longer novel with more room for exploring theme and character to a fuller dimension.

Humour is also a major component of Ellis's writing. "I find lots of humour delightful," she explains, "from pratfalls to highly attenuated *New Yorker* cartoons. I like dry and wet humour. I really enjoy stand-up comedy and slapstick." Characters in Ellis's novels are surrounded by a low-key comic warmth, ranging from a sense of play and silliness to subtle irony and satire. The wit is both verbal and situational. Running jokes shared in families and among friends act as a private short-hand language, defining family closeness, the affectionate play that binds relationships, as in the teasing between Jessica and her father in *The baby project.* Jess's dad's tongue-in-cheek dinner-table monologue is an example of the running family gag:

> 'Jessica, *please,*' dad's voice filtered through. 'Could you pay some attention to eating? Dinner with this family is getting to be like eating with an order of silent monks, what with Mr. Wired-for-Sound over there and a daughter who is trying to find the answer to the universe in her peas. We could have a little conversation, you know. Some families share things at dinner. Some families discuss world affairs. We could even assign a topic if nothing leaped to mind. How about gerbils? You, the youth of today, could share a fresh modern perspective on gerbils. We, the older generation, could share experiences of gerbils of the past. I, for example, could tell you about my career as a door-to-door gerbil salesman.' . . .

> 'Your mother could talk about the computer applications of gerbils and then we could share some heart-warming stories of the gerbils we had when we were first married.'

> (*The baby project* 15–16)

Parody also has a place in Ellis's broad range of humourous writing, from *The baby project*'s tenant Charlene's attempts at country-and-western song-writing which drift up the hot air register:

> 'Like two socks from the dryer
> We used to stick together,
> But you left me for another
> But you left me for another
> And I'm living cling-free

> Cling-free, cling-free,
> That's the way it's gonna be,
> Cause you left me for another
> And I'm living cling-free.'

> (*The baby project* 85)

Eccentricity of character and outrageous situations are common elements in Ellis's writing. This gives her an

opportunity, she says, to use a "sharper, more pointed wit. Charlene in *The baby project* and Ernie in *Pick-up sticks* march to different drummers. I have a low tolerance for other writers making up wacky characters for the sake of it. In my own writing I try to create major, whole-rounded characters most of the time. But at the periphery I like to find room for little cartoons."

The affectionate and sensitive portrayal of country-and-western singing Charlene and mentally-challenged Ernie, however, is quite different from the sharp satirical depiction of the Yuppie uncle's family in *Pick-up sticks.* Whereas Ellis depicts Mrs. Manning, the bigot in *Next-door neighbours,* with humanizing, insightful perception, drawing her a strapped-in lonely misery, in *Pick-up sticks,* some satirized figures come perilously close to stock characterization. Ellis addresses this: "The part about the Yuppie family got me in trouble with some critics and it was the part I enjoyed writing almost the most. I find it oppressive to be fair. It felt liberating to write about this family. I didn't want to make the uncle a deep person with a past; I just wanted to play."

In both her critical and creative writing, Ellis works toward a sensitivity that incorporates the child reader. She never forgets that children's books are read by real people. That knowledge, so obvious yet so often overlooked, lends value to her critical writing, and authenticity and appeal to her fiction. Ellis comments, "I'm pretty aware that I'm writing for children, for pubescent children. I have strong ethical feelings as a children's writer. I would never write genre fiction for children. I would be appalled. I couldn't do it. I'm very idealistic about writing well for children. But, in a sense, it's not for them. It's for me. I became a writer because I want to do something significant in the world. I didn't really become a writer for a career."

She considers her inner child as part of her characters and a critical reference point: "My child self, a girl about twelve, is still alive in me. I do reach back to her to check things out. My characters are a fictional construct of Jessica, Peggy, Polly and myself. Children's responses to my writing are surprising and touching. I like exploring their perceptions of what I have done. One girl in Quebec told me, 'When I'm reading your books I feel like I'm the person in them'. I was moved to tears. What is stimulating to me as a writer is communicating with another human being, creating the experience for the reader of feeling, 'Yes, that is what I've always thought, always felt'. If I can do that two or three times in a book, I feel I have that connection with a reader. And I figure I'll have a better chance with kids, of catching those fresh perceptions of life because children, as readers, aren't jaded or overly familiar with them."

Ellis's stories of growth and change offer both the child and adult reader engrossing experiences of complex personal epiphanies, simply and beautifully told. Each of her novels is touched by her craft as a writer and by her compassion as a human being. Ellis's writing grows stronger and richer with every book.

## TITLE COMMENTARY

📖 *THE BABY PROJECT* (1986; published in the U.S. as *A Family Project,* 1988)

### Margaret Steffler

SOURCE: A review of *The Baby Project,* in *Canadian Children's Literature,* No. 47, 1987, pp. 90–1.

Sarah Ellis's *The baby project* is remarkable for its range of tones which elicit diversity in the reader's emotional response. From humourous and critical satirical portraits to depictions of extreme grief and love, Ellis's wit and sincerity are apparent. *The baby project* deals with several contemporary family issues (perhaps too many for the young reader's assimilation) in its focus on eleven-year-old Jessica Robertson's response to the specific challenges and obstacles of her situation—a situation abruptly disrupted and complicated by the birth and death of her sister, Lucie.

Some of the subjects and issues addressed by Ellis include popular child psychology, prenatal conditioning, parents' roles, single parents, emotional illness, education, older mothers, adolescent withdrawal and crib death. Some subjects are treated seriously and thoroughly, with compassion and sympathy: for instance, emotional illness is explained in an extremely striking and sensitive manner. Others, such as crib death, are merely introduced and glossed over. The remaining issues are treated in a humorous manner, and the child's point of view casts aspersions over the adult world, which tends to take itself too seriously in attempts to direct and control experience.

Ellis is at her strongest when she uses Jessica's perspective to expose and gently satirize contemporary language, attitudes and stereotypes. Jessica's response to Mr. Blackburn's request for the use of "a variety of media" in the school project involves a mundane translation: "That meant Mr. Blackburn wanted you to go to the school library and look at filmstrips." Jessica accurately predicts Mum's weekend topics for conversation (derived from parenting articles left in the bathroom) and analyses Mum's attempts to spend "quality time" with her children, as opposed to the "equality time" offered to Jess by the tenant, Charlene.

The non-traditional roles of Jessica's parents are not simply accepted by either Jessica or Ellis, but are examined and criticized, even though the Robertsons have obviously chosen the roles most suitable to their temperaments. Ellis pokes fun at the contemporary stereotypes: Dad, who stays at home, makes egglemon soup and refuses to use canned feta cheese; and Mum, the beautiful, brilliant and athletic engineer, who cannot abide the boring task of ironing. Ellis's point is positive simply in its presentation of these non-traditional roles, but is also realistic in its acknowledgement of problems and conflicts, especially for Susan Robertson, who struggles to be both engineer and mother.

The novel's weaknesses include a rather confusing and compressed time frame, which could be clarified by specifying the length of Lucie's life. Jessica herself pales a little beside some of the more eccentric and captivating secondary characters, particularly Charlene, the dispenser of blue sea-urchin hair and black nail polish. Jessica's precocious friend, Margaret, arguably the most interesting of the characters, unfortunately fades away towards the end of the novel. Finally, *The baby project* concludes on a contrived and predictable note in the reconciliation of Jessica and Simon.

These are minor weaknesses in an unusually humourous and perceptive novel. Sarah Ellis deftly handles the eventual link between Margaret and Jessica, which is based on their shared experiences of hollowness and loss, along with their relinquishment of "that . . . happy in every part feeling." The extreme changes in Jessica's life force her to accept circumstances rather than attempt to escape or control them.

### David Gale

SOURCE: A review of *A Family Project,* in *School Library Journal,* Vol. 34, No. 7, March, 1988, pp. 188, 191.

A new baby is the Robertson *Family Project,* and this Canadian novel deals realistically with the expectations and emotions of the event. Ellis paints a sure picture of the 11-year-old protagonist, Jessica, as she happily faces the changes that her new sister brings into her life. She successfully focuses on the details of change, and in so doing creates an honest portrayal of family life. When the baby dies of crib death, Ellis is also effective in showing the family's response and gradual recovery. Certain chapters, such as the description of a theme birthday party, are hilarious. The quirky natures of Jessica's parents are unusual, and all characterizations are ably handled. It is refreshing that all members of this family really care about each other. The pacing of this book is erratic, in keeping with the priorities in the Robertsons' lives: meandering as they await the birth, hectic following the baby's death. In her telling, Ellis presents a credible depiction of important family events, in turn funny and sad.

### *Kirkus Reviews*

SOURCE: A review of *A Family Project,* in *Kirkus Reviews,* Vol. LVI, No. 5, March 1, 1988, p. 361.

When 11-year-old Jessica and her teenage brothers hear that their parents are expecting a new baby, they are delighted—Jessica even makes the baby the focus of a school project she's doing with best friend Margaret. Two-thirds of the book concerns the family's adjustments—some major, some amusing, but all undertaken with love—to Lucie's arrival. Then, suddenly, Lucie is a victim of crib death, and the family's strength is given a new test as her loss seems to divide them even as her birth had drawn them together—until, slowly, each finds a way to reach out to another and into the family reservoir of love to find the strength to go on together.

In Ellis's skillful hands, what could have been a routine problem novel becomes a powerful exploration of a warm, secure family, each humorous, believable portrait drawn beguilingly off-center, pinpointed with realism as vivid as Mahy's, but in Ellis's distinctive voice. Her choices of images and turns of phrase are delightfully unexpected, giving a sense of life rediscovered at the turn of every page; and—best of all—readers should find the book as approachable as a Cleary or a Byars.

**Betsy Hearne**

SOURCE: A review of *A Family Project,* in *Bulletin of the Center for Children's Books,* Vol. 41, No. 8, April, 1988, p. 154.

Eleven-year-old Jessica does a school project in preparation for the coming of her new baby sister, whom she and her two older brothers anticipate and welcome with enthusiasm. Jessica, in fact, has a special touch with baby Lucie, and she is shattered when Lucie is a victim of crib death. This is a story of a family—already changed by the oldest son's departure and stressed by the second son's rebellious adolescence—pulling through a crisis that traumatizes the mother to the point where she can hardly function. Although Jessica's point of view is consistently maintained, each complex character develops in a different way, which makes the novel an ambitious one. There are a few points when the mother's rigidity is perhaps overemphasized (she often talks in capital letters), and the tenant downstairs seems one character too many. In general, however, the cast is subtly portrayed, especially the rebellious brother, and there are some memorable scenes that will touch young readers with a realization of the resilience that is crucial in a loving family.

**Mary Hedge**

SOURCE: A review of *A Family Project,* in *Voice of Youth Advocates,* Vol. 11, No. 2, June, 1988, p. 85.

While at a family meeting, 11 year old Jessica, youngest member of the Canadian Robertson family, learns that her mother is going to have a baby. This news makes Jessica feel happy, sad, and scared at the same time. She tells her friend Margaret and they decide to do their class project on babies. The family's preparations for the birth and life after baby Lucie arrives in the summer have their typical ups and downs. The unexpected shock comes when Jessica's dad comes to get Jessica early from a slumber party because Lucie has died from crib death. Dealing with the death is more upsetting for the whole family than preparing for or living with the baby. Jessica's mother has trouble dealing with ordinary things and her 14 year old brother Simon, the only character who is rather stereotypical, remains sullen and obnoxious. The book ends, though, on a positive, hopeful note.

This is a realistic look at an average family dealing with a difficult problem. The shock of the sudden death is especially realistically portrayed. Fortunately, the family's grief is never overwhelming and there is frequently a bit of humor in their conversations and actions. Jessica's courageous and cooperative attitude is inspiring.

The book, the author's first, was previously published in Canada as *The Baby Project.* I highly recommend this as one of the best young adult problem novels.

## NEXT-DOOR NEIGHBOURS (1989; published in the U.S. as *Next-Door Neighbors,* 1990)

**Joan McGrath**

SOURCE: A review of *Next-Door Neighbours,* in *Quill and Quire,* Vol. 55, No. 9, September, 1989, p. 23.

Being "the new kid in town" is trying for any youngster; but for a shy minister's daughter fresh from the country, it's agonizing. Out of sheer nervousness, Peggy immediately gets off on the wrong foot with the "in" crowd at her new school. Her first real friend in Vancouver is Sing Lee, the Chinese gardener from next-door who rescues her lost cat; but this pleasant relationship causes difficulty with the vinegary old woman who is his employer. Steeped in the prejudice of an earlier and cruder day, Mrs. Manning is in the habit of referring to the refined, fully adult Sing as her "houseboy" and generally treats him with reprehensible lack of respect. She suspects the motives of anyone, including Peggy and her family, who does not both endorse and share her unpleasant attitudes and behaviour. When Sing assists Peggy with a puppet project, his participation brings about an abrupt and unjust dismissal. Through her brave though unavailing efforts to defend her friend, Peggy learns a good deal about the possibilities of rising above one's own discomfort and timidity.

The anti-racist elements of the story are mild, perhaps because it is a period-piece of sorts, set in 1956. The pickled-in-brine old lady who causes a good deal of unhappiness through her selfish bigotry is portrayed almost as an object of pity—which, after all, may be appropriate. She is also shown to suffer more through her self-imposed isolation than Sing does as a result of her closed-mindedness. The youngsters, Peggy and her fellow-puppeteer George, are lively and likable. Ellis has a deft descriptive touch, a way with a quirky phrase, and a convincing child's-eye view of hypocritical adults.

**Maggie de Vries**

SOURCE: A review of *Next-Door Neighbours,* in *Canadian Children's Literature,* Nos. 57–8, 1990, pp. 149–50.

Like Margaret Drabble's *The radiant way,* Sarah Ellis's second novel *Next-door neighbours* takes its name from a grade-school primer. And Ellis, like Drabble, has laden her title with irony.

We get to know three next-door neighbours in Ellis's book. The protagonist Peggy's open, trusting and unusual friend, George Slobodkin, is pleased to discover that he bears this title, although he lives next-door on the lane rather than the street. Sing Lee, the Chinese "houseboy," lives next door and is a genuine friend. Yet he is shut away in the basement and treated like an untrustworthy servant by Mrs. Manning, the only real next-door neighbour in the book.

Here lies the irony. For Mrs Manning is a blustering fool, a character never to be found in a children's reader or a Mr. Rogers neighbourhood. Sarah Ellis creates no stock characters and, without straying from Peggy's viewpoint, she manages to show Mrs. Manning's human side. She is lonely, pathetic and frightened and from these spring her cruelty, bigotry and lack of insight.

Peggy is new in the neighbourhood and this carries an added burden because she is excruciatingly shy. She complicates her life by telling a grand lie to a group of girls on her first day of school, thus isolating herself. School becomes torture and that leaves her family and her neighbours. Through her relationships with George, Sing and Mrs. Manning she grows enough over the summer holidays to face the girls at school in September and to put her lie behind her.

As Peggy enters back into this intense world, her friendship with George wanes. He is not lost from her life, but Ellis recognizes growth and change and places Peggy exactly where she would be at this point. Thus *Next-door neighbours* comes full circle, starting and ending with school.

Perhaps the circle is a little too perfect; we are carried a little too far into Peggy's future and are provided with several too many neatly-wrapped packages. But it is nice to see everything work out and the magic that is woven throughout the book far outweighs a slightly pat conclusion.

At the centre of *Next-door neighbours* is the puppet show which Peggy and George prepare together and which Sing and George's father make possible with their help and suggestions. The project is beautifully simple, but fraught with the obstacles that children would face under the circumstances. And it radiates consequences: great, terrible and inescapable.

Adult readers may find a note of nostalgia in this book, for it is set in 1956. It is not quite clear why Ellis has chosen the '50's instead of the '80's, but perhaps this is not an important question to answer since the year will not come between a child and the story.

*Next-door neighbours* is a gripping, powerfully-written novel fit to join Sarah Ellis's award-winning *The baby project* on the shelf; fit also to stand side by side with its titular companion, *The radiant way.*

## Barbara Elleman

SOURCE: A review of *Next-Door Neighbors,* in *Booklist,* Vol. 86, No. 13, March 1, 1990, p. 1340.

With great trepidation, Peggy faces a new school after her minister father takes a church in western Canada. Overanxious and scared, Peggy blows a chance for friendship: she inexplicably tells her classmates that she has a horse. When the lie is discovered, Peggy is icily ignored. To fill her loneliness, she reluctantly agrees to participate in a puppet-show competition with George (the immigrant son of the church's caretaker), though at first she thinks he is a pain. After a disastrous attempt to make puppets on their own, the two find a mentor in Sing Lee, the Chinese gardener and houseman of Mrs. Manning, a wealthy next-door neighbour, who, they discover, treats the man abominably. When Sing comes to their show, where Peggy and George win a much-deserved first prize, Mrs. Manning fires him. Only months later does Peggy find out what has happened to their gentle, kind friend. In this story about the many kinds and layers of friendship, Ellis, author of *A Family Project,* subtly examines the ways prejudice, feelings, and responsibility for one's actions affect making and losing friends. She etches personalities that are likable amid their strengths and weaknesses and creates family dynamics that fit smoothly and believably into the plot; the well-rounded, realistic portrayal of a minister is highly welcome in a field where clergy are often badly portrayed. For children, undoubtedly, the biggest draw will be Peggy and George and their interactions. Ellis writes with a firm hand—ever in touch with her theme her characters, her plot, and her audience.

## *Kirkus Reviews*

SOURCE: A review of *Next-Door Neighbors,* in *Kirkus Reviews,* Vol. LXVIII, No. 6, March 15, 1990, pp. 422–23.

Ellis' marvelous debut (*A Family Project,* 1988) would be hard to match, but its admirers should be happy with this cleanly written, perceptive second novel.

It's 1957; Peggy (12) and her family have just moved to Vancouver. Painfully shy, Peggy gets off on the wrong foot with the girls at school when she's caught in an uncharacteristic, boasting lie. She does make two friends: the aging Chinese "houseboy," Sing, of the haughty old woman next door; and George Slobodkin, 11, son of a Russian émigré who is caretaker of her father's new church. When Peggy and George enter a summer puppet contest, Mr. Slobodkin provides a Russian folk tale, and Sing helps by suggesting shadow puppets and critiquing their show. But when Sing attends the performance without his employer's permission, the lady reveals the extent of her tyranny and prejudice: Sing is fired, and the kids are left to learn just how callous his treatment has been.

Wonderfully individual characters are created here, as in the earlier story, by an accumulation of unique, revealing detail: the overearnest hat George insists on wearing even though it makes him the bullies' target; the hilarious homemade insults with which Peggy's family defuses animosity ("Cranky old sump pump"). A wealth of memorable scenes—poignant, suspenseful, funny—make every page a pleasure. Another warm, thought-provoking story from a fine author.

**Nancy Vasilakis**

SOURCE: A review of *Next-Door Neighbors,* in *The Horn Book Magazine,* Vol. LXVI, No. 3, May-June, 1990, p. 334.

In this quiet, satisfying story set in Canada in 1957, an unusual friendship among three social outcasts is played out. A clergyman's daughter, Peggy moves with her family to a large city parish where she starts off on the wrong foot at school by bragging about the nonexistent horse she used to own. The lie is almost immediately discovered, and for the rest of the school year she is shunned by the girls in her class. Shy Peggy, ostracized because of her one big lie, is forced into a grudging alliance with George Slobodkin, the immigrant boy-next-door who wears weird "little man" clothes and is teased by the other boys because of his grating adherence to the truth at all costs. This tenuous duo is counseled by Sing, the kind and lonely Chinese gardener who resides in the basement of the other house next door to Peggy's own. The story is told from Peggy's point of view; through her, the reader is drawn into the lives of these three as they combine forces to put on a puppet play. Out of this creative exercise and the friendship that it nurtures, each of the participants gains newfound strengths. Sing leaves his prejudiced employer, who had treated him shabbily for years, and George stands up to the local bullies. Peggy gradually overcomes much of her shyness as she learns that no one is immune to failure and self-doubts. Her discovery at summer's end that her worst tormentor at school has problems at home is not as surprising as it might have seemed earlier. This carefully constructed story with excellent characterizations and a plot that isn't flashy but moves along quickly never wavers from its child-centered perspective.

## 📖 *PUTTING UP WITH MITCHELL: MY VANCOUVER SCRAPBOOK* (1989)

**Joan McGrath**

SOURCE: A review of *Putting up with Mitchell: My Vancouver Scrapbook,* in *Emergency Librarian,* Vol. 18, No. 2, November-December, 1990, pp. 60–1.

Elizabeth and her little brother Mitchell are visiting Granny in Vancouver. *Putting up with Mitchell* or *My Vancouver scrapbook,* is Elizabeth's version of the trip, of the visits to the Aquarium, the Art Gallery, Chinatown, etc., and of what a nuisance it is to have a brother. Some of Granny's stories about Daddy when he was

a little boy teasing his sister, prove that Mitchell is a chip off the old block. This dramatically illustrated, brightly tongue-in-cheek account of a wonderful family holiday might just possibly inspire some record-keeping among its readers. Maybe Mitchell should keep a diary next time.

*Kirkus Reviews*

SOURCE: A review of *Putting up with Mitchell: My Vancouver Scrapbook,* in *Canadian Children's Literature,* No. 61, 1991, p. 107.

In *Putting up with Mitchell,* Brighouse Press has produced the perfect souvenir of a family trip to Vancouver—a mock scrapbook of a young girl's visit with her Granny. In it, Elizabeth makes note of her impressions of all the sights they visit, and of the antics of her exasperating four-year-old brother Mitchell. Author Sarah Ellis adroitly avoids the pitfall of the geography textbook approach ("Billy and Suzy Visit Tokyo") by getting the voice of the big sister just right: "Mitchell bought a box of Cracker Jack, and the prize was a kazoo. He kazoo'd all day. People looked at us. . . . I wonder what it would be like to be an only child." Granny, a robust, energetic woman who has no trouble keeping up with her two grandchildren, is drawn without any tinge of liberal condescension to old people.

## 📖 *PICK-UP STICKS* (1991)

**Barbara L. Michasiw**

SOURCE: A review of *Pick Up Sticks,* in *Quill and Quire,* Vol. 57, No. 11, November, 1991, p. 25.

*Pick Up Sticks* is an easy read. The pages seem almost to turn themselves as 13-year-old Polly learns the difference between price and value. Topical buttons are there to be pushed: the mother single by choice; the fruitless search for affordable housing; the acquisitive yuppies; the bored, destructive teens; the mentally handicapped friend who finds a contributing role; and many more. To these are added the more universal experiences of rebellion against parental values, broken friendship, and fear for one's personal safety.

Polly and her mother have two months to find a new home when the house they share with Mrs. Protheroe and her mentally handicapped son, Ernie, is sold to a developer. Their only prospects, a sterile high-rise where the manager is rent-gouging, a squalid basement conversion, and accommodation with janitorial duties in an illegally-restricted apartment building, are rejected by Polly's mother. She, unlike Polly, regards her factory studio as an emergency alternative until they can find the right home. When Polly's increasing anxiety explodes in anger, she blames her mother and her idealistic values for their homelessness and she fantasizes about rescue by her unknown father.

It takes six weeks as a guest of her financially successful aunt and uncle, alienation from her best friend Vanessa, abandonment at night in a warehouse area by her cousin, and escape from a slowly pursuing car to bring Polly to the haven of her mother's studio and the security of a renewed, more appreciative relationship with her mother.

The characters, other than Polly, remain stereotypes and even Polly's individuality is only partially realized. Consequently, the novel leaves the impression that the many genuine concerns it raises have significance only for their trendiness rather than for the reality they reflect.

## Lissa Paul

SOURCE: A review of *Pick-Up Sticks,* in *Canadian Children's Literature,* No. 67, 1992, pp. 87–9.

*Pick-up sticks,* the third novel by Vancouver author Sarah Ellis, is an important book. It won a 1991 Governor General's award, a tangible sign of the status she deserves. Besides being a novelist, Sarah Ellis is a librarian and critic. She knows books. I've always admired her critical capacity to state clearly the issues at the heart of any text she discusses, and then be generous in her assessment. A lovely habit in a reader, one I try to emulate in my reading of her work.

Sarah Ellis conveys the details of contemporary urban life with anthropological precision. She is brilliant at making us focus on the bits and tatters of landscape that usually float invisibly by. When we look with Polly, the thirteen-year-old heroine of *Pick-up sticks,* at the ads for "Advanced Rolfing" and "Vivation Therapy (Formerly Integrative Rebirthing)" on the notice board of the library where she works part-time, we see the bizarreness of the signs we usually ignore. Ellis also makes us focus on the faces we otherwise tend to shun, or on the faces of adolescence we'd rather forget or not acknowledge. There is Polly's neighbour Ernie, a developmentally handicapped man who joyfully participates as he watches reruns of "The Beverly Hillbillies." There is the old lady with the tea cosy hat who belongs to the co-op crowd.

And there is Polly's friend, Vanessa, who has a crush on her high-school English teacher. Vanessa wears a purple ski mask as a disguise on the day she spends gazing at his house. Here, Ellis's use of the purple ski mask deftly transforms the common episode of the adolescent crush into something that reveals its simultaneously comic and embarrassing qualities. But this is where I run into problems with the book. The image overbalances.

Polly makes an art project mask out of faces cut from magazines. The mask becomes a weighty Symbol of False Faced Bourgeois Society. It becomes a reflection of the morality Polly learns to reject in the characters of: her uncle Roger, a businessman of the camel-hair coat and cellular car-phone variety who lives in a house lifted from the pages of *Better Homes and Gardens;* his suitably decorative wife, Barbie (I'm tempted to add the "doll"); and worst of all, his daughter Stephanie, The Bored Teenager, a member of an increasingly common urban phenomenon, The Middle Class Gang who steal from the poor and prey on the downtrodden.

Polly chooses to stay with Roger and his family for a time (while her mother tries to find an apartment for them she can afford on her earnings as a stained-glass artist) and taste some of the physical comfort and convenience money can buy. But Polly only realizes money can't buy happiness when a nightmare ride with her cousin Stephanie and her terrorist gang drives the lesson home.

What worries me is the way *Pick-up sticks* divides on binary lines. Is it better to live in a messy apartment with spaghetti sauce "slowly blipping, decorating the wall with a fine red spray," than in a big house with a "clean and tidy kitchen, eating microwave heat-in-a-bag cannelloni"? Although the plot of *Pick-up sticks* does not turn only on dinner, the distinctions between cheap, messy spaghetti sauce and upmarket clean cannelloni tend towards the oppositional forms of structuralist anthropology.

What I long for in *Pick-up sticks* is the kind of barometric sensitivity to childhood friendship Ellis demonstrates in *Neighbours,* her second novel. There the struggle between wanting to be part of the in-crowd and wanting to be kind is played out more delicately. Maybe what I really long for is Sarah Ellis's next novel, so I can find her anthropological precision threaded with her apprehension of the subtleties of human relationships.

## Hazel Rochman

SOURCE: A review of *Pick-Up Sticks,* in *Booklist,* Vol. 88, No. 10, January 15, 1992, p. 931.

"Why did you choose to be a mother if you can't do it right?" 13-year-old Polly yells at her single-parent artist mother. All of Polly's embarrassment and anxiety about their unconventional life-style erupts when their old rental apartment house is sold to developers, and they can't find a place they can afford. However, a few weeks spent with her rich relatives in their home humming with appliances and tension send Polly back to the shabby muddle of her mother's studio. Not that Canadian writer Ellis indulges in heavy, simplistic messages. She does weight things against the conservatives, exposing their bigotry while mocking their affectation (Polly's aunt has a PFC, a personal fitness consultant, who keeps her "strong, stretched, and centered"). But Ellis also mocks the mother's socially conscious co-op ("Inspirational posters masking-taped to the mustard walls advised sharing and caring"). The character of Polly's middle-aged neighbor Emie, who can't read but loves to memorize postal codes and TV theme songs, is drawn with humor and compassion. There's a forced attempt at a "story," as Polly's spoiled cousin takes her on a vandalism spree, but what will grab kids is the sharp and affectionate view of the way we live now.

## Barbara Hutcheson

SOURCE: A review of *Pick-Up Sticks,* in *School Library Journal,* Vol. 38, No. 3, March, 1992, p. 237.

A short but satisfying novel about a girl's coming to terms with her unconventional mother. Polly is unsettled to learn that she and her single mother must move from the house they've lived in for all of her 13 years. Her concern mounts as her mother is unable to find an affordable apartment, and unwilling to accept a position managing a building that doesn't rent to nonwhites. In a panic, Polly accepts her affluent uncle's invitation to move in with his family, only to find that while they are materially better off, their lives are lacking in the things that really matter. She discovers that as in the child's game of pick-up sticks, every element in life touches every other and cannot be disturbed without affecting the whole. Ellis has filled her story with a wealth of well-drawn characters, believable situations, and neatly balanced tension and humor, all against an economical but vividly painted backdrop.

## Ellen Fader

SOURCE: A review of *Pick-Up Sticks,* in *The Horn Book Magazine,* Vol. LXVIII, No. 2, March-April, 1992, pp. 208–9.

Thirteen-year-old Polly hates change, yet it seems inevitable when she discovers that their landlady has sold the house in which she and her mother live; they now have two months in which to find another affordable apartment. Polly's mother, a rather unconventional soul who chose to have a child without being married, pursues some hilarious as well as depressing leads for housing. Polly is unable to withstand either the anxiety of the situation or her anger about her mother's precarious artist life-style and decides to live temporarily with her mother's well-off brother and his family. Their emotionally sterile home life—Ellis calls their house crowded and empty—provides an effective counterpoint to the warmth and love of Polly's life with her mother. A traumatic, disastrous incident with her selfish, shoplifting cousin and her friends brings Polly back to her real home. Readers will rejoice in Polly's heartwarming reconciliation with her mother and will feel reassured that the changes in Polly's future will be that much easier because of their love for each other. A splendid cast of supporting characters adds interest and humor. Ellis's writing is lean and child-centered; her insights are perceptive and have an unmistakable ring of honesty. Another gem from the author of the excellent *Family Project* and *Next-Door Neighbors.*

## OUT OF THE BLUE (1994)

## Janet McNaughton

SOURCE: A review of *Out of the Blue,* in *Quill and Quire,* Vol. 60, No. 11, November, 1994, p. 36.

On the cusp of her 12th birthday, Megan Hungerford's life is clam and happy. Her mother has returned to school and her father, a freelance writer, reads Sherlock Holmes aloud every evening. Megan even gets along with her lively young sister, Betsy. Tolstoy was wrong: happy families are *not* all alike. Sarah Ellis's talent lies in part in her ability to show how a happy family deals with difficulty, whether that family consists of a single mother and child as in her 1991 Governor General's Award-winning *Pick-Up Sticks,* or of the more conventional two parents and two children we find here.

In *Out of the Blue,* this typical family is suddenly transformed by the arrival of a new member. Not a baby, but a 24-year-old doctoral candidate in astronomy named Natalie. Megan's mother, pregnant when she was 17, gave Natalie up for adoption at birth. Betsy is enthusiastic about the unexpected existence of an older half-sister, but Megan isn't. It doesn't help that her mother is completely enthralled with her new-found daughter. Determined to show that she is mature enough to handle the situation, Megan holds her feelings in. Gradually, as she becomes accustomed to Natalie, she begins to reconcile herself to the presence of someone new in her family. Megan remains distanced from her mother, however, until a misunderstanding causes her to blurt out her anger.

The plot of *Out of the Blue* is fairly mundane and not particularly fast in its pacing. It is a tribute, then, to Ellis's skill as a writer that this book is so hard to put down. The characters and their relationships are vivid, fully realized, and difficult to forget. The only false note is in the characterization of Megan's mother. Even her preoccupation with her new-found child does not explain how she could be oblivious to Megan's angst for so long, especially as she is not a selfish or uncaring person. This small criticism aside, *Out of the Blue* delivers to Sarah Ellis fans the superior quality they have come to expect from her.

## Julie Cummins

SOURCE: A review of *Out of the Blue,* in *School Library Journal,* Vol. 41, No. 5, May, 1995, p. 106.

The shock not only comes out of the blue, but it also casts a blue haze over 12-year-old Megan's perfect life. When her mother announces that she has rediscovered the child she had at 17 and gave up for adoption, everyone but Megan seems thrilled. When Natalie, now a 24-year-old Ph.D student in astronomy, invites the family to be part of her wedding, Mom becomes crazed with catering plans, 5-year-old sister Betsy is excited at being a flower girl, and Dad is supportive. Megan struggles with her emotions, searching for a "sense of family and self" at their island cottage, which is filled with generations of memories and serves as a reflective backdrop. When she finds a Japanese fishing float, it becomes a symbol for her confused state and a resolution for her feelings. Finely crafted characterizations convey Megan's resentment, Betsy's precociousness, and Mom's preoccupation with melding present and past. Experience and emotion are interwoven in poignant descriptions like "she stayed inside herself like peanut butter in a jar." Another portrayal of a contemporary family forced to refocus, written by an author who is in touch with real life and relationships.

## Stephanie Zvirin

SOURCE: A review of *Out of the Blue,* in *Booklist,* Vol. 91, No. 17, May 1, 1995, pp. 1572–3.

When 12-year-old Megan's mother suddenly takes off her "let's-get-things-organized coat" and becomes "this soft, slow person" who sings soppy songs, Megan knows something's up. And indeed it is. It seems Mum has made contact with the daughter she gave up for adoption many years ago, meaning Megan has a 24-year-old half-sister—a surprise that challenges Megan's trust in grownups and shakes up her childhood world. Ellis's handling of the family dynamics is quiet and sure, and her characters (with the exception of sentimental Mum) are fresh, appealing—and imperfect. It's no real surprise that Megan decides to accept Natalie. What is unusual is Megan's motivation for doing so. Her decision isn't rooted in sisterly affection; rather, it stems from Megan's understanding of how Natalie must have felt growing up and Megan's sudden discovery that Natalie is the sort of interesting person it's always nice to know. No angst-filled drama here; instead, readers get a solid, credible adjustment story.

## Maeve Visser Knoth

SOURCE: A review of *Out of the Blue,* in *The Horn Book Magazine,* Vol. LXXI, No. 4, July-August, 1995, pp. 456–57.

As Megan's twelfth birthday approaches, she attributes her mother's strange, secretive behavior to a hoped-for surprise present. Instead, her secure world is turned upside-down. Megan learns that as a young woman her mother gave birth to a baby girl and gave her up for adoption. Now, twenty-four years later, that child, Natalie, has sought out her birth mother. Megan's mother, with the encouragement of her husband, begins to forge a relationship with her oldest daughter, and Megan and her younger sister, Betsy, must adjust to this new situation. Betsy accepts Natalie immediately, but Megan can not reconcile herself to knowing that she may no longer be first in her mother's affections, and she worries that there are other lies and secrets awaiting her. Gradually, Megan moves beyond her enormous hurt and defensive dislike of Natalie to a tentative acceptance. She overhears one day her mother describing her daughter's "know-it-all stage" and is furious until she discovers that her mother was talking about Natalie, not Megan. During a subsequent conversation, Megan discovers that it has also been difficult for her mother to get used to the changes brought about by Natalie's existence. With renewed security in her place in the family and her importance to her parents, Megan is able to make room for Natalie in her life. Sarah Ellis writes, as usual, with grace and empathy. *Out of the Blue* is a sensitive and rich family story in which very real troubles are tempered with humor and love.

---

Additional coverage of Ellis's life and career is contained in the following sources published by Gale Research: *Contemporary Authors New Revision Series,* Vol. 50, and *Something about the Author,* Vol. 68.

# Nikki Grimes

## 1950-

African-American author of poetry, fiction, and nonfiction.

Major works include *Growin'* (1977), *Something on My Mind* (1978), *Malcolm X: A Force for Change* (1992), *From a Child's Heart* (1993), *Meet Danitra Brown* (1994).

## INTRODUCTION

A distinguished black author who writes for children and young adults, Grimes is best known for her works of poetry and fiction that feature young African-American characters with whom readers can identify. She is also credited with writing an objective and well-researched biography of Malcolm X and a fictionalized biography of Mary, the mother of Jesus Christ. Drawing upon scenes from her own childhood, Grimes is noted for successfully conveying the black experience and universal themes such as friendship, tolerance, family and community relationships, and children surviving adolescence. Although Grimes was criticized for her lack of character development in her earlier books, in later works she is often praised for her sensitive and warm treatment of characters, her poignant text, and her upbeat poetry. Committed to writing for children, the author once remarked that "the responsibility for creating quality literature and learning materials for black children rests with the black writer. I, for one, have accepted that responsibility and, while I do not write for children alone, I write for children first."

### Biographical Information

The daughter of a violinist and composer, Grimes was born in New York City in 1950. She began writing when she was about six years old, and by the time she was a teenager, Grimes decided she would become a professional writer. While attending Rutgers University, Grimes worked as a talent coordinator for Blackafrica Productions and then as an English instructor from 1971 to 1974. Graduating from Rutgers with a Bachelor of Arts degree in English in 1974, Grimes stayed on at the school as a researcher until 1975. An avid student of languages, Grimes has been a freelance writer and photographer since 1975. Many of her childhood experiences and emotions are found in a number of her works, including *From a Child's Heart, Something on My Mind,* and *C is for City* (1994). "In general, my fiction is autobiographical," the author revealed. "My life and travels have been difficult, but, in surmounting those difficulties, I have learned much that I wish to share. There's no better way to do that than through my work." In addition to her books, the author

frequently contributes poetry and fiction to adult collections and periodicals.

### Major Works

Grimes's first novel, *Growin',* features Yolanda (nicknamed Pump), an African-American fifth grader who likes to write poetry. Still adjusting to her father's death and a move to a new neighborhood, Pump gets into trouble at school and at home. Eventually she, along with other characters in the story, learns to be more tolerant. Critics credited Grimes for her writing style and warm story but felt the characters required more depth and emotion. In her first book of poetry for children, *Something on My Mind,* Grimes included a series of prose poems that reflect the black experience as well as various childhood emotions such as fear, joy, yearning, and concern. The book received a Coretta Scott King award for its striking illustrations by Tom Feelings.

In *Malcolm X: A Force for Change,* Grimes examines the life, contributions, and aspirations of the famous Black Muslim leader who was assassinated in 1965. Grimes's comprehensive research did not escape critic Jeannette Lambert, who complimented the author on the number of details included in the work. Her next book, *From a Child's Heart,* is comprised of thirteen sentimental poems, written as prayers to God, which reveal the hopes and needs of young African-American children. Written in an "authentic" childlike voice, Grimes admits in her introduction that she extracted prayers and memories from her own childhood to share with her audience. Most critics enjoyed the sentimentality and deeply felt text in addition to the sensitive and realistic artwork by Brenda Joysmith. *Meet Danitra Brown,* another collection of thirteen poems, features narrator Zuri Jackson talking about herself and her admiration for her good friend Danitra Brown. Again, critics were delighted with the simple narrative poems that blend so well with the artwork by illustrator Floyd Cooper.

## Awards

Grimes received a Ford Foundation grant for Africa in 1974-75. *Something on My Mind,* illustrated by Tom Feelings, received a Coretta Scott King special illustration award in 1979.

---

# TITLE COMMENTARY

## 📖 *GROWIN'* (1977)

### Publishers Weekly

SOURCE: A review of *Growin',* in *Publishers Weekly,* Vol. 212, No. 20, November 14, 1977, p. 67.

Grimes, a distinguished black poet, presents her first novel, an interesting and heartening story if not an altogether successful one. Pumpkin's father dies and her grief is magnified when she and her mother have to move. She misses her best friend and the support her father had given her, as she tried to write poems dismissed as mumbo-jumbo by her mother. In a new school, Pumpkin is at first the target of bullying Jim Jim. But the two become good friends, sharing their artistic aspirations. They also get into trouble, which deepens their resentments of unsympathetic adults and classmates. Eventually, dangerous adventures (too many) bring all involved into a climate of mutual tolerance. It may seem strange that a girl like Pumpkin, with literary yearnings, refuses to learn good English.

### Jack Forman

SOURCE: A review of *Growin',* in *School Library Journal,* Vol. 24, No. 4, December, 1977, p. 49.

There's too little substance and spirit in this short novel about the friendship between two Black elementary school classmates—Jim-Jim, a bully who is soft and kind deep down and dreamy narrator Yolanda (nicknamed "Pump") who likes to write poetry. Pump and Jim-Jim play hookey together and get caught in a school fire because they disobey a drill, but the effect of these mishaps on them goes unexplained. Many other potentially interesting scenes lack any development: Pump's reaction to the accidental death of her father, to whom she was very close, is passed over in two paragraphs. In addition, Grimes does not sufficiently flesh out her characters—Jim-Jim never really comes across as a terror, for example, though she is a bit more successful in describing obsessive writer Pump's rapprochement with her mother when she finds poetry the older woman had once written. Packaged in a colorful and attractive cover, the novel promises much more than it delivers.

### Kirkus Reviews

SOURCE: A review of *Growin',* in *Kirkus Reviews,* Vol. XLV, No. 23, December, 1977, p. 1266.

The black ghetto setting and conspicuously non-sexist relationship gives some utilitarian points, where such are counted, to this undemanding story of the friendship between Pump, who moves to a new neighborhood when her father is killed in an accident, and Jim Jim, the tough kid she stands up to on arrival. There's a period of "testing" (so described) and then real trust, when Pump shares her poetry with him and Jim Jim, whose toughness is merely a good defense, reveals his devotion to drawing. And there is adventure a-plenty—in an abandoned building, a river with a tricky current, and a burning school from which the neighborhood shady lady rescues them . . . to the chastened gratitude of previously head-wagging parents. This last leads to a sentimental full-cast finale; till then Grimes keeps it light and easy, but *Growin'* would have to do a lot of stretching before any real feelings were tapped.

### Zena Sutherland

SOURCE: A review of *Growin',* in *Bulletin of the Center for Children's Books,* Vol. 31, No. 8, April, 1978, p. 127.

"Mama can't stand me, and you know it! Nothin' I do ever pleases her," Pumpkin (Yolanda) had said, and her gentle, loving father had assured Pump that Mama loved her just as much as he did. Then Daddy was killed in a car accident, and Pump had to live with Mama's scolding and, when they moved, go to a new school. Although Pump's relationship with her mother is the binding factor in this story, it's chiefly an episodic account of a black girl's childhood, her friendship with Jim Jim, and the growing sensitivity and understanding that burgeon in preadolescence. The writing style is competent, the story has warmth, but the characters, although believable, have little depth.

## SOMETHING ON MY MIND (1978)

### Publishers Weekly

SOURCE: A review of *Something On My Mind,* in *Publishers Weekly,* Vol. 213, No. 22, May 29, 1978, p. 51.

Tom Feelings's sensitive drawings of black children intensify the moods expressed in the prose poems by Grimes. The artist and the lyricist couldn't reveal the thoughts of the boys and girls portrayed here more acutely if they were inside their subjects' skins. A teenaged boy sits on the steps of his city apartment home and thinks about what his daddy says, that growing up is mostly waiting. A desolate little girl wishes that "she" wouldn't always send her out to play instead of talking to her. Frankie Lee and friends make believe they'll find a place where they can be just at home and not have "to feel worse than white people." The book can make you ache but it can help you understand, as well, something important. Too many among us are starving for what most Americans take for granted.

### Booklist

SOURCE: A review of *Something On My Mind,* in *Booklist,* Vol. 74, No. 22, July 15, 1978, pp. 1732–33.

Melancholy flows through this series of prose poems that light on childhood's moodier dreams and wishes: "Waiting / for summer to end. / I've used up all the fun. / I wish school would start again / so there would be something to do." These and other blue or bitter thoughts— "She sent me out to play again. . . . One day I'll be too big to send out to play. / What will she do then?"—are set off by [Tom] Feelings' skeletal drawings and sepia watercolor paintings. The pages are striking—good paper, spacious design—and there's pleasure in admiring his acuity with simple line and his strong sense of composition. However, such striking sketchbook art doesn't breathe needed life into the language, which lacks music and the surprise of memorable insight; while the drawing is spare, the poems are somewhat flat. It's really the artwork that centers the book here, accompanied by a surrounding textual conversation.

### Kirkus Reviews

SOURCE: A review of *Something On My Mind,* in *Kirkus Reviews,* Vol. XLVI, No. 14, July 15, 1978, p. 747.

Grimes' short, eminently accessible poems about everyday feelings and everyday activities (hanging out, being cool, waiting) never strain for effect, but they never say anything out of the ordinary either; and her sympathetic approach is sometimes just sentimental. One poem ends, "The only thing that's better/ is Mama's kiss and hug"; and another whole poem reads, "Pretty./ That's what Daddy says I am/ whenever he comes/ to get me./ I love him and I'm glad/ he's gonna come today./

Oh, I wish he'd hurry up!" [Tom] Feelings' soft black-and-white illustrations provide pleasing, sensitive accompaniment. . . .

### Ruth M. McConnell

SOURCE: A review of *Something On My Mind,* in *School Library Journal,* Vol. 25, No. 1, September, 1978, p. 137.

Free verse by a young poet puts words to a series of sketches and portrait studies of Black American youngsters by a noted illustrator. The imagined thoughts reflect the Black experience but also convey the universal marking-time, growing pains, and perplexities of youth in poignant, funny, and sad ways. A child remembers her grandmother sitting on the porch; a young teen ponders the practical use of schooling; three little children at a gate, "Talking make-believe," say where they'd like to travel; and boys hanging out at the ball park wish "one of them was good enough/ to be a star one day" so "that he could come back/ and shine for us." A few of the sketches [by Tom Feelings] were in the artist's autobiographical *Black Pilgrimage* but here take on new life in these handsome reproductions in black-and-white on rich cream-colored paper. The bouquet of faces on the cover, reminiscent of Symeon Shimin's work, sets a tone of sensitive realism that is maintained throughout.

### Zena Sutherland

SOURCE: A review of *Something On My Mind,* in *Bulletin of the Center for Children's Books,* Vol. 32, No. 2, October, 1978, p. 30.

As the book's jacket makes clear, the black and white drawings of black children by [Tom] Feelings were used by Grimes as bases for prose poems that interpret the pictures. The drawings are sensitive portraits, some beautifully shaded and soft, others looking like deft, unfinished sketches. The poems vary in depth and treatment, some fragmentary and others imbued with poignant emotion; all are serious, some reflecting the black experience and others—most of the selections—capturing universal longings or reactions of childhood.

## FROM A CHILD'S HEART (1993)

### Kirkus Reviews

SOURCE: A review of *From a Child's Heart,* in *Kirkus Reviews,* Vol. LXI, No. 20, October 15, 1993, p. 1329.

Thirteen subtly cadenced, accessible poems in an authentically childlike voice: messages confided to God as to a trusted friend. Each reveals a telling hope, ambition ("I want to be/a credit to the human race"; or, "I don't want to get the chance/just 'cause the color of my skin keeps me from fitting in . . . Give me the hardest step, I'll learn it./Make me number one, Lord. I'll earn it"), internal debate ("I need a miracle . . . I should study . . . ? . . . Then You'll help me remember what I've learned?/ Well that sounds fair"), fear, plea ("Lord,/Please give my Grandma one more year . . . she's been my mom and dad as far back as memory goes/and she knows the ins and outs of being free inside"), or joy. The implicit advice is frequently bracing, but gracefully delivered and never overbearing. [Brenda] Joysmith's sensitive, realistic pastel drawings of pensive young African-Americans at work and play are beautifully composed and quietly luminous; now in various private collections, they date from 1984 to 1992. A lovely, deeply felt book.

## Publishers Weekly

SOURCE: A review of *From a Child's Heart,* in *Publishers Weekly,* Vol. 240, No. 42, October 18, 1993, p. 73.

With an emphasis on upbeat family relationships, the 13 poems in this collection call to mind the easy sentimentality evoked by Norman Rockwell paintings. According to the note at the beginning of the volume, Grimes wishes to "share" the "prayers of [her] childhood" when she "talked to God about [her] hopes, [her] fears, [her] longings, and all the ordinary, everyday concerns that touched [her] life." Unfortunately, many of the poems are so coy and precious, and so adult in perspective, that the "prayers" often seem more like sermons directed at a young African American audience rather than offerings "straight from the heart" of a child, as the poet claims. "I'm little now," says the child in the opening poem, but "I believe I want to be / a credit to the human race." A child who has a book report due and a math test asks for "a miracle from [God]" but then says, "Say what? / I should study for the test? / Read the book? Do my best?" A young dancer asks God to be chosen for a solo "'cause I'm good," and not "just 'cause the color of my skin keeps me from fitting in." More successful than the poems, [Brenda] Joysmith's soft-toned pastels of children and their families offer positive portraits of friends and families.

## Meg Stackpole

SOURCE: A review of *From a Child's Heart,* in *School Library Journal,* Vol. 39, No. 12, December, 1993, p. 104.

Grimes has composed prayerful verses to give voice to the subjects in pastel drawings (done between 1985–1992) by the African-American artist Brenda Joysmith, who paints a pretty world of healthy and well-groomed children. Youngsters are shown nestled close to their parents, bending their heads together with playmates, and lost in contemplation or daydreaming. Grimes's prayers, on the other hand, express yearning (in direct dialogues with God) for more time with a single mother, any friend in a new neighborhood, work for a laid-off father, parents who do not fight, or a longer life for a grandmother. The situations are common enough, but here their poetic voices

seem false and not well matched to the art. An earnest religious sensibility pervades. *There Was a Place* by Myra Cohn Livingston does a better job of evoking the feelings of children in painful family situations, while *And God Bless Me,* selected by Lee Bennett Hopkins, offers poems of gratitude. Walter Dean Myers's *Brown Angels,* Ashley Bryan's *Sing to the Sun,* Eloise Greenfield's *Honey, I Love,* and Grimes's own **Something On My Mind** are all full of vibrant, truthful, and accessible poems about the experiences of African Americans and all young people.

## Betsy Hearne

SOURCE: A review of *From a Child's Heart,* in *Bulletin of the Center for Children's Books,* Vol. 47, No. 6, February, 1994, p. 188.

"Sis always says/ 'If you're gonna do something, do it right.'/ So when I do my homework every night,/ I draw my letters straight and neat in my notebook./ I know the teacher may not take the time to look,/ but Sis says do it anyway, even if nobody else can see—/ except You, Lord, and me." That's the tone and tenor of these thirteen poems reflecting inner conversations between African-American children and the God whom they variously confide in and petition. There's a modicum of rhyme, a conscious if informal sense of innocence, and more than a little sentimentality, which is echoed in the soft, idealized pastels that face each page of verse. The pictures [by Brenda Joysmith] are well drawn, with a kind of Norman Rockwell nostalgia that will please fans of the poetic messages packaged here.

## 📖 MALCOLM X: A FORCE FOR CHANGE (1992)

## Publishers Weekly

SOURCE: A review of *Malcolm X: A Force for Change,* in *Publishers Weekly,* Vol. 240, No. 1, January 4, 1993, p. 74.

Grimes's distinctly partisan account of the African American leader conveys his remarkable drive but fails to mediate the controversies surrounding him. Whether discussing the tragedies that shaped Malcolm's childhood, the criminal activities of his youth, his affiliation with the Nation of Islam or his eventual rejection of separatism, Grimes rarely provides enough of either a historical or social context to help the reader assimilate disturbing information. For example, the Nation of Islam's teachings (among them, that whites comprise a "devil race") are presented without interpretation. Evidence of her own biases may escape her audience's notice, but she clearly conveys her passion for her subject and thereby recreates some of the excitement surrounding Malcolm. For a more objective treatment with greater historical perspective, see Walter Dean Myers's *Malcolm X: By Any Means Necessary.*

## Sherri Forgash Ginsberg

SOURCE: A review of *Malcolm X: A Force for Change,* in *Kliatt Young Adult Paperback Book Guide,* Vol. 27, No. 3, May, 1993, p. 23.

Malcolm X was assassinated in 1965 but his remarkable influence and work is alive 28 years later. Malcolm Little grew up in abject poverty in Lansing, Michigan. His father died under mysterious, sinister circumstances and his mother was left to care for eight children. Mrs. Louis Little at times resorted to boiling dandelions in order to feed her family. She was humiliated and demoralized by the social welfare system designed to aid her family. Ultimately she succumbed to mental illness and was institutionalized while her children were sent to different locations. Malcolm was placed in a comfortable family environment and established himself as a smart and popular student. However, when a teacher told him he could not become a lawyer because he was black, Malcolm became restless and unruly. He took off for Boston to live with his sister and eventually resorted to crime and landed in prison. In jail he discovered the Muslim religion which dramatically changed his life.

This is a terrific book to acquaint the younger readers who are unwilling or unable to tackle *The Autobiography of Malcolm X.* Malcolm's work empowered African Americans and changed their lives as well as white Americans.

## Jeanette Lambert

SOURCE: A review of *Malcolm X: A Force for Change,* in *School Library Journal,* Vol. 39, No. 8, August, 1993, p. 196.

An incisive look at the life and accomplishments of Malcolm X. The author obviously has been diligent in her research, apparent in the number of details she provides. The evolution of Malcolm X from an impoverished youth to a leader who tried to rectify racial injustices by focusing on black pride is handled in a commendable manner. What results is not a glorification of the man, but rather a serious examination of his contributions and aspirations. Grimes does not dwell much on his personal flaws; she does relate what impact some of his decisions had on his leadership and philosophy. The quality of the few black-and-white photographs is questionable; they seem merely decorative rather than integral to the book.

## C IS FOR CITY (1994)

## Maria B. Salvadore

SOURCE: A review of *C is for City,* in *The Horn Book Guide,* Vol. VII, No. 1, July-December, 1995, p. 28.

From *A* to *Z,* rhythm and alliteration effectively describe the joys of a city. The rhyming text is accompanied by highly detailed illustrations in glowing neon colors, de-picting a pristine New York City. Additional items that start with the featured letter fill each page, and these have been carefully listed at the back of the book. Both the text and the art create a finding game in this cleverly conceived book.

## MEET DANITRA BROWN (1994)

## Hazel Rochman

SOURCE: A review of *Meet Danitra Brown,* in *Booklist,* Vol. 90, No. 12, February 15, 1994, p. 1085.

A series of simple poems tells a friendship story in the voice of Zuri Jackson, who admires her spirited buddy, Danitra Brown. Their relationship is upbeat but unsentimental. They have lots of fun together riding bikes and jumping rope, and they help each other out with chores and problems. Zuri is sorry one time when she betrays her friend's secret, but they make up, and Danitra comforts Zuri when she feels bad that she has no dad around. Zuri loves the way her friend ignores the neighborhood taunts about her thick coke-bottle glasses; in fact, Danitra's proud example helps Zuri when the kids tease her about her very dark skin (her Mom tells her to say, "The blacker the berry, the sweeter the juice"). [Floyd] Cooper's double-page spread oil-wash illustrations in rich shades of brown and purple are reminiscent of those he did for the poetry anthology *Pass It On.* He sets the individual portraits within a lively city neighborhood, in changing seasons, indoors and out. We feel the girls' energy and their bond, in joyful games and in quiet times together.

## Kirkus Reviews

SOURCE: A review of *Meet Danitra Brown,* in *Kirkus Reviews,* Vol. LXII, No. 8, April 15, 1994, p. 557.

In a lively cycle of 13 poems by the author of ***Somethin' on My Mind*** (1978), Zuri Jackson celebrates her vibrant best friend Danitra: "the most splendiferous girl in town . . . She's not afraid to take a dare./If something's hard, she doesn't care./She'll try her best, no matter what." Danitra shares work, play, and confidences with equal verve, knows how to defuse a mean tease or comfort a friend, and loves to wear purple. In expansive double spreads, Cooper visualizes the girls' city neighborhood in glowing impressionistic pastels while focusing on subtly modeled close-ups of them in their many moods. The joyous portrayal will appeal to a broad age range (the friends are depicted as 10 or 12 years old); older readers may enjoy going on to Jean Little's equally upbeat portrait of Kate Bloomfield, *Hey World, Here I Am!*

## Barbara Osborne Williams

SOURCE: A review of *Meet Danitra Brown,* in *School Library Journal,* Vol. 40, No. 5, May, 1994, p. 108.

A collection of 13 original poems that stand individually and also blend together to tell a story of feelings and friendship between two African-American girls. Grimes creatively uses the voice of Zuri Jackson to share tales of the girls' moments of admiration, pain, self-assurance, pride in their cultural heritage, sadness, disappointments, play, and their thoughts and feelings about future dreams and aspirations. [Floyd] Cooper's distinguished illustrations in warm dusty tones convey the feeling of closeness. The poignant text and lovely pictures are an excellent collaboration, resulting in a look at touching moments of friendship with universal appeal.

## Betsy Hearne

SOURCE: A review of *Meet Danitra Brown,* in *Bulletin of the Center for Children's Books,* Vol. 47, No. 11, July-August, 1994, p. 357.

With a smooth, scatterbrush effect in browns and russet reds, [Floyd] Cooper offers a filmy artistic backdrop for these thirteen poems, all about narrator Zuri's best friend Danitra. The girls are African American, and the neighborhood is inner-city, but the friendship will seem familiar to a broad spectrum of readers: Zuri admires Danitra, gains support and protection from her company, and sometimes fights with her. The verse is naive and tuned to tell a story, the rhyming determined but rarely strained: "Danitra's scared of pigeons. I promised not to tell,/then I opened my big mouth and out the secret fell." Zuri's few shadowy moments and flashes of insecurity are as natural as the dense hues of the illustration; yet in total effect, the illustration is as upbeat as the poetry, with skillful drafting especially evident in facial expression and body postures. While some kids may get impatient with Danitra's idealized persona, for many children—especially those afraid of more formal or lyrically complex poetry—this book will prove a satisfying introduction and sturdy friend.

## Ellen Fader

SOURCE: A review of *Meet Danitra Brown,* in *The Horn Book Magazine,* Vol. LXX, No. 4, July-August, 1994, p. 467.

Danitra Brown, "the most splendiferous girl in town," and her best friend Zuri Jackson are the focus of this collection of thirteen poems by Nikki Grimes. Danitra wears purple every day—"Purple socks and jeans and sneakers, purple ribbons for her hair. / Purple shirts and slacks and sweaters, even purple underwear!"—because queens in Timbuktu never dressed in any other color. Zuri admires Danitra's independent spirit and is quick to defend her friend when she is teased about her thick glasses. Danitra is equally considerate of Zuri's emotions. When Zuri feels excluded on Parents' Night because "I've got Mom and me only," she receives the support she needs—"Danitra knows just what to say to make me glad. / With her around, I'm never lonely." The two girls share many special times, acting out plays, riding bicycles, and jump-

ing rope. The poems do not present a completely idealized portrait of their time together. Zuri reveals that Danitra is afraid of pigeons, and the exposed secret strains their friendship. But Zuri's apology saves the day with Danitra, who loves to write rhymes and stories and boasts that she is going to win the Nobel Prize. "I double-dare anyone to roll his eyes. I know she'll do it!" One of the most poignant poems, which explores Zuri's sensitivity about her skin color, is **"Sweet Blackberry."** Zuri's mother offers this retort when kids at school tease her: "'Next time, honey, you just say, / The blacker the berry, the sweeter the juice.'" Floyd Cooper's full-color paintings throb with the energy of a big city and with the warmth and exuberance of the girls' dynamic relationship.

## Lee Bennett Hopkins

SOURCE: A review of *Meet Danitra Brown,* in *The Five Owls,* Vol. IX, No. 1, September-October, 1994, p. 14.

In the first of thirteen rhyming poems, the character Zuri Jackson tells readers: "You oughta meet Danitra Brown/ the most splendiferous girl in town." Danitra, a young African American girl, is a spunky, poetic protagonist, one who is not afraid to take a dare, only wears purple like queens in Timbuktu, doesn't mind her big, thick bifocals, prefers jeans to dresses, and aspires to win the Nobel Prize.

Like Danitra, [Floyd] Cooper's full-color paintings are equally splendiferous. City landscapes vibrate from the pages enhancing the verses. Readers will enjoy the warmth and friendship the two girls exude and will certainly not want to miss meeting Danitra Brown.

## Cyrisse Jaffee

SOURCE: "A World of Words," in *Women's Review of Books,* Vol. XII, No. 2, November, 1994, pp. 31–2.

"Multiculturalism" has become the latest publishing trend, as schools and libraries struggle to provide materials for an increasingly diverse population. Books by and about Native Americans, Hispanic Americans, Asian Americans and many other ethnic groups are eagerly sought by editors; making sure a book is non-sexist is not always a top priority. ("Non-sexist" sometimes seems to be in the eye of the beholder; a book can be praised for having a woman as a main character, even if she is portrayed as passive, helpless, or boy-crazy.) Occasionally, a book is well-received because it fits a multicultural "niche," despite a halting narrative, gender stereotypes, or other flaws. But many titles, happily, meet both criteria. They provide young girls—and boys—with characters they can cheer on, identify with and learn from.

One such recent book is the delightful *Meet Danitra Brown* by Nikki Grimes, with illustrations by Floyd Cooper. Independent, smart and determined, Danitra Brown— "the most splendiferous girl in town"—is the kind of girl you'd indeed want to meet. Told in verse by the well-known African American poet and children's book writer, this lively picture book offers younger readers an affectionate portrait of friendship and individuality. In the title poem, Danitra is "not afraid to take a dare./If something's hard, she doesn't care." She also wears bifocals that are "big and thick and round." In the poem **"Coke-bottle Brown,"** even when "dumb old Freddy Watson" makes fun of her, Danitra tells her friend Zuri, who narrates the book, "Can't waste time on some boy who thinks it's funny bein' mean./Got books to read and hills to climb that Freddy's never seen."

The poems capture the importance of the friendship between Zuri and Danitra. **"Ladies of the House"** explains that when Danitra's mother is sick, Zuri helps Danitra with her household chores; in **"Mom and Me Only,"** when Zuri feels angry on Parent's Night because she doesn't have a mom and a dad, Danitra reminds her that Zuri's mother "loves you twice as much. Is that so bad?" (Zuri also has to endure the teasing of some of her schoolmates because of her "double chocolate fudge" skin. In **"Sweet Blackberry,"** her mother tells her "Next time, honey, you just say,/The blacker the berry, the sweeter the juice.") Danitra, proud of her African heritage, wears purple to emulate the queens of Timbuktu in **"Purple."** The language—like Danitra—is filled with energy and rhythm, ideal for reading aloud. Enhanced by Floyd Cooper's warm, full-color illustrations in brown and gold tones. . . .

## 📖 *PORTRAIT OF MARY* (1994)

### *Kirkus Reviews*

SOURCE: A review of *Portrait of Mary,* in *Kirkus Reviews,* Vol. LXII, No. 14, July 15, 1994, p. 935.

Children's author Grimes does an adult turn with this mild historical fiction about the mother of Jesus.

Largely narrated in the first person, the novel tells the familiar story of Mary in a simple, pious way that is sure to please fundamentalist believers. Coming of age in the backwater of Galilee, ruled by the evil and tyrannical puppet-king Herod, Mary is attracted to the carpenter, Joseph, by his muscular good looks and his love of God. She is betrothed to him when she is visited by the Archangel Gabriel, who announces that she has conceived a child by the spirit of God. She envisions opprobrium and rejection as a result of this "illegitimate" pregnancy, but Joseph stands by her and vows to keep the matter private between them. Forced to flee to Egypt to avoid the mass infanticide ordered by Herod, they return only after the monarch's death. Jesus, the son she bears, impresses all those around him, and Mary remembers the promise of Gabriel and the old prophecies, but she still doesn't fully understand. Finally, Jesus embarks on a ministry of which she is no real part. She sees him only occasionally and is confused when he spurns her. She watches helplessly as he is arrested and executed. When he is raised from the

dead, in fulfillment of the prophecies, Mary, like Doubting Thomas, refuses to believe it until she has seen it with her own eyes—after which she emerges believing and exultant. Passages from the Gospels punctuate the text and serve to give it a homogenized story line culled from disparate parts of the biblical tradition. Attempts to add resonance to the bare-bones account by portraying Mary's inner thoughts are only sometimes successful.

Boy meets girl. Girl gives birth to Messiah. Messiah dies. Messiah lives. Enough said.

### Susan Salter Reynolds

SOURCE: A review of *Portrait of Mary,* in *The Los Angeles Times Book Review,* September 11, 1994, p. 6.

Nikki Grimes, author of several children's books including a biography of Malcolm X, began this project as a series of poems about the life of the mother of Jesus Christ. The poems became a theater piece that was performed for church audiences and coffeehouses, and finally took the form of this narrative. A combination of Scripture and storytelling, in the end this is another story of child loss and faith. Mary, picture of grace and sacrifice, believes in the visions and dreams that she and her husband must act upon; marrying in spite of the pregnancy, moving to Egypt to escape the slaughter of the innocents in Bethlehem, hearing the proclamations from prophets and wise men on the fate of their son. Of course, there's never enough detail in this story; no amount of pomegranates or wet hay or lentil stew will drag it below the level of myth, but it breathes life into the story to be able to picture Mary's daily life and her hopes and fears for her son ("Why, he would be the best carpenter in all Jerusalem, if Joseph had his way"). In the Notes and Acknowledgments, Grimes describes the few places where she played with history and myth and Scripture—most important, a section in which the risen Christ visits his mother. "I cannot imagine," writes Grimes as a mother who has lost a child, "that Jesus would have visited his friends one final time . . . and not have done as much for his beloved mother."

### Ilene Cooper

SOURCE: A review of *Portrait of Mary,* in *Booklist,* Vol. 91, No. 2, September 15, 1994, p. 114.

A small, graceful look into the heart of Mary, the mother of Jesus. With the New Testament and other sources as a basis, Grimes constructs a fictionalized biography narrated by Mary herself. It begins with Mary as a confused and frightened young woman, unsure of how to react to the mystical forces that are buffeting her life. It is really not until after Jesus' death, when her son appears to her, that Mary begins to comprehend the wonder of her life and the miracle of resurrection. Grimes' Mary is a fully realized character who reacts with the same unease, confusion, and despair that most would in her situation. Yet without even being quite sure what it is she is placing her faith in, Mary holds—sometimes by her fingertips—to the vision that was given to her before Jesus was born. A compelling narrative, both as fiction and as interpretative religion.

**Additional coverage of Grimes's life and career is contained in the following sources published by Gale Research:** *Contemporary Authors,* Vol. 77-80.

# Ruth Krauss

## 1911-1993

American author of picture books, plays, and poetry.

Major works include *The Carrot Seed* (1945), *The Happy Day* (1949), *A Hole Is to Dig: A First Book of First Definitions* (1952), *A Very Special House* (1954), *I'll Be You and You Be Me* (1954).

## INTRODUCTION

A well-respected and prolific writer of children's stories, Krauss is renowned for works that display humor, cleverness, and an awareness of the thoughts, desires, and language of young children. Her most popular creations are a series of picture books with brief texts that present a simple, undeniable truth as seen from a child's perspective. Her writing, whether in poetry or prose, contains a rhythmic, lyrical quality that in many cases is said to recreate the patterns of childhood speech. Krauss's writings are also esteemed for their consistent experimentalism. She was one of the earliest authors to observe and record the language of young people, using their help to create such ground-breaking books as *A Hole Is to Dig* and *I'll Be You and You Be Me*. The former work, Krauss's first collaborative effort with illustrator Maurice Sendak, is considered a landmark in children's literature for its incorporation of the actual words and ideas of children. Krauss has, however, disappointed some critics, who have observed that her unique and clever manner might be unappreciated by small children, or have felt that her texts are more buoyed by the talent of her illustrators than by her own efforts. Still, Krauss's influence on children's literature has been extensive, and her humorous, whimsical, and creative portrayal of a child's world has, in the words of Jean F. Mercier, earned her "lasting fame with the creation of timeless works, clearly understood and valued by everyone who speaks the *lingua franca* of childhood."

### Biographical Information

Krauss was born in Baltimore, Maryland, in 1911. Her childhood interests included the study of art and music, in addition to a love of reading, all of which her parents encouraged by allowing her to leave public school after the eighth grade in order to devote herself to the study of the violin and the arts at the Peabody Institute in Baltimore and later at New York City's Parsons School of Fine and Applied Art. After studying anthropology at Columbia University and poetry at the New School of Social Research in New York, she began writing for children and published her first work, *A Good Man and His Good Wife,* in 1944. Her second picture book, *The Carrot Seed,* was the result of a collaboration with her husband, writer-illustrator and comic-strip artist Crockett Johnson.

This and her other early children's books were well-received by critics. The same was true of several works she produced in the 1950s illustrated by the now-famous artist and children's author Maurice Sendak. Such books as *A Hole Is to Dig, A Very Special House,* and *The Birthday Party* established both Krauss and Sendak as major figures in the field of children's literature. In the 1960s, Krauss continued her success with experimental writings—some for adults—including poetry, poem-plays designed for the theater, and more sophisticated works such as *The Cantilever Rainbow* (1965). Her literary production slowed in the 1970s and 1980s, though she continued to write. Krauss's last published work before her death in 1993, the poem *Big and Little* (1988), was a return to the style and technique of some of her earlier works.

### Major Works

Krauss's writings for children demonstrate a range of technical development highlighted by a sustained concern to portray the world from the child's point of view with humor and sensitivity. *The Carrot Seed* is representative of her writings in the 1940s, and bears stylistic and thematic affinities with her other early works, such as *The Great Duffy* (1946) and *The Growing Story* (1947). Each consists of a very brief text, numbering less than one hundred words, and follows an inquisitive little boy as he discovers some facet of the world around him. The boy in *The Carrot Seed,* a fable about the importance of confidence and hard work, refuses to lose faith in the hope that the carrot seed he has planted will grow. His perseverance pays off when the seed finally sprouts, contradicting the doubting pronouncements of his parents and other adults, and produces an enormous carrot. *Bears* (1948) and *The Happy Day* are two works that focus entirely on animals. In the former, Krauss produces a short, rhyming text that features bears engaging in a variety of activities. In the latter, she and illustrator Marc Simont tell a story of springtime as the animals dance and play in the snow after discovering the first flower of the season. *The Backward Day* (1950) displays Krauss's emphasis on childlike humor as a young boy decides to play a joke by doing all of his ordinary activities, such as walking and dressing, backward. *A Hole Is to Dig: A First Book of First Definitions* is based on Krauss's observations of sometimes clever, often humorous, childhood definitions of everyday things. The results range from "a castle is to build in the sand" and "a seashell is to hear to the sea" to "a tablespoon is to eat a table with." *A Very Special House* explores the contours of childhood imagination, as a little boy dreams of a magical house, where everything from writing on walls to jumping on beds is permitted—a theme that Krauss explores further in *I Want to Paint My Bathroom Blue* (1956). *Somebody Else's Nut Tree, and Other Tales from Children* (1958) and *A Moon or a Button* (1959) are both collections of stories and thoughts culled from the minds of children, informed by a child's sensibility. *Open House for Butterflies* (1960), a sequel to *A Hole Is to Dig,* likewise reflects Krauss's attempts to record the poetry of children's interpretations of the world. *The Cantilever Rainbow,* one of Krauss's earliest attempts at the poem-play aimed at an older audience, contains eighteen lyrical pieces—free-wheeling, clever, and occasionally absurd meditations based upon a sun motif. In *What a Fine Day For. . .* (1967), a kind of nonsense book, Krauss encourages children to take delight in the worlds of poetry and music. *I Write It* (1970) dramatizes a simple theme, a child's joy in writing his or her own name. *Little Boat Lighter Than a Cork* (1976) relates the voyage of a baby traveling in a walnut-shell through a dream-like fantasy world. Her last work, *Big and Little* (1988), poetically explores the concepts of large and small while displaying the importance of love relationships through a child's eyes.

## Awards

Krauss received Spring Book Festival honor citations for *The Carrot Seed* in 1945 and *I Can Fly* in 1951; *A Hole Is to Dig, I'll Be You and You Be Me, I Want to Paint My Bathroom Blue, The Birthday Party,* and *Open House for Butterflies* were all named to the *New York Times* Best Illustrated Books of the Year lists. Marc Simont and Maurice Sendak each earned Caldecott Honor citations

for their illustrations for *The Happy Day* and *A Very Special House,* respectively.

---

# GENERAL COMMENTARY

## Lee Bennett Hopkins

SOURCE: "Ruth Krauss/Crockett Johnson," in *Books are by People,* Citation Press, 1969, pp. 121–24.

I spent a hilarious summer afternoon with Ruth Krauss and her husband, Crockett Johnson. Their home is situated in a small Connecticut town on the north edge of Long Island Sound. As I approached the house, Mr. Johnson was standing outside, apparently waiting for me. He is a big man—tall, husky, and completely bald, just like the famous character Barnaby whom he created. Looking at me and chuckling Mr. Johnson exclaimed, "I draw people without hair, because it's so much *easier*! Besides, to me, people *with* hair look funny." Discussing New York he said, "I'm probably the only person you've ever met who was born on East 58th Street in New York City." On living in Connecticut he remarked, "It was a nice neighborhood here until the young fogies moved in and spoiled it. The lake is so crowded now that there isn't even enough room to go sailing." He continually interrupted his conversation with guffaws of laughter.

Soon Ruth Krauss joined us on the sun porch. At the precise moment she entered, a clap of thunder exploded, lightning flashed, clouds darkened the sky, and rain began to pour from the heavens. As we were all being nicely drenched, Miss Krauss looked at me and said in a most relaxed manner, "Oh, hell-o. Do you think we should move inside?"

Miss Krauss is as funny and as clever as her many books. She was born in Baltimore, Maryland, studied art and music at Peabody Conservatory, and graduated from the Parsons School of Fine and Applied Art in New York City. She also studied anthropology at Columbia University. Her books are milestones in the field of children's literature. Children simply adore them. One of the reasons for this, perhaps, is that Miss Krauss studies boys and girls.

When preparing *A Hole Is to Dig: A First Book of First Definitions* (1952), she carefully observed children around the community. "I went to the beach every day and would ask five- and six-year-olds the question, 'What is this for?' or 'What is that for?'—questions about things that children held personally dear to them. Actually I got the idea from child psychologists who write that five-year-olds are pragmatists. I wanted to see if they were right! The kids thought I was crazy," she laughed. "I asked one boy what a hole is for, and he looked at me like I was nuts, frowned, and walked away from me. Another child, however, said 'A hole? A hole is to dig?' And that's how the title was born."

The first children's book Mr. Johnson illustrated was his wife's *The Carrot Seed* (1945), which is typical of her work in that it contains very few words. "I wrote it in 45 minutes" she commented. It tells a simple tale of a boy who planted a carrot seed. His mother, father, and big brother all tell him it won't come up. The child, however, ignores the negative advice, gives it great care, "And one day a carrot came up just as the little boy had known it would." When *The Carrot Seed* was published, a copy was sent to San Francisco where the United Nations was being organized. "I guess the message came through. Look what it did for the U.N.!" she laughed.

Mr. Johnson has since collaborated with his wife on several other books including the comic *How to Make an Earthquake* (1954). "Do you know what the librarians did with *How to Make an Earthquake*?" he asked. "They catalogued it with other how-to books such as how to collect stamps and how to sew a seam," he roared.

Mr. Johnson has also written and illustrated the famous "Harold" series, beginning with *Harold and the Purple Crayon* (1958), amusing tales that relate the adventures of a small boy who "draws" himself in and out of curious situations. Also to his credit are *Ellen's Lion* (1959), and *The Lion's Own Story* (1963), his personal favorites.

The work habits of this husband-wife team vary. Miss Krauss stated, "I'm haphazard, flighty, and eccentric. I'm fresher in the morning and like to work on the kitchen table." Mr. Johnson declared, "And I can work any hour of the day. I'm a steady worker."

The Johnsons do have a serious side to them. Mr. Johnson is avidly interested in executing geometric paintings—paintings that require the mathematical computations of a computer. His large canvasses, covered with dramatic color, have been exhibited in a New York gallery.

Miss Krauss is a serious student of poetry and has been devoting much of her time to writing poem-plays. Several seasons ago she had *A Beautiful Day,* 17 poem-plays strung together, produced off-Broadway and directed by Remy Charlip. Mr. Johnson described the reception the play received. "I caught the second night's performance. At the end of the play the audience cried out 'Bravo! Bravo!' and wild applause rang from the theatre's rafters. I have never heard such response. 'Isn't this wonderful?' I asked Ruth. She merely looked at me disappointedly and remarked, 'I'm crushed! This audience is not as enthusiastic as the one we had last night!'"

Miss Krauss also teaches poetry at a local art center and is doing poetry workshops at Daytop Village, an institution for the self-rehabilitation of narcotic addicts.

My day in Connecticut turned out to be filled with fun, good humor, and interesting anecdotes. I even learned that Crockett Johnson is not really Crockett Johnson!

"Crockett is my childhood nickname. My real name is David Johnson Leisk. Leisk was too hard to pronounce—so—I am now Crockett Johnson!" he exclaimed.

Before I left the sun came out. Even today I can hear the strains of Ruth Krauss's "hee, hee, hees" and Crockett Johnson's "ho, ho, hos" whenever I pick up *A Hole Is to Dig* or *Barnaby*!

## Anne Martin

SOURCE: "Ruth Krauss: A Very Special Author," in *Authors and Illustrators of Children's Books: Writings on Their Lives and Works,* R. R. Bowker Company, 1972, pp. 247–55.

With the removal of fairy tales from the nursery, and the advent of the realistic "here and now" type of story, there has been some lament that there is no longer any "imagination" in books for young children. Many adults have felt that the pre-school child is being brought up almost exclusively on a literary diet of steam shovels, trains, tugboats, tractors, and the like, which might serve to limit his outlook on life to its narrowly technological and mechanical aspects. Perhaps in reaction to this tendency, or perhaps merely accidentally, there has recently developed a new kind of imaginative picture book literature, not dependent on the stylized conventions of the fairy tale, which draws its inspiration from children's own fantasies, desires, word play, and sense of humor.

One of the pioneers in this development was Margaret Wise Brown whose seemingly rambling, pointless, and "silly" stories made many parents shake their heads in wonder at the odd tastes of their young children who were enchanted with these books. At present, other authors are striking out into new writing patterns of their own on the picture book level. One of these is Beatrice Schenk de Regniers, whose highly individualized style has evoked a great deal of interest and discussion. Perhaps the most controversial (among adults, at least) is Ruth Krauss who has probably gone further than any other author in experimenting with the form and content of picture books.

After reading through Miss Krauss' books, one may first be impressed by the wide range of mood and purpose. There is the quiet determination in *The Carrot Seed,* the whimsical word play in *Bears,* the warm tenderness in *The Bundle Book,* the boisterous fun in *A Very Special House,* the practical (and impractical) advice to bored youngsters in *How to Make an Earthquake.* In spite of this variety, there seem to be certain underlying assumptions about children which have shaped the style and content of all of Miss Krauss' books. While such assumptions are only implicit and are never formulated into a doctrine, they might be stated somewhat along these lines:

That children are neither cute darlings to be patronized, nor miniature adults to be civilized, but rather lively, well-organized people with codes, ideas, and ambitions of their own which often need a chance to be worked out.

That children are fascinated by language—the trying out of nonsense syllables, the defining of familiar terms, the groping for expression of feelings, the striving to communicate ideas.

That children, like older people, have special dreams and desires which can only be gratified by fantasy, and that they love to indulge in these day dreams.

That children have an exuberance and joy in daily living, and an irrepressible sense of the ridiculous which may differ radically from an adult's idea of what is funny.

That these assumptions are so clearly conveyed in her picture books, indicates that Miss Krauss has made good use of some special abilities and advantages. It is clear from her material that Miss Krauss has had close contact with young children which permitted her to observe carefully their patterns of speech, make-believe games, and ways of telling stories or narrating events. She has an ear for the kind of word play and nonsense talk that brings immediate response from children, and an unusual insight into some of the complicated emotions and relationships beneath children's verbal expressions. Along with the craftsmanship to organize her material effectively so that it becomes meaningful and enjoyable to the child reader, Miss Krauss has added one extra dimension—the experimental attitude. When her material demanded it, she has permitted herself to depart from the conventional form of children's books in an attempt to create new, more suitable forms. Since pictorial representation is of primary importance in books for young children, Miss Krauss has been fortunate in the collaboration of good artists whose illustrations serve to represent, clarify, and even interpret the action and mood of the texts. Probably the best way to illustrate all the foregoing assertions is to examine rather closely the content and style of the books themselves.

Three of the earlier books seem to be definitely related in theme and execution. These are *The Carrot Seed, The Growing Story,* and *The Backward Day.* All are written in a casual but concise style (*The Carrot Seed* almost abruptly in terse, single sentences on each page) and all tell an uninterrupted story without digressions or explanations. All have an atmosphere of calm but single-minded drive towards a climax. In each book, an unnamed "little boy" is obsessed with a particular idea or plan which he follows through purposefully and successfully to the end. In *The Growing Story,* the little boy is determined to find out whether he himself is growing like the animals and plants around him, and, after a summer of discouraging doubts, he triumphantly shouts out his proof when he tries on his winter clothes, "Hey! . . . My pants are too little and my coat is too little. I'm growing too." In *The Backward Day,* "A little boy woke up one morning and got out of bed. He said to himself, 'Today is backward day.'" This gives him the opportunity of doing such wonderfully peculiar things as walking downstairs backwards, wearing his underwear over his coat, and saying

"goodnight" at breakfast time. In both these books, the boys' families are amazingly patient and cooperative. In *The Carrot Seed,* however, the little boy has to pursue his project of planting and caring for a carrot seed against the scorn and disbelief of his whole family until, in a highly effective understatement, comes the emphatic climax, "And then, one day, a carrot came up just as the little boy had known it would" (dramatized by a humorous illustration of a giant carrot on a wheelbarrow).

These may seem like trivial plots to adults, and hardly worth writing about, but to a young child it is tremendously exciting to know that he is part of a growing world, or that sometimes he may be right and his elders mistaken, or that by his own actions he may, at least temporarily, change the established habits of daily life. These ideas open up a whole realm of speculations to the child about his own place as an autonomous individual, no longer completely dependent on adults, capable of initiating and completing projects of his own. At the same time, there is the humorous acceptance of limitations. In *The Backward Day,* after a maximum exploitation of his lovely idea, the little boy realizes its impractibility (and perhaps also its gradual monotony) and is permitted to make a dignified withdrawal of the whole cumbersome business by merely starting the day all over again, this time frontwards.

With the possible exception of *The Growing Story* which lacks the light touch of the other two, these books can also be enjoyed purely at the story level without any deeper implications. The appealing, wide-eyed stoic in *The Carrot Seed* (incidentally, this, like many of the other books, is illustrated by Crockett Johnson, the author's husband and well-known creator of Barnaby) is lovable just for himself, and the blandly described details of what is involved in doing things "backward oh backward oh backward oh backward oh backward" are completely satisfactory in their own right. Whatever other implications there may be, they are injected subtly enough so that the reader may be aware of them or not, according to his own capabilities or desires.

In just the same way, *The Bundle Book,* where a pleasant young mother spends a long time guessing just what the "strange bundle" on her bed might be, can be enjoyed merely as a guessing game (and what young child doesn't love to play at hiding and "fooling" his parents) and for Helen Stone's soft, accurate illustrations of the squirming bundle. But beyond the fast-moving story line there emerges a strong and almost inescapable feeling of a real and unsentimental love relationship between this mother and her child, a feeling with which the young reader can easily identify because this love relationship, or lack of it, with his own parents is one of the most important things in his life.

In contrast to these books, *The Happy Day* and *Bears* make their appeal purely on the fun and nonsense level. The text of *The Happy Day* is perhaps somewhat disappointing. In rhythmically relating the story of several species of hibernating animals which discover a miraculous flower growing in the snow, the text becomes almost monotonously repetitious with its constant refrain of "They sniff. They run. They run. They sniff." Fortunately, the suspense is sustained and the climax heightened by Marc Simont's admirable black and white illustrations of warm, sleepy, furry animals suddenly galvanized into swiftly graceful action. The contrasts of warmth and cold, sleep and rapid motion, search and discovery, come through in spite of a rather artificial plot.

The ingenious, tongue-tickling text of *Bears,* however, is quite equal to Phyllis Rowand's masterful illustrations of ridiculous, lovable bears of all sizes and amazing capabilities. These "bears, everywheres" are a special species, closer to teddies than to zoo bears, as they slide down bannisters "on the stairs," are lost in suds while "washing hairs," and do practically anything as long as it rhymes. The only possible false note may be the inclusion of "millionaires" whose top hats and cigars are quite meaningless to two- and three-year-old readers, but that's an insignificant objection. *Bears* is the kind of book that young children can look at repeatedly, finding previously undiscovered details in the pictures, "reading" and giggling at the text, even inventing more rhymes in the same vein.

All the previously discussed books are written in a straightforward, economical style, the writer being an objective author telling a story. *I Can Fly,* Miss Krauss' contribution to the Little Golden Book series, might be considered a transition piece. It marks a shift away from the style of the earlier books toward the experiments with a first person narrative in a child's own idiom of speech and thought carried out in *A Hole Is to Dig, A Very Special House,* and *I'll Be You and You Be Me.* Very close in spirit to *Bears, I Can Fly* is an invitation to make-believe and mimicry full of delightfully silly rhymes ("Who can walk like a bug? Me! Ug ug") very much like the ones children improvise all the time. The ending is an inspired burst of "Gubble gubble gubble, I'm a mubble in a pubble. I can play I'm anything that's anything. . . . " Illustrated in Mary Blair's witty, colorful pictures, this book is probably one of the most successfully executed of the very inexpensive picture books. Where *I Can Fly* tentatively approaches a child's way of talking and playing, there is a real evolution in the other three books from a reflection of a child's world in *A Hole Is to Dig* to an increasingly abstract representation of children's desires and feelings in *A Very Special House* and *I'll Be You and You Be Me.* All three are illustrated in Maurice Sendak's expressive black and white drawings which are sensitively responsive to the changing form of the texts.

*A Hole Is to Dig* contains a group of unrelated definitions of familiar objects and concepts in a child's world, expressed in the way children would, and in most cases probably really did, explain these terms. For older children and adults, this book is a funny and even touching experience because the definitions are such a curious combination of incredible narrowness of understanding and a vastly profound vision of what is true and important. Thus we can smile at "a face is so you can make

faces," but we can only hold our breaths at "a dream is to look at the night and see things." In our harried life of household worries about orderliness and sanitation, it is well to be reminded that "dogs are to kiss people," or that "mud is to jump in and slide in and yell doodleedoodleedoo." There are also bits of that pre-school age humor which can be so exasperating to adults, such as "a tablespoon is to eat a table with," followed by an appropriate pantomime, probably at great length. Perhaps this book has almost more to say to older people than to young children. For the child who lives within these concepts, the book is enjoyable because it is a true picture of his world. For the adult who has pigeonholed familiar objects too easily and thoughtlessly, it is a glimpse into a kaleidoscopic range of meanings.

*A Very Special House* depicts another aspect of the child's life—his dream world, as opposed to the real world in *A Hole Is to Dig.* This lively fantasy embodies all the exciting things a particular little boy would like to do in a house of his own, and they are also the things that are usually most disapproved by parents and teachers. Walls are to draw on, chairs are to climb on, doors to swing on, beds to jump on. The house is filled with rioting, scurrying animals (and a giant) with which to share secrets, play wild games, and shout delicious nonsense words like "ooie ooie ooie." The climax is a mad confusion of shouting and mischief where "nobody ever says stop stop stop." Yet all the time the little boy knows that this special house is "right in the middle—oh it's ret in the meedle— oh it's root in the moodle of my head head head." He is content just to think about it, and, to show that he was just fooling anyway, he punctuates his stream of imagination with a crazy jump in the air which lands him "bung" down on his bottom, at which he exits with a happy, shamefaced smile. Obviously, the child reader can also gain a harmless release of his disapproved desires on the verbal, imaginative level. The humor in text and pictures is of the slapstick variety, though there are also several nasty digs at the social conventions of the adult world.

It is an amazing feat that Miss Krauss has successfully depicted a world of riot, chaos, and confusion by employing a strictly disciplined, rhythmical, almost lyrical style in symmetrical form. The text begins and ends on the note of clowning to the sound of "dee dee dee oh," and the real narrative begins and ends with the chant of "I know a house—it's not a squirrel house, it's not a donkey house . . . " The build-up from a rather calm description of the house, through an increasingly excited portrayal of activity, until the noisy climax, is achieved through the skillful change from long complete sentences, to interrupted thoughts, to irregular short phrases, and finally to the large print repetition of a single word. The deceptively easy, natural flow of the monologue is actually accomplished only by means of an extremely controlled style, carefully worked out to the last nonsense syllable.

In connection with *A Very Special House* it is interesting to mention an earlier book by Ruth Krauss which, though very different in purpose and style, somewhat foreshadows her later books. *The Big World and the Little House* is a self-conscious, almost moralistic attempt to describe the relationship between the world and the individual. The style is uneven, and there is an awkward juxtaposition of varying ideas and moods. But there is also something of the poetic, rhythmical quality of *A Very Special House* in many passages such as:

> Inside the house there were no beds, no tables, no chairs. No rugs were on its floors, no pictures on its walls. No smoke was in its chimney. At night it was part of the dark.

A more startling resemblance lies in some of the ideas which were later developed more fully in *A Very Special House,* though of course in a different context. In the little house "you could put your feet on the chairs and it didn't hurt them," and grandma painted the walls "with one wall special for drawing pictures on. It was also special for washing them off." Perhaps the "special house" had its genesis in the "little house," four years before its actual creation.

Turning from *A Very Special House* to *I'll Be You and You Be Me* is somewhat akin to turning from *Portrait of the Artist as a Young Man* to *Ulysses.* In both cases there is the tremendous step from a challenging but easily understandable plot line to a fragmentary, constantly shifting point of view and emphasis. It would certainly be ridiculous to make a real comparison between Ruth Krauss and James Joyce, but there is no doubt that this book is an experiment with a completely new art form for children.

The general themes of the book may be vaguely described as feeling tones—loving, liking, dreaming, wishing, wanting, happiness, and probably a few others. In order to express these, Miss Krauss uses a variety of literary forms, including stories, poems, monologues, a play, a parody, a near-parable, and even "a mystery." Within this large variety of forms there are basically two kinds of writing: first, the same child-like material with which Miss Krauss proved herself to be so proficient in *A Hole Is to Dig* and *A Very Special House,* and, secondly, and adult expression of what the child may be feeling, an apparent attempt to express for the child some things that he feels deeply but doesn't, or perhaps can't, often discuss.

The first type of writing, which makes up the bulk of the selections in this book, is represented by such items as the monologue by an older child about a baby:

> he can't talk yet
> but I can understand him—
> even when he's over at his house and he
> yells and nobody knows what he means—
> I know. I could tell other people for him . . .

The second type of writing can be most clearly exemplified by such fragments as "A horse that's lost could be dreaming of the girl that's going to find him." In this passage there is again an echo of *The Big World and the Little House* in the intensity of feeling that doesn't quite

come across. Perhaps that is because an adult, using adult symbolism, is speaking not as an adult writing for children, but as a child representing supposedly childish feelings. The result can not be genuine expression for either child or adult.

Because the themes of this book are so large and generalized, there seems to be a lack of focus and unity, although most of the individual pieces are significant and self-contained. It would have been a shame to exclude such gems as "I think I'll grow up to be a bunny before I grow up to be a lady," and its inclusion could probably be justified in terms of the theme of friendliness and intimacy, but there is no one feeling or direction strong enough to pull all these little pieces into a comprehensive whole. Thus this experiment comes dangerously close to being an ordinary collection, not because the form itself is necessarily unwieldy, but because the internal structure has not been sufficiently integrated. Yet there is a degree of freedom in the development of theme and mood in both text and illustration (at one point the artist draws a complete dream sequence which is not described in the text at all) which is almost impossible in the more traditional books for children. While this book is not altogether equal to its conception or to the excellence of some of its individual parts, it certainly points the way to new creative art forms in the field of writing for children.

Miss Krauss' latest book to date, *Is This You?,* is less impressive than her other work. Similar in purpose to her earlier *How to Make an Earthquake,* this book is of the how-to-amuse-yourself variety in that it gives instructions for producing an original book. But while *How to Make an Earthquake* contains a number of ingenious ideas, some of them undoubtedly originated by children and explained in the familiar pattern of children's make-believe ("one person has to be the World. And then somebody has to be the sun . . ."), *Is This You?* is built on the single pattern of ludicrous possibilities. Thus to the question "Is this how you take a bath?" one illustration depicts a little boy in a bird bath, and another in a hippopotamus pool. Some breakfast eating suggestions include a piano leg and an earthworm. While some of the combinations are genuinely funny, the rigid pattern produces an effect of rather forced humor, and the kind of book the child is instructed to make comes close to the dull, standardized composition topics of "My Family," "My Home," "My Friends," etc. In spite of the book's cleverness and amusing illustrations, it forces the reader into specific and stereotyped responses. In *How to Make an Earthquake,* on the contrary, there is much scope for imaginative play. Many of the ideas may have a very familiar ring to parents and teachers. Few children can resist the delight of playing parent and subjecting their adult "child" to an ordeal of this sort:

> Then you take the child by the hand and say, "You
>     *have* to.
> Come on. Let's go."
> And the child says, "No no no." And the child
>     cries.
> But you make the child go to the party anyway . . .

The detailed descriptions of such common childhood amusements as making "mish-mosh" out of odd bits of food, elevate these to the status of important projects and real games. Even a quite young child can get much satisfaction out of following step by step directions, especially when they are written in language close enough to his own so that he can understand them easily.

Since *Is This You?* is not a story book and is somewhat out of line with most of Miss Krauss' writing, it gives little indication of the direction she intends to follow. It remains to be seen whether she will revert to some of her earlier styles, or continue to work along the lines of *I'll Be You and You Be Me,* or perhaps strike out into completely new areas of experimentation. Whatever path Miss Krauss will take, it is almost certain that young readers will leave analysis, criticism, puzzlement, and amazement to the adults. For them a Ruth Krauss book "is to look at" over and over again, to quote from and laugh at and talk about, and even (going along with Sendak's illustrations) to hug lovingly and to drop off to sleep with.

## Barbara Bader

SOURCE: "Ruth Krauss; Ruth Krauss and Maurice Sendak," in *American Picturebooks from Noah's Ark to the Beast Within,* Macmillan Publishing Company, Inc., 1976, pp. 416–33.

Ruth Krauss, who was taking courses in anthropology at Columbia, went to Harper's with the idea for a book on race relations, and the outcome was the sturdy nonsense of *A Good Man and His Good Wife.* She joined the Writers' Laboratory at Bank Street, and listened to children there and on her own; and out of their speech, formed poetry. With the merest prompting she seems to have grasped intuitively what the great Russian children's poet Kornei Chukovsky spent his life studying, "the whimsical and elusive laws of childhood thinking"; and there is no surer guide to her work, unbeknownst, than Chukovsky's summation *From Two to Five.*

"Once there was a good man and his good wife," the story begins, and it might be "The Husband Who Wanted to Do Housework" or any of the many old tales of married couples, folkore's domestic comedy. "The details of his awkwardness furnish the amusement for the story," writes Stith Thompson [in *The Folktale,* 1946], "and these may be expanded at will." Moreover, continues Thompson, writing on folktale types, "The fool is frequently so literal-minded that he follows instructions even in the most inappropriate situations," and he cites "the best-known tale of this type," "What Should I Have Done," otherwise known as "Lazy Jack" (Jacobs) or "Prudent Hans" (Grimm). It is what one sees in *A Good Man and His Good Wife,* but it is not nearly all.

The couple's cottage, Ruth Krauss writes, has "white walls and red curtains and lots of little cubbyholes and handyshelves"—construing 'handyshelves' as the twin, in sense

and in sound, of 'cubbyholes,' the way children are wont to do. Comes the nonsense, and we're in on the game, for we can spot instantly—in Ad Reinhardt's two-color cartoons—just what it is that the poor husband is hunting for; and perceive that, no matter what it is, it's not where it should be. For—more nonsense—"I get so tired of the same things in the same place," says his wife. All right, he'll do something about it, he'll take her at her word; "And that was how the good man cured his good wife of a bad habit." Not unlike the way kids confound their elders, sometimes innocently, sometimes not, by taking their words literally too.

Out of print for some time, *A Good Man and His Good Wife* was revived in 1962 with conventional illustrations by 'the 1956 Caldecott winner, Marc Simont' (*A Tree Is Nice*), an ironic switch considering Ad Reinhardt's emergence, in the years following the original edition, as a leading abstract painter; and a loss for a book that remains nonetheless a wonderfully satisfying amalgam of folk-thought and child thinking.

There followed *The Carrot Seed,* child fable without peer. To tell it, tight and true as it is, one would have to have recourse to Ruth Krauss's words, so let us have Ruth Krauss's words as written and printed:

A little boy planted
a carrot seed.

His mother said, "I'm afraid
it won't come up."

His father said, "I'm afraid
it won't come up."

And his big brother said,
"It won't come up."

Every day the little boy pulled
up the weeds around the seed
and sprinkled the ground with
water.

But nothing came up.

And nothing came up.

Everyone kept saying it
wouldn't come up.

But he still pulled up the
weeds around it every day
and sprinkled the ground
with water.

And then, one day,

a carrot came up

just as the little boy
had known it would.

In the few nouns and verbs, the strategic 'ands' and 'buts,' is the essence of story; in the repetitions and rhythms, the essence of storytelling; in the interplay of silence and stress, storytelling and poetry, overlapping. And as it might in a poem, and should in a poem for young children, each sentence or line carries an image, a way of writing that perfectly suits picturebooks. But for a picturebook the image can be, as effectively, one of inaction—"But nothing came up. / And nothing came up"—which, pictured and spaced out, marks time dramatically (remember Angus, "for exactly THREE minutes, by the clock" not curious about anything at all); or, to dramatic purpose too, one of gradual gathering action—"And then, one day," (the ground breaks) "a carrot came up" (towering green fronds) "just as the little boy had known it would" (giant red carrot).

From a monochromatic cream and brown, the book bursts into color with the appearance of no ordinary carrot; and that extraordinary carrot, the equivalent of Jack's miraculous beanstalk, is more than the vindication of the little boy's confidence, it is power. Besides knowing how, one has to know what to say, whether in words or in pictures; and in pictures, few if any said more—with less—than Crockett Johnson, "creator of Barnaby" and Ruth Krauss's husband.

As few words as there are in **The Carrot Seed,** there are fewer in **Bears;** and there were mutterings about a book that said nothing but *bears, bears, bears.* It came, as it happens, the year after a book called *Nothing But Cats, Cats, Cats,* which, you may recall, had a good bit to say; but I am reminded also of an ad that Eunice Blake ran at Nelson: "You Can Never Have Too Many ANIMAL STORIES," it read cheerily, "So We Have Published . . . " an entire list of them. Just bears too, a muchness of bears, is not to be belittled; or, as the flap copy puts it: "Here is a whole, solid, wonderful book of nothing *but* bears."

> Bears, bears, bears, bears, bears.
> On the stairs
> Under chairs
> Washing hairs
> Giving stares
> Collecting fares
> Stepping in squares
> Millionaires
> Everywheres
> Bears, bears, bears, bears, bears.

It is the way children play with words, and with notions of things, rhyming them endlessly, ringing changes on the same sound, the same something; and the more non-sensical the result, the funnier it seems to them. But it begins in a correspondence they feel between sound and sense, or meaning: any old absurdities—bears laying bricks, shaking hands—wouldn't do. They wouldn't do as well, either, if they weren't things kids are close to—climaxing with that magic word 'millionaire.'

Not all, as some claimed, but much falls to the pictures, which cannot be real and ought not be whimsical—hence the value of Phyllis Rowand's natural artifice. Her bears are the funnier, and bearier, for being the same bear in

assorted sizes and poses, and for their wide-eyed solemnity. Stepping in squares, they have purpose, aplomb; millionaires, they are debonair; and collecting fares—a neuter, a stumper—they are busy conductors and playful children both. But there's a sense in which they're children being bears collecting fares, stepping in squares—everywheres.

Rhyming is easy and insidious and popular, but Krauss uses rhyme only when she has a reason to; small and simple as her texts are—deceptively simple, in truth—each is shaped by the nature of the contents.

Chukovsky remarks on the child's "priceless urge to establish the causal connection between separate facts," so that he associates, willy-nilly, things that occur simultaneously or that bear a resemblance to one another. In tenor, in movement, *The Happy Day* is the most spontaneous of books, a natural that would appear to defy explanation; but behind it, comprising it, are simultaneous similar occurrences—what do they signify? what are they leading to?

> Snow is falling.
> The field mice are sleeping,
>
> the bears are sleeping,
>
> the little snails sleep in their shells;
> and the squirrels sleep in the trees,
> the ground hogs sleep in the ground.
>
> Now, they open their eyes. They sniff.
> The field mice sniff,
>
> the bears sniff,
>
> the little snails sniff in their shells;
>
> and the squirrels sniff in the trees,
> the ground hogs sniff in the ground.
>
> They sniff. They run.
> The field mice run,
> the bears run,
>
> the little snails run with their shells,
> and the squirrels run out of the trees,
>
> the ground hogs run out of the ground.
> They sniff. They run.
>
> They run. They sniff.
>
> They sniff. They run. They stop.
> They stop. They laugh.
> They laugh. They dance.
>
> They cry, "Oh!
> A flower is growing in the snow."

In sum, various animals sleep, sniff, run, find the first

flower growing in the snow; and it is yellow; a bright flat yellow flower against furry, fleecy black and gray and white, a child's flower-emblem bringing an end to winter.

It is a story contained, as it were, in five species, a string of verbs and an image; contained but not confined. 'Bears are sleeping' is a lullaby line, one of those phrases—envisionings—that have a special hold on children (later the basis of whole books); the 'snails in their shells'—sleeping, sniffing, running in their shells—are the unexpected, the amusing, the touch of nonsense. The animals' 'sniff' at the first whiff of spring is the spark, touching off action, curiosity; and a bit of onomatopoeia that, whether reading or listening, one imitates instinctively. So it goes to the last lines, in 'accidental' rhyme.

The pictures are prescribed: a set of the animals, in fixed order, sleeping, then sniffing, then running; or snug in their dens, popping out, taking to their heels—each of which is funny animal by animal as a sequence, and gathers force and momentum as bears and mice, snails, squirrels, ground hogs stream across the pages en masse, only to come to a halt, the lot of them, around a single small flower. A book pictured, one could say, in the writing too (Krauss had studied art), but written for such pictures as will fill it with life; as Marc Simont's quick and personable animal performers do.

Year by year the books appeared, marked by no special predilections, no particular manner or style, not then. They were—unusual praise—books children liked and adults appreciated.

*The Backward Day* takes us back to *A Good Man and His Good Wife,* but only so far. Getting up, a little boy says to himself, "Today is backward day"; and proceeds to put on his coat. Over his coat goes his suit, over his suit, his underwear: "Backward day is backward day." So backward goes he down the stairs (taking care to look over his shoulder), into the breakfast room, past his place and his chair; backward he turns his father's chair, and tucks his father's napkin at the back of his collar. "Goodnight, Pa," he greets his father, and "Goodnight," his father replies; and in a trice the whole household is turned around. The little boy is the one to right things. "Time to go to bed," and back up the stairs, backward, he goes—"backward oh backward oh backward oh backward oh backward and . . ." back into bed. Then it's time to get up again, to put on his underwear, suit, shoes, socks: "BACKWARD DAY IS DONE!"

The topsy-turvy nonsense that *A Good Man and His Good Wife* keeps at a distance, story-like, to laugh at, is transposed to the home as a reversal of the established order of things; or, as the jacket puts it more pointedly, "the conventional routine of the household is turned upside down." This we would label, not unreasonably, 'child psychology': the little boy, in control, upsets the applecart with impunity and then, of his own volition, rights it. Meanwhile we enjoy the incongruity with him.

Nursery rhymes, Chukovsky observed, abound in topsy-turvies—children ice-skating on a hot summer's day, a blind man gazing while a deaf man listens; and he searched for a reason for their persistent popularity, a psychological basis for the pleasure children take in any violation of the established order. As he tells it, his small daughter came to him one day, after she had mastered to her great satisfaction the fact that a dog goes bow-wow, a cat goes meow, and cried out—"looking mischievous and embarrassed at the same time"—"Daddy, 'oggie—meow!"

"That is," Chukovsky continues, "she reported to me the sensational and, to her, obviously incorrect news that a doggie, instead of barking, meows. And she burst into somewhat encouraging, somewhat artificial laughter, inviting me, too, to laugh at this invention.

"But I was inclined to realism.

"'No,' said I, 'the doggie bow-wows.'

"'Oggie—meow!' she repeated, laughing, and at the same time watched my facial expression which, she hoped, would show her how she should regard this erratic invention which seemed to scare her a little.

"I decided to join in her game and said:

"'And the rooster meows!'

"Thus I sanctioned her intellectual effrontery. Never did even the most ingenious epigram of Piron evoke such appreciative laughter in knowledgeable adults as did this modest joke of mine, based on the interchange of two elementary notions. This was the first joke that my daughter became aware of—in the twenty-third month of her life. She realized that not only was it not dangerous to topsy-turvy the world according to one's whim, but, on the contrary, it was even amusing to do so, *provided that together with a false conception about reality there remained the correct one. . . .* "

The emphasis is added, in accordance with the stress that Chukovsky himself places on verifying and self-examination, and additionally on self-appreciation, as explaining the value that the absurd, the incongruous—all manner of nonsense—has for a child. "*Others* do not seem to know that there is ice only in winter, that it is impossible to burn one's tongue with cold porridge . . . that mute people are incapable of crying 'Help.' *He,* however, has become so sure of these truths that he can even play with them."

He knows, as surely, that a carrot does not grow to the size of a watermelon; but what a good joke on the doubters to pretend so.

*The Backward Day,* with another, younger 'make-believe,' *The Bundle Book* (1951), brought to an end what one might call, *pace* Graham Greene, 'the entertainments,' for the next year there appeared the first of the inside-child books, *A Hole Is To Dig.*

RUTH KRAUSS AND MAURICE SENDAK

The year was 1952 and the dominant note was, collectively, color, size, design. Honors went, too, to the anecdotal: Lynd Ward's *The Biggest Bear* won the Caldecott, among the runners-up was *One Morning in Maine*.

In *Infant and Child in the Culture of Today* (1943), [Arnold] Gesell observes that at five or six, the child "is likely to define a word in terms of use. The wind is 'to make the clouds come,' it is 'to push the ships,'" Gesell's interest is in the child's thought processes, his route to understanding cause and effect (at four, "Trees blow," they make the wind). Ruth Krauss, alerted, took notice of the definitions themselves and of what they said about how children felt. She asked children their meanings for words and tried out her own definitions on them; "A mother is to hug you" was vetoed—"A mother is to cook your food." The ones they approved she took to Harper's, jotted on 3 x 5 cards, as the basis for a book.

A first illustrator, Mordvinoff, could see nothing in them; but in Maurice Sendak's sketchbook were drawings of Brooklyn children that made Ursula Nordstrom think "he would be perfect for it," and Sendak, young and new— Marcel Aymé's *Wonderful Farm* (1951) was just behind him—took to the idea from the start. Author and editor sifted the definitions for those they liked best, some that they discarded ("Buttons are to keep people warm") Sendak championed, for what he could do with them; and from the three-way hook-up came *A Hole Is To Dig*, "A First Book of First Definitions" and a novelty all around.

"Here is a children's book without gaudy four-color pictures which can charm its more pretentious competitors right off the map," Marshall Lee wrote in that month's [*Publishers Weekly*] design review. "Wonderful little drawings printed in black on an India stock [buff] with type in rust brown on a small square page produce an enchanting effect."

Less apparent, perhaps, but no less noteworthy is what Ruth Krauss does with the definitions. Were one to set down the separate lines in some approximation of the way they appear in the book, one would have a kind of verse-drama for many voices, for there are sounds that repeat, words and phrases that recur, and thoughts that expand throughout—to say nothing of the exchanges, explicit and implicit, among the children as pictured. As two successive openings:

Hands are to hold.
    A hand is to hold up
    when you want your turn.
    A hole is to dig.

The ground is to make a garden.
    Grass is to have on the ground
    with dirt under it
    and clover in it.
        Grass is to cut.
    Maybe you could

hide things
in a hole.

Plainly to be seen in each instance are a theme or motif, and variations, with large type for the large-picture legend or dominant note, if there is one, and smaller sizes of type for parallel thoughts or offshoots or, sometimes, like-sounding nonsense—as "Hands are to eat with," mischief in itself, springs upon us "A tablespoon is to eat a table with." The patterns are many and unpredictable, no more to be anticipated than the sequence of motifs. But the book isn't *A Hole Is To Dig* for no reason: a hole is to hide things in, 'maybe,' besides, or "to sit in," "to plant a flower," "for a mouse to live in," "to look through" (a knothole), and lastly, conclusively—"A hole is when you step in it you go down," and if you're a small Sendak child, bid fair to disappear. The finale is a parade winding across the two pages, "The sun is so it can be a great day"; the afterword, "A book is to look at," to crawl over, to doze on and have pleasant dreams.

Like the word-meanings, the drawings are observations— as distinct from formalized illustrations. Like the words, too, the figures seem to dance through the pages; Krauss had studied music as well as art, Sendak has often spoken of his indebtedness to it. But it is life and more than life that he is depicting. "Mashed potatoes are to give everybody enough" might have been set at the family dinner table where the idea was born; instead we have a steaming mountain of (meatless) mashed potatoes and around it, stamping and banging their spoons, children of all sizes: a mashed-potato pandemonium. "Dogs are to kiss people" is, in turn, a kiss-fest, with sixteen pairs of kids and pups looking like Central Park of a summer afternoon. Or take "A party is to say how do you do and shake hands"—and curtseying, bowing, scraping, squeezing, sniffing are big children and miniature children, baby children, boy children, dogs, a cat, oh so serious and comical in party hats. "A face is so you can make faces" asks, as it were, for a demonstration, "Rugs are so you don't get splinters in you" is wide open, a natural playground; but the others are fantasy-scenes of Sendak's making, a penchant, a vision, peculiarly his and, early and late, enormously fruitful.

He multiplies meaning everywhere, whether by giving the line "The world is so you have something to stand on" to a lone boy and girl, arms entwined, or by adding to "Hands are to make things" and "Hands are to eat with," a small acrobat, evidence that hands are to stand on too. He amplifies, that is, and extends; but he is starting not with a story which has inherent implications, but with expressions, to which he gives meaning, a particular implication, or with ideas, to which he adds one or more of his own—at the last, to the idea that "A book is to look at" the idea of a book on the floor to burrow into and, finally, to fall asleep on.

Ruth Krauss, he testifies, "pointed out that I was giving the kids who would read the book middle-class attitudes toward their roles. I had the boys doing what boys were expected to do and girls doing what *they* were expected to do. God forbid a boy should be jumping rope! Of course, that isn't the way it is, and at the last minute I made some quick changes." At the party, to be sure, one of the boys is curtseying while his girl partner bows.

Without the reminder, however, one might not notice the avoidance of sex typing as such because there are so few sex *roles,* only boys and girls together jumping in the mud, rolling in the snow, doing dishes, dancing on their toes—the last two, granted, usually sex-typed but here as natural a common pursuit as the first. There are no families, that is one thing: it is a world of children, and a world of children acting spontaneously. There are no expectations, strictures, norms, hence no established order to violate. Back of the Noisy Books was, in part, Margaret Wise Brown's recognition that it was natural for kids to make noise. Back of *A Hole Is To Dig,* implicit in the attention to kids' definitions, is acceptance of the meanings they're liable to give to words, and that whether they're being pragmatic ("The sun is to tell you when it's every day") or projecting their feelings ("The sun is so it can be a great day") or—from either or both—flouting convention. "A face is so you can make faces," and, as a protesting librarian was reminded, children will whether we want them to or not; "Mud is to jump in and slide in and yell doodleedoodleedoo"—not, mind you, to make niggardly mud pies. There's as much pensiveness, though, as acting crazy—more; more kisses, certainly, than snubs or taunts. There is, in fact, almost everything except conventional behavior; the book is absolutely without hypocrisy.

The time, again, was 1952. In the 1950s and early 1960s the prevailing assumptions of psychology and sociology, that man was plastic—pliant, pliable—and that society was in equilibrium, were joined, as Kenneth Keniston has written [in *Youth and Dissent: The Rise of a New Opposition,* 1971], "in the theory of socialization and acculturation. Malleable man was said to be related to stable society through a series of special socializing institutions like the family and the education system, whose primary function was to 'integrate' the individual into society. Specifically, families' and schools' chief job was to teach children the social roles and cultural values necessary for adult life in that society." When Keniston himself studied alienated students at Harvard in the late Fifties and early Sixties, he found in them a focus on "sentience, awareness, expression, and feeling," and, corollary, a desire for a kind of experience—unstructured and unconstrained— "which is above all characteristic of early childhood," [as he wrote in *The Uncommitted: Alienated Youth in American Society,* 1965]. By 1968-69, the disaffected have become the dissidents, and Keniston is writing [in *Youth and Dissent*] not of deviant behavior but of a revolution of consciousness: "a special personal and psychological openness, flexibility and unfinishedness"; "the stress on the expressive, the aesthetic, and the creative; the emphasis on imagination, direct perception, and fantasy"; "a revolt against uniformity, equalization, standardization, and homogenization"; and so on.

All children had come to look like Sendak children, Ur-

sula Nordstrom (and others) remarked in the early Seventies. To an extent, this is the way art recasts nature: after Grant Wood, we see Grant Wood farmers; after Renoir, Renoir women. It is true too that there always were such shaggy, dumpy little boys—as against the strapping towheaded all-American tyke; and that picturing them is, on Sendak's part, just so much more individualism. Still, at the start longer hair on boys and unkempt looks in general represented individuality as well—the right to be different, to be imperfect, the wish to be valued for oneself rather than for one's resemblance to an Ivy League or Jaycee model. Children came to look like Sendak children physically in the aftermath of young people's taking on much of the open, instinctual Krauss-Sendak spirit; and though we cannot call the books contributory in any measurable sense, where they were known they cannot but have been nurturants. At the very least they were prophetic.

*A Very Special House* is just what one of the youngsters in *A Hole Is To Dig* would have dreamed up; and there he is, doing his little dance, singing his little tune, not in advance of the title page, a herald or harbinger, but after, as a part of the book proper. A little boy in bright blue overalls, all alone, dancing—a revolutionary act; and then skipping, bouncing, swinging through the pages, chanting, shouting, grinning, chortling, while the doodleeoo drawings, like the ones he crayons on his wall to begin with, bring the very special house to life. It's a life, he tells us, and a house, that's not anything, not anywhere, but "right in the middle" ("oh it's ret in the meedle—oh it's root in the moodle") "of my head head head." But neither is it expressly, antiseptically encased in a dream: bouncing, beaming even as he tells it, the little boy tumbles through the air and straggles off. Are they so different—wishes, hopes, dreams?

*A Hole Is To Dig* was unique, and it was copied; *A Very Special House* is the extension, the implementation of much that is broached in *A Hole Is To Dig* and, less 'inspired,' more *formed,* it is by contrast assimilable. The relationship between *Hole* and *House* illustrates, as well, a salient feature of the Krauss-Sendak partnership, the way each built upon the work of the other, not in a single book only but book by book in the course of their collaboration.

The wonderful early Krauss books, the ones written to a child's measure, are constructed almost invariably on a one-to-one basis—one image or action per line per picture; and whether or not they grow (*Bears,* for instance, doesn't), they are sequential or, more properly, serial. A collection of definitions might have taken the form of a picture dictionary, the model of a one-to-one serial form, but it wouldn't have been in the least *A Hole Is to Dig.* By grouping the definitions and varying the groupings, an interplay of thoughts was set up, simultaneous and fluid; and Sendak, further, makes of the groupings now a tableau, now one-two-three 'frames,' now a kite trailing odd thoughts, now an arrow, a pointer—followed wordlessly by more more more. The stage was set for ripostes and asides, and for the baby's "boodlyboodlyboodly"; for changes of definition, new meanings, for a baby silently sucking his toes while, in the spotlight, "Toes are to dance on."

"Dee dee dee oh-h-h" dances the *Very Special House*'s little boy, and once inside he's all over the place, climbing and drawing, snoozing and swinging at once; and so, soon, are the turtle and the rabbit and the giant he brings home " . . . and I'm hopping and I'm skipping and I'm / jumping and I'm bumping and Everywhere is music— and / the giant spilled his drinking and it went all down the floor / and the rabbit ate a piece out of my very best door / and Everybody's telling for more More MORE." It runs on, it erupts, it runs together—like a dream, daydream or night-dream or play-dream; and the disarray, the flux, the indeterminacy were essential to the personal and private fancies that were to chiefly occupy Ruth Krauss thereafter.

Then and later, directly or through intermediaries, artists took up the pictorial ideas that Sendak himself returns to repeatedly and develops. He isolates the single child, making of his imagining a more immediate and individual experience; and so, for story-telling emphasis, does Blair Lent. Sendak uses silence, or virtual silence, for free movement and a final fillip (after having, in effect, created silence by free movement in *A Hole Is to Dig*); and Mary Chalmers uses silence, and a last look, to specific dramatic effect. Put *A Hole Is to Dig* and *A Very Special House* together and you have the makings of *Rain Makes Applesauce*—exploding all over the page, carrying a feedback-refrain; but only the makings, the impetus. They were ideas—and not formulas—that allowed of varied original application.

The wellhead that *A Very Special House* was for artists, *I'll Be You and You Be Me* was for authors. It is the book in which the talk of small children is transmuted into a style that is Ruth Krauss's too, the embodiment of the thought of small children. *I'll Be You and You Be Me:* it fits.

What it says bears thinking. This book, the jacket tells us, is about love and friendship, but it "is also about something beyond love and friendship—a feeling of togetherness that it is impossible for an adult to describe but which children will recognize." Recognize is the proper word, for they won't be told, mostly, they'll be shown. The dream-giver makes his rounds, and each child marches off with a best-of-all dream; a little girl stands alone under a vast sky—"she is waiting for her friend, waiting and waiting"; a wedding party is a maypole dance, a game of tag, a bowl of chicken soup. A little boy making a poem makes a dream (without words) of a magic bird that flies him to the sun, to the moon, over seas and towns, and home to his mother—who is waiting. (There is good waiting, and not so good.) But they are not meant to be described either, these light-fantastic pages, where the pictures say things that can't be put in words, and the words say things that can't be put another way; and a poem is a poem ("dopey") and a play is a play (with an audience) and a story is a story ("and now listen") and one story is

a mystery; and there's a "Dance For a Horse" and, opposite, "a new holiday and a good song / if you have a monkey for a friend friend friend." (The holiday, naturally, is Monkey Day, and you sing "Happy Monkey Day, dear Monkey . . . ")

Within the book is enough for a dozen books (there was, later, a *Monkey Day*); it is like a notebook-sketchbook that Krauss and Sendak made together, a scrapbook of her images and his, now complementary, more often conjoined: I'll write for you and you draw for me. And because he could draw fantasy sequences, she wrote a poem for a little boy that ends with the words "a dream I made," after which comes the dream of the magic bird. But because the words "she is waiting for her friend, waiting and waiting," expand even in the saying, he pictures the little girl holding a bunch of flowers in an empty, endless meadow.

Because, too, the wedding party is so engagingly, unaffectedly comical, the definition of love, opposite, has less the waxen aspect of any attempt to say that love is this or that. It is difficult if not impossible to read it now without also reading in it what-came-after: Love Is a Special Way of Feeling, Happiness Is a Warm Puppy, et al. One can say easily enough that Love Is a Special Way of Feeling is slop, that Happiness Is a Warm Puppy is a pet-store slogan, the one everything and nothing, the other a sometime thing; and then perhaps see what is different about Ruth Krauss's terms of definition—that for one thing they're not categorical but actual: the word defined 'in terms of use' (Gesell) as per *A Hole Is to Dig.*

But out of them came, by abstraction and ascription, the others—looking alike, passing as child thoughts; and entered the language. The words defined in *A Hole Is to Dig* are concrete nouns, objects—a dream is the nearest to an intangible. But the definitions are invested with feeling, which *I'll Be You and You Be Me* took as its province, spinning out little stories, variations on fellow-feeling; and suddenly feelings were a subject—and an object. All kinds of feelings, for neither is *I'll Be You and You Be Me* a repository of only kindly thoughts: the kids who made faces in *A Hole Is to Dig* are acting out their aggressions now. "There are six friends and they all put on each other's coats. It is winter and they run in the snow. Then they begin to fight. Then they are unfriends. Then they yell at each other 'You give me back my coat!' It is winter—right in the middle—and they are running in the snow."

That's "A Story," and books were made afterward of little more (entitled *Let's Be Enemies,* for one); and little stories were made that, like the poets and dreamers in *I'll Be You and You Be Me,* children might tell to themselves.

First by Ruth Krauss. "This is the story of Charlotte and Milky Way, her horse," Charlotte begins, and were there not quotation marks we would still know it was she, so gravely does she tell it, and dramatically and ingenuously, in a mingling of Biblical phrases, matter-of-fact observations, and pathos. The pathos arises in the threat to sell her beloved Milky Way:

> Then a big man comes, who is her father,
>     and says,
> he won't make a good race horse so we will
>     sell him.
> Then Nathan can go to college when he is grown.
> —That's the little brother.
> Now just sorrow is coming in
> Now just sorrow is coming in

And when Daddy accedes to her pleas, "the flowers appear on the earth," the "multitude" rejoice.

In the gloom, Charlotte and her father are washed out, almost colorless; happiness restores the rose to her dress, and body to the scene. Alone in early morning and at evening, she and Milky Way are ethereal, sharers in a dream; but overleaf, the moonlight brighter, Charlotte waving good-by, "horses eat all night when they're not sleeping."

Somewhat evanescent and tenuous though it may be, **Charlotte and the White Horse** is not precious and it is not solemn; it is, in fact, a nice complement to Crockett Johnson's little-boy's-dream *Harold and the Purple Crayon,* which appeared at the same time. Both have, in their own way, their heads in the clouds and their feet on the ground.

Subsequent Krauss-Sendak books are, for various reasons, less successful. In **I Want to Paint My Bathroom Blue** (1956), Sendak's dreamer never does touch base, that is part of the trouble. **Somebody Else's Nut Tree** (1958) is subtitled "and other Tales *from* Children" which suggests, per the stress added, both its strength—freshness of vision—and its major weakness—many of the stories are truly ephemeral. Opposite each, printed in toto, is an animated sequence which attempts to put it into pictures, an effort foredoomed insofar as few— "The Little Queen" made commoner is a notable exception—consist of concrete images or invoke direct experience.

A late little Krauss book says it; **I Write It** (1970), it says, "On a piece of paper I write it . . . "

> On my finger nails small skies
> On pitchers of milk
> I write it
> On carousels
> On park benches
> On shells . . .
>
> On you, waves
> I write it
> I write my name

The brimming pictures are by Mary Chalmers, the names are yours and mine and everyone's, the signature is unmistakably Ruth Krauss.

## Maurice Sendak

SOURCE: "Ruth Krauss and Me: A Very Special Partnership," in *The Horn Book Magazine,* Vol. LXX, No. 3, May-June, 1994, pp. 286–90.

Before children's books grew up and took on some of the unsavory commercial characteristics of their elder sibling, grown-up books, there was Ruth Krauss. There were some few others, too, of course, but Ruth, along with Ursula Nordstrom, editor of children's books at Harper and Brothers, dominated the landscape when I came on the scene in the early fifties. That ancient book world was populated with giant women—grand, inspired, towering women who invented the American children's book from scratch. Back then, most publishing-type guys wouldn't be caught dead in a "kiddie-book" department, and when they did show up (after we'd grown up and the whiff of Big Bucks reassured their masculinity), the better part of the business was all but dead.

In those cottage-industry days of the mid-forties, Ruth and her painter, writer, illustrator, cartoonist, and all-round ingenious husband, Crockett Johnson, teamed up and created that perfect picture book, **The Carrot Seed,** the granddaddy of all picture books in America, a small revolution of a book that permanently transformed the face of children's book publishing. **The Carrot Seed,** with not a word or a picture out of place, is dramatic, vivid, precise, concise in every detail. It springs fresh from the real world of children, the Bank Street world of listening to children and recording and re-creating their startling speech patterns and curious, pragmatic thinking processes. These explorations at the Bank Street School in Greenwhich Village, pioneered by Margaret Wise Brown, were turned into hilarious, nutty, immortal poetry by Ruth Krauss, fresh from her anthropology courses at Columbia and the Writers Laboratory at Bank Street. In full charge of her intuitive grasp of all things related to real children (as opposed to children's book children), this vivacious, sexy, high-living lady suddenly appeared and conquered all. How could she fail? Ruth broke rules and invented new ones, and her respect for the natural ferocity of children bloomed into poetry that was utterly faithful to what was true in their lives.

She had the gleeful cooperation of that other "giant," Ursula Nordstrom, who was only too ready to encourage Kraussian mayhem and break into new forms. And I was the lucky kid who was taken up and apprenticed to those two happy hooligans. I found myself drawn into that yummy cottage industry, cooking up the most amazing dishes with my two new mamas and my new big papa, Dave (alias Crockett) Johnson. And it all took place in Connecticut, in Ruth and Dave's big rickety frame house by a river with a boat. So, with all the ardent thoughtlessness of youth (I was twenty-three), I pretty much abandoned my good but grumpy Brooklyn parents, who had no boat and little confidence in my ability to earn a living.

Ruth and Dave became my weekend parents and took on

the job of shaping me into an artist. I was a good apprentice, and *A Hole Is to Dig,* in 1952, was my official baptism into picture books. I remember the porch table covered with a million (it seems) bits of Krauss words and thinkings, encircled by my little scratchy, dumpy doodles. Ruth and I would arrange and rearrange and paste and unpaste and Ruth would sing and Ruth would holler and I'd quail and sulk and Dave would referee. His name should be on all our books, for the technical savvy and cool consideration he brought to them. There was an impressive silence about Dave (he was the most giant of all!), and after Ruth had gone to bed I'd hang around with him, hoping he'd open up and waiting for my weekly reading list.

Ruth wasn't so patient, or quiet, and she could frighten me with her stormy tirades. It was hard for such a fiercely liberated woman to contend with a potentially talented but hopelessly middle-class kid. In the end, she slapped me into shape—almost literally. When Ruth approved of a sketch, I was rewarded with the pleasure of her deep belly laugh, which rose upward and exploded in little-girl giggles. But her disapproval could be devastating. There was the awful weekend when we were near completion of *A Hole Is to Dig,* and both of us were worn thin with the whole messy business of pasting, doing, and undoing and Ruth began raging at something she'd missed and only just discovered in a number of my pictures. She accused me of assigning the kids middle-class roles: boys doing boy things, and girls (even worse!) doing girl things. "God forbid, a boy should jump rope!" screamed Ruth. Panic-stricken, I made some very hasty changes. There are, alas, some suspiciously hermaphroditic-looking kids lurking in the pages of *A Hole Is to Dig.* The very last little picture, the girl sleeping on a book, was originally a boy. Why did Ruth insist I change him to a girl? Perhaps because the two vignettes above him/her are of two little boys and she wanted a girl to finish off the triumvirate of book-loving kids? I didn't ask questions.

My favorite Krauss is *A Very Special House,* published in 1953. That poem most perfectly simulates Ruth's voice—her laughing, crooning, chanting, singing voice. Barbara Bader, in her *American Picturebooks from Noah's Ark to the Beast Within,* sums up that text: "It runs on, it erupts, it runs together—like a dream, daydream or night-dream or playdream; and the disarray, the flux, the indeterminacy were essential to the personal and private fancies that were to chiefly occupy Ruth Krauss thereafter." "Thereafter" was the series of books Ruth and I collaborated on, eight in all. They permanently influenced my talent, developed my taste, and made me hungry for the best. But nothing was so satisfying as *A Very Special House;* those words and images are Ruth and me at our best. If I open that book, her voice will laugh out to me. So I will leave it shut a while.

Is there anyone who grew up in the late forties or the fifties who doesn't treasure the memory of the fresh, bubbling, no-nonsense nonsense of *I Can Fly* and the somber, ethereal shades and biblical rhythms of *Charlotte and the White Horse* and the supreme inventiveness of

Crockett Johnson's *Harold and the Purple Crayon* (*Harold* and **Charlotte** were published in the same year, 1955) and all the other Krauss and Johnson masterpieces? Yet the death of Ruth Krauss on July 10, 1993, went unnoticed, aside from a small obituary, a mere *footnote* riddled with errors published in *The New York Times* five days later. We writers and illustrators of children's books are *footnotes* to the book business and are of interest only when we generate lots of money or, even more astonishingly, when we appear on the best-seller lists.

This condescension says more about the status of children than it does about us hard-working professionals. Those kids so brilliantly celebrated, loved, and congratulated in Krauss book after Krauss book are, in truth, powerless little tots of no special interest to any group, political or otherwise. As always, there is endless tongue-clucking coming from government, but little else. We are numbed by the daily reports of children getting murdered on the way home from school, by abuses committed in the best and worst neighborhoods. Children are stoical and suffer silently. What choice do they have? We kiddie-book folk oddly share their humiliation. Apart from parents, we are often the first to greet them in this life, the first to magically empower them. What a mighty role we play, and how often we hear praise, usually incoherent, from those grown-up kids who blush and sniffle and cannot recount those long-ago secret moments spent with our books. We snagged them before they could even talk. Ruth is their great champion, and with all due respect to those fine people who shared the obituary page with her, it is likely that she will be remembered best.

When I last visited Ruth, I was struck by her extreme frailty and her startling, strong, snow-white hair that fell thickly down her back to the floor. She was a child again, with her staring, suspicious eyes. I mentioned Dave and she murmured: "Poor baby." She frowned and looked troubled. Then, just as quickly, her face cleared and she smiled gently, shyly. How often I'd seen that transformation. I took her face in my hands and kissed her on the mouth. And I was rewarded once more with her growling belly laugh that rose up into a cascade of little-girl giggles. This was the same seductive Ruthie, the high-flying Ruthie who gave all of herself to her art. What a lucky kid I was.

---

# TITLE COMMENTARY

📖   *THE CARROT SEED* (1945)

*Virginia Kirkus' Bookshop Service*

SOURCE: A review of *The Carrot Seed,* in *Virginia Kirkus' Bookshop Service,* Vol. XIII, No. 8, April 15, 1945, p. 180.

Even tiny children love to see things grow, and this is a

picture book about a carrot seed that grew. The publishers, in choosing Crockett Johnson, creator of Barnaby and Mr. O'Malley, as illustrator, have picked the ideal person for the job. Barnaby seems to tickle the funny bone of three to six as much as he does their elders. This is the story of a small boy who plants a carrot seed, waters it and cultivates it and ignores the scepticism of his elders. Faith (and care) win out and it comes up, the biggest carrot in many counties. A good humored tale—pictures in two and four colors.

### New York Herald Tribune Weekly Book Review

SOURCE: A review of *The Carrot Seed,* in *New York Herald Tribune Weekly Book Review,* May 20, 1945, p. 8.

There are just 101 words in this narrative, all told: its pictures utilize comic strip technique of the high grade or O'Malley type; you can go through it in less than no time. the judges at the Spring Festival contest, by spontaneous, unanimous, decision, sent a copy to the San Francisco Conference. Here's the scenario. A little boy planted a carrot seed: nothing happened. One by one everybody told him it wouldn't come up. He kept right on watering it and one day it did come up—just as the little boy had known it would.

And now you see why six enlightened citizens sent this little parable to the Golden Gate.

### Ellen Lewis Buell

SOURCE: "Young Gardener," in *The New York Times Book Review,* July 18, 1945, p. 18.

The older you are the more you will appreciate this book. But the very young will understand it too, for who knows better than they the substance of things hoped for? And who likes better to confound the skepticism of grown-ups? So it was with the little boy who planted a carrot seed. Father, mother, big brother told him it wouldn't come up. But every day he watered it and weeded. And one day it did come up. You see it all: the superior cynicism of the onlookers, the stubborn confidence and the pride of faith justified in the small believer, portrayed in pictures which are as economical of line as the text is with words. You don't need trimmings to understand this parable.

### Mary Lou Burket

SOURCE: "Growing Things," in *The Five Owls,* Vol. III, No. 4, March-April, 1989, p. 63.

[The] boy in **The Carrot Seed** is one of the tenacious children in literature. He plants a seed, he expects it to grow, despite the fact that everyone who counts—his mother, his father, his older brother—tells him it won't. Of course, he isn't just hopeful; he's hardworking, too, weeding the ground and sprinkling it with water. But the

sustaining point the author, Ruth Krauss, makes is that it's his faith, not his effort, that really matters. When the reward bursts from the soil, Crockett Johnson, who drew the pictures, makes it glorious: a bright, solid, unmistakable carrot every bit as large as the gardener. One could hardly wish for a better introduction to what cultivating plants is all about—or for a more agile example of picture book art—than this spare and witty forty-year-old book.

## THE GREAT DUFFY (1946)

### Virginia Kirkus' Bookshop Service

SOURCE: A review of *The Great Duffy,* in *Virginia Kirkus' Bookshop Service,* Vol. XIV, No. 19, October 1, 1946, p. 490.

A delectable book for the distracted parent who wants to wean small sons from too constant demand for the comics. Mischa Richter of *New Yorker* fame catches the spirit of the indomitable small boy in a big traffic-ridden world. Tommy was too small to go all the way to school alone. In pointed gray and black sketches the artist conveys the mother's decision. And so the scene changes. Tommy becomes a super-boy, in gorgeous colors and comic strip adventure. As the great Duffy he has an exciting before breakfast adventure with motor cars and planes, crowded streets and airports—adventures which catch the 'Walter Mitty' touch. And an understanding mother allows him time to switch back to the black and grey of daily life at home, which is after all not so bad. An imaginative handling of real small boy psychology. A love of a book.

### Marjorie Fischer

SOURCE: A review of *The Great Duffy,* in *The New York Times Book Review,* November 10, 1946, p. 3.

Here is the child's equivalent of "The Secret Life of Walter Mitty." A small boy is told by his mother that he isn't big enough to walk to school alone. So, between dressing and oatmeal, Tom voyages by submarine, plane and parachute, rescues a puppy—and still leaves for school on time. Children frustrated by size, and with imagination, will understand the story, and all parents will get it. The pictures, rather confusingly run together without benefit of margins, have the glorified and cockeyed reality of [Mischa] Richter's cartoons, and the text is free and easy, a montage of radio and movie adventure stories. For small children and parents name of Mitty.

## THE GROWING STORY (1947)

### Virginia Kirkus' Bookshop Service

SOURCE: A review of *The Growing Story,* in *Virginia Kirkus' Bookshop Service,* Vol. XV, No. 17, July 1, 1947, p. 335.

The author of some of our very favorite juveniles (*A Good Man and His Good Wife, The Carrot Seed, The Great Duffy*) has again given us a satisfying, lovely text that will get repeated reading with four to six year olds. A little boy helps mother put away his winter clothes; he asks if he will grow during the summer; he watches the chicks grow tall and feathery, the puppy become a dog, the seeds grow into corn and flowers, the pears grow big and ripe. But in the mirror he looks just the same. Then comes fall—and the clothes come out again, and he sees for himself that he has outgrown his pants and his coat. Appealing pictures [by Phyllis Rowand are] modern and stylized without sacrifice of a certain tenderness that never degenerates into being wishy washy.

### May Lamberton Becker

SOURCE: A review of *The Growing Story,* in *New York Herald Tribune Weekly Book Review,* September 14, 1947, p. 14.

If the five-year-old for whom you are choosing a story is like others of his age he finds the rate of his own growth a matter of warm interest. Here is a little story all about this one matter, as it affected a little boy, a puppy and some chicks.

They were all very little when the story begins. You see him surrounded by tall trees and houses that seem to him taller than we find them, for he is always looking up. The grass grows, the corn begins to grow, the chicks rapidly grow and mother puts away the little boy's winter underwear. Then he looks in the mirror and tells mother that the chicks are up to his knees and the puppy to his middle, but he's just the same: can he be growing? So, with delightful full-page pictures, in colors—every other page in four colors—the season rolls on till the chicks have grown up, and so has the dog, and our hero still is a little boy. His mother takes out his winter underwear, for the days are cold. "Hey!" cries the little boy as he puts them on. "My pants are too little and my coat is too little. I'm growing too!"

All this time the growing that goes on in all nature takes part in pictures and text, but, of course, the little boy to whom it is read will be the real hero.

### Frances C. Darling

SOURCE: A review of *The Growing Story,* in *The Christian Science Monitor,* November 11, 1947, p. 16A.

*Growing Story* by Ruth Krauss, who did the amusing *Carrot Seed* last year, has full-page, comical illustrations by Phyllis Rowand. All summer long the little boy watches the dog and the chickens and the flowers by the barn grow bigger and taller and he keeps wondering about himself. At last when he takes out his old winter clothes he finds the pants too short and the coat too tight and he

knows then he has been growing too. Simple, but satisfying to young readers who will enjoy the little story and the truth behind it.

### Lillian Gerard

SOURCE: A review of *The Growing Story,* in *The New York Times Book Review,* November 16, 1947, p. 42.

The phenomenon of growth, combined with a child's interest in himself, makes this a fascinating story, easy to read aloud and discuss. It concerns a boy, a puppy and some chicks, all of whom pass through the growing stages even as the seasons change and all things ripen and mellow. As the boy observes the wonders of nature he also wonders about himself. Will he grow, too? And because growing is a process the child cannot feel, he can only be sure that he is taller when winter comes again, and his clothes are tighter and shorter, and his arms and legs are longer and stronger. These experiences make a pleasant book, deftly illustrated with full page, four-color drawings, scaled to size and exaggerated for effect.

### Patricia Cianciolo

SOURCE: "Using Illustrations in the School," in *Illustrators in Children's Books,* William C. Brown Company Publishers, 1976, pp. 94–123.

A long time favorite with four-, five-, and six-year-olds is ***The Growing Story*** which was written by Ruth Krauss. The text, and the precise but simple line drawings by Phyllis Rowand, depict a little boy watching many things grow—grass, flowers, chickens, and a puppy, among other things. He doesn't realize until he puts on his warm clothes in late autumn that he, too, has grown. Identification with the book character who is involved in a situation as common as this will be easy for the young reader. He will appreciate more fully that he, too, is growing up. ***The Growing Story*** can be used to help the young reader accept with ease and grace the physical changes that are taking place within him.

###  📖 *BEARS* (1948)

### *Virginia Kirkus' Bookshop Service*

SOURCE: A review of *Bears,* in *Virginia Kirkus' Bookshop Service,* Vol. XVI, No. 20, October 15, 1948, p. 552.

This is fun—not only because teddy bears are very dear to small hearts, and this is all bears—not another creature in it; but because the nonsense words are just the sort of repeats on sound that the child who is starting to put words into a pattern will find enchanting.

## Louise Seaman Bechtel

SOURCE: A review of *Bears,* in *New York Herald Tribune Weekly Book Review,* November 14, 1948, p. 6.

"Bears, bears, bears, bears, bears—on the stairs—under chairs—washing hairs—giving stares—collecting fares—stepping in squares—millionaires—everywheres—" the total text of a merry little book which I find delights small children. the bears are rather oddly drawn to my taste, but not to theirs. Anyway, it's the fun that counts. Wait till you have to choose which bear you are—maybe you will prefer to be the one lolling in a cloud in "everywheres," or the one sitting on a flag-pole or the one that hops out of the mail box. Really very funny and surprising.

## Anne Thaxter Eaton

SOURCE: A review of *Bears,* in *The Christian Science Monitor,* December 21, 1948, p. 11.

*Bears,* story by Ruth Krauss, pictures by Phyllis Rowand, is just that. "Bears, bears, bears," says the text (one or two or three words to a page of pictures), "on the stairs, under chairs, collecting fares . . . everywheres." And there indeed the bears are, not entirely realistic, but undoubtedly bears and engaging bears at that. The pleasant absurdity of the idea and the rhyming words—exactly the kind of rigmarole the young child makes up for himself—will please children from three to seven. An amusing picture book made in a spirit of gayety and frolic.

## 📖 THE HAPPY DAY (1949)

### *Virginia Kirkus' Bookshop Service*

SOURCE: A review of *The Happy Day,* in *Virginia Kirkus' Bookshop Service,* Vol. XVII, No. 17, September 1, 1949, p. 463.

A lovely book, which scarcely needs the captions, for the idea is evident in [Marc Simont's] enchanting pictures in soft blacks and whites, with one touch of color at the end. The pictures show the world of nature asleep, the squirrels in their trees, the ground hogs in the ground, the snails in their shells, and the ground blanketed in snow. And then something awakes them, and you see them coming out to find out for themselves—as the small fry find for themselves at the end of the book. Possibly a book that has more perfection to an adult than to a child, but somehow I think children will grow into it, too.

## Elena Baker

SOURCE: A review of *The Happy Day,* in *The New York Times Book Review,* September 25, 1949, p. 32.

The animals are asleep and it is snowing. They wake up and they sniff. The squirrels run out of the trees, the ground hogs run out of the ground, the field mice run, the snails run, and the bears run. They all stop and laugh and dance when they find the marvelous thing—one yellow flower.

The appearance of snow; the animals sleeping and waking up; the running search and the discovery are wonderfully portrayed in large black-and-white illustrations. Many pre-school children will love the small animals and the big, genial bears, the snow and the action. Though the recurring word patterns in large type are excellent for beginning readers, these older children are generally too scientifically minded to accept such things as snails who run, sniff, and dance unless the miraculous is built up to an even greater degree than in this book.

## Louise S. Bechtel

SOURCE: A review of *The Happy Day,* in *New York Herald Tribune Book Review,* November 13, 1949, p. 6.

The author of the very brief but unforgettable text of *Bears* now gives us another book in which bears predominate. Again her text is as brief as possible, only about one hundred words. On big pages we see all the woods creatures sleeping in their holes in the snow or in the ground or in trees. Then come pages on which they all open their eyes and sniff. You will love the one where "the little snails sniff in their shells." Then they all begin to run. They sniff and run, they run, they sniff, and in the last big double-page picture they are gathered smiling or open-mouthed in a circle. They cry, "Oh! A flower is growing in the snow!"

The wonderfully snowy black and white scenes, the fuzzy creatures so well drawn and printed make a lovely winter picture book for the nursery age.

## Frances C. Darling

SOURCE: A review of *The Happy Day,* in *The Christian Science Monitor,* November 15, 1949, p. 13.

Snow is falling, and so the animals curl up in their winter homes—the field mice and the bears and the groundhogs all snugly sleeping until the day when the first whiff of spring comes through the forest. *The Happy Day* of this snowfall is described by Ruth Krauss in short, clear phrases which Marc Simont has illustrated in beautiful pictures, all soft grays and white. His drawings are full of action and beauty of design, especially those double pages where the animals race through the snowy woods toward the joyful surprise which ends the story.

## Anne Carroll Moore

SOURCE: A review of *The Happy Day,* in *The Horn*

*Book Magazine,* Vol. XXV, No. 6, November-December, 1949, pp. 520–23.

*The Happy Day* by Ruth Krauss, with pictures by Marc Simont, is a large-size picture book in black and white of animals taking their long winter sleep—field mice, bears, squirrels, snails in their shells, ground hogs, all in snowy scenes of serenity and beauty in which they wake up at the end. I think it a picture book children will love to own as a welcome change from activities to nature itself.

### The Atlantic Monthly

SOURCE: A review of *The Happy Day,* in *The Atlantic Monthly,* Vol. 184, No. 6, December, 1949, p. 103.

*The Happy Day,* by *Ruth Krauss.* This is far and away the best of this year's picture books. As we open, the bears are sleeping, the field mice are sleeping, the snails are sleeping, not to mention the squirrels and the ground hogs. Just why they wake up in such a hurry and dash off, all in one direction, is a secret. Marc Simont's illustrations contribute enormously.

## THE BIG WORLD AND THE LITTLE HOUSE (1949)

### Virginia Kirkus' Bookshop Service

SOURCE: A review of *The Big World and The Little House,* in *Virginia Kirkus' Bookshop Service,* Vol. XVII, No. 21, November 1, 1949, p. 603.

This is a book with a purpose—but not too emphatically that to lose out as a quite charming story of how a family brought a house back to life. At the start of the story—told in pictures by Marc Simont and expanded captions by Ruth Krauss—the little house is neglected, tumble-down, the prey of storm and loneliness. The pictures express this dismal quality. Then comes a family, three generations and pets as well—and the house begins to take on life, and at the end becomes a home rather than just a shell of a house—a part of its surroundings—and, through radio and television and telephone, a part of the world. It is this phase that doesn't quite come true to the adult reader, who realizes that the contribution is a receptive one, not a contributing one—and the family remains identified with the house rather than the world. But this doesn't much matter in a book which has its own story.

### Bulletin of the Children's Book Center

SOURCE: A review of *The Big World and The Little House,* in *Bulletin of the Children's Book Center,* Vol. III, No. 2, January, 1950, pp. 16–17.

The author sets out to achieve two purposes—the concept of home and the concept of the world. In neither is she successful—but she has managed a pleasant picture book, beautifully illustrated, that will please children even though they do not grasp the full meaning of the text. Used as a picture book to be enjoyed for the rhythm of the prose, the interest in the family reclaiming an old, abandoned house, and the color of the illustrations it should be successful—and it is possible that an occasional child will get the full import of the text.

### Lois Palmer

SOURCE: A review of *The Big World and The Little House,* in *New York Times Book Review,* January 15, 1950, p. 14.

The little house was a dilapidated old shack with rain and wind blowing through it until a family moved in and industriously began to make it into a home. Everybody worked: father, mother, children, grandpa and grandma. Soon the little house had new doors and new window panes. The roof was mended and there was shiny fresh paint indoors and out. Now the little house had become a gay, happy part of the big world and the family was ready to share with all the people of the world their contentment.

While the story and pictures of this book express a deep, sincere feeling, it is difficult to judge whether the 5-to-10-year-olds for whom it is written will find enough action in both to please them. It is a good book, certainly, for a family to share together. A few comments from the grown-ups will add a great deal to the children's enjoyment of the story. The family and world relationships brought out in this story offer good material for discussion groups.

### The Christian Science Monitor

SOURCE: A review of *The Big World and The Little House,* in *The Christian Science Monitor,* May 10, 1956, p. 17.

Obviously when a children's book is reissued it is usually because it's such a fine book people have been asking for it.

That is just the case with this second issue of *The Big World and The Little House.* It's an appealing story of how a family moved into a deserted house and turned it into a home. They brought clocks (the kind that don't run and the kind that do), they dug a pond to reflect the stars, chipmunks came and with it all an understanding of what home is and even a glimpse at world-mindedness.

Marc Simont's pictures are enormous and jolly. Combined with the story they make the book both enjoyable for the four-to-eight-year-olds and full of meaning.

*"Portrait of the Author as a Young Star," from* Under Twenty, *written and illustrated by Ruth Krauss.*

**Margaret Sherwood Libby**

SOURCE: A review of *The Big World and The Little House,* in *New York Herald Tribune Book Review,* May 13, 1956, p. 35.

The lovely big color pictures on every page, well reproduced, match the humor, the poetic realism and the universal feeling of the text. In easy prose, whose charm reaches children from five to eight, we hear of a family who make a lonely house into a home. We know how each of them felt about the house as a home, and, gently, at the end, comes the hint that there is a still greater feeling possible about the whole world being a home. It is surely a book that will live long.

**Myra Pollack Sadker and David Miller Sadker**

SOURCE: A review of *The Big World and The Little House,* in *Now Upon a Time: A Contemporary View of Children's Literature,* Harper & Row, 1977, p. 19.

**The Big World and the Little House** (1949), by Ruth Krauss, depicts a warm, active family making a desolate house into a home, one that is integrally related to the rest of the world. The little house is all alone on a big hill, without trees or flowers for company and without doors or windows to keep out wind and rain. A large family comes to this lonely house and sets to work to make it into a home. They paint and plant, put in furniture that can be played on, and even reserve one wall for the children to draw on. This picture book emphasizes the theme that a home is a special place created with love, and for some people home is the whole world.

> Home is a way people feel about a place. These people felt that way about the little house. Some people feel that way about a room, which is just part of a house.

Some people feel that way about a corner—which is just part of a room that is part of a house. Some people feel that way about the whole world.

## 📖 THE BACKWARD DAY (1950)

*Virginia Kirkus' Bookshop Service*

SOURCE: A review of *The Backward Day,* in *Virginia Kirkus' Bookshop Service,* Vol. XVIII, No. 18, August 1, 1950, p. 413.

The appeal of this little book is its nonsense for the little boy who wakes to decide that "Today is backward day" carries through his dressing backwards, walks backwards, sits backwards at the breakfast table—and is joined by his father and mother and little sister. He lands himself right back in bed, and, with backward day gone, is all ready to start the day properly. The idea will amuse when the tedium of too much routine is overpowering, and also show that a joke is a joke and not to be kept up indefinitely.

**Ellen Lewis Buell**

SOURCE: A review of *The Backward Day,* in *The New York Times Book Review,* September 10, 1950, p. 36.

Any child with a smidgen of humor will understand perfectly the game which the little boy plays in this picture book. Youngsters—and reminiscent grown-ups—will know exactly how he felt when he woke up one morning, said to himself "Today is backward day," put on his clothes in reverse order and went down the stairs backwards. Of course, not everyone has a family so willing to cooperate as was his. Together they play out the game to its unexpected but logical conclusion. This is written out of a true appreciation of a child's imagination and humor. Both text and pictures [by Marc Simont] are so much fun that parents may as well be prepared for an immediate performance.

*The Christian Science Monitor*

SOURCE: A review of *The Backward Day,* in *The Christian Science Monitor,* November 11, 1950, p. 9.

A slight little bit of nonsense that will tickle the small fry. The pictures are simple and direct. The little boy who dresses backward and exchanges a morning "Good night" with his family, all of whom sit backward at the table will be a bit of gay foolishness in the family conversation for many a day, lightening tension and turning incidents into play. Makes a hit with pre-schoolers.

**Rochelle Girson**

SOURCE: A review of *The Backward Day,* in *The Satur-*

*day Review of Literature,* Vol. XXXIII, No. 45, November 11, 1950, p. 40.

This book, printed in deep blue and green as well as a particularly deep black, tells of a little boy who decided that it was a "backward day" and that everything should be done in exactly the opposite way from which it is usually done. He put his coat on first and his underclothes last. He sat in his father's chair at the breakfast table, turned away from the table instead of toward it. He said "goodnight" instead of "good morning" and went downstairs and upstairs backward. It was obviously a great relief to his family when "backward day" was over. The illustrations are striking and lovely in design. The idea will probably amuse youngsters.

**Louise S. Bechtel**

SOURCE: A review of *The Backward Day,* in *New York Herald Tribune Book Review,* November 12, 1950, p. 9.

That lovely picture book of last year, **The Happy Day,** has a successor, by the same author and artist, Ruth Krauss and Marc Simont, called **The Backward Day.** It is an amusing conception, which many a small boy may have started, but never carried quite as far as this one. Somehow it doesn't quite "come off," even with the undoubted brilliance of the Simont pictures.

***Bulletin of the Children's Book Center***

SOURCE: A review of *The Backward Day,* in *Bulletin of the Children's Book Center,* Vol. IV, No. 2, January, 1951, p. 13.

When the little boy got up in the morning he decided it was a backward day, so he dressed backwards (starting with his coat and ending with his underwear), went down stairs backwards, and sat in his father's chair with his back to the breakfast table, Then, of course, he had to go back to bed since that is the logical way to start a backward day, and when he got up the second time it was a normal day. His family joins in his make believe to the extent of greeting each other backward and sitting with their backs to the table. The story will appeal to young children who are feeling rebellious at their regimented lives and will, at the same time, show the limits to which rebellion can go.

📖 *I CAN FLY* (1950)

**Margaret F. O'Connell**

SOURCE: A review of *I Can Fly,* in *New York Times Book Review,* May 8, 1966, p. 40.

*I Can Fly* returns in a slightly larger format with Mary Blair's same impudent illustratons in bright, brassy colors. The ebullient text, full of alliteration and rambunc-

tious sounds, really must be read aloud. Beginning readers can tackle it by themselves with minimal help.

📖 *THE BUNDLE BOOK* (1951)

***Virginia Kirkus' Bookshop Service***

SOURCE: A review of *The Bundle Book,* in *Virginia Kirkus' Bookshop Service,* Vol. XIX, No. 19, October 1, 1951, p. 575.

The sweetly soft, pastel illustrations by Helen Stone are lovely, but may appeal more to Mother rather than the toddler, in this delectable story-game for very little children and their mothers. The strange "bundle" on the bed made Mother wonder what it was. Was it a bundle of laundry? a monkey? a bird?, but all the guesses were very funny and very wrong, until the bundle popped out and yelled "It's ME!", and that is just what Mother wanted all along. The warmth of cherished "secret fun" infuses this gentle story which has a gleeful humor the toddler will recognize and appreciate.

**Louise S. Bechtel**

SOURCE: A review of *The Bundle Book,* in *New York Herald Tribune Book Review,* November 11, 1951, p. 12.

Two famous names appear on **The Bundle Book.** Ruth Krauss, author, and Helen Stone, artist. A two or three-year-old plays a little game with Mother. What's in the bundle on the bed? On each page Mother guesses, and Baby answers, till the last happy page where the bundle yells "It's ME." Miss Stone's pictures have charm, a bit on the Laurencin order, but we do not think they would carry the idea with enough amusement to the very small child. However, the game is worth the attention of mothers.

**Lois Palmer**

SOURCE: A review of *The Bundle Book,* in *The New York Times Book Review,* November 11, 1951, p. 42.

All who enjoyed **The Carrot Seed** and other books by Miss Krauss will respond to the excitement of the author's latest story. Here a "mysterious" bundle appears and mother tries to guess what it can be. When the bundle, the mother, the reader and the young listener can't bear it any longer, the cover falls off the bundle and the voice yells, "It's ME!"

Once again the author has presented her story in a warm, friendly, homey style within the scope of the young child's appreciation.

Helen Stone's drawings show a lumpy bundle ever on the move and obviously delighted with itself, and a young mother who enters into the spirit of the game.

## Jennie D. Lindquist and Siri M. Andrews

SOURCE: A review of *The Bundle Book,* in *The Horn Book Magazine,* Vol. XXVII, No. 6, December, 1961, p. 403.

"One morning a mother saw a strange bundle under the blankets in her bed. 'What is it?' she said to herself. 'What can it be?'" She guessed first one thing and then another but never the right thing, and in the end the bundle had to pop open and show Mother what it was. Just the right amount of suspense for the nursery age and Helen Stone's lovely drawings in three colors make this a good choice for very little children, who will enjoy playing the "bundle game" themselves.

## 📖 A HOLE IS TO DIG: A FIRST BOOK OF FIRST DEFINITIONS (1952)

### Virginia Kirkus' Bookshop Service

SOURCE: A review of *A Hole is to Dig: A First Book of First Definitions,* in *Virginia Kirkus' Bookshop Service,* Vol. XX, No. 14, July 15, 1952, p. 401.

When a book of imaginative nature such as this comes along, we get all excited, expect it to be top flight. Though the definitions in this "First Book of Definitions" may bring a few squeals of delight from the young mind making its first associations between the things he knows and what they make him think about—they are not up to the level of warmth and humor of Ruth Krauss' other work. Attractively laid out, each small page has on it one or two phrases—each accompanied by the miniscule drawings of Maurice Sendak reminiscent of the old British picture books. The funniest definition: "Hunh! Rugs are so dogs have napkins". An ordinary definition, and there are a lot like this one: "A mountain is to go to the top". One that calls for a mental leap: "A prinicpal is to take out splinters". A just plain silly one: "Little stones are for little children to gather up and put in little piles". Lastly, some imaginative ones, and these will set kids smiling and perhaps thinking up a whole lot of their own: "A castle is to build in the sand", "A hat is to wear on the train", "Eyebrows are to go over your eyes", "Buttons are to keep people warm". They are cute and they are thought provoking. What they should be is more thought provoking.

### Bulletin of the Children's Book Center

SOURCE: A review of *A Hole is to Dig: A First Book of First Definitions,* in *Bulletin of the Children's Book Center,* Vol. VI, No. 1, September, 1952, p. 7.

An unusual and exciting book with all the elements of a true classic. Here are words used as young children might think of them in terms of their own experiences. The author has that rare ability to reproduce children's words and expressions so that they are completely childlike but never childish or condescending. There is a logic to the definitions (i.e. Eyebrows are to go over your eyes; A mountain is to go to the top; Hands are to hold, etc.) that will appeal to children and a humor that both children and their parents will enjoy. Sendak's lively illustrations are a perfect complement to the text and will bring forth chuckles from children and adults alike.

## Ellen Lewis Buell

SOURCE: A review of *A Hole Is to Dig: A First Book of First Definitions,* in *The New York Times Book Review,* September 7, 1952, p. 31.

Aided, and, in a sense, edited, by young children, Ruth Krauss, always an original author, has produced a unique book. At least, I know of nothing quite like it, although it bears a certain kinship to Ethel Berkeley's *The Size of It* and *Ups and Downs.* Here are interpretations of everyday objects in direct relationship to the child's experience. Forgetful grown-ups may be shocked at the child's unconscious egoism, but once they have remembered back it will seem quite reasonable that "a sea shell is to hear the sea" and "a principal is to take out splinters." Some definitions are startlingly logical as "the world is so you have something to stand on," and "a party is to say how-do-you-do and shake hands."

A revelation to grown-ups as to children's impressions, this could also be the basis of a wonderful game of questions and answers which would set children thinking. Maurice Sendak has illustrated it with drawings bouncing with action and good humor.

## Jennie D. Lindquist

SOURCE: A review of *A Hole is to Dig: A First Book of First Definitions,* in *The Horn Book Magazine,* Vol. XXVIII, No. 5, October, 1952, p. 315

Entirely original in approach and content is this "first book of first definitions" in which Miss Krauss, with the help of children themselves, gives us such gems as "a seashell is to hear the sea"; "cats are so you can have kittens." The illustrations are perfect whether they are making it clear that, of course, "buttons are to keep people warm"; or picturing the small boy who feels he has thought of an excruciatingly funny definition: "A tablespoon is to eat a table with." Like [Fritz Eichenberg's] *Ape in a Cape* this can start children off on a fascinating game.

## Louise Bechtel

SOURCE: A review of *A Hole is to Dig: A First Book of First Definitions,* in *New York Herald Tribune Book Review,* November 16, 1952, p. 5.

"The world is so you have something to stand on . . . The sun is to tell you when it is every day . . . Eyebrows are to go over your eyes . . . A floor is so you don't fall in the hole your house is in . . . Cats are so you can have kittens . . . A dream is to look at the night and see things."

Miss Krauss made up some definitions, inspired by a line in a book by Dr. Gsell. She tried them out on two groups in nursery schools, and kept for her book those the children approved. She added a few of their own remarks, and arranged the whole in an order with a childish logic of its own, which gave the illustrator a merry time. The tiny book with its hundreds of funny, tiny children, has immediate appeal to the eye. Perhaps its best listening audience is those a few years older who will be able to say what THEY would give as definitions.

We regret that a paragraph from the publicity note did not provide a page or two. It says that two definitions not included are those of "mother" and "father." The author had written: "A mother is to hug you." and "A father is to pick you up and throw you about." The children said: "A mother is to cook your food," and "A father is to earn money." Thus the children proved themselves as pragmatic as Dr. Gsell had expected, and not as sentimental as Miss Krauss.

**Margaret Ford Kieran**

SOURCE: A review of *A Hole is to Dig: A First Book of First Definitions,* in *The Atlantic Monthly,* Vol. 190, No. 6, December, 1952, p. 100.

[This book] could hardly be classified as a book for boys and girls—rather it is a book about them—[but] I single it out because, to me, it contains the quintessence of childlike impressions.

*A Hole Is to Dig* it's called, and one cannot read it without marveling at the easy way young people strip a definition of everything but the essentials. What is a lap, for instance? "Why, a lap is so that you won't get crumbs on the floor." And the sun? What is that? "The sun is so that you can have every day." In just as fine an economy of phrase I learned that "cats are so you can have kittens" and that "buttons are to keep people warm." All these findings are noted in a tiny volume compiled by Ruth Krauss, with impish illustrations by Maurice Sendak.

**Sam Leaton Sebesta and William J. Iverson**

SOURCE: "Realistic Fiction," in *Literature for Thursday's Child,* Science Research Associates, Inc., 1975, p. 246.

When authors and artists attempt to enhance the ordinary by clever interpretation, the result ought to be evaluated in terms of honesty as well as invention. *A Hole Is to Dig* by Ruth Krauss consists of clever definitions ("The world is so you have something to stand on"). Although popular with adults, this book may not be appreciated by children, who often miss the whimsy. Yet the spirited drawings by [Maurice] Sendak probably transmit the book's real intent to young readers.

## 📖 *A VERY SPECIAL HOUSE* (1953)

### *Bulletin of the Children's Book Center*

SOURCE: A review of *A Very Special House,* in *Bulletin of the Children's Book Center,* Vol. VII, No. 4, December, 1953, p. 30.

Ruth Krauss has again captured the true essence of a child's imagination and set it forth in language that has appeal for both the child and the adult who will be reading the book to the child. The "very special house" is a child's imaginative house where he can do as he pleases and "nobody ever says stop, stop, stop." The rhythm of the text demands to be read aloud and there is delightful nonsense in both the sounds of the words and their context. Sendak's illustrations are perfect for the text, pointing up both its imaginative qualities and its humor.

**Margaret Ford Kieran**

SOURCE: A review of *A Very Special House,* in *The Atlantic Monthly,* Vol. 102, No. 6, December, 1953, p. 97.

Now we come to a slim little picture book by Ruth Krauss illustrated by Maurice Sendak. *A Very Special House* it is called. If you recall *A Hole Is to Dig,* which they did last year, you will get ready automatically for chuckles and cheers. Miss Krauss really penetrates a child's mind. She knows he wants wild animals and she knows he wants them jumping over all the furniture—which is pretty well messed up by cracker crumbs anyway. It's a lighthearted book and I loved it, but I have a strong feeling it will win the approval of fond uncles and aunts more than of parents. It's not quite orthodox, as this excerpt shows.

The child says: "I'm bringing home a giant and a little dead mouse. . . . Everywhere is music and the giant spilled his drinking and it went all over the floor . . . and everybody's yelling for MORE MORE MORE!"

You can see it is no handbook for deportment, but in the blowing-off-steam department it deserves an award—and, as I say, I loved it.

**Virginia Haviland**

SOURCE: A review of *A Very Special House,* in *The Horn Book Magazine,* Vol. XXIX, No. 6, December, 1953, pp. 452–53.

Here, as full of bounce as *A Hole Is to Dig* and

even richer in ideas fascinating to small children, is another collaboration perfectly in tune for them. The little boy of this story knows just what a Very Special House should be. It would have a bed to bounce on, a table "very special where to put your feet feet feet" and it would be a place to bring any friends—a lion, a giant, some monkeys. Best of all, it would always suggest "MORE MORE MORE"; "NOBODY ever says stop stop stop." [Sendak's] exuberant drawings running over each page are made for lingering looks and chuckles.

### Linda Kauffman Peterson

SOURCE: "A Very Special House," in *Newbery and Caldecott Medal and Honor Books: An Annotated Bibliography,* by Linda Kauffman Peterson and Marilyn Leathers Solt, G. K. Hall & Co., 1982, pp. 300–01.

The illustrations of Maurice Sendak's 1954 [Caldecott] Honor Book transform Ruth Krauss's story of a child's imaginary house into a menagerie of domesticated and wild animals, crayoned walls, and abused furniture. This is indeed a very "special" house in which beds are made for jumping on; in which animals romp and wander, freely munching on furniture; and in which all the action moves to the musical rhythm of the words and pictures.

Sendak's line drawings expand upon the repetition of Krauss's words and share in the mounting rhythm of the song of the story. After the lion eats all the stuffing from the "chairs chairs chairs" and keeps "going snore snore snore," the chorus chimes in for "MORE MORE MORE," and no one *ever* says "stop stop stop." The cumulative effect of this imaginary noise, outrageous destruction, and sheer delight of the participants is a very healthy release, especially as the young child admits that this very special house exists only in the middle of his "head head head."

Sendak's attention to detail, even in this early work, helps fuse the text and pictures, which reinforce each other as they go. At the height of the melee, each animal engages in his own version of eccentric behavior, only to leave the young child alone in quietude at the close of the story. What makes the book effective and worthy of Honor Book status is in part due to Sendak's characteristic style. His attention to detail expands the text when the words do not, and he creates a sense of his enjoyment and the characters' as well. What might have fallen down as a weak text is strengthened by the artist, even though the book employs only black line drawings, interspersed with the blue and white figure of the young child, on ochre-toned backgrounds.

Sendak's abilities as an artist of children's books manifest themselves here, for his appeal is to the child, and all things forbidden become possible in the hands of this artist.

### HOW TO MAKE AN EARTHQUAKE (1954)

### Rae Emerson Donlon

SOURCE: A review of *How to Make an Earthquake,* in *The Christian Science Monitor,* May 13, 1954, p. 15.

At long last a way has been found to keep a peanut balanced on one's nose. Let me quote a passage from a precious book, *How to Make an Earthquake,* by Ruth Krauss: "Put a sticky raisin on top of your nose. Then, take a peanut and stick it on top of the raisin. That's all." And how, we ask, can it be demonstrated without a little practice?

This is a book of more than just make-believe. It contains much educational activity for the five-to-sevens. For example, to make the world go around, one person in the middle is the world, others are the stars and clouds and rain, each revolving in his proper orbit. Here is a really clever way to teach some basic principles and spontaneous action.

On the other side, the play side, there is given a way to make sitting an interesting thing to do. That can be an accomplishment for the parent of a five-year-old: "One way is to lie on your back in a big chair and put your legs up the back of the chair." Other ideas with just the right blend of sense and nonsense: "Mishmosh" can be made from leftovers, bracelets from the fancy tops of socks—and earthquakes erupted as one sits in the sand.

### Lois Palmer

SOURCE: A review of *How to Make an Earthquake,* in *The New York Times Book Review,* May 23, 1954, p. 24.

Once you have learned to make an earthquake, according to the directions on Page 5, you will find thirty-two other new ways of having fun in Ruth Krauss' book. Crockett Johnson's illustrations are as amusing as the author's ideas. Everyone in the family will want to balance a peanut on his nose when he sees how carefully the little boy in the picture is doing it. Another drawing shows a boy learning to make sitting interesting. Grown-ups won't try this one, but children will, especially when watching a television. There are stunts and games to play with other children, some to play by one's self and others to play with grown-ups. A few are serious, many are delightfully silly—all are fun and very satisfying.

Miss Krauss' close understanding of what tickles young children, of how they like to mix reality with make-believe, makes this a new kind of how-to book—a good one for parents to buy, for the nursery school to add to the teacher's library and for the visitor to bring to young children.

## Louise S. Bechtel

SOURCE: A review of *How to Make an Earthquake,* in *New York Herald Tribune Book Review,* May 30, 1954, p. 8.

Except for Margaret Wise Brown, Miss Krauss (Mrs. Crockett Johnson) has been one of our most thoughtful observers of very young children. First she reflected their favorite kinds of story telling in picture books (*Bears, A Happy Day,* and *I Can Fly*). Then she made a real hit with *A Hole Is to Dig,* and now, again using her notes on the children's own words, she reports on "things to do" which, at about three to five, are considered hilarious.

Perhaps this is firstly for parents, to cheer them as to some activities of their own pre-school rascals. Some may wish to skip such items as making a supper dish called "mish-mosh", or "making guests think they are going to swallow bugs." But for a stodgy, unimaginative child, such ideas as drawing with your toes, making the world go round, dancing in the sky, are delightful "How to make a book" has been widely quoted but this item, like the sandpile earthquake, will sound less original to children themselves. And we have found several sturdy, active children of four definitely scornful; they have plenty such ideas of their own, and would much rather listen to a story.

## *Bulletin of the Children's Book Center*

SOURCE: A review of *How to Make an Earthquake,* in *Bulletin of the Children's Book Center,* Vol. VIII, No. 1, September, 1954, p. 4.

Thirty-three suggested activities for young children, many of them the nonsense kinds of activities that children find so excruciatingly funny. The activities, in themselves, are well chosen and have an originality not often found in books of this type. Unfortunately their manner of presentation is wholly adult rather than childlike. The book is written in the tone of an adult laughing at children and lacks entirely the childlike qualities of language and humor that have made Miss Krauss' earlier books so popular with children and adults alike. The directions for most of the activities are so wordy and so supercillious in tone that the child will fail to get the point of what he is supposed to do. Crockett Johnson's illustrations are much more successful than is the text in both their humor and in their ability to convey the ideas which the author is wishing to put across.

## 📖 *I'LL BE YOU AND YOU BE ME* (1954)

### *Virginia Kirkus' Bookshop Service*

SOURCE: A review of *I'll Be You and You Be Me,* in *Virginia Kirkus' Bookshop Service,* Vol. XXII, No. 19, October 1, 1954, p. 678.

Ruth Krauss' imagination mellows with successive books. *A Hole is to Dig* left us unconvinced that it was really a child's book, but this collection of odd rhymes and sayings has everything; it tickles the funny bone while making grown-ups sense in a child's turn of phrase more than the surface meaning of the words. Predominant are themes of friendship, wishing, and the imaginative turnabouts that make real things real by making them what they are not. Examples may illustrate what gives the book its flavor such as . . . ". . love is you give them a leg off your gingerbead man. No, two legs. And the head!" Or another "I wish I was a mouse so I could run over the table." Tiny as Maurice Sendak's drawings are, they pack their own particular wallop. Good things come in small packages.

## Ellen Lewis Buell

SOURCE: A review of *I'll Be You and You Be Me,* in *The New York Times Book Review,* October 31, 1954, p. 36.

Like her memorable and widely quoted collection of definitions, *A Hole Is to Dig,* Ruth Krauss' new book draws its inspiration directly from children. Its theme is love and friendship as experienced and expressed at that age when the dividing line between the two is much thinner than in later life. So "love is the same as like, only you spell them different—only more of the same, sort of—love has more stuff, in it!" Emotions vary from wistful hope to tenderness, to certainty of affection given and received. And just to prove that not all is sweetness and light, there is a short short story—very realistic—about six friends who became unfriends during a complicated arrangement of swapping coats.

Not all the objects of affection are human. Here is expressed a child's deep affection for a toy or an animal, and there is even a "poem by a tree for some bugs." Certain of the comments and ideas seem extraneous to the main theme—or else they are oversubtle for a mere adult. Doubtless, though, children will grasp their meaning immediately. And anyone of any age will find the reality of childhood in Maurice Sendak's pictures. Small, delicately drawn, they have a force and an ebullience out of all proportion to their size.

## Louise S. Bechtel

SOURCE: A review of *I'll Be You and You Be Me,* in *New York Herald Tribune Book Review,* November 14, 1954, p. 32.

What a book! Probably the best combination thus far of the Krauss selective reporting on the talk of small children, with the Sendak genius for carrying out their ideas or carrying them further, in hundreds of tiny figures. It is a Krauss-Sendak scrapbook, more or less on the theme of love and friendship as the nursery age expresses it in very brief stories, plays. "poems," "mysteries," dreams, and many potent exclamations stuck into corners of pages.

There is no doubt that hundreds more thoughts were collected from the thirty-six children (unless "Ursi" is Mrs. Krauss' editor) to whom the book is dedicated. Also, there is no doubt that their talk as selected is clear to us because of the editing. It still may not be "clear" to all small children, and each will appreciate the words with a different speed of comprehension. But the irresistible succession of busy, tiny pictures, the pages with no words at all, the pages with only one picture to dream upon for quite awhile ("she is waiting for her friend, waiting and waiting" and "a horse that's lost could be dreaming of the girl that's going to find him") will demand re-looking, by ages three to five.

Here is a rare combination of dream, humor and pathos; play together and play alone; normal everyday doings and special, original kinds of "love." Because there are both boys and girls (each with truly characteristic likes or loves), because we are indoors and outdoors, and meet horses, monkeys, toys, the clothes so important to children, the book gives us a child's world in the round, a happy world where one shares shouting, singing, dancing for joy, jumping over the world together. The definition of love you must discover, with its play marriage pictures opposite. Here's the story with probably the most wonderful pictures: "I used to love monkeys more, but now I love horses—just my one ear is a monkey's now and the rest of me is a horse. I can sleep standing up because horses do—but I can still live in a tree or hang by my tail."

How often I have seen a very small child seal up a secret paper gleefully in an envelope that is treasured a long time. Now I know what might be inside, from the page called "if I want, I can give it to a friend." It says: "Some grass and some ocean and some dark for daytime and some sun for nighttime and a hug—I put them down together on a piece of paper—I could hold it in my hand—I could keep it in my pocket." Then, in small type, the tiny friend at the seaside says: "You could roll it in a little ball and poke it in a shell."

### Virginia Haviland

SOURCE: A review of *I'll Be You and You Be Me*, in *The Horn Book Magazine*, Vol. XXX, No. 6, December, 1954, p. 427.

A treasure to be shared by child and adult about love and friendship on the nursery level, in language that belongs to childhood—thoughts about copying each other, trading and sharing, making gifts, being twins. "Love is you give them a leg off your gingerbread man. No, two legs. And the head!" The contents jump along as does the mind of a child—a poem, a dream, a little play, a fairy tale, "a love song for elephants," nonsense rhymes. The tiny sketches in lines, in borders or in full page are blithe and bouncing in the manner of those in *A Hole Is to Dig*.

### IS THIS YOU? (1955)

### *Virginia Kirkus' Service*

SOURCE: A review of *Is This You?*, in *Virginia Kirkus' Service*, Vol. XXIII, No. 4, February 15, 1955, p. 125.

Brain teasers for small fry, from an expert at them, adds up to a book of one's own that might make *its* author pleasantly more aware of immediate surroundings. "Is this you?", "Is this where you live?" asks Ruth Krauss and then follows up with all sorts of crazy impossibilities you can just hear the kids saying "Noooo!" to and laughing. Then she tells you to draw a picture of the real answer—your school, your house, what you want for a birthday present, etc. Droll pictures by Crockett Johnson.

### Elsie T. Dobbins

SOURCE: A review of *Is This You?*, in *Library Journal*, Vol. 80, No. 1, April 15, 1955, p. 994.

This is a perfect book of its kind for any child from four to six. It is full of nonsense in text and pictures, showing humans in ridiculously impossible positions and suggesting that the young reader or listener draw the correct picture answer. When he has finished the book, he will have drawn a picture of his own life. Libraries will want to buy in reinforced binding. Recommended especially for preschool age.

### Ellen Lewis Buell

SOURCE: A review of *Is This You?*, in *The New York Times Book Review*, April 17, 1955, p. 28.

It would be a literal-minded youngster indeed who could resist this invitation to autobiography. Ruth Krauss and Crockett Johnson begin this daffiest of do-it-yourself books with a picture of dejected snow figures, ask blandly "Is this your family?", follow it with other startling examples and then suggest that you draw a picture of your own family. In the same fashion they proceed to other fundamentals of living, such as "Where do you live?" "Is this your friend?", arriving eventually at the all-important title question. If the reader follows suggestions he will have, by this time, a homemade autobiography.

The absurdities of bathing in a bird-bath, a piano leg for breakfast, a bed in a grocery window—dramatized in Crockett Johnson's pictures—will undoubtedly set children off on their own variations of this game. At the same time they will be gaining a deeper realization of the familiar things of life. A very funny book that says more than it seems to.

### Dan Wickenden

SOURCE: A review of *Is This You?*, in *New York Herald Tribune Book Review*, August 14, 1955, p. 7.

"Is this your family?" asks the first line, above a cartoon of three dejectedly-melting snowmen. "Is this?" asks the second, beneath the portrait of a wide-eyed but obviously royal family—even the dog wears a crown. "Is this?" asks the third, of a picture of two gingerbread men, one of whom has sustained a bite in the side.

So Ruth Krauss' questions and Crockett Johnson's zany pictures go on, from one category to another: dwelling places, food, names, schools, preferences in birthday presents, methods of traveling and bathing and sleeping. And then the grand climax: "Is this you?" Are you a rag doll, a clown, a mouse? And after each set of questions and cartoons, the child is asked to draw his own answer, until at the end he has composed an autobiography in pictures.

Children of just the right age will probably find *Is This You?* excruciatingly funny. But the novelty may wear off rather fast, and the book as a whole seems aimed less at lone readers or listeners than at groups of youthful artists.

### *Bulletin of the Children's Book Center*

SOURCE: A review of *Is This You?*, in *Bulletin of the Children's Book Center*, Vol. IX, No. 1, September, 1955, p. 9

A nonsense picture game for the 5-7 year-olds. The book is divided into sections: your family, where you live, what you eat for breakfast, your name, your friend, how you take your bath, etc., with each page asking one or more questions of the child. The cartoon-like illustrations by Crockett Johnson suggest silly answers to each question. "Is this you?" is answered by a picture of a rag doll, a clown, a sphinx, a TV artist, a face on a nickel, a face in the moon, a mouse, a knight in armour. At the end of each section of questions, the author suggests that the "reader" draw a picture representing his own answer to the questions. All of the drawings may then be fastened together to make a book. Several of the pictures would probably have little or no meaning for the very young child. However, there is a rollicking type of humor in the combination of picture and text which will appeal to the older pre-school child, especially if the family joins in the fun. An excellent book for use on auto or train trips.

## *CHARLOTTE AND THE WHITE HORSE* (1955)

### *Bulletin of the Children's Book Center*

SOURCE: A review of *Charlotte and the White Horse*, in *Bulletin of the Children's Book Center*, Vol. IX, No. 10, June, 1956, p. 114.

Highly imaginative story of a small girl and her make-believe white horse. The little girl takes care of the horse from the time it is a colt, persuades her father not to sell it, and thereafter rides the horse each morning and grooms and feeds it each night. The story is too subtle for any except the most imaginative children. The pastel colors of Sendak's illustrations capture the dream-like quality of the story.

## *I WANT TO PAINT MY BATHROOM BLUE* (1956)

### *Virginia Kirkus' Service*

SOURCE: A review of *I Want to Paint My Bathroom Blue*, in *Virginia Kirkus' Service*, Vol. XXIV, No. 16, August 15, 1956, p. 569.

With help again from Maurice Sendak, here is another book of the things one dreams about rather than does—like painting the bathroom blue and sprinkling seeds all over the sunny earth and having a whole house for all one's friends. The little boy in this reminds one of a ballet dancer, leaping from thought to thought and suddenly making it materialize with a touch of his magic wand.

### Olive Dean Hormel

SOURCE: A review of *I Want to Paint My Bathroom Blue*, in *The Christian Science Monitor*, August 30, 1956, p. 7.

"I want to paint my bathroom blue—my papa won't let me paint it blue . . . I want to paint my kitchen yellow and my sitting room white with turtles and all my ceilings green." This is a charming bit of fantasy for imaginative small children, the kind that sets them to dreaming and satisfies something that wants expression deep down inside. Maurice Sendak's ethereal blues, sunny yellows, and urgent greens do just that.

### Margaret Sherwood Libby

SOURCE: A review of *I Want to Paint My Bathroom Blue*, in *New York Herald Tribune Book Review*, September 9, 1956, p. 6.

Here is the wistful little boy who wants to paint his bathroom blue drawn in fresh and charming water-colors by Maurice Sendak. He floats, paint brush in hand, in a dream of blueness or flies eagerly up a pink stairs toward the horse in his bedroom. This artist, whose own book, *Kenny's Window*, won an honor award in the New York Herald Tribune Book Festival this spring, shows here what joyous things he can do with bright, clear color. Ruth Krauss has fashioned the text, a trifle for the very young, composed of a few phrases describing a child's dream house, phrases that echo as this author's always do, very skillfully, the patterns of the children's own speech. There is the singsong rhythm of "the doorknob, the dearknob, the door little dearknob" and the clumsy awkwardness of "like Mother is blushing because two of her children put their feet in the cake." Both will amuse the nursery group.

## Lois Palmer

SOURCE: A review of *I Want to Paint My Bathroom Blue,* in *The New York Times Book Review,* November 4, 1956, p. 38.

Once again in few words Ruth Krauss reveals the innermost feelings of little children. A little boy would like to paint his bathroom blue but his papa doesn't agree. The boy can't paint his bathroom blue or his kitchen yellow or cover the living room walls with pictures of turtles. There are many other things that he would like to do—big things, wonderful things, exciting things. Maurice Sendak's pictures show the happiness and activity of the little boy as in his pretend world, he accomplishes all his big ideas. Children will understand that it is all wishful thinking on the part of the little boy but it is so pleasant to contemplate that they will pretend along with him.

## Zena Sutherland

SOURCE: A review of *I Want to Paint My Bathroom Blue,* in *Bulletin of the Children's Book Center,* Vol. XI, No. 6, February, 1958, p. 60.

A small child tells how he would paint his dream house if he were allowed full rein. The impossibility of such a situation is indicated in his statement that his father would not allow him to really do this, but that does not deter him from expressing his desires in terms that give vent to his imagination and are not bound by adult reason or logic. The illustrations reflect what the rooms would look like if the child had his way. The utter illogic and impossibility of the book make it one that will be limited in appreciation to those adults and children who like this type of unbridled imagination.

## THE BIRTHDAY PARTY (1957)

### Virginia Kirkus' Service

SOURCE: A review of *The Birthday Party,* in *Virginia Kirkus' Service,* Vol. XXV, No. 3, February 1, 1957, p. 65.

David was bored. He'd been "everywhere"—to the beach, to the corner—but not to a birthday party. He comes home to an apparently deserted house. Then he opens the dining room door—and there it is—a surprise party for David. Tiny drawings by Maurice Sendak against a backwash of ochre depicts the world of the small fry with crisp charm. Guaranteed a hit for the 3 to 5 year olds.

## Margaret Sherwood Libby

SOURCE: A review of *The Birthday Party,* in *New York Herald Tribune Book Review,* May 12, 1957, p. 28.

Charming and artistic as the other books have been on which Ruth Krauss and Maurice Sendak have collaborated, we have always thought of the texts as very clever reporting of little children's language, perhaps of some children's secret thoughts, rather than words holding delight for the children themselves. However, their newest book, **The Birthday Party,** is perfect for a child audience. In about a hundred words (hand-lettered a few to a page) and tiny appealing pictures, a momentous event in a child's life is told. We can see the three or four-year-olds breathless, as David, who had been EVERYWHERE but had never been to a birthday party, comes home one day and searches an empty house until he reaches the dining room. We can imagine how their eyes will shine at his wonderful surprise. Here is a tender loving glimpse of an important first experience.

## Jennie D. Lindquist

SOURCE: A review of *The Birthday Party,* in *The Horn Book Magazine,* Vol. XXXIII, No. 3, June, 1957, pp. 212–13.

A little book of a size small children like to carry around, with a surprise ending to delight them, about David who had been everywhere—to the beach, the woods, even "to the corner alone." Everywhere except to a birthday party. The lovely pictures are the kind sometimes called "deceptively simple." At first glance there seems not to be much detail in them; yet every one is very expressive, particularly of the way David is feeling at the moment, whether he is on the sands at the beach, puzzled because he cannot find anyone at home in his house, or present at last at the gayest of birthday parties.

## Mary Louise Hector

SOURCE: A review of *The Birthday Party,* in *The New York Times Book Review,* June 30, 1957, p. 18.

A little boy named David who had been everywhere but never to a birthday party wanders into one just getting under way in the dining room—in honor of his own birthday. Maurice Sendak's illustrations are captivating—real but stylized, with an effect of kindliness, verve and humor. Ruth Krauss provides 114 pseudo-childlike words, and few of them are worth the time of younger readers. Mr. Sendak's illustrations don't really need the words; collected under the title of *The Birthday Party,* they alone would have suggested the story.

### 📖 MONKEY DAY (1957)

#### *Virginia Kirkus' Service*

SOURCE: A review of *Monkey Day*, in *Virginia Kirkus' Service*, Vol. XXV, No. 12, June 15, 1957, p. 410.

Monkeys and more monkeys, presents, parties and paper hats are skillfully blended in a merry lap-sized book by the practised hands that gave us *Bears*, etc. Here are a little girl who loves monkeys, and the wedding of monkeys and flocks and flocks of baby monkeys. Phyllis Rowand must have had fun doing her engaging sepia drawings of the curly-tailed and large eyed monkeys and their frolicking capers. Such books, made up of elements young children cherish, are fun and make them *want* to be able to read. Fine reading for first and second graders, too. Not unlike *Millions of Cats*, this is for a distinctly older group than the author's earlier works.

#### Margaret Sherwood Libby

SOURCE: A review of *Monkey Day*, in *New York Herald Tribune Book Review*, November 3, 1957, p. 11.

Again it seems that Ruth Krauss has built a simple little phrase into a series of happenings that very little children will savour with delight. She used the phrase first in *I'll Be You and You Be Me*. It is "Happy Monkey Day." Lo! Now, on the first page of this big, flat picture book, a companion to *Bears* there is a demure brown monkey sitting waiting to celebrate *her* day, (We are told she is a girl monkey.) There are presents, of course, and the best present is a boy from "the girl who loves monkeys." Now there can be a wedding! After a birthday, nursery and kindergarten children love nothing better than to have pretend weddings. Here are the monkeys, with all the essentials, a pair, one with a veil, the other with a present, and the wedding song:

> Hope you happy wedding
> Hope you happy wishes
> Hope you happy Baby Monkey
> Hope you love and kisses.

Did the baby monkey arrive? Of course. But that is not ALL. Ruth Krauss and Phyllis Rowand have made the fun cumulative and the "girl who loves monkeys," and all young readers can enjoy monkey days and weddings galore.

#### George A. Woods

SOURCE: A review of *Monkey Day*, in *The New York Times Book Review*, November 17, 1957, p. 59.

*Monkey Day* by Ruth Krauss is the occasion for showering presents on the little primates. The gift of a boy monkey to a girl monkey leads to formal nuptials and a kind of over-production with hundreds of monkeys cavorting over the pages. Phyllis Rowand's ballet-like stances of the humans and anthropoids are well-done but incline toward the monotonous in a silly, excessive story of monkey-cult devotion.

#### Mabel Berry

SOURCE: A review of *Monkey Day*, in *Library Journal*, Vol. 82, No. 13, December 15, 1957, pp. 3242-43.

Monkey Day is a boy-monkey. A wedding follows and then dozens and dozens of baby monkeys. The whole process is repeated the next Monkey Day with boy-monkeys for the girl-monkeys and girl-monkeys for the boy monkeys and weddings for all. Although Ruth Krauss has given us delightful picture books, this is in poor taste. Sepia drawings on cluttered pages add to the confusion. Not recommended.

#### *Publishers Weekly*

SOURCE: A review of *Monkey Day*, in *Publishers Weekly*, Vol. 204, No. 13, September 24, 1973, p. 187.

Few writers can so authentically mirror the thoughts, feelings and fancies of the special world of children as Ms. Krauss. Few readers will be able to resist her latest whimsy. "The monkey is happy because it is Monkey Day. Everyone is bringing presents. The monkey is a girl." Among the gifts—from, a man, a woman and a "big child"—the best is a boy-monkey brought by a little girl. The monkeys are wed and the girl eagerly awaits the birth of a baby monkey and more and more baby monkeys, more and more Monkey Days. Ms. Rowand's delicate, old-fashioned pictures add much to the book.

### 📖 SOMEBODY ELSE'S NUT TREE: AND OTHER TALES FROM CHILDREN (1958)

#### *Virginia Kirkus' Service*

SOURCE: A review of *Somebody Else's Nut Tree: And Other Tales from Children*, in *Virginia Kirkus' Service*, Vol. XXVI, No. 4, February 15, 1958, p. 133.

On the shaky foundations of words said by children Ruth Krauss has evolved inconsequential flights of fancy. They are not stories, nor are they verses. They are passages which wander—about a little girl turned into a queen by a good fairy, about a boy who flies in a little ship, breaks his leg and is taken to the hospital—all in language somewhat like Gertrude Stein. An attempt to be childlike achieves inanity.

#### Margaret Sherwood Libby

SOURCE: A review of *Somebody Else's Nut Tree: And Other Tales From Children*, in *New York Herald Tribune Book Review*, May 11, 1958, p. 27.

Ruth Krauss and Maurice Sendak have truly "captured

the realm of childhood" in the new collection of rhythmic pieces illustrated with subtle and expressive little figures which progressively tell the story. Here are a dozen and a half "tales from children," filled with happiness, sheer bubbling happiness, in gay words and processions of tiny prancing children and animals: happy eggs, happy marbles, a rainbow of happiness, even rain that "rained Happy Everafter." Except for the title verse nothing, absolutely nothing, can stay wrong. Even after the little little fish ate the little fish that ate the Big fish "they all went off swimming together," while tigers remain even if there "never were more lions Evermore." We think this is a wonderful book for adults, a gift from children interpreted by Ruth Krauss, to provide glimpses of their deepest longings and satisfactions and, in the end, of their sorrow when they find the little nut tree they thought nobody else could find "was somebody else's nut tree."

### Ellen Lewis Buell

SOURCE: A review of *Somebody Else's Nut Tree: And Other Tales From Children,* in *The New York Times Book Review,* June 22, 1958, p. 16.

Anyone who knows Ruth Krauss' *A Hole Is to Dig* and *I'll Be You and You Be Me* is aware of her remarkable talent for drawing from children their own ideas—sometimes only semi-articulated—and giving them form and substance. This book is in the same vein—eighteen short stories, reworked from words she heard said by children, but unlike *A Hole Is to Dig,* which was just about perfect, this one is uneven, for all its lovely imagery and rhythms.

There is, for instance, the title story (which comes last). Its switch ending left this reader a little breathless and baffled, as it did a select group of children of assorted ages. So did **"The White Boat,"** heavy with symbolism, and a number of others. On the other hand, such vignettes as **"A Girl at a Party," "The Little Queen"** and **"The Boy and the World"** clearly express a child's delight in a sense of coziness and in the warm reassurance of parental love. And for sheer fun there are **"The Girl on the Silver Horse"** and **"The Kitten and the Lion."** The simpler stories are certainly worth the price of admission, but older readers-aloud had better be prepared with good explanations for some of the others.

### A MOON OR A BUTTON: A COLLECTION OF FIRST PICTURE IDEAS (1959)

#### Virginia Kirkus' Service

SOURCE: A review of *A Moon or A Button: A Collection of First Picture Ideas,* in *Virginia Kirkus' Service,* Vol. XXVII, No, 3, February 1, 1959, p. 85.

Sometimes Ruth Krauss manages to capture the evolution of an idea in a schoolroom with complete charm and veracity. Sometimes her sense of fun is so captivating

that an abstract idea is transformed into concrete entertainment. But this book misses fire. If the children in the Rowayton school had been given a concept and transferred it to paper, the result might well be what this conveys. But why give the concept to [illustrator] Remy Charlip—and ask him to reproduce the idea as he conceives of a child's presentation? It seems to lose reason for being; the theme of nonsense has run away with the book. It would seem likely that the picture book age child would reject this.

### Mabel Berry

SOURCE: A review of *A Moon or A Button: A Collection of First Picture Ideas,* in *Library Journal,* Vol. 84, No. 1, May 15, 1959, p. 48.

Although Ruth Krauss has written a number of delightful picture books, this is disappointing. Each page contains a picture with a word or line of text giving the author's idea of the way a child might depict an object or situation. It is too bad that the pictures and interpretations were not actually those of a child. Many will be confusing to the preschooler for whom the book is intended. Not recommended.

### Rose Laura Mincieli

SOURCE: A review of *A Moon or A Button: A Collection of First Picture Ideas,* in *Library Journal,* Vol. 84, No. 1, May 15, 1959, p. 48.

A little book consisting of childlike pictures with captions which evoke ideas in young children's minds which might lead to group conversation among preschoolers, though, due to the small size of the book, it would be limited to use with not more than about six children at once. Illustrated by Remy Charlip; a circle suggests the moon or a button, many windows may mean a visit to the city, or a house in the country make one think of Grandmother's house, etc. Rather new type of picture book for a special use with ages 3–5.

### Ellen Lewis Buell

SOURCE: A review of *A Moon or A Button: A Collection of First Picture Ideas,* in *The New York Times Book Review,* June 21, 1959, p. 22.

Subtitled "a collection of first picture ideas," Ruth Krauss' latest book is a series of pictorial jokes and freewheeling fancies, inspired in part by school children and drawn by Remy Charlip. It would be interesting to know just where the children's ideas left off and those of the author and artist began. Most of the pictures are childlike, as well as charming and amusing, especially "A witch's valentine"— a heart with a jack-o-lantern face; "Kisses drying"—a row of x's hanging from a clothesline; and "Something very little"—the tiniest of black forms on a white page. But certain others, such as "Grandmother's house," "A city child in the country" and "A visit to New York City," seem a little self-consciously symbolical. And this raises the point as to how much inspiration an adult should give to young children. It is fine for the latter to exchange their own ideas and jokes but it seems unnecessary to provide pictorial ideas for children who are at that stage when most of them draw as naturally as they walk or laugh.

**Margaret S. Libby**

SOURCE: A review of *A Moon or A Button: A Collection of First Picture Ideas,* in *New York Herald Tribune Book Review,* September 6, 1959, p. 9.

Remy Charlip has drawn childlike pictures in black and white and gray tones to illustrate some ideas Ruth Krauss gleaned from the children of Rowayton Public School. The pictures are as fascinating to look at as children's own drawings. They have the same logic mixed with irrelevance, the same ability to show feelings and relationships. Perhaps they will open the way to fresh ideas and interpretations by other children, but most young children are so bubbling over with originality that they do not need models or inspirations. What they do need is grown-ups like Ruth Krauss and Remy Charlip who appreciate the charm of their work without trying to alter it or twist it to adult standards.

## OPEN HOUSE FOR BUTTERFLIES (1960)

### Virginia Kirkus' Service

SOURCE: A review of *Open House for Butterflies,* in *Virginia Kirkus' Service,* Vol. XXVIII, No. 7, April 1, 1960, p. 288.

The charm of this verbal free-for-all cannot be disputed, but coming as a sequel to *A Hole is to Dig,* this second book by Ruth Krauss and Maurice Sendak to some extent lacks the spontaneous charm of the first. Based on the assumption that children delight in their own verbal jokes, Ruth Krauss defines various situations and words—"Pins never unfit you" . . . "a baby is so you could be the boss" . . . "a baby makes the mother and father—otherwise they're just plain people". Charming, funny, sometimes wise, the text supported by the irresistible diminutive drawings of Maurice Sendak will find an appreciative audience, in many cases, among the readers at whom it is directed, and, as frequently, will be championed by their parents.

**George A. Woods**

SOURCE: A review of *Open House for Butterflies,* in *The New York Times Book Review,* May 8, 1960, p. 30.

*Open House for Butterflies* by Ruth Krauss is a companion volume to her 1952 classic, *A Hole Is to Dig.* This new book, which appears to have been culled from the sayings of precocious children primarily for the benefit of sophisticated adults, offers snippets of wisdom and practical philosophy. "A baby is so you could be the boss," "pink means nightie" and "when you're very very tired just throw your tired away," are some of the gleanings. Not only does its point and pur-}pose escape me but it also baffled six children to whom it was carefully, hopefully read. They all, however, loved Maurice Sendak's abundant and enchanting miniatures.

**Pamela Marsh**

SOURCE: A review of *Open House for Butterflies,* in *The Christian Science Monitor,* May 12, 1960, p. 1B.

Ruth Krauss and Maurice Sendak—she writes the smiling lines, he draws the smallest, most animated children—combine exhilaration with quietness in *Open House for Butterflies.* There is nothing gentler than the resting boy—"Everybody should be quiet near a little stream"—unless it be the tiny beaming child—"A baby makes the mother and father—otherwise they're just plain people." But these children, like real children and April weather, don't stay the same for long. They caper across a double-page spread—"Look I'm running away with my imagination"—and "A baby dances with its feet in the air." Like its predecessor, *A Hole Is to Dig,* this book of child definitions will endear itself to those adults conscripted by the 3–7's to "read it to me again."

**Betty Miles**

SOURCE: A review of *Open House for Butterflies,* in *Saturday Review,* Vol. XLIII, No. 29, July 16, 1960, pp. 37–8.

This sequel to *A Hole Is to Dig,* although less well organized than its predecessor, offers another collection of children's statements that are pure and sudden and illuminating. But it is adults who need illumination. To a young child the comment that "grownup means to go to nursery school" is flatly logical. To an adult it has a poignancy no child could understand.

Youngsters consistently see and feel things directly, and find nothing unusual in their point of view. The child who greets a summer morning with "It's a good day for barefooting!" and says of a suede jacket, "It feels like liver," is not aware of speaking poetically. The child who demands, "Mother, who are *they* when *they say?*" is not aware of being philosophical. And the child who gasps out admiringly, "Jane's hair is so pretty—it goes way down to her *anus!*" is not aware of the delightful incongruity.

Children are spontaneously artful in their artlessness. For this very reason they are confused when their own way of looking at the world is presented to them, bound and formal, in a book. **Open House for Butterflies** is likely to confuse young children. But for older brothers and sisters, for adolescents, for parents and librarians and teachers and pediatricians and every other kind of grownup besides, Miss Krauss's words are like windows open to sudden freshness. And Maurice Sendak's pictures recall, and embrace, the quite magic world we know perfectly well is too fragile and too merry to exist outside of nostalgia.

Here, then, is a juvenile one can recommend wholeheartedly for adults. Perhaps we have real need of this kind of book; the adult novel seldom offers so pure a vision of childhood. Meanwhile, one must regret having no more of the children's books Miss Krauss used to write with such verve and insight: **The Carrot Seed, The Growing Story, The Big World and the Little House** were real juveniles, the kind that real children beg to have read to them in real living rooms.

Children should be, after all, the *raison d'être* of the children's book. It is to be hoped that neither the author's sincere desire to speak to adults, nor ignorance or dismissal or exploitation of children, will ever obscure that fact.

### George Shannon

SOURCE: A review of *Open House for Butterflies,* in *Los Angeles Times Book Review,* July 16, 1960, p. 8.

The story of childhood is one of energy, discovery and a growing sense of self. Few children's books recount this better than **A Hole Is to Dig** and its companion, the **Open House for Butterflies,** both by Ruth Krauss and Maurice Sendak. The latter, recently reprinted, asks one of the many children who act out stories and play with words in these pages: "If you went out and forgot your pretend friends, where would you go when you went back for them?" And another: "If you run out of cereal, can you run into it again?"

Giving body and breadth to these young voices, Sendak's pen-and-ink illustrations evoke the spontaneous choreography of children at play. Together, Krauss and Sendak have created a lasting celebration of childhood's importance. Or, as one child puts it: "A baby makes the mother and father—otherwise they're just plain people."

📖   *MAMA, I WISH I WAS SNOW—CHILD, YOU'D BE VERY COLD* (1962)

### Virginia Kirkus' Service

SOURCE: A review of *Mama, I Wish I Was Snow—Child, You'd Be Very Cold,* in *Virginia Kirkus' Service,* Vol. XXX, No. 2, January 15, 1962, p. 53.

It is hard to find conviction in the concept here. Children may wish they were birds or squirrels or fish—something denoting action in another element, but how often do they want to be a chair, the sun, a fireplug, a piece of paper? Or how much would they be influenced by the mother's matter-of-fact description of what the obvious result would be? There seems little here for identification. And too often, the responses transcend the young child's understanding. Woodcuts by Ellen Raskin and the forced modern rhyme and rhythm patterns are not enough to override the text shortcomings. A disappointment from the usually dependable Ruth Krauss.

### Zena Sutherland

SOURCE: A review of *Mama, I Wish I Was Snow—Child, You'd Be Very Cold,* in *Bulletin of the Center for Children's Books,* Vol. XV, No. 8, April, 1962, pp. 127–28.

An interestingly illustrated picture book with an unusual text, all of which is in the same form as the title. Some of the comments have humor: "Mama, I wish I was a chair." "Child, you'd be sat on." Many of them, however, have latent concepts that are rather complicated for a read-aloud audience: "Mama, I wish I was a piece of paper." "Child, you'd need to be a tree first." The book has imaginative quality, but it seems doubtful that it is of the sort to be appreciated by small children.

### *The Christian Science Monitor*

SOURCE: A review of *Mama, I Wish I Was Snow—Child, You'd Be Very Cold,* in *The Christian Science Monitor,* May 10, 1962, p. 2B.

***Mama, I wish I was snow—Child, you'd be very cold,*** by Ruth Krauss, illustrated by Ellen Raskin, falls between stools. It doesn't quite manage the whimsey that adults have relished in Miss Krauss's previous **A Hole Is to Dig** and **Open House for Butterflies.** Nor is it likely to strike responsive chords in even the more imaginative child. Its title is derived from Garcia Lorca, and the whole effort has a kind of quaint translated flavor as if it contained old Spanish sayings that don't quite come off in English. Sorry. Will await more butterflies.

### *Saturday Review*

SOURCE: A review of *Mama, I Wish I Was Snow—Child, You'd Be Very Cold,* in *Saturday Review,* New York, Vol. XLV, No. 19, May 12, 1962, p. 36.

The little Spanish poem by Garcia Lorca, reproduced in the front of this book is charming; whether the idea remains so as enlarged upon by Ruth Krauss is another matter. Parents whose children wish they were chairs, paper, a fire plug (of all things!) *are* going to need "new insights," as the description of the book suggests.

It is, of course, a game in dialogue, and a resourceful mother may be able to go on with the playing of it indefinitely. The woodcuts [by Ellen Raskin] are interesting as design, and colorful. But a seven-year-old would be bored by the whole thing.

## George A. Woods

SOURCE: A review of *Mama, I Wish I Was Snow—Child, You'd Be Very Cold,* in *The New York Times Book Review,* Part II, May 13, 1962, p. 5.

I'm afraid however, that Ruth Krauss' **Mama, I Wish I Was Snow—Child, You'd Be Very Cold,** inspired by a poem by the Spanish poet Federico Lorca, is going to leave children very cold indeed. The book is composed of a series of "I wishes," such as "Mama, I wish I was a piece of paper," with the answer, "Child, you'd need to be a tree first," and "I wish I was autumn," followed by "you'd be full of apples." There is some absurd humor here, poetic response too, all of it executed in imaginative fashion. But it is, unfortunately, imaginative beyond the child's ability to appreciate.

## A BOUQUET OF LITTLES (1963)

### Zena Sutherland

SOURCE: A review of *A Bouquet of Littles,* in *Bulletin of the Center for Children's Books,* Vol. XVIII, No. 6, February, 1964, p. 96.

A small read-aloud book with small-figured, stylized illustrations [by Jane Flora] that have a medieval quality. The cataloging in rhyme of small things suitable to other small things is appealing but repetitive: "A little bell best fits a little ring, A little bee best fits a little sting, As my small branch best fits my little swing, a little la la la best fits a little sing / a little here best fits a little there / a little fountain fits a little square / A little water fits a little well / a little blue best fits a little bell / a little word best fits a little spell / a little roar best fits a little shell. . . . " The ways in which words are used may confuse some small children, but those who enjoy word play will be happily challenged.

## THE CANTILEVER RAINBOW (1965)

### Virginia Kirkus' Service

SOURCE: A review of *The Cantilever Rainbow,* in *Virginia Kirkus' Service,* Vol. XXXIII, No. 18, September 15, 1965, p. 986.

It was off-beat off Broadway first and it comes as a surprise to find these poem-plays and happenings being listed by the publishers at the 11 to 13 age level. But it's really not such a shocking surprise, after all. There is exceptional humor here, different and fresh, visual and vital. You also have to run to get with it, and kids do manage to run better than adults. When there was a Greenwich Village vogue for this sort of production, part of the pleasure in attending was to hear the comments of the more earnest, intense members of the audience. Some of them were desperate to locate an exact, profound revelation of cosmic truth. That attitude seems as deadly as its obverse, which would dismiss the whole undertaking without recognizing its ability to entertain, stir the mind to puzzlement and finally, to influence art. Here's an example of the sort of poem play that drives commentators to take extreme positions in praise or blame: *A Beautiful Day.* "Girl: What a beautiful day! The Sun falls down onto the stage. End." The woodcuts of Antonio Frasconi lend a strong, happy support and follow the sun theme of the poems. The audience doesn't wait, it's in the process of being formed and the book's greatest use among youngsters will probably come from talented teachers. It should also find its way to what seems to us the most logical appreciative readership—college students with a taste and curiosity for the avant garde.

### The Christian Science Monitor

SOURCE: A review of *The Cantilever Rainbow,* in *The Christian Science Monitor,* November 4, 1965, p. B11.

In one of the charming poems that make up **The Cantilever Rainbow** Winnie the Pooh and William Shakespeare carry on a dialogue in rhyme, building up to a slightly mad unison chorus on the pleasures of being a cloud. It is Ruth Krauss being most typically untypical. There is a good deal of E. E. Cummings in her, a light touch of Gerard Manley Hopkins, and the general look of a Marx Brothers movie. Hers is a kind of poetry of the absurd—free-wheeling and chancy but by no means undisciplined. The sun is the chief motif around which Miss Krauss orbits, and Antonio Frasconi's woodcuts adorn her verse like fiery Hispanic sunbursts. This brilliantly original little book is catalogued for 13's and up.

### Lillian Morrison

SOURCE: A review of *The Cantilever Rainbow,* in *School Library Journal,* Vol. 12, No. 4, December 15, 1965, p. 5527.

Eighteen sun-inspired poems accompanied by approximately the same number of strong, sunny, full-page illustrations. The pieces are funny, clever, imaginative in a Dada way, and often quite lovely and lyrical. They include a few instant poem-plays, as original as they are short, and several duets, one of which combines *Winnie the Pooh* and Shakespeare successfully. Teenagers, especially the brighter and more sophisticated ones, with a taste for the zany, will find the book delightful and mind-quickening. It may need introduction.

## 📖 THIS THUMBPRINT (1967)

### Kirkus Service

SOURCE: A review of *This Thumbprint,* in *Kirkus Service,* Vol. XXXI, No. 11, June 1, 1967, p. 641.

If you have an uninhibited imagination (like Miss Krauss) a violet fingerprint can suggest anything—a singer, a dog, an Indian, a cowboy. With pen and ink she turns prints into people or surrounds them with people, tacks on a label, a sentence or a funny poem, and calls it a page. Much of the humor is adult, most of it is lively, offbeat— and pointless, all of it is artistic. Original nonsense that will probably be response-less.

### Harriet B. Quimby

SOURCE: A review of *This Thumbprint,* in *School Library Journal,* Vol. 14, No. 1, September, 1967, p. 110.

A series of unrelated phrases and partial nursery rhymes are cleverly illustrated [by Krauss] with purple ink thumb prints and simple black lines. The result is a kind of participation book presumably designed to pique the young child's imagination and sense of humor. Unfortunately, the lack of any unifying element beyond the thumbprints and the intrusion of some forced humor, and the occasional change in focus (to hand and pinkie prints) keep this from being as successful as it might have been. For use with small groups at school and at home.

## 📖 WHAT A FINE DAY FOR . . . (1967)

### Kirkus Service

SOURCE: A review of *What A Fine Day For . . .,* in *Kirkus Service,* Vol. XXXV, No. 21, November 1, 1967, p. 1317.

*What a fine day for . . .* anything you can think of. "A mouse and a cat and a ball and a bat / a ball and a throw, a stop and a go" and lots more says the text that Remy Charlip has lettered with clever line figures (across a succession of pages that look like a package of poster paper), says the song that Al Carmines has written as accompaniment. It's a song with an open end, the remainder to be supplied by children caught up in the free-swinging nonsense. The three collaborators are active in children's theater in and around New York, and this is less a book for routine circulation than a very original device to arouse group participation, with music (and chord indications) for an experienced pianist. Teachers from nursery school up will want to have a try.

### Barbara Gibson

SOURCE: A review of *What A Fine Day For . . .,* in *School Library Journal,* Vol. 14, No. 6, February 15, 1968, p. 70.

Young children will undoubtedly enjoy the bright colors and rhythms of this delightful bit of nonsense composed of couplets, such as "What a fine day for / A bunny and a hop / A go and a stop." Ruth Krauss has again created a world in which young listeners can become involved. This book has great possibilities for use in both language arts and music, as the words have been set to music on the last six pages; also, children are encouraged in the delight of creating their own lyrics.

## 📖 THE LITTLE KING, THE LITTLE QUEEN, THE LITTLE MONSTER AND OTHER STORIES YOU CAN MAKE UP YOURSELF (1968)

### Barbara H. Gibson

SOURCE: A review of *The Little King, The Little Queen, The Little Monster and Other Stories You Can Make Up Yourself,* in *Library Journal,* Vol. 94, No. 10, May 15, 1969, p. 2090.

The title of this little book (6" x 5") is intriguing; unfortunately, the content is disappointing at best. In the first story, a little boy wants to be a king, the Good Fairy grants his wish, his mother and father are horrified, he wishes to become a little boy again, the Good Fairy grants his new wish, and everyone lives happily ever after. The same story is repeated with a little girl who wants to be a queen and a little monster who wants to be a little boy. By the third time around the plot has lost its zing, and the suggestion that listeners might want to make up their own stories following this pattern has little appeal. In general, this lacks the zest of Miss Krauss's other books, such as *The Growing Story* (1947). The illustrations, too studiedly child-like, are merely an adult's scribbling, and other adults, looking for material to spark children's creativity, could much better rely on stories they can make up themselves.

## 📖 I WRITE IT (1970)

### Kirkus Reviews

SOURCE: A review of *I Write It,* in *Kirkus Reviews,* Vol. XXXVIII, No. 7, April 1, 1970, p. 377.

Everywhere *I write it:* "On a piece of paper . . . On my looking-glass and on snow . . . "; "On the air / I write it / And no one can see it / But I know it's there." Touseled Kate Greenaway miss or plump Indian maid or neighborhood boy: "On my finger nails small skies / On pitchers of milk / I write it / On carousels / On park benches / On shells." Where skyscrapers loom and planes loop-the-loop, where shaggy donkeys graze, and "On you, waves / I write it / I write my name." Without punctuation or termination, without limitation of time or place, nimbly, buoyantly . . . jubilantly asserting the *me* that is Felicity or Isaac or Pedro or Sean (from the multilingual signatures on the last page).

## Publishers Weekly

SOURCE: A review of *I Write It,* in *Publishers Weekly,* Vol. 197, No. 17, April 27, 1970, p. 79.

A small book that contains an enormous helping of joy, for what can match the joy a child discovers in writing? Especially, as in this story, writing his own name? Especially, too, as in this book, the joy captured in words by Ruth Krauss, the *Hole Is to Dig* Ruth Krauss, and in pictures by Mary Chalmers, the *Throw a Kiss, Harry* Mary Chalmers.

## Zena Sutherland

SOURCE: A review of *I Write It,* in *Bulletin of the Center for Children's Books,* Vol. 24, No. 2, October, 1970, p. 29.

A small book, a single thought, a charming interpretation. The text is continuous, happily cataloging the many ways and places that "I write it," and the precise, beguiling figures of children show that it is a universal activity. On the last pages are scribbled and printed all the names of the children who have so enjoyed the thrill of achievement, the satisfaction of having learned to write their own names. The writing is breezy and blithe, the theme appealing.

## EVERYTHING UNDER A MUSHROOM (1974)

### Publishers Weekly

SOURCE: A review of *Everything Under A Mushroom,* in *Publishers Weekly,* Vol. 205, No. 5, February 4, 1974, p. 72.

The spirit of Ruth Krauss's unique version of childhood has been caught by Margot Tomes, which is to say that her drawings are complementary and complimentary to the text. A small part of the author's latest book appeared in *Somebody Else's Nut Tree and Other Tales from Children* (1958) but that shouldn't stop people from snapping up this one. It's difficult to describe the inspired nonsense here; the book is a series of glimpses of little ones at play—all under a mushroom. "Once there were two nothings. The one was a girl nothing. The other was a boy nothing. Then, they were born." Under "little fairy little wish," we find a girl saying, "I wish I was a cherry tree" and a boy saying, "I wish I was springtime" and a droll third party saying "I wouldn't wish to be spaghetti." It all adds up to enchantment.

### Kirkus Reviews

SOURCE: A review of *Everything Under A Mushroom,* in *Kirkus Reviews,* Vol. XLII, No. 6, March 15, 1974, p. 294.

To this reader at least a sub-mushroom setting is a handicap to overcome, and Ruth Krauss' scattered snatches of childlike conversation only increase the risk of preciosity. Most of the way, however, she manages to maintain a precarious balance in her rhyme full of "littles" (" . . . little smile little frown little street little town . . . little fairy little wish little spaghetti little dish . . . "), which marches across the top of each page while Margot Tomes' barefoot toddlers come and go below, carrying props for their exercises in make believe. "Here comes a firefly for when the moon goes off" says one bearing a candle, and another with petals on her head announces "here comes a wild flower! WOOF." There are other comments dropped here and there—"I'll be the little street and you be the little street cleaner" (the speaker pictured prone, while a companion sweeps him with a broom) or "I wouldn't wish to be spaghetti"—and it all does take place under a mushroom, to the likely satisfaction of whimsical grownups and children too young to care why.

## Karla Kuskin

SOURCE: A review of *Everything Under A Mushroom,* in *The New York Times Book Review,* May 5, 1974, p. 46.

A big beige mushroom stands at the center of each spread in *Everything under a mushroom* by Ruth Krauss, pictures by Margot Tomes. Above the mushroom runs a line of rhyming words such as "little one little two little cow little moo." Below a group of children act and comment on the action. The drawings are strongly reminiscent of those Maurice Sendak did in early Ruth Krauss books but the pages are laid out confusingly and there is no path for the eye to follow with ease. Too few phrases are spontaneously poetic while too many lack a needed spark. The author aims to directly touch the hearts and imaginations of children. Although I do not think she succeeds here very well she is a step ahead of many who write for children and never try.

## Zena Sutherland

SOURCE: A review of *Everything Under A Mushroom,* in *Bulletin of the Center for Children's Books,* Vol. 27, No. 11, July-August, 1974, p. 180.

Every double-page spread carries a large picture of a mushroom under which there are a variety of activities, and on each page there are four words. The text begins, "Little one little two, little cow little moo, little cow little calf, little street little town . . . " All the while, children are playing below and there are small signs: "I'll be the little street and you be the little street cleaner," or, "Here come a firefly for when the moon goes off." There's never any plausible excuse for the mushroom, but the imaginative play of the children, the rhyming text, and the attractive illustrations are appealing.

## 📖 *LITTLE BOAT LIGHTER THAN A CORK* (1976)

### *Publishers Weekly*

SOURCE: A review of *Little Boat Lighter Than A Cork,* in *Publishers Weekly,* Vol. 210, No. 11, September 13, 1976, p. 99.

A tiny book has resulted from the outsized talents of Ruth Krauss and artist Esther Gilman. It's as gentle as a lullaby, just right for introducing the joys of books to toddlers. The little boat is a walnut shell which sails with its baby passenger safely into small streams, big rivers, the bottom of oceans, up among the Arctic icebergs and through more waters. Along the way, the voyager meets dolphins, white whales, mermaids, sea dragons and other friendly creatures. The poetic text is soothing; the drawings are just right. They are pencil sketches, with the yellow sail of the brave craft the only note of color throughout.

### Helen Gregory

SOURCE: A review of *Little Boat Lighter Than A Cork,* in *School Library Journal,* Vol. 23, No. 5, January, 1977, p. 84.

A minuscule book offering a gentle if pointless tone poem illustrated with soft charcoal drawings touched with lemon yellow of a baby floating in a walnut shell past mermaids, dolphins, etc. It won't waste anyone's time since it takes less than a minute to read and peruse the pretty pictures, but Sendak's entire Nutshell Library can be purchased for less than this unmemorable extravagance.

## 📖 *SOMEBODY SPILLED THE SKY* (1979)

### *Publishers Weekly*

SOURCE: A review of *Somebody Spilled the Sky,* in *Publishers Weekly,* Vol. 215, No. 4, January 22, 1979, p. 370.

It's seldom that today's tots are treated to creations by Krauss. They are bound to read and reread her forthcoming opus, a must-have like *A Hole Is to Dig, The Carrot Seed* et al. Abetting her unparalleled amphigories are [Eleanor] Hazard's crazy drawings in blue and white, pictures that the poet's lines sometimes swirl around, chase or embrace. What makes Krauss's inventions irresistible is her genius for echoing the daft but unassailable logic of children. "A Girl at a Party" is an example: "There was a girl at a party / and she was very beautiful. / Her face was beautiful. / Her dress was beautiful. / Everybody said, 'How beautiful!' / And she was rich too. / But the other girls at the party didn't care / because they all had warm bathrobes."

### *Kirkus Reviews*

SOURCE: A review of *Somebody Spilled the Sky,* in *Kirkus Reviews,* Vol. XLVII, No. 6, March 15, 1979, p. 324.

"Drizzle tonight off the east coast of my head," reads Krauss' weather report, assuring old admirers that her head still grooves to its own isobars; and "b Ballet" encourages readers to let go too: " . . . be a button they push you and the moon comes out." Besides the ballet, she comes up with offbeat operas ("little kid opera" consists almost entirely of "Bow wow wow" repeated), plays ("Bells" has a man deliver the sun to a little girl's apartment), songs, and a "sonnet" in which each of the 14 lines consists of the one word NO. (The title, perversely, is "Ten Nos," and the pictures show ten naughty rabbits provoking them.) Not everything here is new; for example, "be ginning on paper," which ends "I write my name," reaches back to Krauss' 1970 picture-book-length *I Write It,* and **"A Beautiful Day"** (complete text: "GIRL: Whata beautiful day! / THE SUN falls down on the stage.") is straight from **The Cantilevered Rainbow,** published in 1965 for ages 13+. Reviewers then found the selection too avant-garde for teenagers, and perhaps it will find a wider audience in the freer picture-book world—though who's to know if it will say more to this age group? But the main problem here is that [Eleanor] Hazard's illustrations aren't wiggy enough to make the most of it. Her children cavort jubilantly, and her animals—the rampaging rabbits, lambs romping in poppies, dogs cutting up in a classroom—are cute enough for a more everyday show of high spirits. But she throws away the title line with a blue splot, and overall her ordinary-looking black line and pale blue pictures betray a literal, linear sensibility when what is called for is the abandon of Bileck's *Rain Makes Applesauce.*

## 📖 *WHEN I WALK I CHANGE THE EARTH* (1979)

### *Booklist*

SOURCE: A review of *When I Walk I Change the Earth,* in *Booklist,* Vol. 76, No. 4, October 15, 1979, p. 335.

Without strain, Krauss' longpoem becomes philosophically and metaphorically engrossing. Change is both subject, method, and metaphor: " . . . oh my suffering shoes / created one so much out of them." Thought and action, cause and effect, frame and content, perspective and potential, present and future simultaneously make a world full but different, as "a dream bends when the night in it dissolves." Even Krauss' poetics participate: pace, viewpoint, and voice in flux from andante to allegro, concrete to symbolic, impersonal narrative to first-person statement. In stasis, movement.

## MINESTRONE: A RUTH KRAUSS SELECTION (1981)

### Publishers Weekly

SOURCE: A review of *Minestrone: A Ruth Krauss Selection*, in *Publishers Weekly*, Vol. 220, No. 8, August 21, 1981, p. 55.

For over 30 years, Krauss has been known for her unique contributions to children's books, creations that delight grownups and boys and girls of all ages. This is a generous collection of memorable poems, inimitable stories, drawings based on thumbprints, etc. Here are the inspired, unarguable definitions like "The sun is so it can be a great day"; "A baby makes the mother and father—otherwise they're just plain people." Open any page at random and discover the fruits of an unchained imagination such as "There was a girl at a party and she was very beautiful. Her face was beautiful. Her dress was beautiful. Her feet were beautiful. Everybody said, 'How beautiful!' And she was rich too. But the other girls at the party didn't care because they all had warm bathrobes." The book will surely be among the new bestsellers.

### Holly Sanhuber

SOURCE: A review of *Minestrone: A Ruth Krauss Selection*, *School Library Journal*, Vol. 28, No. 3, November, 1981, p. 94.

The author's latest book is a collection of playlets, short pieces (e.g., "The world is so / you have something / to stand on"), adult-interest verse (e.g., "When you break your heart it changes / all exits are open arriving like a sky"), encores of her "Thumbprint" character and the texts of several previous children's books. The author seems uncertain of which age group she wishes to address. The content is at war with itself, as is the physical format, which might appeal to grades six and above. The rhymes are facile and shallow. Filled with forced whimsy, they're downright dumb, so bad as to be embarrassing (e.g., "in the head / I love you / in the feet / I love you / in the night / where is the telephone? / I love you / is there no telephone? / I love you . . . "). The author strives to be childlike and the results are childish and condescending. What text was adequate when accompanied by outstanding illustrations proves itself too weak to stand alone.

### Ruth M. Stein

SOURCE: A review of *Minestrone: A Ruth Krauss Selection*, in *Language Arts*, Vol. 59, No. 6, September, 1982, p. 606.

"Sing a little song / dance a little dance / hang on to your hat / hang on to your pants here we go-o-o-o-o-o." You'll find mini-plays, definitions, short prose texts, and other samples of Kraussian verse. Many are reprinted old favorites to be discovered by new readers. Remember her red thumbprints with the pen-and-ink additions? If I begin quoting, I'll never stop. Definitely for sharing. Calmer than Silverstein, and for a younger audience. I love them both. Shel S. is the more universal of the two, with less whimsey and a mightier wallop.

## BIG AND LITTLE (1988)

### Barbara Elleman

SOURCE: A review of *Big and Little*, in *Booklist*, Vol. 84, No. 18, May 15, 1988, p. 1610.

Relationships from a child's perspective are presented with lyrical simplicity through sparse text and lush pastel illustrations. Developing from unsophisticated spatial comparisons—"big fields love little flowers"—to interpersonal associations—"big monkeys love little monkeyshines and I love you"—the childlike images mount in tenderness as the boy is seen romping alone, playing with his sister, attending his cat, and, at book's end, helping tend her newborn kittens. Rich with the hues and scenes of the changing seasons, the illustrations vividly portray the affection and warmth of this book, which begs to be cuddled up with and shared.

### Leda Schubert

SOURCE: A review of *Big and Little*, in *School Library Journal*, Vol. 34, No. 11, August, 1988, pp. 82–3.

Krauss' intimate poem explores concepts of big and little through images such as "big sorrows love little tears" and "big fields love little flowers." Each set of concepts ends with a reassuring "and I love you." [Mary] Szilagyi's full-color illustrations portray a sturdy boy, sometimes joined by other family members, playing through three seasons at a rural seaside community (with Manhattan occasionally in the background). He plants a tree, plays ball, finds sea shells, reads a book, and flies a kite. . . .

As the poem ranges from abstract to concrete, it should be comforting to small children, who will sense love and protection.

---

Additional coverage of Krauss's life and career is contained in the following sources published by Gale Research: *Contemporary Authors*, Vol. 141; *Contemporary Authors New Revision Series*, Vol. 47; *Dictionary of Literary Biography*, Vol. 52; *Major Authors and Illustrators for Children and Young Adults*; and *Something about the Author*, Vols. 1, 30, 75.

# Marcus Pfister

Swiss illustrator and author of picture books.

Major works include *The Sleepy Owl* (1986), *Penguin Pete* (1987), *The Rainbow Fish* (1992), *The Christmas Star* (1993), *Rainbow Fish to the Rescue* (1995).

## INTRODUCTION

Both an illustrator and writer of picture books for pre-schoolers and early primary graders, Pfister receives more praise for his eye-catching watercolor illustrations than for his stories. Generally speaking, his storybooks, written in his native German tongue, feature animal protagonists and explore emotional ground from which most books for the young typically shy away. Pfister's most notable creation to date is *The Rainbow Fish,* the book in which he first used watercolors combined with an iridescent-foil technique to visually capture the reader's attention. Finding friends, sharing, courage, and helping one another in a time of need are among the themes Pfister addresses in his plots. "For me," says Pfister, "there is one major criterion in determining the value of a book: If it brings adults and children together and makes them interact intensely, then it has achieved its purpose."

### Biographical Information

Born in Berne, Switzerland, Pfister grew up the third of five children. While attending art school in Berne, Pfister worked for an advertising agency; in 1981 he moved to Zurich to become a graphic artist for another agency. Wanting to travel, Pfister took a leave of absence from work in 1983, and toured the United States for six months with his wife, Kathrin. While on vacation, the aspiring artist decided to go back to the agency part-time and devote his spare hours to his own work. The result of this effort was his first self-illustrated book, *The Sleepy Owl.* Pfister achieved a heightened success in 1992 after producing *The Rainbow Fish,* which has sold over four million copies. The popular and prolific children's author and illustrator once again resides in Berne with his wife and three children.

### Major Works

In the picture book *The Sleepy Owl,* Little Owl and her human friend Tom realize they can't play together because of their different sleeping patterns. To resolve the problem Tom paints an owl face on his kite to let Little Owl know he is still her friend. Several critics were impressed by Pfister's artwork, but not his story; as

a reviewer in *Growing Point* noted, "The story is minuscule, the wash and ink pictures broad in composition and rich in colour." Similar assessments followed the publication of *Penguin Pete,* the first of a series which describes the adventures of Pete—the smallest penguin in his colony—as he learns to walk, fly, and eventually, swim.

*The Rainbow Fish,* the first book in which Pfister employed his signature holographic foil stamping, tells the story of a selfish fish who won't share his beautiful iridescent scales with the other fish. After becoming an outcast, the rainbow fish learns to share his scales and, therefore, makes many friends. Again, most critics found the unique artwork eye-catching and the story predictable. *The Christmas Star,* a story about the shepherds, kings, and animals following the twinkling star to baby Jesus, and *Dazzle the Dinosaur* (1994), a tale of friendship towards and acceptance of a dinosaur that has a shiny spine, also employ the foil technique. In the glittery *Rainbow Fish to the Rescue,* the sequel to *The Rainbow Fish,* the newly accepted fish leads a rescue mission to save an outcast fish from a shark.

## Awards

Pfister received the Critici in Erba Prize at the Bologna Children's Book Fair and the Christopher Award, both in 1993, for *The Rainbow Fish*. *The Rainbow Fish* was also a Book of the Year for a children's book selection by the American Booksellers Association in 1995.

---

# TITLE COMMENTARY

## WHERE IS MY FRIEND? (1986)

### Anita Silvey

SOURCE: A review of *Where Is My Friend?*, in *The Horn Book Magazine*, Vol. LXII, No. 5, September-October, 1986, pp. 583-84.

With the exception of Rosemary Wells's brilliant books about Max and Ruby, board books for the preschool set have almost exclusively explored concepts and the identification of objects and numbers. Refreshing, because it delves into the realm of emotion for the very young, the book shows a lonely porcupine searching for a companion. He gazes longingly at cacti, a nut, a brush, and a pincushion—which have been cleverly drawn to look almost like porcupines—but only at the end of the minidrama does the creature locate a friend. Although the drawings of the porcupine's face, hands, and feet are more cartoonlike than is necessary, the page design is clean and spare, and the final drawing of two porcupines nestled together with quills touching is absolutely endearing. The book is a fine example of the growing group of board books that bring a range of experience in book form to the very young.

### Louise M. Zuckerman

SOURCE: A review of *Where Is My Friend?*, in *School Library Journal*, Vol. 33, No. 2, October, 1986, p. 156.

Each of these bland board books is a slight, uninspired story with one-dimensional, uninteresting color illustrations. The best of this lack-luster series is *Where Is My Friend?* The friend-seeking porcupine has a certain amount of appeal and is drawn with some humor. The objects he encounters (cactus, brush, seed pod) are all large enough for a toddler to focus on. Unfortunately, not many of them will be able to *identify* most of the objects. Compared to Eric Hill's "Spot" books, which show how a high level of interest can be maintained in a short, simple board book, these four books could change the category name to "bored" books.

## THE SLEEPY OWL (1986)

### Gail L. Cox

SOURCE: A review of *The Sleepy Owl*, in *Canadian Children's Literature*, No. 44, 1986, p. 97.

*The sleepy owl* tells the story of a little boy and an owl who want to play together. Owing to their opposite sleeping times they must agree to be friends apart. The dreamy watercolours add a lovely atmosphere, but because of the weak plot the book is best left alone. North-South books suffer a little from a stilted translation into English.

### Margery Fisher

SOURCE: A review of *The Sleepy Owl*, in *Growing Point*, Vol. 25, No. 3, September, 1986, p. 4691.

In this elegant picture-book the shape of an owl's face is repeated on the kite which consoles Tom after the bird has refused to wake in daylight to play with him; even when he lends her his alarm clock the trick backfires, for the rest of the owl family resents being woken in the day time. The story is minuscule, the wash and ink pictures broad in composition and rich in colour.

### Susan Scheps

SOURCE: A review of *The Sleepy Owl*, in *School Library Journal*, Vol. 33, No. 6, February, 1987, p. 73.

When Little Owl awakes one evening to find that her friends have gone off without her, she flies down to a house and taps on the window. Young Tom wakes up, gives her his alarm clock, and promises to play with her the next afternoon. Little Owl cannot wake up when the alarm goes off, and when she doesn't come, Tom paints an owl face on his kite—a flying friend that looks like Little Owl. When she sees the kite, Little Owl knows that Tom is her friend. The bird's large yellow-ringed eyes shine from amidst her jewelled pastel watercolor feathers. The predominately dusk-toned illustrations on their blue and gray night backgrounds (several given texture by sponge applications of color) crisply contrast to the text on a stark white facing page or a white border beneath the illustration. The appeal of the illustrations will ensure the popularity of this trite but pleasant story.

## PENGUIN PETE (1987)

### T. R. Hollingsworth

SOURCE: A review of *Penguin Pete*, in *Children's Book Review Service*, Vol. 16, No. 7, February, 1988, p. 73.

Pete, the smallest penguin in the flock, is a non-swimmer who deeply wants to swim in the ocean with the others. When a number of birds land on his iceberg, he finds a

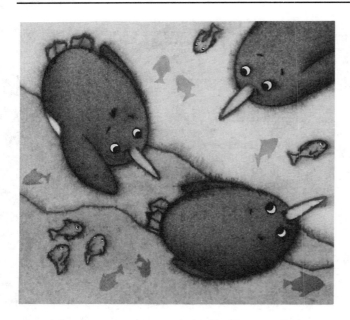

*From* Penguin Pete, *written and illustrated by Marcus Pfister.*

friend who is even smaller. Steve, his bird friend, can fly and poor Pete can't do that either. Eventually he learns to swim. The muted watercolors add to the weak, contrived story that lacks suspense and complications.

**Jane Gardner Connor**

SOURCE: A review of *Penguin Pete,* in *School Library Journal,* Vol. 34, No. 7, March, 1988, p. 174.

Pete is the smallest penguin in his colony, and he is eager to grow up quickly so that he can swim in the sea. This story tells about his small adventures, including his efforts to walk gracefully, his friendship with a bird who tries to teach him to fly, and finally his first day swimming. The events between the beginning and end of the story seem to be incidents designed to flesh it out rather than integral parts of plot. Pete's success at swimming is so natural that it doesn't create much of a climax, making this a pleasant but unexciting story. It is unfortunate the story is so flat because the illustrations are humorous and appealing. Pfister has created big-eyed, short, squat penguins and set them against a soft background using mostly white, gray, blue, and lavender to capture Pete's icy world. Delightful endpapers showing Pete in various positions provide an inviting opening to the book.

## PENGUIN PETE'S NEW FRIENDS (1988)

**Kathryn Weisman**

SOURCE: A review of *Penguin Pete's New Friends,* in *School Library Journal,* Vol. 34, No. 11, August, 1988, p. 84.

Pfister continues the adventures of **Penguin Pete,** a young Antarctic penguin. Pete is angry when he cannot go fishing with the bigger penguins. He decides to go fishing on his own and falls asleep atop a whale who takes him to play with an Eskimo boy, an elephant seal, some sea lions, and finally back home again. The soft child-like illustrations will appeal to very young listeners as will the simple plot line, although adults may be put off by the discrepancy of placing Eskimos in the Antarctic.

## PENGUIN PETE AND PAT (1989)

**Publishers Weekly**

SOURCE: A review of *Penguin Pete and Pat,* in *Publishers Weekly,* Vol. 235, No. 15, April 14, 1989, p. 68.

Penguin Pete, previously encountered in **Penguin Pete** and **Penguin Pete's New Friends,** romps with some dolphins on his way back to his home colony. Later he finds true love with a blue-beaked girl penguin named Pat; they get married and have a baby by book's end. Readers will neither understand Pete's head-over-heels attraction for Pat, nor will they care. The plot and the characters—despite Pfister's buoyant watercolors—just lie on the page.

## SUN AND MOON (1990)

**Regina Pauly**

SOURCE: A review of *Sun and Moon,* in *School Library Journal,* Vol. 36, No. 7, July, 1990, p. 63.

This story offers clichés and stilted writing about a conversation between the Earth and the lonely Sun who would like to have a friend (oddly, the Earth behaves like a friend, but never offers to be one). The conversation is repeated between Earth and Moon. And, surprise, the Moon and the Sun agree to become friends. They meet momentarily (an eclipse) and agree to get together more often. The illustrations—like the story—are a little hard to believe. The drawings are flat and without perspective, while the colors are wonderful shades of greens and yellows and blues. They can't make up for the poor writing and an unconvincing story.

**Judy L. G. Eyerer**

SOURCE: A review of *Sun and Moon,* in *Children's Book Review Service,* Vol. 18, No. 14, August, 1990, p. 162.

As the sun and moon struggle to deal with the loneliness which accompanies their positions in the sky, a wide range of celestial events are introduced in a simple and enjoyable manner. **Sun and Moon** could be presented merely as a pleasant tale or could be used as a springboard into or accompaniment to a child's introduction to astronomy. The pastels give the story a dreamy feeling and complement the text perfectly.

## 📖 *SHAGGY* (1990)

**Margery Fisher**

SOURCE: A review of *Shaggy*, in *Growing Point*, Vol. 29, No. 6, March, 1991, p. 5489.

A comic design of a dog with an endless string of sausages on the end-papers sets the tone for a lively sequence when a junk-yard dog plagued by rats concludes, after accidents and disasters over a theft from the butcher, that the cats' offer of help should not have been scorned. Soft stippled paint in offbeat spinach green, coffee brown and mauve guides us through the streets and the yard in an idiosyncratic view of urban enclaves.

**Dorothy Houlihan**

SOURCE: A review of *Shaggy*, in *School Library Journal*, Vol. 37, No. 3, March, 1991, p. 177.

A predictable, pedantic story about friendship. Shaggy, a junkyard dog, enjoys his untethered lifestyle but for the rats that also live in the dump, taking his food and disturbing his sleep. When a cat volunteers to rid Shaggy's home of rodents in exchange for shelter, the dog turns down the offer, refusing to share his home with anyone. Yet one day, after Shaggy steals a string of sausages that the rats in turn pilfer from him, he swallows his pride and begs the cat for help. She agrees, saying, "What are friends for?" They retrieve the sausages and presumably live happily ever after. Pfister's inelegant blend of indistinct watercolor backgrounds and cloyingly cartoonish animals fail to lighten the heavyhanded message. The text contains inconsistencies—Shaggy steals food, but believes the rats shouldn't take his cache; the dog and cat can speak to each other, but apparently not to the rats or even to other dogs; the cat calls herself Shaggy's friend, but he has done nothing to earn the honor. Avoid this obvious, unengaging tale.

## 📖 *HOPPER* (1991)

**Joan McGrath**

SOURCE: A review of *Hopper*, in *School Library Journal*, Vol. 37, No. 9, September, 1991, p. 239.

*Hopper* is a tiny white hare with one blue-tipped ear. He is tired of winter, ice and snow, cold feet, and nothing but bark to eat, but his mother lovingly reassures him that the joys of spring will return. This quiet picture book has very little in the way of plot, but features a wealth of large, misty watercolors in luscious pastel shades that are as soft and cuddly as a child's favorite blanket. *Hopper* conveys the same all-encompassing sense of security and warmth as does that classic of the nursery by Margaret W. Brown, *The Runaway Bunny*, and will be appreciated by the same audience.

## 📖 *I SEE THE MOON: GOOD-NIGHT POEMS AND LULLABIES* (1991)

**Carolyn Phelan**

SOURCE: A review of *I See the Moon: Good-Night Poems and Lullabies*, in *Booklist*, Vol. 88, No. 4, October 15, 1991, p. 444.

This picture book showcases 12 poems for sleepyheads. Mainly British in origin, they include traditional rhymes and lullabies, poems by Blake, Rossetti, Nesbit, and Stevenson, and the African American song "Kumbaya." Pfister's colorful paintings, usually starry evening scenes in muted hues, life the words out of everyday reality into a twilight zone of dreams between waking and sleeping. A sweet, soporific choice for bedtime reading.

**Ronald Jobe**

SOURCE: A review of *I See the Moon: Good-Night Poems and Lullabies*, in *School Library Journal*, Vol. 38, No. 2, February, 1992, p. 83.

A nocturnal dozen to read at bedtime. Poems by Blake, Rossetti, Nesbit, and Stevenson are featured, accompanied by watery, dreamlike illustrations that present an intriguing mood of evening and rest. Exquisitely composed scenes highlighted by curious details (e.g., a bell hanging from a crescent moon) are juxtaposed against timeless vistas (e.g., a bed and window frame floating amidst the stars). Beautiful as they may be, they do not have much relevance to the text.

## 📖 *HOPPER HUNTS FOR SPRING* (1992)

**Carolyn L. Shute**

SOURCE: A review of *Hopper Hunts for Spring*, in *The Horn Book Guide*, Vol. III, No. 2, January-June, 1992, p. 243.

When Hopper's mother tells him that "'spring is coming at last,'" Hopper the bunny takes his mother's words literally and eagerly bounds away to meet his new playmate. Soft-edged illustrations with dominant shades of blue and purple aptly suit this charming and childlike end-of-winter story.

**Anne Connor**

SOURCE: A review of *Hopper Hunts for Spring*, in *School Library Journal*, Vol. 38, No. 7, July, 1992, pp. 62–3.

Hopper's mother tells him that Spring is coming, and he rushes off to meet what he hopes will be a new friend. Upon this frail premise, the story unfolds as the little rabbit looks in a hole, a cave, and in a hollow tree for Spring. Along the way he meets a mole and is befriended by a bear with whom he shares a honey feast. The snow-white bunny finally returns home and his mother sets him straight. While the double-paged, dreamy watercolors are quite lovely, the flat story destroys any appeal this book might have. There is no humor or depth of feeling, and children will not derive much enjoyment from Hopper's misunderstanding. All but the very youngest listeners will find the adventure inane.

## THE RAINBOW FISH (1992)

### Ellen Fader

SOURCE: A review of *The Rainbow Fish,* in *School Library Journal,* Vol. 38, No. 11, November, 1992, pp. 75–6.

Children will be immediately drawn to this book that features an iridescent, metallic-looking main character whose "scales were every shade of blue and green and purple, with sparkling silver scales among them." Adult suspicions of the gimmick overwhelming the story quickly fade as the plot unfolds: none of the other fish will have anything to do with the Rainbow Fish, who always swims by superciliously and refuses to give away any of his special garb. He is lonely and without admirers until a wise female octopus advises him to give away his scales. Rainbow Fish then discovers that sharing brings happiness and acceptance. The delicate watercolors of underwater scenes are a perfect foil to the glittering scales that eventually form a part of each fish's exterior. This is certainly a story written to convey a message, but in its simplicity, it recalls the best of Lionni. Besides, what three-year-old doesn't need reinforcement about sharing?

### Publishers Weekly

SOURCE: A review of *The Rainbow Fish,* in *Publishers Weekly,* Vol. 239, No. 48, November 2, 1992, p. 70.

Despite some jazzy special effects achieved with shimmery holographs, this cautionary tale about selfishness and vanity has trouble staying afloat. Rainbow Fish, "the most beautiful fish in the entire ocean," refuses to share his prized iridescent scales—which, indeed, flash and sparkle like prisms as each page is turned. When his greed leaves him without friends or admirers, the lonely fish seeks advice from the wise octopus, who counsels him to give away his beauty and "discover how to be happy." The translation from the original German text doesn't enhance the story's predictable plot, and lapses into somewhat vague descriptions: after sharing a single scale, "a rather peculiar feeling came over Rainbow Fish." Deep purples, blues and greens bleed together in Pfister's liquid watercolors; unfortunately, the watery effect is abruptly interrupted by a few stark white, text-only pages.

### Carolyn Phelan

SOURCE: A review of *The Rainbow Fish,* in *Booklist,* Vol. 89, No. 9, January 1, 1993, p. 811.

Proud of his shimmering silver scales, Rainbow Fish disdains the plainer fish who asks him to share his treasures. When word of his refusal gets around, Rainbow Fish finds that the other fish swim away at his approach. A wise old octopus advises him to share his scales. When he does, Rainbow Fish finds that the more he gives to others, the happier he feels. The plot is rather predictable, but the artwork certainly catches the eye. Incorporated into the fluid, watercolor paintings, iridescent foil catches every light and radiates colored sparkles that would be the envy of any fish and will fascinate preschoolers. A gimmick? Well, yes, but in context it works. A popular choice for picture book displays.

### Kate Kellaway

SOURCE: "Dancing with Owls," in *The Observer,* April 9, 1995, p. 19.

Beauty is only fin-deep, at least that would seem to be the moral of this *huge* and glamorous book. It is twice the size of a normal picture book and the rainbow fish is covered in glittering diamante scales; he is fat, shiny and magnificent. But he's also unhappy, lonely in his pride until he gets the point. Life and luck are to be shared—he starts to dole out his scales. On a scale of one to ten, this book scores ten.

## THE CHRISTMAS STAR (1993)

### Christine C. Behr

SOURCE: A review of *The Christmas Star,* in *The Horn Book Guide,* Vol. V, No. 1, July-December, 1993, p. 97.

An oddly adapted version of the Christmas story, in which the stars in the night sky converge to form the Christmas star that leads shepherds, kings, and animals to the Christ child. The artless text is obviously a vehicle for the illustrations, which feature glittery foil stars, palaces, crowns, and gifts combined awkwardly with soft color washes.

### Publishers Weekly

SOURCE: A review of *The Christmas Star,* in *Publishers Weekly,* Vol. 240, No. 38, September 20, 1993, p. 40.

Using the same shimmering holographic foil found in *The Rainbow Fish,* Pfister's star provides this book's soft-edged illustrations with sparkle. A fairly conventional text tells how the radiant star leads shepherds, kings and animals to Bethlehem, to witness the Nativity. Pfister's technique has grown more sophisticated since *The Rainbow Fish;* here, the silver star appears to "reflect like the sun off the golden domes" of a palace, and each king's gift has its own, distinctive pattern.

## School Library Journal

SOURCE: A review of *The Christmas Star,* in *School Library Journal,* Vol. 39, No. 10, October, 1993, p. 47.

A pleasant, unremarkable retelling of the familiar gathering of shepherds, kings, and animals. One by one, each group discusses the news they've heard of the coming of the baby who will be Lord and King. And one by one, they see the brilliant star glowing overhead and follow it. The quiet story and soft, blended watercolors in pastel shades of blue, green, and tan are overwhelmed on almost every page by sparkling, appliquéd paper in the shapes of stars, shining castle domes, and kingly thrones and presents. This technique competes with the text and illustrations for readers' attention.

## D. A. Young

SOURCE: A review of *The Christmas Star,* in *The Junior Bookshelf,* Vol. 57, No. 6, December, 1993, p. 228.

The story of the birth of Jesus and the Epiphany is told here with magnificent full page illustrations handsomely embellished with glittering "holographic" foils which will, surely, catch and hold the attention of the very young child who is listening to the story being read aloud as a special treat.

His earlier book *The Rainbow Fish* illustrated in the same style has been a best seller and I think *The Christmas Star* will be equally successful.

## PENGUIN PETE, AHOY! (1993)

## Bambi L. Williams

SOURCE: A review of *Penguin Pete, Ahoy!,* in *School Library Journal,* Vol. 40, No. 1, January, 1994, p. 97.

While exploring, Penguin Pete happens upon an abandoned ship. Once aboard, he meets Horatio, the ship mouse. After eating in the storeroom, they explore the ship, climbing ropes to view the depth of the sea, get tangled in an old fishing net, and play hide-and-seek. Pete goes for a swim, while non-swimmer Horatio boards a lifeboat, which starts to sink, and the penguin scurries to save his new friend. The story ends with Pete swimming across the waters waving good-bye and promising to visit again—and to teach Horatio how to swim. The simple text allows room for discussion. Children will find security in knowing that others fear swimming, and in a friend like Pete who provides support and encouragement. The pastel watercolor illustrations bring the string of adventures to life. While the characters are cartoonlike figures, their facial expressions convey human emotions of joy, uncertainty, and anticipation.

## CHRIS & CROC (1994)

## Publishers Weekly

SOURCE: A review of *Chris & Croc,* in *Publishers Weekly,* Vol. 241, No. 22, May 30, 1994, p. 56.

The Creator of *The Rainbow Fish* serves up a tepid, rambling friendship story about a boy named Chris and his stuffed-toy crocodile. Somewhere between Lyle and Barney lingers Croc, in a kind of stuffed-toy-as-playmate limbo. Alternating between bored baby-sitter and mischievous conspirator, Croc yawns, "You're not doing too well, my boy," when Chris teeters clumsily on his roller skates. Then, after gleefully suggesting that Chris strap on a few pillows to cushion him like a hockey player, Croc hypocritically warns the boy that his mother "is not going to be happy to see those pillows." A few episodes later, Croc crashes to the ground after parachuting from a tree branch, but the reluctant Chris devises a way to save face in front of his daring pal. Their day together ends on a raffish note: Croc is shown devouring the spinach which Chris deems "yuck." Despite Pfister's diverting watercolors, the story's channel-surfing structure and sloppy characterization rarely coalesce.

## Louse S. Murphy

SOURCE: A review of *Chris & Croc,* in *School Library Journal,* Vol. 40, No. 9, September, 1994, p. 192.

The cheerful illustrations in this Swiss import feature a freckle-faced redhead of about five and his long-suffering pet, a stuffed crocodile. Chris drags a reluctant Croc along on his search for something to do. They rollerskate and pretend to play ice hockey (using mom's white pillows for padding). A game of catch ends in disaster as Croc bites through Chris's new beach ball. The pair even try skydiving with the deflated beach ball as a parachute. Finally, it is time for dinner and Croc nobly eats Chris's spinach, an act of true friendship. The illustrations have some interesting watercolor effects and are better realized than the story. With too many words on most of the pages and the lack of a unified story line, the narrative drags from one boredom-fighting scheme to another. Readers will end up with the same task as this duo—looking for something else to do.

## DAZZLE THE DINOSAUR (1994)

## Christine C. Behr

SOURCE: A review of *Dazzle the Dinosaur,* in *The Horn Book Guide,* Vol. VI, No. 1, July-December, 1994, p. 50.

A young dinosaur with a set of glittering spines on his back sets off with his sister to find and conquer the dreaded Dragonsaurus. Young dinosaur fans may appreciate the confusing bevy of real and imaginary dinosaur species, as well as the gimmicky foil spines, but the would-be climactic rescue scene is far from dazzling.

### Publishers Weekly

SOURCE: A review of *Dazzle the Dinosaur,* in *Publishers Weekly,* Vol. 241, No. 40, October 3, 1994, p. 69.

The appeal of this somewhat run-of-the-mill story is boosted by the use of a reflective overlay on the tiny prehistoric hero's spines—the same technique that brought best-sellerdom to Pfister's *The Rainbow Fish.* Readers first meet Dazzle as a sparkly egg that has mysteriously appeared in Mother Maiasaurus's nest. He hatches at the same time as little Maia, and they become fast friends, exploring the valley where they live and dodging its many dangers—including the blood-thirsty Tyrannosaurus Rex. Dazzle vows to rout the evil Dragonsaurus who drove the Maiasauruses from their valley, a quest ensues, and the flashy hero's shiny spines save the day. Pfister's soft pen-and-wash illustrations, rendered in soothing hues of lavender, soft green and blue are pretty, though oddly bland—with the exception, of course, of Dazzle's shiny spines. There is some fact woven into this fantasy, but these wide-eyed dinosaurs have more in common with Barney than with the exhibits of a natural history museum.

### Alexandra Marris

SOURCE: A review of *Dazzle the Dinosaur,* in *School Library Journal,* Vol. 41, No. 1, January, 1995, pp. 91–2.

Two young dinosaur friends, Maia (a Maiasaurus) and Dazzle (who has a row of iridescent, foil-stamped spines on his back), set off to reclaim their ancestral cave from a mean Dragonsaurus that has taken over. They scare him away with an implausible tactic and then, in an anticlimactic ending, lead the other dinosaurs back to the peaceful valley. Blues and blended greens predominate in the watercolor illustrations. The cartoonlike creatures have wide eyes; Maia has long, curly lashes. Dazzle's spines hint at a magical element that is never really delivered. A dazzle-less production.

### Lauren Peterson

SOURCE: A review of *Dazzle the Dinosaur,* in *Booklist,* Vol. 91, No. 11, February 1, 1995, p. 1011.

The reflective illustrations Pfister used in *Rainbow Fish* are successfully used again in this charming prehistoric tale. Food and water are scarce in the valley where young Dazzle (so named because of the glittering spines along his back) and his friend Maia live. It hasn't always been that way, though. Until vicious Dragonsaurus came along, the dinosaurs lived in a cave with its own fresh spring and roamed a valley filled with delicious trees and ferns. Together, Dazzle and Maia set out to chase the nasty beast away and regain their rightful home. The plot is fast paced and imaginative, and the shimmering artwork is integral to the goings-on, not merely decorative. The popularity of the subject matter among young children, coupled with the unusual look of the pictures, will ensure the book a warm reception at story time, followed by lots of requests to read it again.

## PENGUIN PETE AND LITTLE TIM (1994)

### Lauren Peterson

SOURCE: A review of *Penguin Pete and Little Tim,* in *Booklist,* Vol. 91, No. 8, December 15, 1994, p. 760.

In another delightful episode in the Penguin Pete series, papa Pete proves to be a real 1990s dad, letting mom sleep while he takes Tim out for a fun-filled winter adventure. Mischievous little Tim bombards Pete with snowballs, rides on an old dogsled, tumbles down a hill, and goes for a swim with some seals. The lighthearted fun turns a bit more serious when a blinding snowstorm separates Tim and Pete, but Tim shows the strength of the father-son bond and the unwavering trust he has in his dad by not panicking and remembering his father's advice: "If you ever get lost, stay right where you are and I'll come and find you." Pete's winter wonderland is beautifully depicted in soft pastel washes of lavender, gray, blue, and green with occasional splashes of sunny gold and orange. This endearing father-and-son team will warm a child's heart on the coldest winter day.

### Kirkus Reviews

SOURCE: A review of *Penguin Pete and Little Tim,* in *Kirkus Reviews,* Vol. LXIII, No. 24, December 15, 1994, p. 1574.

On this particular snowy day, Penguin Pete takes his son, Tim, out for a walk. They have a snowball fight, go sledding, and slide down long slopes together. Suddenly, Tim loses his father in the snow. He is found by a seal who invites him for a swim. Tim knows that he must remain in one place when he is lost so that Pete can locate him, but he mischievously disobeys. Eventually his father finds Tim and they happily make their way home. The unclear message in this book may mislead the young reader. Tim's blatant disregard for an important rule doesn't even merit a lecture from Pete, and Tim leaves the incident none the wiser.

The adorable illustrations are the only appealing thing about this dull, confused penguin tale.

### Lynn Cockett

SOURCE: A review of *Penguin Pete and Little Tim,* in *School Library Journal,* Vol. 41, No. 2, February, 1995, p. 79.

Penguin Pete and his son Tim start the day with a walk

*From* The Rainbow Fish, *written and illustrated by Marcus Pfister.*

in their icy, polar world, engaging in a snowball fight and taking a ride on a dogsled. Snow begins to fall, and as the wind howls, Tim looks up to find that his dad is nowhere in sight. Soon a friendly seal offers to take him for a dip in the frigid water, and after a brief swim he returns to land and awaits the reunion with his father. The short, choppy sentences make for a quick, yet uneven read. Tim's statement to Pete that "I didn't think you were ever going to find me" seems out of place, since the tiny creature spent most of his "lost" time swimming contentedly with a seal. Watercolors applied to wet paper create a soft, snowy atmosphere—a perfect setting for the story. The penguins, however, don't rise above the look of fuzzy stuffed animals. They appear stiff and their facial expressions rarely vary enough to convey personality or mood. In all, a disappointing effort.

### The Junior Bookshelf

SOURCE: A review of *Penguin Pete and Little Tim*, in *The Junior Bookshelf*, Vol. 59, No. 3, June, 1995, p. 96.

Penguin Pete and his son Tim enjoy games in the snow. They throw snowballs at each other, try out a dog sled, and finally reach the water. Tim sets off to swim with a seal but is happy to return to the security of his father and home. The illustrations create appealing images of snow

and icy water, with two likable penguin characters. The brief text would be suitable for quite young pre-school children. It is about the warmth of family affection rather than a lifestyle in the icy wastes. The theme of father and son playing together adds another view of Pete's life to those seen in previous books.

## 📖 *HANG ON, HOPPER!* (1995)

### Judy Constantinides

SOURCE: A review of *Hang On, Hopper!*, in *School Library Journal*, Vol. 41, No. 6, June, 1995, p. 94.

After staying too long at his friend Scamp's house, Hopper the bunny tries to take a shortcut home by swimming across a stream. When he gets into trouble in the water, Scamp tells him to hang onto a branch and goes for help. Hopper drifts downstream to a beaver's dam, where he makes a new friend and learns a lesson as well: water is dangerous when you don't know how to swim. Illustrated in lovely pastel watercolors somewhat in the style of Garth Williams's work, this is a simple story that gently preaches water safety while entertaining readers. Pfister has written other "Hopper" books, and no doubt the youngest audiences will welcome another. Slight, but pretty, and with a worthwhile message.

## 📖 *RAINBOW FISH TO THE RESCUE!* (1995)

### Publishers Weekly

SOURCE: A review of *Rainbow Fish to the Rescue!*, in *Publishers Weekly*, Vol. 242, No. 29, July 15, 1995, pp. 229–30.

Rainbow Fish, that glittery piscine, is back, this time with another moral to impart. Readers will remember how he learned to share in the original tale (*The Rainbow Fish*), doling out his shimmering scales to all the have-nots, and this story finds him and his sparkling school of friends at play—but bent on excluding a little striped fish who wants to join in all their games. Rainbow Fish is a little ashamed, remembering as he does what it feels like to have no friends. So when a shark appears and imperils the dejected interloper, it's Rainbow Fish who leads the rescue mission. The main appeal of Pfister's books is not the stories but the pretty pictures—pastel watercolors peppered with holographic foil-stamp overlays that glimmer and gleam—and this new volume amply serves up more of same.

### Betty Teague

SOURCE: A review of *Rainbow Fish to the Rescue!*, in *School Library Journal*, Vol. 41, No. 9, September, 1995, p. 184.

When a little striped fish approaches the established school of fish, each of whom has one silver scale, and asks if he can play, he is turned away because he is not equipped to play "flash tag." Although Rainbow Fish remembers how it felt to be excluded, he does not come to the rescue until later when the school escapes a snapping shark's jaws, leaving the striped fish to fend for himself. Then Rainbow Fish spearheads the school's diversionary maneuvers and leads the smaller fish to safety. The next game is changed so that the new member of the group can join in. Pfister uses the same ocean-hued watercolors and foil-stamped scales that he used to illustrate *Rainbow Fish.* The faces of the fish reflect the emotions of the text, from derision to fear. The shark is appropriately fearsome. Although it is not mandatory to have read the earlier title first, it would be helpful in order to understand his recollection of his loneliness before he shared his scales and became one of the group. The gently implied themes of sharing and friendship in the first story are expanded here to include courage. Groups may be inspired to talk about befriending others, even if they are different, or about doing what is right, even if it is not popular.

**Carolyn Phelan**

SOURCE: A review of *Rainbow Fish to the Rescue!,* in *Booklist,* Vol. 92, No. 2, September 15, 1995, p. 176.

A sequel to the enormously popular *Rainbow Fish,* in which our hero makes friends by sharing his sparkling scales with his plainer cousins, this picture book continues the theme of belonging. When Rainbow Fish and his friends exclude a little striped fish from their game of flash tag simply because he doesn't have a flashing scale, Rainbow Fish wants to help. Unfortunately, he's afraid that he'll lose his friends if he goes against the flow. It takes a threatening shark for Rainbow Fish to rally his friends to the rescue and for the fish to accept the newcomer. Parents and teachers will find the book a good vehicle for discussing courage in the face of peer pressure. Children will find the iridescent silver highlights in the watercolor artwork beguiling and the emotions played out underwater familiar from the playground.

**Anne Freier**

SOURCE: A review of *Rainbow Fish to the Rescue!,* in *Magpies,* Vol. 10, No. 5, November, 1995, p. 12.

Is it as good as the first? This is the immediate question asked when a sequel title appears. This is particularly true when the first book created such an impact with its readers to become an instant and widespread favourite.

*Rainbow Fish* was first published in 1992. It was a unique book that literally 'dazzled'. Its most outstanding features were the silvery fish scales and fin flashes stamped with diffraction foil circles which catch and bounce the light to reveal sparkling rainbows of colours and the intense background watercolours of turquoise and electric blues, mauves, indigo, lush greens, soft and glowing rose, coral

and golds which delicately yet dramatically create serene underwater scenes.

The story of how the Rainbow Fish, *'the most beautiful fish in the entire ocean'* learnt to share his most prized possessions—his shimmering scales—to make friends, won a rather 'dazzling' string of awards including the 1993 Christopher Award, the 1993 Bologna Book Fair Critici in Erba Prize and the International Reading Association/ Children's Book Council Children's Choice for the same year. It proved not just to be a book for the critics but for its legion of readers. Young readers received it with wide-eyed wonder and parents and teachers welcomed this parable-like tale which reinforced the value of sharing and seeing past possessions in the search for true happiness. It was a storyteller's dream and certainly a hard act to follow. How would the character shape up in Rainbow Fish 2?

*Rainbow Fish to the Rescue* continues the story in the same shimmering style and extends and develops the moral tale read in *Rainbow Fish.* Again we meet the school of fish, each with their sparkling scale frolicking in their reef home in the deep blue sea. They have found happiness living and playing together but exclude a little striped fish from their games because he doesn't have a special scale. The other fish turn their backs on him. By means of the piscatorial equivalent of a thought bubble Rainbow Fish reflects on the 'personal growth' he experienced when he divested his pride. This is a clever one-page version of the 'story thus far' which gets everyone up to speed. In the midst of his musings dangers suddenly loom in the menacing figure of a shark. The sparkling silver scale fish find safety in a narrow crack in the reef whilst the little fish is stranded. Just as it seems he will become the shark's lunch, Rainbow Fish convinces the others to help and leads a rescue mission. They swarm straight for the shark, confusing it and saving the little striped fish from the jaws of death. The grateful fish is welcomed into their circle, their unity not through the common denominator of their shimmering scales but simply by their brotherhood. If Rainbow Fish's first lesson in the original story was to find humility and true friendship then this new adventure sees him actually risking his life to save a stranger. Again we see a strong reinforcement of the Golden Rule/Do Unto Others principle and a happy and satisfying ending. There is some minimal loss of visual impact as the scales are now dispersed across the pages instead of clustered on the central character. This is compensated somewhat by the use of more double-page spread watercolour backgrounds and more variance in the tones and feathered bleeding of brilliant colours to produce a strong spread of backdrops. Even though it attempts to capture the essence of the original story via flashback, I think it misses the mark slightly and I recommend you to read the original first.

I lingered over and stroked the pages, and yes, I took every opportunity to tilt and lift the pages so I could glimpse the rainbow effect. But the foils are not simply an empty visual device nor is it just soppy schmaltz as both story and device will evoke a strong audience response from readers of all ages. When I kept trying to locate my review copy invariably my six-year-old would be found re-reading it. Her noble defence simply, 'I could read this book lots of times'. I'd have to agree—its vivid pages tell a gentle tale with wide appeal.

---

**Additional coverage of Pfister's life and career is contained in the following source published by Gale Research:** *Something about the Author,* **Vol. 83.**

# Geoffrey Trease

## 1909-

English author of fiction, nonfiction, autobiography, and plays.

Major works include *Bows against the Barons* (1934), *Cue for Treason* (1940), *No Boats on Bannermere* (1949), *This Is Your Century* (1965), *The Phoenix and the Flame: D. H. Lawrence, a Biography* (1973), *Song for a Tattered Flag* (1992).

Major works about the author include *Nottingham: A Biography* (by Trease, 1970), *A Whiff of Burnt Boats: An Early Autobiography* (by Trease, 1970), *Laughter at the Door: A Continued Autobiography* (by Trease, 1974), *Geoffrey Trease* (by Margaret Meek, 1960).

## INTRODUCTION

A prolific and distinguished creator of a wide variety of books for young people—including mysteries, school stories, travel writings, history, and biographies—Trease is acclaimed for his pioneering efforts to write juvenile historical fiction using a contemporary style with parallels to modern issues. His first action-packed stories about ordinary people who lived in extraordinary times, written primarily for adolescents, were viewed as a refreshing change from the stilted language, long-winded descriptions, and romanticized aristocracy associated with historical fiction up to that time. Trease also introduced genuine heroines in his works. Defying the conventional separation of boys from girls in books for young readers, he chose times and places where girls could be educated, sufficiently free to participate in adventures, and able to demonstrate their natural wit and spirit on a par with boys. Trease's school stories were innovative in other ways, focusing on the day school rather than the boarding school, including parents as well as teachers, and showing the characters growing older in the sequels, a new development for the genre.

Trease has also penned biographies of Byron and D. H. Lawrence for high school students that not only combine his love of history and literature but capitalize on his experience with the theater and bring his subjects to life for his young adult audience. "Realism, I suppose, is what I have always aimed at," the author has commented. "I am not a 'children's writer' in the sense that I concern myself with any insulated 'magic world of childhood'— it is the adult world which absorbs me and which I want to present and interpret to the young reader inexorably growing up into it." A respected critic as well as a writer and lecturer, Trease wrote *Tales out of School: A Survey of Children's Fiction* (1949) to define the substance and standards of the field. Margaret Meek concluded in her monograph on the author: "[Trease] has closed the gap

between entertainment and didacticism, showing that in the children's story they merge happily together, and he has bridged the gulf between the comic and the classic in a way for which teachers can never be grateful enough. He has taught his fellow writers that if they are to earn their lauds as minor artists, only sound adult standards of integrity will do, all this with a seriousness of purpose and a sense of humor."

### Biographical Information

Born the youngest of three sons to a wine merchant in Nottingham, England, Trease grew up in a happy family in legendary Robin Hood country. The only nonathlete among his siblings, he passed his time making up stories, creating his own magazine, and acting out plays in his backyard. His interest in drama, while it did not lead to acting or playwriting as a career, later helped with the construction of his fiction and his dialogue. Although Trease loved history as a student, he won a junior scholarship in Classics and majored in Greek and Latin. At Oxford, where he again won a scholarship, he resigned before graduation, resolving to become an author rather than an academician. Moving to London, he tried social work in the slums, hack journalism, and a stint as an unqualified teacher, all the while determined to become a published writer. Trease married a fellow teacher and, pressed for money, contacted a left-wing publisher with the idea of writing a children's book about Robin Hood fighting the evils of feudalism. The publishers were enthusiastic, and the book—*Bows against the Barons*—was a resounding success. Before World War II intervened, Trease wrote several plays for adults which received favorable notices. He then served four years in the British Army, ending up in India, where he wrote his first radio dramas for British children with fathers in the East. Once home, the author began to publish steadily a number of works, ranging from school stories to nonfiction to historical fiction about such diverse periods as the French Revolution, the Russian Revolution, medieval Norway, and ancient Athens. For adults, he has written novels, biography, autobiography, and scholarly histories of Italy, London, and Nottingham. Trease balances his writing schedule with travel and lecturing on the importance of children's literature, and even in his eighties has produced several well-received works.

### Major Works

In his first book, *Bows against the Barons,* Trease chose the popular hero Robin Hood not only to take advantage of his Nottingham-born familiarity with the area and legend, but to herald a new historical view of a commoner inciting rebellion against his betters, a perspective diametrically opposed to the romantic tradition of Merrie England's pomp, pageantry, and class bias and superiority. Besides spicing his historical fiction with plenty of suspense, drama, and contemporary issues, Trease added another new element: adventurous girls. Kit, his vivacious heroine in *Cue for Treason,* set in Elizabethan times, runs away from an arranged marriage to join a theatrical troupe; she disguises herself as a boy who acts female roles, as was customary in those days. *No Boats on Bannermere* was another departure from literary tradition: unlike boarding school stories about secret feasts and hidden passageways, *No Boats,* the first of five books in a series, deals with four ordinary children and their everyday lives in day school and out, their joys and frustrations, social and sexual developments, and growth into adulthood. In *This Is Your Century,* Trease attempted to satisfy the curiosity of his daughter and others of her generation about the two world wars, revolutions, periods of prosperity and depression, scientific advances, and political upheavals of the twentieth century that he himself had seen but which appeared as history to the young. *The Phoenix and the Flame: D. H. Lawrence, a Biography,* undertaken at the request of high school teachers, was completed without going into any graphic details about Lawrence's torrid love affairs but in such a manner that the more sophisticated reader could read between the lines and the less knowledgeable remain innocent. As with his earlier biography of Byron, he was able to give young readers some idea of the person behind the works they were studying and a well-researched background of the period in which

the author lived. *Song for a Tattered Flag,* one of his more recent works, takes a contemporary event, the last days of Nicolae Ceausescu's Romania, and makes it come alive with appealing characters and a lively plot featuring a visiting youth musician caught up in the spontaneous people's revolt against dictatorship.

### Awards

Trease's play *After the Tempest* won the Welwyn Festival Award in England in 1939. *This Is Your Century* received the *New York Herald Tribune* Spring Book Festival Award for nonfiction for older readers in 1966.

---

## AUTHOR'S COMMENTARY

### Geoffrey Trease

SOURCE: "Problems of the Historical Storyteller," in *The Junior Bookshelf,* Vol. 15, No. 6, December, 1951, pp. 259–64.

To the critic, historical fiction must seem one of the easiest branches of the author's craft. Plots and characters are ready-made, adventures abound, colours are richer, language and sentiments nobler than today's. . . . Set against such advantages, what are a few hours spent browsing in the Quennell's useful volumes, to "get the costumes right"? . . .

In preferring to write conversations in more or less standard English, avoiding both archaisms and anachronisms, I have felt that the most important thing was to establish the living warmth of the characters and diminish the distance between them and the suspicious young reader. I believe this choice of style can equally well be justified on historical grounds. A recent correspondence in the *Times* about the 'period voice' affected by the B.B.C. in nineteenth century plays brought out the point that the Victorians, though more precise and artificial in their public delivery, spoke in private life very much more like ourselves than actors would have us believe. So, too, if the historical fiction-writer were to reconstruct his dialogue from the less affected private letters and diaries of the past, and above all from the verbatim records of State Trials and similar proceedings, he would be even less inclined to write, with Stevenson in *The Black Arrow,* "Shalt have a quarrel in thine inwards, boy!" or "Alack, I am shent!" or (with an eminent living writer) "Wot you what?" The plain English of Raleigh (who could turn a phrase if he cared to, as when he spoke of the dead queen as a "lady whom Time hath surprised") suggests that one can go back at least as far as the Elizabethans without finding everyday conversation so very different from that of today. As for remoter periods, surely we must take refuge in the convention which permits foreigners, whether Roman gladiators or Gestapo agents, to converse in English? Either Robin Hood must speak standard modern English or he must use some pre-Chaucerian variety which no normal child will understand. There is no logical justification for anything between.

But—and this is where experience brings doubt—*is* the young reader logical? Is there not within him perhaps a natural and admirable thirst for the colour and music of wild words? Does he not prefer, in his private games, to scream: "Down, varlet, or by my halidom—!" rather than: "Stop it, you fool, or else—"? May it be that, triumphing over all considerations of History and English, Wardour Street tushery appeals on entertainment grounds, because it gives the reader something he wants and which we have not yet learnt to provide otherwise?

In the same way I now find myself asking a question which would never have occurred to me in the old days: Does historical accuracy matter? . . . Which in the long run has done most for a child—a painstakingly accurate reconstruction, in which all the evidence is so well balanced that neither heroes nor villains can be distinguished as such, or a turgid, swashbuckling narrative which, while possibly leaving some minor misconceptions, has certainly left one abiding impression, that History after all is fun? . . .

Suppose then that accuracy is desirable but not the prime essential. What *is* it, anyway? In one's first books one is delighted to get one's material details right—to check on a boy's underwear (if any) in 1400, on the time taken by the Exeter to London coach in 1686, on the possibilities of laburnum overhanging an Oxford wall in 1643. Then, with reflection, come questions harder to answer than what the characters ate and wore. What did they feel and think? Can their psychological processes be reconstructed with any confidence? Is it not just as wild guesswork as Henry Williamson's attempts to imagine the life of an otter or a salmon? . . .

However scornfully we may dismiss [presenting characters who are little more than modern persons in fancy dress] as an insult to the adult reader's intelligence, we may feel that it is sometimes hard to avoid it in juvenile literature. It is still our national policy to bring up boys and girls with an absolute standard of ethical values. At the age when they are reading historical adventure-stories they can hardly be expected to grasp more sophisticated conceptions of relativity. How then can we present them with "authentic" historical heroes, who combine admirable feats of daring with acts of repellent cruelty? The temptation to endow one's medieval or Renaissance heroes with additional modern virtues, such as kindness to animals, consideration for servants, modesty in dress, and reluctance to commit private homicide, is extremely hard to resist. After all, the first requisite of a hero is that he can be admired.

A special—but a specially frequent—example of this dilemma is presented by heroines. If they are to appeal to the modern young reader, they must possess much of that spirit and independence which characterise the girl of today. In some historical periods this can be squared with the facts: too often, it cannot. If our heroine is to be mobile, if she is to be available for adventures, we are all too often driven to the expedient used (for a different reason), by the Elizabethan dramatists: once again the tresses must be snipped and the delicate limbs encased in boyish hose. So convincingly indeed, that in *The Black Arrow* Dick Shelton can spend over fifty pages with Joanna, including a night in the woods, without noticing the disguise. Whether or not this is equally convincing to the adolescent reader today, the repetition of the device becomes wearisome to the writer, yet hard to avoid. The most difficult problem of this kind I have personally met was in a story of classical Athens. How—without suppressing the almost Oriental attitude of the ordinary Athenian to women—could I introduce a girl with sufficient liberty of action even to meet the boy-hero, let alone have any adventures? Add that, for the sake of a happy ending to their friendship, she must be the lawful daughter of a citizen, not a disreputable alien or slave, and the problem is almost insoluble. It is fun solving such puzzles, but, if one writes with a respect for the facts of social history, they are uncomfortably common.

One final question: how far can, and should, the storyteller work against the rooted prejudices of the young reader? My own instinct is to answer, "just as far as his conscience prompts him," but he should be warned that it is an uphill task. "I'm awfully sorry," I was once told by a B.B.C. producer who had serialised several of my books in Children's Hour, "but I daren't do your new one. All the listeners would be up in arms. You see it's anti-Cavalier!" It was hardly that, actually; it was an attempt to present my own belief that, in every ten people during the Civil War, there were approximately one Cavalier, one Round-head, and eight others just longing for it to stop. I suspect that children are almost equally prejudiced in favour of Jacobites and French aristocrats, but I have not yet had the chance to prod them and find out.

**Geoffrey Trease**

SOURCE: "Why Write for Children?," in *School Librarian*, Vol. 10, No. 2, July, 1960, pp. 102–4, 107–8.

Years ago, when collecting material for a book on children's fiction, I approached several popular authors with this question, framed in slightly more delicate terms: 'Why, except for the money, do you write for children?' It seemed to me a fair question, and one which every author should ask himself if nobody else does. I am putting it to myself here.

As I grow older, and I would like to think a little less dogmatic, I realize how much room there is, in the all too generous output of juvenile literature, for a variety of reasonable answers. But I think there is one particular dividing-line, based on temperament and attitude to life, which separates writers into two main camps. Many adult readers of children's books too—publishers, reviewers, librarians, teachers, parents—whose own preferences influence the choice of books which finally reach the child, have a natural attraction to one side or the other.

What is this fundamental difference? I would like to quote, rather than try to paraphrase, something I wrote in the *New Statesman* last year: 'Some, like Carroll and Grahame,' wrote for children 'because they rejected or at least regretted the adult world, and sought relief in an imaginative relapse into childhood. Myself, though, I find the adult world a splendid—if often terrible—thing. I have a quite old-fashioned urge to tell the new boys about it, to communicate information and enthusiasm, re-create the past, interpret the present, and help them understand their surroundings and themselves.'

Perhaps this was no more than stating the obvious fact, that some people prefer fantasy, others reality. But I think there is more to it than that. There seems to be among the English a special (some would say an excessive) nostalgia for the nursery, much less marked in the literature of other nations. There is a reluctance not so much to grow up—as boys and girls we are keen enough to do so—as to let the next generation grow up. 'Let them enjoy themselves while they can' is the pessimistic maxim of many English parents, implying that enjoyment and maturity are incompatible. Fantasies of violence and horror are acceptable, but in realistic writing the young reader must be shielded from all experiences more poignant than sand between the toes and strawberry jam for tea.

I remember the late Wilson Midgley, editor of the old *John o' London's,* remonstrating with me about one of my **'Bannermere'** books. He had taken it home to review himself, he said, because he always enjoyed anything about the Lake District—but why, oh why, must I spoil everything by hinting, however lightly, at the affection developing between the grammar school boy and the high school girl? Time enough, surely, for that sort of thing when . . .

There spoke the authentic voice of English tradition. In contrast I recall the thirteen-year-old school-girl who told me that her favourite among my books was **Black Banner Abroad.** I asked why. Her vehement answer nearly blew me backwards. 'Because the boys in it dance with the girls!' In her, possibly, spoke the authentic voice of the generation I was writing for.

Actually, when I started writing for children, I was not concerned with this particular aspect of helping them 'understand their surroundings and themselves'. In 1933 we had 'Books for Boys' and 'Books for Girls', a hard-and-fast distinction which some old-fashioned bookshops and libraries still try to preserve. I recall how, in 1935, the then editor of the *B.O.P.* took an article on my visit to the Soviet Young Pioneers' camp at Artek—but begged me to soft-pedal the fact that half the campers were girls. I did my best, for in those days I was more interested in breaking down some of the other taboos, political, racial, and so on, and I felt I could not fight on every front at once. The girls soon got into my stories, of course, but in the early days they behaved themselves in the best tradi-

tion of English juvenile literature, i.e. like boys, and did nothing to impede the progress of the rattling yarn.

Those first books were propagandist. **Bows Against the Barons** (still in print, with such minor changes as I was able to make just after the war) gives a fair idea of what I was trying to do in the nineteen-thirties. I was sincere but crude, writing from instinct rather than knowledge. At school I had never studied English History after my thirteenth birthday. What I have learnt since has come from writing books and reading other people's and (during one brief, impudent but not unsuccessful period) teaching it to School Certificate level. But it was not mainly the gradual process of self-education in English History which caused the propagandist impulse to weaken and die. Apart from advancing years and world events, I was a good deal influenced (even if none of the men were) by the discussion groups I had to run in Army Education.

So now, and for many many years past, if I admit an urge to 'communicate information and enthusiasm, re-create the past, interpret the present' and so on, I am thinking (I hope) along the same lines as a teacher. He has his own opinions, his pet theories, his moral standards, his individual view of life. He cannot prevent their colouring his lessons. But he has a professional ethic which compels him also to present to his pupils the alternative arguments and conclusions, the awkward but relevant facts which do not square with the theory he favours. 'The completely unbiased teacher no more exists than the unbiased historian, but G. M. Trevelyan's well-known essay shows us what a world of difference lies between the unscrupulous controversialist and the conscientious, though humanly fallible, interpreter of accepted facts. The children's author should, I think, have the same professional ethic as the teacher. He will sometimes find it harder to live up to, if only because children prefer black-and-white characters and do not like their stories slowed down by debates, but that is the ideal he should keep before him.

Any adult, addressing himself to children whether at the blackboard or at the typewriter, has certain advantages over them and cannot escape certain responsibilities. He must at times come down off the fence and give a lead—even a judge has to direct the jury. So, with due sense of those responsibilities, the author will present his own interpretation of the world. So long as, like the teacher, he does not abuse his advantageous position to preach party politics or sectarian religion, he should be free. Those controversies, however, *are* best left for treatment in adult literature, where writer and reader meet on equal terms.

Anybody reading one of my own stories should easily be able to detect the more specific motives which prompted its writing. **Trumpets in the West** sought to teach children that there was once a time when England was the most musical country in Europe. **Silver Guard** was an attempt to correct the romantic royalist vision most children have of the Civil War: if I had written it ten years earlier it would have been a fervent piece of Roundhead propaganda, but by 1947 I was attempting a more objective approach. **The Crown of Violet** was born of a life-long passion for classical Athens and a desire to communicate a little of it to the children who would never learn Greek. *Word to Caesar* owed something to the modern fumblings towards European unity: I wanted children to know that there had once been a time when a man could travel from Britain to Byzantium without crossing a frontier. Also I felt that most authors from Kipling onwards had shown us too much Roman Britain and too little Rome. *Mist Over Athelney* was similarly inspired by two motives, one historical, one topical. The first was to correct the still-prevalent idea that the Anglo-Saxons had only an inferior civilization; and the second sprang from the popular feeling in 1957 that England was finished and emigration was the only hope for youth. There had been a good deal of emigration in the year 878, too, but some people, notably a man named Alfred, had stayed behind.

To the writer of the book such considerations as these provide the real driving force. The young reader may, and probably should, be quite unconscious of them. He demands a story and must be given one. But that story must not be given perfunctorily. It must not be jam on a pill. Along with the author's intellectual enthusiasm he must share quite genuinely in the young reader's enjoyment of excitement and mystery. The old phrase, 'a child at heart', is a good one. The children's writer needs to be that, yet at the same time an adult in mind. He cannot choose his theme and then say, cold-bloodedly: 'Now I suppose I must dramatize it all in twenty breath-taking chapters'. He must enjoy those chapters—the disguises and escapes and stratagems—just as much as (on a different level) he enjoys the necessary historical research. And just as much as, he hopes, the boys and girls will enjoy them too.

So, for myself, I write for children not only to say something but also for the pleasure of telling the story.

It is not, of course, pure effortless joy. What work is? The junior novel, like every other art-form, imposes its own limitations, and the eleven-plus audience, like every other audience, makes its special demands. It is sometimes a relief to turn to the writing of an adult novel—to feel that one can safely slacken pace, develop character, digress a little, permit oneself the pleasures of irony, satire and allusions which would be lost on the younger reader. But, no less, there is refreshment in turning from the novel and its own exacting demands to the child-audience with its less jaded palate and open-minded welcome. To switch from one form of writing to the other is like resting one set of muscles and bringing another into play.

Just as Shakespeare knew that his audience liked spectres and sword-fights, yet managed to say what he wanted to say in *Hamlet,* so we cannot ignore the basic ingredients our readers require. That is not to say that we must continually serve up 'the mixture as before'. The treasure-hunt, for example, is one of the basic themes in juvenile fiction. It is only objectionable when it is presented in a thoroughly hackneyed form and as a fantasy solution to the problems of the characters. I confess cheerfully to having used the treasure-hunt motif in at least six of my thirty-odd children's books, but only in one case, *No Boats on Bannermere,* do the young finders derive any personal financial benefit, and then only to a modest extent which does not affect the plot. In the other books I varied the theme. The treasure became the unique copy of an ancient Greek comedy (*The Hills of Varna*), an eighteenth-century shorthand diary (*Black Banner Players*), a missing father (*The Secret Fiord*), the restoration of national honour (*Black Banner Abroad*), and the establishment of historical truth (*The Gates of Bannerdale*).

Thirty books (forty, with non-fiction) lay any author wide open to the charge of over-writing, though he might well cry, looking round him, that he was astonished at his own moderation. I write less quickly nowadays (*The Hills of Varna* was written in five weeks) and try to restrict production by writing novels and radio-plays, giving lectures and plainly idling. Even so, the ideas insist on bubbling up, 'the old-fashioned urge to tell the boys' (and girls) has a way of reasserting itself, and when all is said the short answer to my original question must be, I suppose, 'because I can't help it'.


**Geoffrey Trease**

SOURCE: "The Historical Novel at Work," in *Children's literature in education,* No. 7, March, 1972, pp. 5–16.

When I began writing historical fiction, right back in 1933, I think the common attitude of the reader was expressed by a schoolgirl called Gillian Hansard. She said, and I quote, because her comments appeared in print: 'Though the details of Scott's novels are not always correct they give one a very good idea of the period, and though they are rather painful to read they always give benefit.' The phrase 'the giving of benefit'—as understood forty years ago—has a rather depressing sound. In those days, children showed a stubborn and pardonable resistance to historical stories which had to be broken down before the storyteller could get anywhere. I would like to think that it is nothing like so strong or so widespread today.

The author has to be clear from the start what *kind* of historical fiction he is going to write. I am not thinking so much of the differences between the adult novel and what I like to call the junior novel rather than the children's story; apart from length, and the possible use of illustrations, those differences become fewer and fewer as the scope and depth of so-called juvenile fiction are enlarged. Those of us who write for both age groups know how little conscious we are of what Rosemary Sutcliff has called 'the quite small gear change' when we turn from one type of work to the other, and most of what I want to say applies to both. The distinction I have in mind concerns first of all the attitude one adopts to the past. I think that most readers of historical fiction—adult readers anyhow—tend to fall into one of two categories. They are concerned with, fascinated by, either the differences between bygone times and their own, or the similarities. Broadly speaking, the former category read to escape from real life; the latter to illuminate it by comparison and recognition of unchanging human characteristics.

The authors in their turn fall into the same two categories. If they belong to the first they are likely to produce the 'costume' novel as I prefer to call it to distinguish it from the true 'historical' novel. They may do an impressive amount of research. We can be pretty sure today that they will get all their dates right and that every button will be in the proper place, though not necessarily fastened, for of late years the old 'cloak and sword' school of fiction has rather given place to what we might term 'bed and bawd'. But as we were long ago taught by the Hollywood film producers, the greatest possible accuracy of isolated detail can still add up to a total effect of psychological falsehood, and that is what happens all too often with a novel conceived in this spirit. Everything has to be larger than life—more colourful, more violent, more passionate, more romantic. Wit, subtlety, understatement, have little place in such novels. They lower the temperature; the reader feels let down. That is why, I think, historical novels in general are intellectually suspect and despised by a sophisticated public which has not examined them closely enough to discern that quite another type exists.

This type is the product of the other category of writers. It is the true 'historical novel', seeking not only authenticity of fact but—so far as it is humanly discoverable—a faithful re-creation of minds and motives. In the last analysis a good historical novel is a good novel, neither more nor less, whose story happens to be laid outside the time limits of living memory. You can subdivide it again if you like. There is the novel which closely follows historical events and introduces famous characters. And there is the novel which we could distinguish as the 'period novel', in which every event and every character is as imaginary as in a contemporary story, but in which the author's aim is to re-create some historical period. But both subdivisions stem from the same approach to history, both can claim in turn the interest of the same writer.

In fact it is often a pleasant relief to turn from one method to another. My own motives in writing have sometimes impelled me towards some of the great subjects that I wanted to tell children about—the French Revolution, the Russian Revolution, Garibaldi. In such cases the chronology of well known events imposes a ready-made framework on the fictitious plot—I found this particularly with my two Garibaldi stories. It is all very labour saving but can also be inhibiting. Although grateful for the splendid material history hands over ready-made—the colourful characters, the dramatic incidents—one sometimes experiences a wonderful sense of liberation when planning the next book as what I have called a 'period novel' in which one admittedly has to do all the work—all the invention of plot and character—but one also has complete liberty of action.

Whichever of these two kinds of novel an author is planning to write, I think it is important that he or she should be in love with the period. Some authors are so deeply, so inexhaustibly, in love with a single century that the affair goes on throughout their working lives and they never feel the need to look elsewhere for inspiration. I myself have to admit not perhaps to promiscuity but certainly to

polygamy. So many aspects of history attract me that I have never been able to confine my attention to one. I have flitted widely between the Athens of Socrates, the fifth century BC, and Saint Petersburg of 1917 AD. But it would be quite easy to lay a finger on the single common factor occurring in every period I have chosen between these extremes in time—the period has to be *literate,* or at least someone in the story has to be literate. I once did a book about the Danes. I could not possibly have emulated the primitive gusto with which Henry Treece so splendidly handled that kind of subject. It's not the splitting of skulls with battle axes that inspires me; it's the opening of minds in a gentler sense. I could only bother with Guthrum because of Alfred.

That particular book, **Mist over Athelney,** will serve to illustrate another consideration that affects my choice of theme. I like sometimes to get two themes into the one story. It's not just economy of effort—two statements for the effort of one; it's not just the growing consciousness that I shan't have time to write all the books I'd like to. It is rather that the interplay of two themes, as in a piece of music, helps to give the story an extra depth and texture. Sometimes those two themes are conveniently embodied in the same historical period. Many years ago, waiting in India for my release from the army, I filled in my time writing a story about the Glorious Revolution which interested the political side of me. But just about that time I had been learning a little about Purcell, and John Blow, and Jeremiah Clarke, and I was full of another enthusiasm to tell English children that there had been a time in history when England had been the most musical country in Europe. Any fellow writer may imagine my glee when I discovered that dates coincided and would fuse my two story lines into one. William of Orange entered London in January 1689, and February saw the performance of the first English opera, Purcell's *Dido and Aeneas.* When I add that the performance took place at a girls' school in Chelsea—which meant that my fictitious heroine could sing in it—you will appreciate that it was truly, in a different sense from usual, 'a turn-up for the book'. *My* book, **Trumpets in the West,** was quickly written in the East and posted home to my wife four foolscap pages at a time. That was as much as would go post free by Forces Air Mail.

It is not often that two suitably interlacing themes emerge so neatly from the period itself. The second theme may be a general one. I wanted for years to write a story of the French Revolution to counteract the aristocratic bias of the romantic novelists. I also wanted to use a character who was to develop into a painter. *He* could have gone into a dozen other historical stories. As it happened, he went into **Thunder of Valmy.** Sometimes the second theme can be modern and highly topical, but suitably transmuted and transferred to another period it helps to give the emotional vitality the story needs. To refer again to my story about the Danes, **Mist over Athelney,** the first theme —the obvious initial inspiration—was the rich, underestimated civilization of those who used to be dismissed as 'our rude Anglo-Saxon forefathers'. But the second theme came straight from the atmosphere of the time when it was written in 1957. We were then experiencing one of our monotonously recurrent economic crises. Each evening the newsreels showed us the queues of would-be emigrants outside Canada House and Australia House. The usual cry was going up, 'England's finished, there's no future here.' And I realized that in the winter of 878 people had been saying just the same—doubtless in the rudest Anglo-Saxon. People in Hampshire and Dorset actually *were* emigrating—packing into ships and crossing the Channel to settle on the other side. They thought it was all over. Alfred was dead, and it was just a matter of months before the Danes overran the last south-western corner of England. People had been wrong then, they could be wrong again. The emotion of 1957 came out in the story of 878.

So the author picks his period. He knows it or he couldn't love it, but the knowledge at this stage can be very superficial. You can fall in love with an unknown girl in a railway carriage, as my father did with my mother, but he had to put in a lot of patient study afterwards.

Authors today need to do a great deal of research. I suppose the standard of sheer accuracy attained by the average historical novelist today has never been equalled in earlier generations. He is writing, of course, for a much better educated public, alert for the slightest mistake. I believe that Victor Hugo once referred to James II of England as 'a jovial monarch', and in another passage somewhere appeared to imply that a 'wapentake' was a kind of Anglo-Saxon policeman. Such casualness would be inadvisable today. Some nineteenth century writers were more conscientious. George Eliot tore up the first draft of *Romola* when she realized how many mistakes she had made, and writing that book is said to have 'changed her from a young woman into an old'. I sympathize with her, though I have never been in quite the same danger. When I look round my own study shelves, full of handy illustrated volumes on every aspect of everyday life in different historical periods, I wonder how on earth people like Scott and George Eliot managed to get as many details right as they did.

On the other hand sometimes I reflect that ignorance could be bliss. There are just too many books now. Somewhere, in some book, someone has recorded everything (if only one knew where to look) and that realization is paralyzing.

I recall a moment of utter despair one evening, walking down the Herefordshire lanes near my house. I was in the middle of *Thunder of Valmy.* I had read, or at least skimmed, about fifty books on the French Revolution. I thought I had got all my facts at my fingertips. I had just finished writing about that historic June morning in 1789 when the deputies were locked out of the hall at Versailles and had to move into the tennis court. I'd imagined a June morning at Versailles—sunshine, sparkle, splendour. And then in the public library I'd come across the fifty-first book, the one I hadn't seen before, the memoirs of the American ambassador at that time, and he'd noted what a miserable wet morning it had been. It

changed the feeling so completely that I had to rewrite the whole passage. And I said to myself, if this is going to happen all through the story, I'm going to give it up. I'll switch to a period where there aren't so many damn documents.

Does it matter? Would anyone spot it? You never know. In *Mist over Athelney,* when I realized that my adventurous young people would have to eat sooner or later, I let them encounter a hermit and share his campfire supper of rabbit stew. That detail passed my learned publishers without comment, it passed the *Times Literary Supplement* and a host of other reviewers. But it didn't pass an eleven year old boy in Aberdeen, who wrote to tell me that there were no rabbits in England before the Norman Conquest.

Even if no one else is going to pounce on a mistake, one hates to make them. They're like a secret burning shame inside, if you only discover them in the published book and it's too late to do anything. But you can't go on researching and checking for ever. You have to ask yourself—as the girl in some historical novels should ask herself but too seldom does nowadays—'How far ought I to go?' You do your best to get things right. You can do no more.

Now I have to admit, and I do so with some reluctance that many a book with unsound history is far better literature than one in which the details are impeccably researched. What's worse, I could go further and concede that some old favourites of bygone age which are no great shakes either as literature or as history have done far more to stimulate an enthusiasm for the past than many books which are their superiors in both respects. They are bad or mediocre books with, in general, good lasting effects. I would put the works of Henty and Harrison Ainsworth into that category. But surely the success of those books lay not in their shortcomings but in their other virtues— they won their public in spite of their faults, not because of them. Falsifying history just to make a better story is to me a confession of artistic laziness and imaginative poverty. The elder Dumas justified it if it led to a good book, not otherwise. He expressed in a characteristically earthy Gallic way: 'One can violate History only if one has a child by her.' I may be thought prudish and pedantic, but I still prefer my own literary offspring to be legitimate.

You have to work at it. Strict adherence to truth can present baffling problems. An example occurred in my own book about ancient Athens, *The Crown of Violet.* I had a boy character and a girl. For the plot to be possible the girl needed a certain freedom of movement to come and go in the city. This is an oft-recurring problem in historical fiction. In the Athens of that date I was up against the blunt fact that no respectable Athenian girl—no citizen's daughter that is—could possibly have gone around like my Corinna; she would have lived a life of almost Asiatic seclusion. I could overcome this difficulty quite simply by making her one of the numerous resident aliens, who were less fettered by conventions. But this solution merely created a new difficulty. I wished to imply, at the end of the story, that the boy and girl would later marry. Yet the law of Athens forbade marriage between citizens and noncitizens. It seemed an insoluble problem. Of course it wasn't. Few problems are if you think long enough. A solution presented itself, and it was a solution supported, though not consciously suggested, by one of the traditional plot situations and denouements of classical comedy. I think the book was improved by sticking to historical truth rather than by taking the quick and easy way out and falsifying it.

Of course none of us can say, with his hand on his heart, that he has never bent the documented record in some trivial detail, for example, by telescoping some period of time and combining two unimportant episodes into one in the interests of dramatic unity. But speaking for myself, I always make even the most minute adjustment of this kind with a feeling of reluctance. One would like to manage without it, but sometimes one just can't. The overall authenticity is what matters. Also the fiction writer has got to produce a picture which *looks* right as well as *being* right. Paradoxically, it can happen that the documented truth sounds false, and the fiction writer, unlike the straight historian, cannot slip in a footnote reference to justify himself. I remember once using the phrase 'What the dickens' in that story of the Glorious Revolution. My publishers challenged it. I replied that Shakespeare had used it in *The Merry Wives of Windsor*. Historically I was right. Artistically I was wrong. The average reader winced at what he thought was an anachronism. You shouldn't make your readers wince. There has to be a measure of compromise.

And there has to be compromise, I fear, on other and more important points. There is the question of what is acceptable to modern taste, and by that phrase I don't mean anything to do with sexual outspokenness, where indeed the 'modern taste' seems to be for highly spiced dishes. No, I mean quite simply how can the author hold his reader's sympathy, how can the reader identify wholeheartedly with the historical character—all of which is absolutely vital, especially when we are dealing with *young* readers—when so much that is authentic and unavoidable, or at least socially acceptable, in the period of the story repels the reader today?

One's Elizabethan heroine probably had black teeth and anything but a sweet breath. The one atmosphere which was probably authentic in most historical eras was of human bodies too little washed and too heavily clothed. It was not only the villains who smelt. Or take our changed attitude to cruelty. What happens to our readers' sympathy if our debonair Regency hero goes, as well he might, straight from partnering the heroine at an elegant ball to the enjoyment of a public execution at dawn? With the young public I should think that the treatment of animals would be one of the worst stumbling blocks, if we represented it with complete historical accuracy. The old squire dies. He may have included in his last wishes—I believe it was commonly done—that all his dogs should be hanged. It would be a foolhardy author who let his hero carry out

that sort of instruction. One can think of countless such difficulties where the author is compelled to present something less than the complete historical picture.

Not every awkwardness is so charged with potential emotion and disgust. There are many little genuine period touches which merely seem odd and may distract the reader, again especially the young reader, such as the way seventeenth century men sat about indoors with their immense hats on. Then there are the things which may strike a modern reader as ambiguous when at the time they were innocent and commonplace, such as the way men used to share a bed. Some of Pepys's most enjoyable conversations on music, careers and life in general seem to have been conducted in this setting, but it is open to misunderstanding if it is used by a novelist.

Psychological authenticity is the great problem. Anyone can find out what people wore and ate. We know how a portcullis worked, and a ballista, and a kitchen spit. But do we know how people's *minds* worked?

I remember as a very young man going up to Naomi Mitchison after a lecture and shyly telling her what her books about the ancient Greeks and Romans had meant to me, *Cloud Cuckoo Land, The Conquered, The Corn King and the Spring Queen,* and I can still recall vividly my utter dismay when she told me she wasn't going to write any more books like that. She had come to the conclusion that she had got the ancient Greeks and Romans all wrong, they hadn't really been a bit like that. I still regret her decision, but I think now that I can understand why she made it. To imagine the *internal* and not just the *external* reality of historical characters is a most daunting enterprise.

Stop and imagine the simplest things. The significance of nightfall when there was no good artificial light; the misery of winter for the same reason, as well as many others; conversely the tremendous liberation of May Day and the lengthening days. Imagine the bodily sensation of cluttering clothes; wet weather before the invention of rubber and plastics. Think of the different sense of time before we had watches with minute hands. There was no really practicable watch, I believe, before Robert Hook invented the balance spring about 1675. Stop and consider how this affects our description of suspense. An officer might conceivably count the minutes before battle was joined at Blenheim; he couldn't really have done so at Naseby. So too with slow communications and consequent anxieties. The invaders might have landed days ago, a man's son might have been born to his wife on the other side of England, a new king might already be on the throne—and there was nothing faster than a galloping horse to bring you the news. It *must* have affected the way people thought and felt.

These, as I say, are the simplest things. Add a few of the complications—taboos, superstitions, religious certainty, medical ignorance. My lord collapses, writhing in agony, and is quickly dead. Today any doctor can tell us various natural conditions which, if not quickly treated with all our modern resources, could prove fatal in such a situation. Our historical characters have no notion of such things, any more than they know malaria is carried by mosquitoes and mental illness is not induced by evil spirits. How many hapless cooks and courtiers must have died horrible deaths for supposedly poisoning their masters who really died of, say, a burst appendix? Spells, astrology, hell fire and horoscopes—these were just some of the things that shaped the thoughts of our ancestors. On the other hand, they were spared the brain washing of the advertisers and they knew nothing of opinion polls.

Is it any wonder that sometimes the conscientious novelist despairs of being able to think himself inside the skin of someone living in an earlier century, when he wonders if he hasn't merely achieved the result he so much despises in other people's books—to create what are really only modern characters decked up in fancy dress? In such moments of depression it is salutary to turn to contemporary writings of some other age—to Byron's letters or the Pastons', Pepys's Diary or Evelyn's, Lucy Hutchinson's memoirs or Boswell's journals, even to some passages from Plato or Aristophanes, Pliny or Petronius or Martial. At once you sense their common humanity—what I meant when I emphasized at the beginning of this article the *similarities* in history, which to some of us make a deeper appeal than the differences, however picturesque. And sensing that common, continuing humanity you take heart again.

So you get your characters, you costume them correctly, you see them in action against a background as accurate as you can make it, you do your imaginative best to endue them with an authentic inner life of thought and feeling. All you have to do now is *write* the book!

Most of the problems now are those common to any kind of fiction. Most of the differences that emerge at this stage *are,* I think, those between the adult and the junior novel. Making every allowance for the great development in breadth of theme, in maturity, in sophistication, of the junior novel in recent years, and making every allowance for changes in the juvenile audience—their conditioning, for example, by television and other media to a quick-witted grasp of techniques, such as the flashback which would have puzzled an older generation of children—making every allowance for all this, I think it is still fair to say that plot and incident retain all their old importance, and that the younger reader, unlike some of his elders, likes a story to have a beginning, a middle and an end—and in that order. And if the adult writer feels bored doing it this way, he might be wiser to work in another field.

We all know that a worthwhile children's book of any type has more than one level. Each reader penetrates as deeply as his years, his sensitivity, his emotional maturity allow. What really inspires the author may be what lies at the deepest level. But he must be prepared for many children to love his book for what he himself regards as the superficial qualities. What I think is vital is that he should never privately despise those superficial qualities and think of them as synthetic decoration—put on, in a calculating spirit, to make the book attractive to the young. It must be a genuine book at all levels. When he is choosing his theme and doing his research his standards can be as adult, indeed as academic, as he likes. When he is writing—when emotion and art begin to take over from intellect—then he must let the child in himself dictate much of the form. I say very deliberately 'the child in *himself'*. Some writers acknowledge the influence of their sons and daughters or other individual children they have specially studied to please. But on the whole a writer should please himself, and a children's writer should not worry and scheme to study children's interests and cater for their demands. He should be a children's writer because he still retains inside himself, perhaps more vividly than the average adult, the vestigial child he once was, and can still enjoy some of the same things that he did then. He may plan his book, as I planned *The Crown of Violet,* with an adult motive—indeed a didactic motive—to inform children about classical Athens and to communicate my own interest and enthusiasm. But in the telling he must, at another level, enjoy the action as genuinely as he wants his readers to enjoy it. To paddle up the shallow river in its gorge, to find a cave with a mysterious girl playing a flute, and then later to get caught up in a plot to overthrow the government—the author himself has got to love every minute of it himself. He is not 'putting it in because the children like it'. He is living it, in imagination, because it is a fantasy which after forty or fifty years still satisfies a hunger of his own.

There is one special problem for the historical novelist, and this applies whatever the age group he is primarily addressing. It is the problem of the vocabulary he should use for his dialogue.

When I came into this field of writing, right back in 1933, the historical adventure story for children was bogged down in tushery. People shouted, 'Quotha!' and 'Ha, we are beset!' and a quotation I specially cherish is '"Yonder sight is enough to make a man eschew lance and sword for ever, and take to hot-cockles and cherry pit," exclaimed the Earl of Pembroke, adding an oath which the sacred character of the building did not in the least restrain.' One of the reasons why historical fiction was then in the doldrums was, I am sure, that even in the leisurely 1930s the child could not be bothered to fight his way through such verbiage.

Should dialogue attempt an authentic period flavour? It is of course possible to construct pastiche conversations for an English story that goes no further back than the eighteenth century and use no single word that has not contemporary authority. It is possible. It is debatable whether such an exercise is worth the effort, or whether it can fully convey what the characters mean, as well as what they are saying. For we can never afford to forget the way in which words have changed their meanings while preserving their appearance. Today, I imagine, a bishop welcomes any sign of 'enthusiasm' among his clergy. He would not have done so in the eighteenth century.

In any case, if we go back to earlier periods, we cannot attempt a faithful reproduction of speech without becoming almost unintelligible. And the effect is to push the characters further and further back into the past, to raise more and more barriers between them and ourselves.

From the moment I planned my very first book I was in no doubt as to my own way of dealing with the problem. The answer had really been given me (I didn't realize it consciously but it was there all right, submerged in my mind) about seven years earlier, when as a schoolboy I had read Naomi Mitchison's story of Caesar and the Gauls. It was only long afterwards, when I dipped into *The Conquered* again, and read Ernest Barker's introduction to my pocket edition, that I knew my debt to Naomi Mitchison. *I* had made Robin Hood speak modern English, without tushery or archaisms, because I felt it was the only way he could speak to the modern child. But it was Naomi Mitchison—even before Robert Graves with his *I Claudius* in the same style, which I had not heard of then—who blazed the trail. As Ernest Barker said in his introduction:

> If the novelist of classical times were to make the speech, dress and other appurtenances true to the text of a classical dictionary, he would hardly make his puppets live or his action move. These ancient figures must break into modern speech if they are to touch us.

They must indeed. Obviously they must not break into modern slang or jarring anachronisms. I believe there was once a Hollywood film showing Henry VIII at the Field of the Cloth of Gold, and one courtier was made to say to another, 'I do hate parties, don't you?' There must be artistic compromise. The ear must be the final judge. A line may be historically right and still sound wrong and if it sounds wrong, it must go as remorselessly as any other kind of blemish. At every moment of the story the reader has got to be simultaneously convinced of two separate things: first that these characters are alive and warm and tangible, as if they were in the room with him; second that they are *not* modern people in this room, but are in another time and place whose atmosphere they have thrown around him and themselves, like some magic pavilion. The achievement of that illusion is really the whole craft of the historical storyteller.

## Geoffrey Trease

SOURCE: "The Historical Story," in *The Horn Book Magazine,* Vol. LII, No. 1, February, 1977, pp. 21–8.

"The trouble is," said my friend gloomily, "a lot of Americans are convinced that the historical novel is dead. They won't even consider a book in that field." My friend is herself American but with wide experience in children's book publishing in Britain, too. "It's maddening," she went on, "and clearly a passing phase. But it's difficult to argue with this kind of received dogma."

A few weeks earlier I had encountered similar views voiced by Americans attending the 1976 International Seminar on Children's Literature, held again in England at its original venue, Loughborough University. A school librarian of long experience lamented the decline of interest in historical fiction, even among good readers. "Back home," she told me, "history isn't taught to children and young teenagers as straightforward history. It's brought into the social studies curriculum along with other disciplines, like anthropology or archaeology, to teach certain concepts."

"Is that necessarily bad?" I said.

I had then just come from a smaller but no less stimulating assembly in Luxembourg. There, in the old Grand Duchy, Miami University had for two summer weeks turned over its permanent European Center to an international workshop on children's literature. I had previously lectured there in 1974. This time I had been interested to find that children's literature had been combined with social studies in a shared program. It had seemed to me a worthwhile arrangement. The social studies people had admitted to learning something fresh, and the exchange of ideas had certainly been two-way.

"No, not necessarily bad," agreed the librarian, "except insofar as the continuity of straight history is lost. Our children learn even American history in a spotty fashion. English and European history suffer still more. The ordinary social studies curriculum leaves many children with only vague generalities."

"A number of teachers," she continued, "are willing enough for children to read historical fiction." Those I had met in Luxembourg had been more than willing. "But more than approval is needed. There must be knowledge of the stories available to complement a particular study. Children require guidance."

A well-known New York editor, Ann Durell of E. P. Dutton, recently warned British writers in *The Author,* the journal of our Society of Authors, about the American children "who do not have the guidance now to be lured into a 'special' book." The specialist who might have guided them, she explained sadly, "has been done away with in the last salary budget cut." Among the "special" books that have suffered from this economy we may suppose that historical fiction looms large.

It seems worth asking the questions: Do we need it? Is the historical story relevant today?

For the writer of such stories—indeed, for all lovers of the genre, these questions pose fresh challenges. Mere unpopularity—some children's instinctive resistance due to reading difficulties and lack of background—is nothing new. When I myself, over forty years ago, began writing historical fiction, it was in the doldrums. It was long-winded, its vocabulary unfamiliar and unreal. Even in 1934 children had begun to groan at all the tushery, the "varlets" and "quothas" and the rest of it. The schools approved of Scott. As a schoolgirl of those days once wrote, "Though the details of Scott's novels are not always correct, they give one a very good idea of the period, and though they are rather painful to read they always give benefit." However, most of the stories children were reading were not by Scott, but by his third-rate imitators with none of the northern wizardry that infused his massive volumes with a compensating vitality. Historical fiction had got stuck at G. A. Henty, and even he had died in 1902. Those of us who began to write it in the nineteen-thirties had to overcome plenty of prejudice among children, but at least we could usually count on the good will of teachers.

Can we always, now? There must be many—especially younger teachers—who, in common with others of their generation, are in passionate or cynical revolt against existing institutions in our society. It has ever been so. But among some people today this disenchantment with tradition, this impatience with evolutionary change, has developed into an anarchic rage. They have no use for historical thinking, even less for historical fiction.

I feel some sympathy with their rebellious emotion. I, too, was once an angry young man, long before that phrase was coined. But in my case rebellion drove me not into contempt for history but into a determination to rewrite it. My first book, *Bows against the Barons,* was born of a wish to retell the Robin Hood story in grimly realistic rather than romantic terms. My second dealt with the Chartist disorders in South Wales and Birmingham in 1839. Both stories were regarded as unacceptably controversial at the time. Only the boldest teachers dared to take them into schools. It gives me some wry amusement to see that today one of the books has achieved the ultimate respectability of a special school edition, while the other, recently translated into French, was at once put on the recommended list by a religious organization, L'Office Chrétien du Livre. The whirligig of Time does indeed bring his revenges.

No, far from being irrelevant to our current ills, historical fiction can be supremely relevant. It was certainly that conviction, not romantic nostalgia for bygone ages, that set me on my own path all those years ago.

The conviction remains as powerful today, though the brash partisan dogmas of the nineteen-thirties are forgotten. When I am casting round for a new theme, it is contemporary relevance that aids my choice and provides the emotional drive. Most often, two things come together like flint and steel to produce the initial spark. One is the historical period or person or event that is for the moment exciting me. The other is the immediate modern significance.

The latter should not be obtrusive. Ideas can be presented more objectively if removed from the realm of current controversy and prejudice. I am glad when the adult book-selector perceives what I am trying to say, but I am content that the young reader get as much, or as little, out of the story as he is equipped to do. It is pleasant to know that sometimes one's point has been taken. "I wondered," wrote a boy from Western Springs, Illinois, "if you might

have injected any part or experiences of your personal life into this book. Although in a different time and place I can see how it is possible to do so."

How right he was! *The Red Towers of Granada,* for instance, is, on the superficial level, a thirteenth-century adventure, with a quest leading from Nottingham Castle to the Alhambra. That book, I well remember, sprang from a desire to tell children about the wonderful Moorish civilization of southern Spain. I have a brief notebook entry, dated May 2, 1960, ending, "these characters might wander southwards to Granada or Cordova and be astonished at the culture of the infidel." Over the next five years, as I can still trace in my notebooks, the idea slowly evolved, nourished not only by reading and by a tour of the cities concerned but also by the emotional impact of what was happening in my own world of the nineteen-sixties. To my cultured Muslims were added equally sympathetic Jewish characters and, since my central figure was, like myself, an English Gentile, the story that finally emerged was an implicit plea for racial and religious toleration. Could anything today be much more relevant?

That is not, needless to say, why children read the book. Nor, equally, was it my sole motive in writing it. The main thing must always be the story itself; the joy in action and suspense and mystery; the interest in human relationships (far beyond mere "toleration"!), in colorful settings and, above all, in language. But the contemporary relevance is not just an extra, tacked on. It lies at the heart of the theme. It is the quality that, however little noticed by the young reader, gives the writer an additional dynamic for his work.

*Web of Traitors,* originally published in England as *Crown of Violet* but renamed for America when I was assured that "no red-blooded American boy would open a book with a flower in the title," was inspired partly by my lifelong passion for classical Athens, Pindar's "shining city with violet crown," and partly by my very contemporary (1952) concern at the way democracies could be overthrown by minorities. As in Athens, 411 B.C. That was the underlying message of the book.

*Popinjay Stairs: An Historical Adventure about Samuel Pepys* is, on the face of it, a picturesque thriller, a tale of murder, blackmail, and general skullduggery in Restoration London, a setting that has always fascinated me and about which I had previously written an adult book, *Samuel Pepys and His World.* The plot deals with corruption in naval contracts and the pressures applied to force an honest public servant into slipping it past his committee. A perceptive adult reader may notice that this tale was written in the early seventies, during a period of sensational exposures on both sides of the Atlantic. I felt that young people would need, as they grew up, to know about such things.

One of my most recent stories, *The Iron Tsar,* was set in 1831 in the repressive era of Nicholas I. He, it will be remembered, was the Russian emperor who liked to conduct his own browbeating interrogations of political prisoners far into the night, dazzling them with massed candelabra (the arc-light being yet unavailable) and clapping dissident intellectuals such as Peter Chaadayev into mental homes. I felt that even a quite young reader would find no difficulty in seeing modern parallels.

Such books involve long research. I have rewritten whole chapters to correct a slight inaccuracy, belatedly discovered. It might make no difference to the story whether a certain morning at Versailles in 1789 was wet or sunny. Perhaps not a single reader would ever notice. But once I had detected the slip myself—in this case from an entry in Thomas Jefferson's diary—I was miserable until I had put it right and got the picture "like it was." If I introduce historical personages into fictitious episodes, I can only justify it if all they say and do is consistent with their recorded behavior on real occasions. And the purely fictitious characters and incidents must similarly accord with the circumstances of the period.

This can raise problems—notably, that of giving girls a fair share of the action in many bygone societies. I was amused when a Canadian girl wrote to me about *Word to Caesar,* which in the United States is titled *Message to Hadrian*: "I liked the way you described Tonia as a Women's Libber." I had not, of course, depicted—much less "described"—my heroine as any such thing, but I saw what had pleased young Wendy out in British Columbia. I had certainly ransacked the social history of the Roman Empire to find how much independence I could justifiably allow a high-spirited teenage girl in the second century A.D.

It was in *Web of Traitors* that I ran into my major obstacle. I wanted boy to meet girl and form a friendship which, I would imply in the closing pages, would lead to marriage in later years. Research showed, however, that in Athens the citizens kept their daughters in almost Oriental seclusion. Alexis could never have run into Corinna outside the home unless she were the daughter of a resident "alien," Greek enough but not Athenian and, therefore, freer to move about. Unfortunately—and here seemed the insoluble difficulty—a pure-bred Athenian like Alexis would not be allowed to marry a noncitizen's child. I had to rack my brains for a long time before I found a twist I could give to the plot that would resolve my dilemma.

Some historical liberties have always been allowed the imaginative writer if the literary result proves worthwhile. "One can violate History," said Dumas in his earthy Gallic way, "only if one has a child by her." Today, perhaps, our standards of scholarship are more strict. We shrink from faking, even to make a better story. I have never thought much of that excuse, anyhow. History has all the raw material the novelist needs. If he knows his job, he will not require to alter the facts.

The modern writer has resources denied to Dumas and Scott and must face a far better informed public. It is not just the professional critic or the historian; I treasure a letter from an English plowman who, having detected a slip in my enumeration of Charles I's family, wrote bluntly: "I like my facts straight, same as my furrows." So today we storytellers must take infinite pains, prowling through museums, plodding through the mud of ancient battlefields, and filling our shelves with books on costume, transport, and everyday life in all their aspects and in every period. The danger is that we fall in love with all our discoveries and allow our plots to get bogged down in the authentic detail we cannot bear to leave out. The reward comes in the response, like a girl's letter from Whitehorse, Yukon: "We all think this novel was fascinating, because it has helped us a lot in our Social Studies course on Rome."

Doubtless her class had plenty of other aids. The nonfiction reference book, beautifully and lavishly illustrated, researched and written by a small team of editors and consultants, often produced and marketed as an international venture, is one of the most impressive phenomena of juvenile publishing in recent years. But while such volumes excel in the depiction of material things, they are not able to convey psychological truth. They can show us the probable equipment of Cleopatra's dressing table, each unguent-pot and pair of tweezers authenticated by a museum exhibit, but they cannot bring Cleopatra and her maids to life as the novelist can.

So, even in the context of social studies, the historical story has an important part to play, and it would be wasteful not to utilize all that the writer has so painstakingly researched and made available to children in attractive form. No less importantly, in schools where (as my librarian friend complained) concentration on social history alone has left children vague about the continuity of events, the historical story can help to fill the gap.

Children—and this is a truism which we neglect at our peril—love a story, a chronological sequence of incidents and situations ending in a climax. It is interesting to learn what people wore in days gone by, what their houses were like, and what they ate. But it is only moderately exciting. Children more often want to know about individual, named people—and what happened to them.

When the children of the twenty-second century turn their minds back to the twentieth, will they confine their interest to our primitive television sets, our quaint automobiles, and the way we heated our homes before solar energy? Or will they want to hear about Hitler and Stalin and all the hundreds of other fantastic characters and dramatic conflicts that filled our era? If these aspects of the past are out of fashion in some schools today, then the historical novel is even more badly needed to make up for the omission.

Are such stories relevant? Let another schoolgirl, writing to me from the Pacific coast, have the last word: "The setting of *Message to Hadrian* is old, but the story relates to battles of today."

## Geoffrey Trease

SOURCE: "Fifty Years On: A Writer Looks Back," in *Children's literature in education,* Vol. 14, No. 3, 1983, pp. 149–58.

Strictly speaking, I suppose it is not fifty years but sixty since I lost my amateur status. I was thirteen when I acquired my first typewriter, and in a few months, with beginner's luck, I had sold three little half-guinea articles to a boys' weekly. But this precocious success was not long sustained. Perhaps the editor, after publishing my confident advice on three quite different hobbies, grew sceptical of my first-hand experience. I was turning anyhow to adolescent verses, camping journals, plays, and other unmarketable creations, and I was twenty before I earned another penny. It was not until 1933, on my twenty-fourth birthday, that with a very modest tally of articles, book reviews, and other oddments behind me, I burnt my boats and resolved to establish myself as a full-time literary man.

Children's fiction formed no part of my plans. I stumbled into it, impelled by a sudden realisation (born of my brash political idealism at the time) that children's literature was all *wrong.* If children were to be nourished on such values, society would lay up for itself a mountain of work to be undone at some date in the future. The 1914 war had revolutionised adult literature, and all the old assumptions were now challenged. So ought we to go on suggesting to children that war was glorious, that the white-skinned peoples were superior, and the British best of all? It would be some years before Orwell's famous essay would proclaim, "Boys' fiction is sodden in the worst illusions of 1910," but before 1933 ended I was tapping out the first chapters of *Bows against the Barons.*

I chose Robin Hood, most obvious of juvenile themes, in reaction against its usual romantic treatment. As a child I had enjoyed the traditional stories, but, even more, the freer invention by A. S. Walkey, a vigorous yarn-spinner early in this century but now undeservedly forgotten. I devoured his serials in old bound volumes of the weekly, *Chums,* and they were as powerful an influence as Henty or Ballantyne. I had never forgotten—I have not now forgotten—Walkey's stirring *Hurrah for Merry Sherwood!* But in 1933 I was anxious, without any disloyalty to my old favourite, to question whether Sherwood could ever have been so "merry" in the real feudal England.

I wrote at white heat, with a crude self-confidence it is now embarrassing to remember. I had one asset: I was Nottingham-born, I had stood on Castle Rock and walked in the dwindling greenwood, I knew of the sandstone caves and passages that still underlie the city and were so handy for my plot. But I did none of the research, local and general, without which I would never contemplate starting a book today. Any one interested can compare the medieval Nottingham of *Bows* with the town as I depicted it in *The Red Towers of Granada* long afterwards.

Anyone can spot howlers in the first edition of *Bows.* I

had a "duke" before they existed in the English peerage. More seriously, the camp-fire talk of my outlaws sounded as though Friar Tuck had returned from Nottingham market with a copy of the *Daily Worker* concealed beneath his habit. The book was propagandist. So, of course, have been many immortal children's books, Anna Sewell's *Black Beauty,* say, and Thomas Hughes' *Tom Brown's Schooldays,* but these illustrious examples prove only that a good enough story can triumph over its intrusive preaching.

This is not to suggest that a children's author is not entitled to "say something," like any other serious writer, but the "something" must be artistically integrated into the story. Twice, in revised editions, I have tried to remove the worst blemishes from the earliest effort, but there is a limit to what can be done without destroying its original vitality. Despite its imperfections the book seems to live on, going round the world in about ten languages. In Roumania it becomes, quaintly sounding, *Umbrele din Padurea Sherwood.* It has proved equally acceptable in the U.S. and in the U.S.S.R., and though it has only recently reached West Germany (Frankfurt, 1982), it has met with a very gratifying reception there.

Looking back over fifty years, I can see other reasons, besides my own shortcomings, for the now so obvious flaws of *Bows.* I had not only to learn my craft by hard, untutored experience, I had to blaze a new trail through what had become the neglected wilderness of juvenile fiction. Little work of distinction had appeared in the preceding two decades. Doctor Doolittle, Just William, and the Pooh books formed, with the early work of Eleanor Farjeon and Alison Uttley, the major contribution. Ransome's holiday stories had just started, but I had not heard of them. In the historical adventure there was no real successor to Henty, who had died in 1902.

I had not heard of Ransome, for the very good reason that new children's books received little serious notice in the press. There was no solid body of criticism. When, as late as 1947, encouraged by the New Education Fellowship, I began a survey of contemporary children's fiction, I had again to start almost from scratch. I could find studies published in the United States, Canada, New Zealand, France and Belgium, but no equivalent in Britain.

If the children's writer lacked critical recognition, his financial inducements were not much better. Grant Richards in 1899 bought *Little Black Sambo* outright for five pounds, and in the 1930s respectable publishing houses thought forty pounds fair for the copyright of a forty-thousand-word book. I was lucky. I got royalties and a modest advance for my first effort, but the practice of outright purchase lingered until after the war. It encouraged over-production, led inevitably to much hasty and mediocre writing, and did nothing to win esteem for a kind of literature already patronised and despised. Our writers today, struck suddenly by the cold blast of economy cuts in the schools and libraries they have come to rely upon, lament that times are hard in 1983. They are indeed. But it was not a bed of roses in 1933, when schools and libraries bought little contemporary fiction, and the living author was often not receiving a royalty anyhow.

The discouragement of meagre earnings in those days was matched for the serious writer by the restrictions on his themes and vocabulary. Older children's books were demarcated, "for boys" or "for girls." Girls, it is well known, ignored the division. Boys were less inclined to. Nurtured on "healthy yarns" of slaughter and horror, they picked up a lot of incidental history and geography but little understanding of the other sex. There were sometimes, of course, chaps' sisters and even other chaps' sisters in minor roles. Henty did not exclude female characters, and, at the end of a long book, might imply or even report a subsequent marriage. But any emotional prelude was excluded. "No, I never touch a love interest," Henty declared (as quoted by Guy Arnold). "Once I ventured to make a boy of twelve kiss a little girl of eleven, and I received a very indignant letter from a dissenting minister."

Fed on such books in my own childhood, I never thought of introducing girls into my earliest stories. Very soon, however, I did. First sisters, then those who emphatically were not. Yet the prejudice lingered in some quarters. As late as 1950 the editor of *John o'London's Weekly*, Wilson Midgley, gently rebuked me in a private letter for "spoiling" **Under Black Banner** with the hint of a budding love-affair on the final page. Such taboos seem unbelievable now, when teenage pregnancy and back-street abortion figure frequently in junior novels, and the writer is free to depict life as it is, and as his readers know from other sources that it is. I shudder to think what dear old Midgley would have said about a recent, excellent book, *The Poacher's Son,* in which the boy not only witnesses but actively assists at the birth of his sister—a realistic, almost horrific episode in which, one might say, no holds are barred.

Sex was only the most obvious of the taboos I remember. Liquor was another. I found the *Boy's Own Paper* very inhibited. In a modern story it disliked any reference—even disapproving—to alcohol, so that it was, except in the historical context of rum-swigging buccaneers, almost literally unmentionable. The supernatural was out: any apparently psychic phenomenon was permissible only if a rational explanation was supplied before the end of the story. This would have ruled out some remarkably fine imaginative books published in the past few years. Authority must not be undermined: schoolmasters could be comically eccentric or pompous, tricks might be played to rob them temporarily of their dignity, but respect for the old school and the older generation should not be fundamentally impaired. Parents, above all, must not be shown with serious human weaknesses. They could be dead or abroad; they were often one or the other, if not both, or the scope for youthful initiative would have been negligible. If, however, parents were present they must also be correct—loving, lovable, and long-suffering. In some ways the restrictions in juvenile publishing were an extension of the guidelines followed in the Lord Chamberlain's censorship of stage plays, which, for instance, prevented the depiction of clergymen in a way that would diminish respect for organized religion, and banned John van Druten's *Young Woodley* in 1928 for fear it would lessen public confidence in the public schools.

The list of restrictions could be lengthened. And it was matched by limitations on vocabulary. Villains might "mutter imprecations," but woe betide the author who submitted a manuscript in which they were quoted. The mildest "damn," or a mention of "hell" or "devil" except in a proper scriptural context, could spark off the kind of outcry that made publishers blench. Realistic working-class speech could not be reproduced, though as working-class settings were rare few people were conscious of the handicap. The natural dialogue of the playground had to be replaced, usually, by a stylized and obsolete slang, carefully refined to avoid offence.

Am I piling it on? It is only because, after twenty or thirty years of freedom, we veterans wonder how on earth we found any satisfaction in writing under so many limitations. But of course we did, and, though we say it ourselves, some good books got written. The creative artist can sometimes thrive on restrictions, whether it be a question of conforming to a sonnet's rhyme scheme or the producer's budget for a television play. When the handicap is not technical, but comes from taboos, stereotyped attitudes, and accepted but questionable values, there is a similar satisfaction in probing the enemy lines to see just what advances *can* be made. So, in those first years, when my overtly left-wing attack barely dented the embattled defences (few teachers outside the Rhondda Valley would have dared to take **Comrades for the Charter** into their schools), I changed my tactics. I wrote, for an anything-but-left publishing house, a story about the first voyage of the East India Company, and managed to say all that I wished to say: that the English had originally gone to India neither to spread the Gospel nor to build an empire, but simply to make fantastic profits.

I never returned, or wished to return, to the oversimplified partisan style with which I had begun. For one thing, after war came in 1939, I was never again in any narrow political sense a partisan. Although I could not rest until eventually I had given my own pictures of the French (**Thunder of Valmy**) and the Russian (**The White Nights of St Petersburg**) Revolutions. I was no longer drawn instinctively towards the barricades. My outlook was broadening even before the war. When it came, I was influenced in a quite unexpected way. After transfer to the Army Educational Corps I was largely occupied with lecturing on my first-hand experiences in Russia and with leading discussion groups on citizenship and current affairs. I had to aim at conscientious objectivity, or at least a demonstrably fair balance to ensure that every point of view was expressed. Sometimes I was forced to play devil's advocate and put forward arguments contrary to my private sympathies. This self-discipline had a lasting effect upon my writing for children. I realised that for an author, as much as for a teacher in the classroom, it was profoundly unethical to present controversial subjects from a biased point of view to immature minds lacking the background knowledge with which to challenge it.

Even in the army I managed, in slack periods, to go on writing. One book was surreptitiously tapped out in the orderly room of an infantry battalion where I was under-employed in His Majesty's service. Another I wrote in the Indian hills as I waited for release. Home at last, I poured out yet another, 60,000 words, in five exuberant weeks of my demobilization leave.

That war, unlike its predecessor, *did* bring a transformation in children's literature. Afterwards, there were whole-sale changes in the personnel and policies of the library services, the schools, the teachers' training colleges, and the publishing houses. This is not to depreciate the pio-neer work of some senior staff in all those fields who, having kept things going in difficult wartime conditions, often past their normal retiring age, were now yielding place to new people and new ideas. We should never forget that, for example, our present excellent Writers in Schools scheme, started by the Arts Council to bring liv-ing authors into contact with their readers, had been pre-ceded by the Children's Book Weeks, sponsored by pub-lic librarians and the National Book League, in the grim-mest years of the war. But mainly of course it was the post-war period, with the immense release of material resources, ideas, and enthusiasm, that encouraged a flow-ering of children's literature which now, alas, we are al-ready beginning to look back upon as a golden age.

In my own favourite field, the historical novel, we soon saw the ripening of a bumper harvest. Long despised, the genre quickly attracted a group of brilliant storytellers such as Rosemary Sutcliff, Cynthia Harnett, and many more. Some came to it after years of work in other fields: for example, Henry Treece had long been known as a poet and Barbara Willard had written many adult novels. Now the children's book was gaining more esteem; it was throwing off the old shackles on its subject matter, and, to be frank, it was beginning to pay properly. As the financial rewards for adult fiction (for a variety of rea-sons) began to tail off, many a talented novelist turned thankfully to the booming juvenile market, where a well-crafted plot, likeable characters, and a moderately cheer-ful outlook upon life were not discredited by fashionable criticism.

The benefits were soon evident in the junior novel, the contemporary as well as the historical. Along with the higher literary standard came stricter scholarship. Senti-mental romance and tushery had to compete with more stories that sprang from conscientious research and a deep, genuine feeling for the period. This wave was apparent from the beginning of the 1950s and brought us a flood of splendid books for about thirty years. It is not quite clear yet whether it has merely broken (like much else in children's literature) on the inhospitable shore of eco-nomic recession or whether it would have expended itself anyhow in the nature of things. Historical fiction makes special demands, and it has always been a minority taste, though the minority has often been a very strong one and its members characterised (many teachers and librarians assure us) by a particular loyalty to their favourite genre. Indisputably, historical stories are in the commercial dol-

drums just now, but it seems to me that, no less indisput-ably, they offer literature of value in a form that can never be totally obsolete. There will always be, please God, the imaginative, intelligent child who will seek his own individual vision of the past through print and not solely through the videotape.

In that faith the historical storyteller labours on. I do, certainly, much as I enjoy working in other fields for a change. Looking back over half a century, I have a wry feeling that I have seen the wheel turn full circle. In 1933 historical fiction was out of favour and had to be revital-ized. Now the battle needs, in some quarters at least, to be fought again.

Over these fifty years I have changed my own views on several points, but (I would like to think) not my basic approach. I am still most attracted to the parallels of past with present, rather than their romantic differences, though of course the colour and contrast of a remote period add legitimate interest on another level. Thus, in writing **The Iron Tsar,** I was passionately concerned with a vital con-temporary issue, the persecution of intellectual dissidents, but whereas, fifty years ago, I might have laid such a story in the present and become instantly involved in accusations of propaganda, I set it in the Russia of the 1830s and based it on well-documented cases such as Nicholas I's imprisoning the poet Chaadayev under med-ical supervision, leaving the intelligent young reader to draw his own parallels from the day's newspaper or TV bulletin. At the same time I was able to combine the grimness of the theme with a setting that moved me, and might move a reader, in an utterly different way: the sheer beauty of Russia as I remembered it from forty years before, the fairy-tale architecture, the forests, the vastly expansive rivers, and the savage scenery hemming the Georgian Military Highway.

I am always happiest working with this double kind of inspiration. I love, for instance, the world of Pepys for its own sake. But it is the obvious contemporary compari-sons that especially inspire me to weave stories against that background: tales of poor theatre folk battling against unscrupulous property developers, of corrupt contractors blackmailing civil servants, and of adventurous young women (like Aphra Behn) striving for professional equal-ity with the men. These are the underlying themes of **Popinjay Stairs** and **The Field of the Forty Footsteps.** And, moving back to Charles I's reign, I wrote **Saraband for Shadows** partly to recreate the vanished magic of the Jacobean masque, partly to say something about the un-changing realities of political intrigue. Children need to know about such things as they grow up into the adult world. The historical novel seems to me to provide anal-ogies from which they can learn agreeably, in their own time, developing their own critical insight.

Though, as a classics scholar, I never had any academic training as a historian in later periods, I have picked up a good store of unsystematic knowledge, and the knack of knowing where to look for any special background infor-mation required. The danger is that one can so easily fall

*Trease (left) with his older brothers George and Bill, c. 1912.*

in love with the information and be tempted to "work it in" when it proves *not* to be strictly required, thereby slowing up the action and putting yet another child off historical novels. Research is essential, but the storyteller must always be in firm control. One of the joys of research is the serendipity factor. You are searching for some fact you need, and you light on a nugget of authentic, quite unrelated information that solves some other difficulty or makes some splendid new contribution to your plot. There should be a separate Muse called Serendipity. She is the historical novelist's best friend.

As one picks up more knowledge, fresh difficulties as well as solutions emerge. One becomes aware of worrying improbabilities. My own nagging headache is the restriction on feminine freedom in so many centuries. I want to give my heroine a fair share of the action—how can I manage it without distorting social history? At first, in *Cue for Treason* and *The Hills of Varna,* I cheerfully fell back on the Shakespeare-sanctified device of male disguise, but a prolific writer has to find other solutions. Real history does in fact afford many documented cases of such transvestite adventures, but, though I resorted to the device again as recently as *Mandeville,* I am always voraciously alert in my historical reading to pounce on any scrap of evidence that will justify the active participation of my heroines at every stage of the plot.

To a lesser extent class often presents a similar problem. A reviewer of this same *Mandeville,* evidently nostalgic for the aggressive attitudes of my earliest stories, seemed regretful that I had introduced lords and baronets. A clear degeneration in my original popular sympathies! (The reviewer should have read more deeply into that book.) We must take history as we find it. I could hardly have sent the worthiest weaver on the Grand Tour to Italy. And in *The Iron Tsar,* similarly, if I was to get my fictitious young heroes into the same room with the autocratic Nicholas, it would be almost obligatory to make them a visiting English nobleman and a Russian count of liberal convictions. In many historical periods "mobility" and "nobility" are linked by more than a similar spelling.

Spelling reminds me of dictionaries, and one other respect in which my work has developed over the decades. If my historical research has become increasingly thorough, so too have I spent more and more time with my *Shorter Oxford English Dictionary.* When I began writing historical fiction I was reacting so violently against tushery that I made my characters converse in modern speech. A fault on the right side—it was primarily important to make those characters warmly alive—but it could sometimes be a fault none the less, admitting some jarring anachronism that shattered the sense of period. Slang and low-life colloquialisms are especially treacherous. Thus, Peter Carter in a recent powerful story about the 1683 siege of Vienna allows a Turkish janissary to exclaim, "Bismillah, what a cock-up!" which may eloquently express the sentiment of all disgruntled soldiers down the ages, but is not perhaps helpful in maintaining the atmosphere of that particular age. I have found no perfect solution for this problem. But, as to diction in general, while retaining all my old antipathy to varlets, minions and the like, I try as far as I can to use words which, though still in everyday use, were already current at the date of my story. Would the producer of my masque in 1636 have spoken of a change in the "cast"? I fly to my invaluable *Shorter Oxford.* He would. "1631." That was a near thing! The typewriter can tap on.

---

## GENERAL COMMENTARY

### Margery Fisher

SOURCE: "Truth and Ginger-Bread Dragoons," in *Intent Upon Reading: A Critical Appraisal of Modern Fiction for Children,* Franklin Watts, Inc., 1962, pp. 225–50.

[We might easily meet] the characters in Geoffrey Trease's . . . recent *Word to Caesar,* set in the second century A.D. Calvus, king of the Roman underworld, with spies operating all over the Empire, is the modern gangster in fancy-dress. For roadside cafés we have wayside taverns, for chases in car and aeroplane, wild horseback rides. The racy dialogue reflects easily, but in a scholarly fashion, the Roman scene. Here is Manlius, the chariot-racer, talking to young Paul on their arrival at Ostia:

'Somewhere to stay?' he echoed, looking thoughtful. 'I'd steer clear of the inns if I were you—Roman inns are no place for a decent boy to sleep in. Why not get a room for the time being, and buy your food as you want it?'

'I'd sooner do that.'

'Rooms take some finding. The city's shockingly overcrowded, and you don't want to land yourself in a slum. Let me see now . . . I know—' He frowned, then gave me a name and address in the Clivus Palatinus. 'They're a very respectable family—one of our drivers, retired now. Mention my name, and they'll let you have one of their rooms. Top floor, I'm afraid, but you won't mind the stairs at your age. Anyhow, it's a good solid building, it won't collapse under you in the middle of the night.'

'Is that usual?' I laughed.

'Happens more often than you think! Too much cheap building—and they stick on too many storeys for the foundations to carry. But this block is sound enough. You needn't worry.' . . .

Present-day writers are doing nothing new, of course, when they cut the cloth of history to fit the form of their own time. Shakespeare's view of Richard III was essentially a Tudor view. Scott wrote in the mood of eighteenth-century Gothic romanticism. Geoffrey Trease, in *Bows against the Barons* (published in 1934), presented Robin Hood under the shadow of hammer and sickle, as a revolutionary trying to inspire an oppressed and stupefied peasantry. His book was written in the spirit of the 'thirties and now seems an exaggerated piece of propaganda, as he would be the first to admit. L. A. G. Strong's study of Wat Tyler's rebellion, *King Richard's Land,* published three years after *Bows against the Barons,* gave a more all-round picture of feudal tyranny. Nor was Trease the first to present the case for the ordinary man. Scott had been aware of it and so had Marjorie Bowen and Herbert Strang in the 'twenties. Trease's effect upon children, and upon the course of historical writing for children, has all the same been far greater than that of earlier writers, because of his gift for choosing his subject so as to show that past and present are comparable, interacting, interdependent. He applies Marxism to history with real genius, and, in his later books, very easily. In *The Hills of Varna,* which is set in the early sixteenth century, he links the Renaissance with the atmosphere of discovery in our own times, and *Cue for Treason,* a spy story of Tudor times, draws a parallel with modern secret service methods. . . .

An historical story must have a point of view, though this may sometimes become a prejudice. Geoffrey Trease recalls how the BBC declined to serialize one of his stories in Children's Hour because it was 'anti-Cavalier.' . . .

[Children] expect to be on one side or the other. An

impartial tale of the Civil War might well be confusing and it would certainly be dull. Trease's own series about this period (*Silver Guard, The Grey Adventurer* and *Trumpets in the West*) is written from the Puritan point of view, though he deals fairly with the Cavaliers.

### The Times Literary Supplement

SOURCE: "Outlaws of the World Unite," in *The Times Literary Supplement,* No. 3378, November 24, 1966, p. 1079.

Thirty-two years after its original appearance, the book with which Geoffrey Trease and the "new" historical novel made their simultaneous debut has been reissued. *Bows against the Barons* has a secure place in the annals of children's literature. . . . Has it anything to say to the children of the 1960s? In so far as young readers like their values clear-cut and uncomplicated, it has. Mr. Trease, in a note to this new edition, calls it frankly a young man's book, and so it is, naive almost to the point of childishness but zestful and packed with action. As history it leans over at an uneasy angle to correct the balance of the conventional period romance of its day. Never were barons more wicked, outlaws more bold and forward-looking. The new edition has splendid new pictures by C. Walter Hodges, depicting Mr. Trease's heroes and villains, as the author sees them himself, in black and white . . .

Mr. Trease has learnt a lot in thirty-two years, and *The Red Towers of Granada* is an infinitely better book than *Bows against the Barons.* It nevertheless strengthens the conviction that Mr. Trease is a writer who has never quite redeemed his best promises. Is he too much determined to write the kind of book he believes his readers demand? The adventures are so contrived, so conventional. They seem grafted on to a narrative structure which is itself admirably and entirely convincing. *The Red Towers of Granada* begins in Nottinghamshire. Robin Hood's gallant band is absent, and the outlaws who waylay a learned Jew are murderous and cowardly. They run like stags when the hero appears, and this is not surprising for he wears the uniform of a leper. The grateful Jew takes Robin into his care, cures him—it is a slight skin infection, not leprosy—and takes him on the long journey to Spain in search of the Golden Essence which will cure King Edward's beloved Queen Eleanor. When Robin returns, with an attractive Moorish bride as well as the Essence, the Eleanor Crosses are already rising on the road between Harby and London. Mr. Trease has a grand subject here, and his glimpses of Jewish and Moorish culture are convincing. There seems however to be an almost calculated triviality in his writing, as if it is pitched at the lowest common denominator of his public.

### Margaret Meek

SOURCE: "Geoffrey Trease," in *Three Bodley Head Monographs: Hugh Lofting, Geoffrey Trease, J. M. Barrie,*

The Bodley Head, 1968, pp. 79–80, 82–5, 88–99, 105–20, 125–26.

[Geoffrey Trease's] first published boys' story, ***Bows against the Barons,*** appeared in 1934. . . .

The story is genuine black-and-white. The hero, Dickon, shot a deer after a day of provocation and ran off to Sherwood Forest, where, as in Shakespeare's Arden, we hear of winter and rough weather. The peasantry are oppressed by bailiffs, lords and abbots, squeezed for money, pressed for military service and they can do no more than put up a brave show of revolt. Robin Hood is celebrated not as the stereotyped romantic hero, but as someone who 'dreamed when the rest of us couldn't see further than our noses'. The heroic ideal shines through an impression of lurking danger. Children enjoy and respond to the clear-cut issues of right and wrong. At this time Trease believed that it was his duty to be a propagandist of social and political realism in opposition to those writers who trafficked in improbability. We find his villains capitalist in utterance, and the heroes are the downtrodden proletariat of the thirties rather than twelfth century peasants, but as an example of shaking up the mixture and telling a clear yarn it has still much to offer. . . .

Trease grasped the appeal of realism and the effect of the adult story for boys. He next tried a school story. ***The New House at Hardale*** appeared in the *Boy's Own Paper* in 1934, and in book form as late as 1953. . . .

The school theme allowed for few variations, for the pattern was confined at that stage to the boarding school. . . . Mystery stories were fashionable, and Trease wrote several before his first adult novel, ***Such Divinity,*** was published in 1939.

Real progress seemed to be along the way of ***Bows against the Barons,*** in historical fiction which told a rattling good story and yet did more. The time dimension, the significance of past events, and above all, the involvement of the modern child in the past, would give depth to the adventure story and take it out of the region of sub-journalism. In ***Comrades for the Charter*** (1934) and ***The Call to Arms*** (1935) the propagandist element survives. These books are still of interest, for they are the first to treat historical themes from a viewpoint other than that of the establishment. Nowhere in history stories before Trease do we find any indication of what stirred up Englishmen, generation after generation, not always unsuccessfully, to assert that they were men with sovereign rights. What could appeal more to adolescents in their attempts to find themselves? . . .

Geoffrey Trease's later books give arguments for both sides [of a conflict], as we shall see, but right from the start the attraction of the historical story as he wrote it is in live issues, involvement, commitment, which alone, we are told, will save us from the sensationalism of the candy-floss world which Richard Hoggart describes in *The Uses of Literacy.*

Commitment also means 'no writing down'. A system of adult values must operate. . . . The children's response was forthcoming, but a writer needs the criticism of his peers. How were they to be made to see that in the tale of everyday life the mainsprings of action are human emotions and personal relationships and involvements, that children feel and suffer, that realism is more than holiday expertise with boat and pony, that sticking to something that has to be done brings more satisfaction than good luck? Some of these points emerged in the first of the main history series, ***In the Land of the Mogul*** (1938), but they were unmistakable in ***Cue for Treason,*** and with it a new era in the adventure story opened. . . .

[***Cue for Treason***] has the marks of the later mature Trease history story as well as the crowded canvas of [G. A.] Henty. For the first time the traditional picture of Queen Bess is linked to the fate of her subjects at the limits of her realm in Cumberland. The songs, sonnets, dresses, play scenes are part of the real world which includes peel towers, lakes, hills and dangerous miners who are a law unto themselves. London is a fascinating but foul-smelling and dangerous place. The characters are round and full, especially the players and Boyd, the Secret Service agent. The gentle Shakespeare and the ruthless Cecil provide the shock of recognition, and the Queen is a sharp-witted old woman with a lot to worry her.

Right from the start the tale has movement, vitality and the suspense that comes from the loading of the circumstantial dice against the hero and heroine who must overcome genuine hazards with determination. The villain is more than a simple traitor, he is a usurper of rights. Trease the propagandist has now given way to the story-teller who has, nevertheless, been concerned to engage our sympathies for the oppressed.

***Cue for Treason*** showed what could be done and how children would respond. They were delighted. The task was now to consolidate the position which had been so hardly won, and the adventure story took on a new lease of life. . . .

Trease uses thematic material at once clearly local and nationally significant in a swift masculine sweep of plot. He suggests that men are prepared to defend first the place where they have their roots, and in the soil of England the historical patterns persist. The theme starts locally and branches out as national interests become clear.

This is particularly so in the novels which have links with ***Cue for Treason: Silver Guard, The Grey Adventurer,*** and ***Trumpets in the West.*** These three stories cover the period of the seventeenth century struggle between the King and Parliament, beginning with the Civil War and ending with the advent of William of Orange. . . . No one runs away to have adventures because life is boring. Instead, the heroes are set on pursuing an even course; Gervase from Boston wants to avoid the Civil War and study medicine at Oxford; Jack wants to compose. When the political situation brings upheaval they say, 'let's have it, get it over, and have a chance to think about our own business for a change'. Now, if this is a device in novel writing like any other, it also shows a change of outlook on the nature of adventure. It suggests that men are, on the whole, home-loving and peaceful, but that there are certain conditions, oppression, wrong, intolerance, under which a quiet life is impossible. The adventures are a challenge to ideas as much as a love of fighting. . . .

This group of novels carries over the social awareness of *Bows against the Barons.* The emphasis is no longer propagandist, but an attempt to put the issues fairly before coming down on one side. The Roundhead cause is made an issue of principle, not a manifestation of Puritanical ill-will. The Cavaliers are no longer the heroes, yet neither are they all silk and show. King James II has few advocates, but he is given a fairer trial than he intended for the seven bishops. The real change in the shift of power to the middle classes is seen in the motives and arguments of Dr Pharaoh, the Bunyanesque character, for whose egalitarian ideas the pillory and galley bench are the inevitable reward. In *The Grey Adventurer* we see how attitudes grow out of a social pattern and persist after the pattern has broken down, as in the relation of master and man in the colonies and the famine that resulted from the failure to believe that the Indians could be trusted.

Without disregarding the need to present black and white issues to boys and girls, Geoffrey Trease succeeds in showing that judgment is not inherent in the events. Those who fought their king regarded it as a serious matter. Religious imposition and the conflict of conscience penetrated even the villages, and for some people, to go to America was a desperate remedy for a more desperate disease. Nor is this gloomy sociology. The vitality of youth permeates it all, and the sieges and battles have no less force and excitement for being described from the less usual (but winning!) side. Everything is not gloriously democratic in the end. . . .

Alexis, the hero of *The Crown of Violet,* is made to go to rhetoric lessons, but he prefers to listen to Socrates whose reputation is not high with Leon, Alexis' father. The plot of this book is a carefully-woven double-stranded one, involving a Spartan conspiracy against Athens and the winning entry in the drama festival. Alexis succeeds in both fields, and Corinna finds her long-lost parents. This stretched even a willing suspension of disbelief on first reading, but the motivation is sound and withstands any hesitancy on the part of the adult reader to accept so much success. Again, the strength lies in the historical context being carried along by the action. Alexis is a gifted young poet, but he is also a boy who has to persuade his father first that he is not troublesome and disobedient. If one thinks that the adults had no chance against the children, one is reconvinced by the soundness of the events: the children are caught when they meddle, and the adults have to be consulted and persuaded before effective military action can be taken. It is an instructive exercise to knock on a plot in Trease's historical novels; they are made to withstand the carping of both children and adults. . . .

[*The Hills of Varna*] has a grip of excitement from start to finish. The feeling tone in this one is memorable in that it conveys just how great was the passion for the new learning. . . . The enthusiasm of the hero and heroine for Greek books is equivalent to the present-day devotion to space travel, and one hopes that the keenness for the sciences will find as good an outlet in a story which conveys the authentic nature of the interest as well as this one does the lasting devotion to the classics. The character of Aldus Manutius is also excellently done. Little first-hand information is available about this printer, so he intrigues the novelist and gives him the stimulus he requires.

The same kind of feeling tone, a sense of historical period made local, comes in *Word to Caesar,* where another journey is undertaken, this time from Bath to Rome. . . . This story has the advantage of another clearly-drawn villain. The intensity of these period tales is due in part to the embodiment of the darker side of the peaks of western civilisation in those who flourish in deceit and treachery. Men like the millionaire Calvus, the Italian duke, and the foppish Hippias show economically and clearly the forces ranged against Roman law, the spread of enlightenment and Athenian democracy.

To counter the emotional poverty which, he says, is 'the saddest flaw in contemporary juvenile books', Trease makes the relationship of the hero and heroine a growing one. He faces the difficulties of writing about personal relationships with tact and sense, taking refuge neither in hilarious extrovert behaviour nor in sentimentality. Jack Norwood in *Trumpets in the West* knows that a baronet's daughter will not find it easy to marry a musician, who is regarded as 'not quite a gentleman'. After their exploit as *fratres coniurati* in looking for the manuscript, Alan and Angela must go their separate ways. Paul will not settle in Bath with Julia, but finds in Tonia a friend then a wife. Adults have come to see that unless these subjects are dealt with in books written for adolescents, their sons and daughters may look for them in a less attractive form elsewhere.

The difference in upbringing between boys and girls provides a good historical 'trace'. The girls are bright, intelligent and worthy of the adventures and able to hold their own, but they are not tomboys all the time; dresses and shoes are matters of concern when they should be. Whereas the boys initiate and carry through the action, the girls deal with people and the heightened sensibility is theirs. In *Mist over Athelney,* Elfwyn, taking money from the Danes, thinks he is taking part of what they had stolen from the English. Judith rejects it: 'one part of her mind told her that it was a low form of cleverness'. Girls used to read the books their brothers brought home: now they find themselves in the adventure story in their own right. Here is another instance of Trease's innovation: he introduced girl characters as active protagonists with their young male counterparts. . . .

The heroes have the hopes and fears of adolescents. A prisoner in Arles, Paul admits that he is afraid, and his first anxiety is to save himself, but as he owes his life to Severus, he thinks it sense that he should lose it by trying to help him. Trease has shown that by admitting fear, indecision and frailty as natural, and by calling on adults to help when their action only would be effective, one increases, not diminishes, the hero's stature.

With the decline of the infant prodigy has faded the nationalist distrust of 'the foreigner'. Here again Trease is implementing his own demands. . . . In *The Silken Secret* (1953), set in Derbyshire with more romantic trappings than most of the earlier books are allowed, the villain is an Italian employed as a landscape gardener. He is anxious to stop the silk merchant from introducing into England the silk-throwing techniques which are the monopoly of the Piedmontese. He has family and national pride, motives which cannot be dismissed as blackheartedness. This is one of the best features in an uneven book, which has the sureness of plot and memorable characters one has come to take for granted. There is also a greater number of stock devices here than in any other, highwaymen, gypsies who poison pies, stilettos, a maze and imprisonment in a cave, as if the author were trying to show that he could use them all and still bring off a creditable historical tale up to his own standard. I find myself watching the mechanism with respect, but do not feel this one vintage Trease. . . .

[*The Barons' Hostage*] is the most overtly didactic of the historical novels, a crowded feudal scene of 1263–65 in which all is bustle, war and government. The family involvements, through which the characters shine out as of old, are complicated, and the events of this confusing time are still confusing despite the excitement of the Lord Edward's escape and the stern character of Simon de Montfort. The shape of the story is held in more closely by the record of events, and although Trease has worked his brief to give boys and girls an idea of what it was like to live at this time . . . , he is more successful when he can thread his own chain of events and use the history as context rather than plot.

The style of adventure in *The Secret Fiord, Word to Caesar,* and *Mist over Athelney* is characteristic of the later period. In *The Secret Fiord* Trease accepts his own challenge and introduces twins, running away, and the long-lost father, all the incidents which he has insisted are overdone in earlier children's books. Here, however, the motivation is strong enough to withstand these elements which avoid the obviousness of cliché. An unforgettable scene in a cathedral town involving the Corpus Christi play, and the escape from the Hanse merchants, show how entertainment and didacticism reinforce each other.

The apparent ease and clarity of outline of these later books owe much to the practised skill of the dialogue. . . .

To combine dialogue and description and to make both organic in a fast-moving plot is to solve the major issues of the historical novel. To do this without loss of integrity and to win the favour of the young is to earn the respect of critics, the praise of parents and the gratitude of teachers. Geoffrey Trease not only fulfils his own demands in this field but also surpasses them in giving new life to an almost outmoded *genre* which was dying for lack of conviction about the adventure of ideas. The felt life of these books is undoubted. They have the vitality and gaiety as well as the idealism and seriousness of adolescence. In respecting his audience, Trease has won for children's stories an abiding recognition they were once about to lose. . . .

The story-biographies included in *The Seven Queens of England, Seven Kings of England* and *Fortune my Foe,* follow the prescriptions in *Tales out of School* where the author speaks with feeling of both the attraction and difficulty of writing about Raleigh and the childhood of kings and queens. . . . In writing history for young people, Trease steps over the line which divides what is known from what is felt, but with an integrity which illuminates rather than detracts from the importance of the facts. The facts are for the textbooks, but they so rarely come alive without inspired teaching. . . . These books fill the gap which separates history from life and will keep an interest alive throughout the period of wrestling with examinations. . . .

Trease had written formula fiction long before the war. . . . *The New House at Hardale* improved the stereotype but left it unchanged in outline. After this came mystery and spy stories. *Mystery on the Moors, The Lakeland Mystery, Detectives of the Dales* depart from the usual mixture by introducing real scenery and the sense of actual location which came out so strongly later in the histories and again in the post-war moderns. These mysteries were neither better nor worse than the average for the thirties. . . .

The out-and-out spy story, *Black Night, Red Morning* (1944) was allowed to lapse when it lost its topicality. The place this time is Russia, and the plot concerns the activity of Russian guerrillas against the Nazis. The urgency of war-time is on this story, and the hero is as heroic and the villain as blackhearted as one ever hopes to meet. It has dated too much to stand revival. . . .

As a craftsman Trease has accepted [the challenge of writing for reluctant readers]. The stories in the book called *The Mystery of Moorside Farm* are stock tales, boy and girl protagonists in adventures concerning a farm, Nazi spies, and a theatrical family. The conventions stick out, the vocabulary is simplified, but the leap to the situations of the main characters is unreal for the backward readers I know, for, more than anything else, they lack experience of story telling. They need a different kind of illusion which gives the appearance of realism, and a quick succession of slapstick situations which produce a comic, custard-pie effect. This does not tempt the serious children's novelist. Trease's strength lies again in the dialogue. It is good that the book exists; we need so many and there are so few. A skilled author like Trease could improve on his earlier performance, but it is not easy to write effectively for the boys and girls, or rather, the young adults who appear regularly in the reports of probation officers. . . .

[The books in the **"Bannermere"** series] are planned and intended to be stories of children 'just like us'. . . . They reassure readers about a world in which other children go to school (day school), play with friends, devise schemes and above all, suffer reverses and frustrations. . . .

Trease is censured for making the Bannerdale children bring culture to the villages; they have a headmistresss who is an expert on Viking remains and a classical head-master of the Arnold species. The answer is not to lower one's sights about scholarship, but to make the experienc-es ring true so that the surroundings do not seem to be the ultimate condition of the adventure. Scholarship is much less a middle-class concern than it was. . . .

Trease, following the example set by Day Lewis's *Otter-bury Incident,* sends his characters to day schools, but standards of good scholarship are the same no matter where, as Mr Kingsford, the Headmaster in the Banner-dale series, would be swift to point out. The boarding schools themselves have had to give up treasure hunts these days and concentrate as much on University en-trance as the rest. . . .

The volumes of the Bannerdale series vary in effective-ness. *No Boats on Bannermere* sets the scene: the Mel-bury family, Mum, Susan and Bill inherit a cottage in Bannerdale and go there to live. Father is 'away' in Can-ada. He is referred to, but not hushedly, and he does not come back. His departure has left his family short of money. The friends are Tim Darren who wants to be a policeman, and Penny Morchard, whose father has a book-shop in Winthwaite, the nearest town. These are the main characters in each book. . . .

To counter his own accusation that children in story books never grow up, Trease has taken the main four from 'elev-en plus' to the career and undergraduate stage. Their adventures throughout each year are set against the nor-mal round of term and holiday. . . . Their responsibilities increase, the scope of their activities widens and their relationships deepen. The balance of home-loving Sue, motherless, harum-scarum Penny, practical Tim, and Bill the thoughtful organiser is a good one, and the reader's identification can shift from one to the other. The scenery of the lakes, the pleasant local feeling of the small town is what most children enjoy. . . .

Each book has a distinctive theme in this general back-ground. *No Boats* sets out to make 'ordinary life mean-ingful and exciting', from going into a new house to dis-covering the ways of fell farmers . . . *Black Banner Play-ers* introduces the two themes which persist in the later books in the series: amateur dramatics, and what the ex-perts call 'adolescent social adjustment'. . . . In this book the theme of how to become an author, the right way and the spurious way, is dealt with, and Bill has a chance to show his mettle when an eighteenth century diary comes

to light and its publication augments the Drakes' small pension.

The general theme of **Black Banner Abroad** is foreign travel, which includes the particular intention of seeing why it is important and exciting for the young. Recollec-tions of school parties abroad fill the reminiscences of journalist schoolmasters and school magazines, but this tale is written from the inside of the expedition. . . . The emphasis throughout is on growing personal relationships and widening experience. The book shows how, when young people go abroad, they become individuals in their own right for the first time, which is why their parents and teachers find them changed when they come back, especially if they have lived with another family. Like Bill, they may also have succumbed to the charms of Gigi, the bewitching character who, despite the author's control, nearly runs off with the story. Some of the best writing of the series is in this book; the performance of Shakespeare in the mothy dark of the amphitheatre is specially memorable. The growing awareness of deeper feelings is handled with forthrightness and tact.

Trease is always at his best when dealing with themes he cares about most. Although this is taken for granted in writing for adults, he would insist that it is also true of the children's author. The effect can be seen by comparing the earlier books with **The Gates of Bannerdale.** Schol-arship, Oxford, historical research and the unforgettable performance of *The Tempest,* are the mainstay of the volume. . . .

Bill is the teller of the tales, and as his chronological age increases, so, mercifully, does his prose style mature. This 'young author' is an uneasy convention to which a great deal must be sacrificed, and I am sure that not enough is gained to warrant it in the early stages, for the descriptive details show the adult author's hand. Sound as the theme is, *No Boats* has a somewhat stagey plot, and the reward motif, that touchstone for all adventure stories, is a disap-pointment, especially after the hard hitting in *Tales out of School.* One must not be entirely swayed by the book's popularity into thinking that it is better than it is. It stretch-es the reader least, and this is not the kind of popularity one covets for it.

When the real difficulties of adolescents begin, when their shortcomings have to be taken into account, then Trease rises to the occasion. . . . [All] their moods give the plots and themes a precision of experience which the first two lack. Sir Alfred, as one reviewer puts it, is a 'cultural villain', and the obstacles to the successful manoeuvre with the War Office are not too convincing. Everyone is so kind and helpful, so *educative,* that I am happier when we pass on to the region of conflicting emotional and intellectual drives, away from the glad animal movements.

But to emphasise the weakness would be to detract from the real achievement of the series. It has implemented the idea that 'school attendance' has become a richer thing, 'school life'. To do this, Trease suggested that 'a handful of good stories might help', and this is exactly what he produced. . . . The lucky accident rarely comes to the rescue of the plot, perhaps only when time and Gigi have stolen the show in **Black Banner Abroad** and the cottage has not been found. On this occasion it is worth it. Trease may not approve of the characters running away with the author, and the length of a children's novel rarely leaves room for it to happen, but this is a success. The class issue is never shirked, although it comes out most where it is most appropriate, at Oxford. The lack of money is what it always is, a nuisance.

The dialogue never really loses its sure touch, but it suffers most in **No Boats** where the curious 'simplification' is not worthy of the author's talent, and the reader is deceived by a false simplicity. I can understand a schoolmarmly complaint about this. It is much better later, but the problem of slang and the contemporary speech of the young is not yet solved; indeed it is perennial with all writers, and the adoption of a new medium, such as that used in *The Catcher in the Rye,* seems to offer a different way of going about it. That is not how adolescents actually talk, but it recreates the illusion successfully, which is better than an unreal realism. . . .

The dialogue has to carry a firm load of description, the growth of character and more than a hint of didacticism. The pills are sometimes thinly coated, but easily swallowed. . . .

A strong sense of values is the backbone of the series. Inherited formula is made meaningful by the clash of issues and different standards of integrity, or even keeping one's self-respect. Learning about different ways of life, about knowledge, and books, all add to the interest in making normal life exciting. Teachers need no longer shake their heads over the handling of adolescent relationships. The difference between boys and girls growing up, a feature we saw clearly in the histories, is skilfully dealt with. . . .

As long as there are children's stories the adults will have to be put somewhere, so it is better if they can be accepted as part of the action. They have to be revolted against; it is not fair to the children otherwise. The Melbury children grow up by having to be responsible for their mother and to see that in the lonely dales they do not have all the fun, although like a good parent she allows herself to be banished to the sales in Manchester. She plays a real adult role, not too interfering, but offering advice when asked and being firm about the social conventions which make children acceptable guests. She shows clearly what Trease meant when he said that the mortality rate amongst parents and relatives was needlessly high. . . .

Does all this add up to 'making ordinary life exciting and meaningful' by confirming what adolescents know of it and stretching their imaginations? Certainly the characters are more 'like us' than books of twenty years earlier which avoided the actual situations around them. Despite claims to the contrary, I think that the good fortune of the schoolboys and girls and their adventurous situations are no more than the average child might look for these days. . . . Here, as in the histories, adventure is as much the result of an enquiring curiosity and a determination to see a job through as the good fortune to be lost on the moors at night, and those who complain that it could never happen to them have not read a set of ordinary children's compositions about what goes on in the neighbourhood at weekends.

The great gap filled by these books is the one between what children read in school and what they like to read. . . . The later volumes stretch the reader without taking him away from the security of what he knows and recognises, and increase his awareness of the value of the experience which is already his, so that his response to life and to books will deepen. The **Bannerdale** books are not beyond the reach of fashion; they will date more quickly than the histories, but meanwhile they offer authentic imaginative experience. . . . [The] **Bannerdale** books are imaginative documentary, carrying, as their author demands that they should, the readers 'from the love of romance to the appreciation of reality'.

Since Geoffrey Trease made his serious effort to write for the *contemporary* young there have been others who have achieved comparable and even surpassing success; but, as Trease began the movement of a new approach to the historical novel for children, so he should also be given the credit for experimenting with the new type of family story which is today a feature on many publishers' lists. . . .

'Fascinating and maddening by turns' is how Geoffrey Trease describes the 'mongrel art form' of the travel book written in a setting of fiction. His child heroes in **'The Young Traveller'** series go to India, Pakistan and Greece with parents conveniently sent on jobs which give them a good excuse to pry around (films and university research), while to tour England in an old car they are joined by two other children from the Commonwealth who help them to see their own country with new eyes. One must remember that the intention is fact, not fiction, for the characters take an 'intelligent interest' sometimes bordering on precocity, and the quotation game can get a little out of hand in books as in real life. Adult readers are probably more sensitive to the mixture of the conventions and amazed by the amount of detail that the writer has managed to include without making it indigestible. Young readers take the setting easily for what it is, and move from sympathetic interest in the motherless son of a newspaper man to the details about the Acropolis without concern for the author, trusting that his craftsmanship will give them the interest and information they want. The facts emerge from the dialogue and from the description given by a character who has a claim to know about what he points out. For India and Greece, two places which he knows well, Trease has an unmistakable place sense which we have already seen in the novels. The historical and romantic elements which fire his imagination come out again in these books in a way which takes them out of the realms of ordinary guide books. The children note and enjoy the everyday things too, food, school, travel, as well as the special highlights of a Greek Easter and an Indian tiger hunt. All this is done with more than journalistic conscientiousness; it takes all his skill as an expert to produce a junior Baedeker. . . .

Just as Geoffrey Trease's sense of place is capitalised in these travel books, his practised hand at dialogue is in demand when we think of plays for children. There are never enough for acting in school, and teachers who have thumbed their way through countless one-act unsuitables of 'The Bathroom Door' variety are delighted with *The Shadow of Spain* where their needs for many parts and sensible dialogue are efficiently met. The three plays in the book will keep the Junior Dramatic Club effectively busy and teach them a great deal about character portrayal and production. . . .

*Tales out of School* ends with a chapter called 'To you— for action', and in the years which have passed Trease has increased the body of his work to an extent which puts him in the first category of writers for children. But more than that, he has made us all, writers, critics, teachers and parents alike, more and more aware of what is involved, and to what extent the children's writer takes on himself the task of helping to make the present generation literate. He has closed the gap between entertainment and didacticism, showing that in the children's story they merge happily together, and he has bridged the gulf between the comic and the classic in a way for which teachers can never be grateful enough. He has taught his fellow writers that if they are to earn their lauds as minor artists, only sound adult standards of integrity will do, all this with a seriousness of purpose and a sense of humour. . . .

It is no mere extension of the habit of being, on the whole, laudatory and approving of writers of children's fiction that has produced this appreciation of his achievement. Geoffrey Trease has fully earned the status that he claims for himself and his fellow writers. The further development of his work is bound to add something to our awareness of what is involved in writing for children.

### Roger Lancelyn Green

SOURCE: "Arthur Ransome and Holiday Adventures," in *Tellers of Tales,* revised edition 1965. Reprint by Kaye & Ward, Ltd., 1969, pp. 83–4, 266–67, 300.

A great cleavage in historical fiction today has divided the aggressively adult novel set in a past age of writers like Robert Graves, Mary Renault and Henry Treece, from those written specifically for young readers. The difference is even more pronounced than that between *Henry Esmond* or *John Inglesant* and the works of Henty: but the writings of our modern Hentys have, perhaps in consequence, taken on a depth of vision and imaginative metempsychosis that sets them far above the historical story-books for boys written by Henty, A. D. Crake, A. J. Church and the rest.

The land was explored and the trail blazed by Geoffrey

Trease, who stumbled into this new byway of history almost by accident, as an 'angry young man' revolting against the traditional story in which our sympathies are always with the Cavaliers against the Roundheads, the Aristocrats against the Revolutionaries. He began his campaign with *Bows against the Barons* (1934), in which he intended that 'the seamy side of Merrie England should be displayed, and Robin Hood represented as a kind of premature Wat Tyler'. Two lesser stories followed, and he then branched off into contemporary adventure and school stories of a less notable quality, but returned to history with *In the Land of the Mogul* (1938) and reached his real kingdom in *Cue for Treason* (1940)—the unforgettable story of the boy who becomes a strolling player in the late Elizabethan period, acts for Shakespeare and helps to unmask a plot against the Queen.

It is not possible to follow Geoffrey Trease through all his historical tales, though the pilgrimage would be a pleasant one—by way of *Silver Guard, The Grey Adventurer* and *Trumpets in the West,* back to an early period in British history with *Word to Caesar, Mist Over Athelney* and *The Secret Fiord.* Nor can we linger over his modern stories in the Bannerdale series, up-to-date family stories with the local grammar schools playing an important part—tempting as it is to compare the *Black Banner Players* (1952) with those in Pamela Brown's *Blue Door Venture* of a few years earlier.

Geoffrey Trease's historical stories are full of excitement and adventure nor, though the historical setting is painstakingly but unobtrusively accurate, are children wafted too far from their own experience, even in *The Crown of Violet* (1952) which leads them back most persuasively to the Athens of Socrates.

### Marcus Crouch

SOURCE: "Foundations," "The Abysm of Time," and "School—Home—Family," in *The Nesbit Tradition: The Children's Novel in England 1945–1970,* Ernest Benn Limited, 1972, pp. 20, 58–9, 60, 162.

The modern historical novel for young people, . . . was launched quite deliberately by Geoffrey Trease with a story about Robin Hood called *Bows against the Barons* (1934). This was not in itself a very good book. In his efforts to present a provocative and unconventional view of the Middle Ages, the young author protested too much; his peasants were uniformly oppressed and virtuous, his barons as monotonously wicked as Sir Jasper in the Victorian melodrama. Geoffrey Trease had, nevertheless, made his point; an historical novel for children might offer an original comment on history and draw parallels with contemporary society. His succeeding books drove home the same lessons with greater subtlety. . . .

Geoffrey Trease had been the conscious inventor of the modern historical novel in the years before the war. His concern was to look at the past afresh, not through the screen of old text-book attitudes and judgements. In the immediate post-war world his work was taken up again both by himself and by a number of other writers. . . .

Geoffrey Trease is one of the best theorists among modern writers for the young. His principles are unexceptionable. His performance has not invariably reached up to his own standards; the bones of his political and social theories are apt to stick through the skin of his novels in an uncomfortable fashion. He was at his best in the decade immediately after the war. *Trumpets in the West* (1947) was written while the author was still in the Forces, and his affectionate pictures of Somerset and the London of Wren were painted among the hills of Central India. The book shows signs of its origins, as well as those of its writer's limited technical equipment. The writing is often naive and cliché-ridden, but the story is beautifully fresh, capturing the challenging spirit in the air of 1688. A year later a very much more mature book appeared. *The Hills of Varna* (1948) is a story of the Renaissance. A slightly contrived plot—plots have never been Trease's main strength—sends Alan away from the shelter of Cambridge into a world bristling as much with ideas as dangers. His journey is a treasure-hunt, but the treasure is not gold or such trash but the manuscript of a Greek satirical comedy lying forgotten in a Dalmatian monastery. Trease manages to share with his readers the intellectual excitement of the quest and its success as well as the more conventional thrills of piracy and banditry. He was less successful in telling the story of the origin of Alexis's play in *The Crown of Violet* (1952). He seemed ill at ease in Socrates' Athens, and the attempt to make the young people of Classical Greece speak in a modern idiom is less happy even than an essay in 'tushery' might have been. ("'You know what Mum is . . . And I do think your old uncle is a dear.' 'He's a scream. Half the time he's scared stiff . . .'") But clearly this was a book which had to be written, and there is some charm in the picture of Athens in its precarious heyday.

Trease's recent work is purged of the crudities of style and thought which mark his earlier writing, but he has bought this technical competence at a high price. The adventuring spirit has faded, and he no longer sparkles with a fresh vision. He still knows how to choose a good and original theme. His two stories about Garibaldi's Italy present, for English readers, an unfamiliar scene. The most satisfactory of his later novels is perhaps *The Red Towers of Granada* (1966). This has the handicap of an awkward plot, but there are admirable portraits of Edward I and his great consort Eleanor, and the author explores thoughtfully the status of the Moors in thirteenth-century Spain and their scientific skills. As always with this writer there is too much plot! The excellent ideas are constantly being swamped by desperate action. . . .

Geoffrey Trease approached the question of the day school from a different position [from A. Stephen Tring (Laurence Meynell)] and in a different topographical setting. In a number of **'Black Banner'** stories he looked at a group of young people of both sexes in a country community of the North-West (*No Boats on Bannermere*, 1954). These are honestly observed and based on sound principles, although a little dull; the scene, however, quickly moved away from school with its limited canvas. The same is true of Trease's later and slighter books about 'Maythorn'.

## Margery Fisher

SOURCE: "Bill Melbury" and "Mark Apperley," in *Who's Who in Children's Books: A Treasury of the Familiar Characters of Childhood,* Holt, Rinehart and Winston, 1975, pp. 45, 203.

Bill Melbury, a schoolboy of fifteen, is determined to be a writer but feels it safer to tell people that he means to teach. When his mother decides to move from the city to the wilds of Cumberland, he and his younger sister Sue find congenial friends in Penny Morchard, daughter of the scholarly bookseller in the nearest town, and Tim Darren, whose efforts at amateur detection help (or so he believes) to forward his ambition to enter the police force.

Geoffrey Trease has chosen his four characters well. Penny's energetic nature, the tenacity that compensates for her lameness, balance Sue's common sense and her enthusiasm for country ways, while Bill's book-learning and Tim's flair for deduction stand them in good stead when they are involved with successive mysteries and activities—Sir Alfred Askew's sharp dealing over an archaeological discovery and a farm sequestered by the War Office (in *No Boats on Bannermere*), amateur theatricals in *Black Banner Players* and *Black Banner Abroad;* while in *The Gates of Bannerdale* Bill, now an Oxford undergraduate, helps to locate the college silver, lost for centuries. Just as Geoffrey Trease set himself to counteract the artificiality of the junior historical fiction of the '30s by more politically alert stories, so in the Bannerdale books he refreshed the tired holiday adventure with its smugglers' caves and hidden treasure by showing boys and girls in everyday life, in the classroom and the kitchen, the local library and the café, and allowing them to entertain natural, gently indicated adolescent feelings for one another. His characters are not helped either by improbable good fortune or by exceptional advantages of mind and body. They are ordinary but individual boys and girls, maturing and changing over the five or six years covered by the books, drawn not in great depth (since this would be unsuitable for the genre) but with such details as are needed to ensure that the events of the stories properly relate to the actors in them.

Without suggesting that Bill Melbury is directly based on the author's self-when-young, it is permissible to point out how closely Bill's ambitions to be a writer and his deliberate gathering of experience parallel the experience of the young Geoffrey Trease. Trease himself has made it clear that he deliberately chooses for his historical novels civilized periods which will supply him with literate characters. No less in the Bannerdale books, books and theatre are a natural accompaniment to life. Then again, for first-person narrative it is necessary (though not all writers do this) to choose a suitable narrator. Because Bill

Melbury wants to write he naturally takes charge of the stories and, in a kind of double bluff, sees the events he is engaged in as potential material for stories. We absorb his view of Penny Morchard, of old Kingsford the grammar school headmaster and Miss Florey, the redoubtable red-headed headmistress of the girls' secondary—a barely retrospective, one-sided, enquiring schoolboy's view. Youthful and instructable (but never naïve), Bill is a likeable, recognizable boy in terms of the '50s—recognizable, in fact, in the '70s as well, for all the supposedly greater sophistication and worldly knowledge of young readers of today. . . .

Mark Apperley at fifteen is ready for active rebellion against his domineering grandmother, who has kept him cooped up on the Worcestershire estate under the tuition of the local curate, obsequious Mr Bilibin. Mark fancies that a letter to an imaginary girl, left unfinished where Mrs Apperley is bound to find it, will ensure that he is sent away to school, but instead, he is packed off, still in Mr Billibin's charge, on a European tour—in 1849 a recognized form of education for the sons of gentry.

So begins a turbulent year in which the sheltered boy is first by chance and then by choice swept into the rising of Garibaldi, the siege of Rome and the rebel army's escape through the mountains. His frustrations are swept aside, his knowledge of the world increased, through his acquaintance with McWhirter, a journalist sending despatches and drawings back to London, with Tessa and Pietro Palma, two young and ardent rebels against French and Austrian domination in Italy, and briefly, the romantic leader himself. Mark returns to England and older and wiser boy after an escapade which proved to be a severe lesson in human relations.

Eleven years later (in *A Thousand for Sicily*), as a young journalist on the *Morning Herald,* Mark attaches himself once more to the rebel army, as an active observer in the sea journey and the capture of Palermo, this time accompanied for part of the time by Julietta Valdesi, half-English daughter of a Sicilian doctor. A predictable, gently romantic ending completes the adventures of a young Englishman who, with the attitudes and opinions of his time, remains understandable today.

In most of his historical novels Geoffrey Trease involves a young fictious hero with an historical personage; in this way he can offer an interpretation rather than a closely considered portrait. Young readers today are more likely to understand the aims and ideals of Garibaldi if they are expressed through the dawning comprehension of a boy who can make the pattern of history seem relevant to our own times.

In the first book about Mark (*Follow My Black Plume*) he is shown to be ingenuous and inexperienced. He sees Garibaldi through a haze of hero-worship, only half realizing that intelligence is as necessary in a commander as the power of personality. Garibaldi, with his cowboy's poncho, red shirt and the black ostrich feathers in his wide hat, seems to Mark a man full of colour, a romantic

hero indeed, 'a big man, barrel-chested, with a reddish-golden beard and a face like a lion's, broad-muzzled, tawny from sun and wind'. The young man of twenty-six sees Garibaldi as an old lion in his fifties, still savage, still capable of quick decisions and bold feats of arms, but saddened by his wife's tragic death and pained by rheumatism. Mark is older too, not at all sure that he wants to be a hero, knowing now the bleak realities and the compromises of war. Geoffrey Trease allows Mark in words, behaviour and verbalized thoughts to offer his own view of Garibaldi very directly. At the same time the way the boy talks with other characters—with the two ardent girls, Tessa and Julietta, with the absurd cleric Bilibin and the cynical McWhirter—tells us as much about him as it does about the minor characters who in their turn add reality to the books.

**Margery Fisher**

SOURCE: "Life Course or Screaming Farce," in *Children's literature in education,* No. 22, Autumn, 1976, pp. 108–15.

Geoffrey Trease showed both taste and balance when he wrote, for readers in the 'teens, studies (they come very near to true biography) of two somewhat unusual subjects, Byron and D H Lawrence. His scholarship and his dry wit make guffaws and genuflection equally impossible. Helped by his own knowledge of a Nottingham still much like Lawrence's, he fulfils the object of the 'Life and Works' genre, to help the young to understand what lay behind those words. Besides, in the case of Lawrence he steers them past fifty years of insensitive misinterpretation to suggest the basic value of the novels:

> Lawrence had begun his lifelong practice of drawing his characters from his own acquaintance. To say this is not to detract from his genius. He was much more than a human camera, aiming an impersonal lens. His eye for external detail was as shrewdly selective as it was keen, but he went far beyond the superficial features that present themselves to the casual observer. Lawrence's wonderful gift—as many who knew him have emphasized—was a deeper capacity for observation and understanding, that penetrated to the very core of the individual. His very hatred of conventional attitudes and artificial poses made him impatient of outer layers. As the critic G S Fraser has put it, he looked for 'the deep drives'. Finding them, identifying them, incarnating them in the person depicted, he gave each character a peculiarly dynamic quality.

That passage may serve to show how Trease dealt with the guffaws. As for the genuflection, he looks directly and firmly at the Lawrence who wrote in later life 'The War finished me: it was the spear through the side of all sorrows and hopes':

> Thereafter he was a different, and to many a less attractive, person. The sense of mission grew more urgent, the manner more arrogant. The metaphor of 'the spear through the side', taken from the Crucifixion

story, shows that Lawrence was beginning to see himself as some kind of Messiah with a sacred duty to set people on a new road, away from the materialism and bourgeois morality he despised. Any obstacle was apt to be seen as persecution.

It is easy to understand Lawrence's feelings, less easy to sympathise with him all the way. He was not the only young writer whose first book brought him a miserable financial reward, and not the only one whose career had been wrenched out of its course by the war. Lawrence might have counted many blessings if he had been given to that sort of arithmetic.

There is nothing predigested or diluted in Trease's two admirable books. He is not bludgeoning his readers into accepting his view but inviting them to examine it as an introduction to Byron's poems and Lawrence's novels.

If really young readers need heroes to live up to, their elders should be able to dispense with routine adulation. Because of the dangers of frankness, most subjects of junior biographical writing are safely dead, and studies of the living are apt to be severely functional and respectful. The most serious danger is, of course, that no boy or girl will develop independent powers of judgment without practice. A lesser evil of the adulatory life study is a total lack of humour, that element that can often take us most surely into the heart of a man. Biographies seldom allow their subjects to be ordinary or absurd. One of the moments I have most enjoyed while working on this article was when I found, in my local library, two books shelved side by side: *Great Prime Ministers* and *Famous Rogues*. Stirred together, they might have made an acceptable dish.

## Bob Dixon

SOURCE: "Class: Snakes and Ladders," in *Catching Them Young 1: Sex, Race and Class in Children's Fiction,* Pluto Press, 1977, pp. 71–88.

Although no-one in Britain can ignore the monarchy—the press and mass media see to that—it's now time to return to the basic class struggle, that between the middle and the working classes, and carry it through to the present day to see where the battle-lines are now drawn up. To take the metaphor further, the monarchy and aristocracy and all the trimmings that go along with them, are best seen, perhaps, as a kind of smoke-screen, obscuring the real struggle.

However, there can be no doubt that the battle was joined in Geoffrey Trease's *Bows against the Barons* (1934) in which Dickon, having killed one of the king's deer, sets off hoping to join Robin Hood in Sherwood Forest. In the forest, he sees a handless corpse hanging from a tree: 'Once it had been a man, whose only crimes had been that he was not born rich and noble, and that he had stolen rather than starve. Now he was a scarecrow to frighten others who might rebel, "forest fruit" for the hirelings of the rich to laugh at.' Dickon eventually makes contact with Robin, who reproves him: 'All right, don't call me

"Sir". We're all equal in Sherwood—comrades.' Soon Dickon realises 'that it was true what these men were saying, that the King and the barons were equally useless to the people.'

Trease's second book, *Comrades for the Charter* (1934) is just as uncompromising as regards its class stance and the unavoidable violence of the conflict. At the outset, the tone is immediately established: 'Dark and sombre . . . was the year 1839. Dark with poverty and misery of the people, starving upon tiny wages to make a few rich men even richer, toiling for as many as sixteen hours a day so that those few rich men might sit idle.' The author even makes reference to 1926, 'when the [Welsh] valleys, which were no longer any use for farming, were no good for mining either—like oranges, sucked dry by the capitalists and thrown aside'. Of Tapper, the finely-drawn Chartist agitator, Trease writes, 'It was obvious that he hated bloodshed, but was being forced to advise it because the Government would take notice of nothing else.' Tapper himself states, 'The capitalists will hang on to the last ditch . . . They'll beat us by the law if they can, and if not, then with shot and shell. They won't give up their soft lives and their riches just because we vote or sign a petition.' The ending is similar in tone to that of *Bows against the Barons*—Tapper tells Owen and Tom, the boys, after the failure and massacre at Newport: 'It's never over . . . Never over. Not until all over the world the peoples are free. You mustn't think of this as just an odd adventure in your lives. It's part of the great war—the only war that was ever worthwhile—the war of the workers against those who've stolen the world!'

Both of these novels, though there's a small degree of coincidence and improbability in the first, are well written and constructed, with a fine sense of drama and suspense.

This same author, in 1953, had published *The Seven Queens of England* with a frontispiece showing 'Her Majesty Queen Elizabeth II at the first Trooping the Colour ceremony after her accession.' Apart from the fact that he has here followed a path similar to that of many writers who came to prominence in the thirties, and, indeed, before and since, we are confronted with something of a literary conundrum which is only borne out by looking at some of Trease's later work, such as *A Thousand for Sicily* (1964), in which he manages to be quite boring, as well as politically short-sighted, with nothing more than the odd gesture in the direction of progressivism. It was, in fact possible to see how things were developing much earlier. In 1940, a significant date in itself, perhaps, Trease's *Cue for Treason* was published, a story set in Elizabethan times, in which the boy narrator, Peter, who goes to the grammar school and comes of 'yeoman' stock which held land from the crown, eventually joins the secret service of the queen. At a critical juncture in the story, Peter tells himself: 'If I gave up now . . . the Queen would be murdered and the Kingdom thrown into anarchy. Thousands of Englishmen would die in the quarrel.'

A great fear of chaos is shown in the novel and, while the

conspirators are noblemen, there's nothing remaining of the sympathetic orientation towards ordinary people which marked Trease's first two books. On the contrary, in *Cue for Treason* four villainous miners are introduced and there is, as well, a reference to a 'drunken German miner . . . jabbering his foreign lingo'. It's perhaps significant that, as far as coincidence and realism go in the structure of the story, this novel is much inferior to Trease's first two works.

For some kind of resolution of Trease's political development, or lack of it, we have to go to his autobiography, called, appropriately, *A Whiff of Burnt Boats.* In it, he describes how, after remarking that even Robin Hood was not allowed to be an ordinary working man but had to be the Earl of Huntingdon, he approached the left-wing publisher, Martin Lawrence, with the idea for *Bows against the Barons.* Trease records that they were delighted with it and, after sampling, eventually published it. After *Comrades for the Charter,* Trease, having, as he admitted, got his foot on the ladder, decided that he 'was not helped by [his] publishers' reputation as specialists in Left-wing literature' so 'we agreed amicably that I should do better to seek my fortune elsewhere', although he remarks that most of the established publishers of junior books 'had a far less generous attitude to their writers'. Trease, by this time, had attended Labour Party meetings and, earlier but without, apparently, any very deep sense of commitment, had worked at Kingsley Hall for a time in a do-gooding, petit-bourgeois, 'humanitarian' kind of way. He apparently never saw leaving his publisher as a question of principle, nor the hack and unethical work he'd done before and continued to do afterwards: puff advertising articles; articles under pseudonyms for religious magazines, even articles for the motoring press, although he couldn't drive a car. Almost scenting criticism, he comments, 'All this was not as unprincipled as it sounds. I never wrote anything against my conscience. I merely packaged my material to suit the customer.' So, we got *The White Nights of St Petersburg* from Trease in 1967 and *The Runaway Serf* in 1968. These show the same sympathies as his first two books. The time, presumably, was ripe again. He had re-packaged *Bows against the Barons* when it was re-issued in a new edition in 1966: 'workers' became 'peasants' or 'neighbours'; everywhere the word 'comrade' was replaced by something else or left out; and Chapter VIII, 'Hammers and Sickles' was retitled 'Friends in Need'. Perhaps this was in line with the dislike for propaganda and the 'passion for objectivity' which Trease, in *A Whiff of Burnt Boats,* says he'd been developing over the years. From this autobiography, a picture emerges of a strange, rather naive, somewhat self-centred person (even his wife remains a very shadowy figure in the background) with little in the way of principles or convictions. He rather writes as an actor acts, taking on different roles, as required.

**Anne Wood**

SOURCE: "Historical Novels—The Hardest Things to Sell?," in *Books for Your Children,* Vol. 17, No. 2, Summer, 1982, pp. 4–5.

Children it seems don't read historical fiction. We are told that publishers find it very hard to sell. Children, that is, in general. Particular children always have, and given encouragement many more would do so. Geoffrey Trease has been writing historical stories for children since 1933 and quietly revolutionised the genre. . . .

Independently Geoffrey Trease came to the conclusion in 1933 that something real could be made of the children's historical story. What about his own home territory of Nottingham for example? Sherwood Forest would have been a grim place in January and Robin Hood's men must have had a desperate struggle against feudal authority. So in 1934 *Bows against The Barons* was published, a first-rate adventure story that nevertheless was true to history despite its socialist leanings. He knew that archaic dialogue put many children off historical fiction. "I did not know that, as I set my Sherwood outlawas talking like ordinary human beings, Robert Graves was simultaneously doing the same with his Romans in *I Claudius.*"

*Bows against The Barons* was a breakthrough, the start of a tradition maintained by Geoffrey Trease but influencing countless other writers. . . .

I have just re-read *Cue For Treason* first published in 1940. Despite one or two convenient twists of plot—two boys, one of them a girl in disguise, seeking work as players in Elizabethan London just happen to be befriended by a rather avuncular Shakespeare for example—it is still a superb children's book. Forty-two years on, Geoffrey Trease would be more subtle but he could not improve the thrill of the first sentence's opening:

> "I asked, weren't we taking the pistol, or anyhow the long, murderous looking pike which has hung across our broad kitchen chimney ever since I can remember?"

The craftsman in the author knows that children deserve and demand a compulsive opening.

Intelligent children who enjoy adventure stories will thrive on a diet of Geoffrey Trease and through their imaginative response to the stories will develop a sense of history. There are also two other outstanding bonuses for Trease readers. One is the immense amount of scholarly research that underpins the cracking good story in every case; though this is never obvious [as the author notes in *Old Writers and Young Readers*]:

> "Research is one of the joys of writing for children but it also has its perils, for too much is as bad as too little. The writer must be aware of falling in love with charming period details that tickle his own adult taste. He must resist the temptation to 'work them in' when they do not further the action and will only slow it down."

The second is the loving realisation of places. Langdale and the Cumbrian Fells are so real in *Cue for Treason* that children could trace the steps of the fictional Elizabethan spies as though they had truly existed. Here is where the exhausted boy-hero swam Ullswater. Here is where he used the last of his strength to topple his would-be murderer off Helvellyn. This wonderfully warm sense of the atmosphere of places is one of the hallmarks of Geoffrey Trease whether he is writing of England, Italy or Russia.

"Children need to discover the treasure under their feet and to gaze on far horizons."

Sometimes when a writer has been a feature of a particular literary scene for a long time he himself can become *"treasure under the feet"* overlooked too often in favour of newer talent. Children's books now have to compete for children's time. It would be a pity therefore if parents and teachers overlooked the opportunity of putting a Geoffrey Trease historical novel in the way of a responsive child. *Cue for Treason* is still a good starting point around the age of ten. . . .

Geoffrey Trease has become a classic writer for children in his own lifetime and it would be a pity if the very stature of his work eclipsed the fact that there are few authors whose novels read so well aloud either at home, on holiday or in the classroom.

### Margery Fisher

SOURCE: "Making Room for the Heroine," in *The Bright Face of Danger*, The Horn Book, Inc., 1986, pp. 228–45.

That most urbane and civilised of innovators, Geoffrey Trease, has shown the way [to include heroines in historical fiction] with his adventuring girls. Their ultimate source might be none other than Shakespeare; they have the gallant gaiety of a Rosalind, the quick wit and flexible mind, the candour of speech and the forthright attitude to life. So that they may enter upon adventures on equal terms with boys, Geoffrey Trease has chosen periods and places where girls could expect to be educated as thoroughly as boys and where a literate society could allow him to give intellectual bite to his tales. The attitude implied towards girls is part of the wider theme of all his work. Whether he sets his story in Renaissance Italy, Tudor England, revolutionary Russia or the European theatre of Garibaldi's campaigns, he promotes a silent but forceful argument for the pursuit of freedom and a liberal outlook. His youthful characters enter upon adventure with a certain idealism added to their instinct for new, active and exciting events.

Trease's approach may be conveniently illustrated in two stories linked neatly though not formally in sequence, *The Hills of Varna,* published in 1948, and *The Crown of Violet,* which appeared four years later. A Yorkshire lad studying in Oxford early in the sixteenth century accepts a mission from Erasmus, who has received news of a lost Greek play, an Aristophanean piece called 'The Gadfly', which exists in a single copy in a monastery by Lake Varna in Dalmatia. At seventeen Alan is no firebrand, though he has been rebuked by his master for settling an argument by violence; as he says, he may love the new learning but he craves action as well as books. To journey through unknown, potentially dangerous lands is a tempting prospect and so is the incentive that unless the unique manuscript is put in the hands of somebody who will give it to the world, in the original and also in translation, the play could well vanish into the private and exclusive library of a wealthy Italian nobleman. The plot is as close to our own times as it is appropriate for the period of the Renaissance and the selection of characters (the lively, resourceful student, the arrogant Duke of Malfetta and his hired bravoes, the liberal-minded printer Aldus Manutius) suits the plot of the book as neatly and naturally as it suits its period.

Skilfully chosen for her role, the heroine Angela d'Asola, Aldus's niece, has grown up with books, languages and a free discussion of social and abstract ideas; she is well able to hold her own in argument with Alan when the disconcerted youth, set on the way from Venice in a trading ship, finds that the girl has stowed away and intends to accompany him. She argues for her rights:

> 'I don't know how girls behave in England—judging by the way you talk sometimes, I wonder if you keep 'em shut up, like the Turks . . . Well, Italy's different. Girls go to school like boys, they learn the same things, and when they grow up they're fit to *do* the same things. It isn't just that we can hold our own with you at Greek and Latin . . . Italian girls have done other things—they've led armies, they've governed provinces . . .'

When Alan offers his own ignoble but characteristic counterargument:

> 'It's not what God intended for women. They should stick to their proper job. All this is sure to make them unfit for it. It'll make them mannish—they'll be growing beards next . . .'

she makes it clear that she has no intention of de-feminising herself, although she has suitably assumed masculine dress for the adventure. Her straight look at arranged marriages leaves the astonished Alan in no doubt that she will accept social convention, when the time comes, and will see to it that she has her own way when it is important that she should.

Matching her companion in courage, in physical endurance and in ingenuity, Angela gently corrects Alan's somewhat limited views of life when the opportunity arises; and when, after escaping more than once from the Duke's men and making a bargain for the play, they lose it at the last moment to the enemy, it is her practical wit that perceives how they can reverse their fortunes. Through their return journey they have read, acted and enjoyed 'The Gadfly' and are well able to dictate the whole work to Aldus's secretaries, and Angela boldly faces the Duke with the argument that as the play *will* be printed, he might as well allow them to borrow the original to correct any errors that might have crept in. All through the tale Angela has behaved not as a hoyden but as a capable, intelligent girl.

The imaginary Greek play was too good a subject to squander on one book, and Geoffrey Trease returned to it in *The Crown of Violet,* ingeniously explaining its provenance while creating another boy-girl partnership in a challenging enterprise. Set in Athens just before 400 BC, when Socrates was exposing social evils and the Theatre Festival was promoting magnificent plays, the story exploits unashamedly the familiar sequence of coincidence and luck, lurking and overhearing, with which the young in fiction expose villainy, in this case through a plot against the State initiated by a vicious, rich aristocrat and sundry foreign associates. A good deal is demanded of the reader in accepting that a boy of fourteen or so could write a comedy good enough to be entered for the annual competition, even though Alexis is given a suitable background—a good education provided by a well-to-do father and an artistic great-uncle willing to put the play forward in his name and find the necessary sponsor to pay for actors, costume and so on.

If Alexis is a peg to hang a story on, rather than an individual, the heroine amply makes up for this. Corinna enjoys a social freedom denied to those respectable girls of Alexis's class whom he would be expected to meet in his private life, because she has not had an enclosed Athenian upbringing. She has travelled widely with her mother, has lived in Syracuse and Massilia, and now has her home in an inn where she is accustomed to meet all kinds of people and to look after herself; although her mother insists on good behaviour, she allows her to wander alone outside the city, and Alexis's first meeting with her is on a hillside where she is playing a flute and is unperturbed at being accosted as a nymph by two schoolboys. When through plausible accidents she and Alexis become aware of the plot being directed by Hippias, she is ready to play her part and at one moment rescues Alexis from being caught by the enemy, but when in order to act the spy, she agrees to attend a crucial dinner-party as a flute-girl and dancer, she takes a naturally feminine view of the situation:

> Some of her self-confidence faded as the week went by. She hated the thought of showing herself off as a public entertainer. Sometimes she went hot and cold, imagining the crowd of guests, the way they would stare and pass personal comments without troubling to lower their voices. She had not spent her whole childhood in common taverns without learning something of life, and her whole nature revolted against the uglier side of it.

> Only her pride stopped her from backing out. She would go through with the plan, she told herself, but, oh! how glad she would be when it was over.

Without pressing emotion too far, Geoffrey Trease allows his heroine more than one side to her character and her good-natured, mature, humorous view of life enlivens the story. Placing Corinna in a section of society where she could reasonably engage in an adventurous move against villainy without sacrificing her honour or her charm as a girl, he puts the final touch to his portrait of her with a very Shakesperean dénouement when it is discovered that she is not after all the daughter of stout Gorgo but of none other than Conon, Alexis's reclusive sponsor, having been exchanged for a boy baby at birth to satisfy his desire for an heir. The rather melodramatic ending does not alter the fact that Corinna, as heroine of a junior adventure, has refreshed its fairly predictable course by her gaiety and her good sense.

Many more of Trease's tales owe their sparkle to heroines of spirited intelligence. In *Popinjay Stairs,* for example, Deborah Fane wins a reputation as a playwright in the early years of the Restoration (though prudently offering her work under the pseudonym Nicholas Arden, to suit the conventions of her day), while a young American travelling abroad with considerable independence expresses in emphatic terms her admiration for the prisoner on Elba and her scorn for British phlegm, in *Violet for Bonaparte.* Judicious compromise leaves Caterina Spinelli safely confirmed in her proper status as a marriageable girl, in *Horsemen on the Hills,* though her education with boys of her own age and the freedom of her kind in Italy in the 1440s help her to play her part in countering the plotting of a rival prince against her father; and Amoret Grisedale, the attractive young heroine of another disguise-adventure (*Mandeville*) ably justifies her claim that girls can endure hardship and outwit enemies as well as boys, when she slips neatly and uninvited into an Italian journey to buy pictures for Charles I. Moreover, her sympathy for Zorzi, a talented dwarf trapped in servitude to a degenerate Italian nobleman, is as emotional as it is practical; there is never any doubt that she is a true member of her sex, and when it comes to a fight for life against their enemies, her weapon is a cauldron of boiling stew where her fellow-adventurer, a lively lad from the London streets, relies on the more orthodox sword. In his unassertive, percipient way, Geoffrey Trease has effectively proved that when it comes to adventure, heroines have as much to contribute as heroes have—but in their own way.

**Marcus Crouch**

SOURCE: "Geoffrey Trease—A Celebration," in *The Junior Bookshelf,* Vol. 53, No. 4, August, 1989, pp. 151–53.

11th August 1989 is the eightieth birthday of that pioneer of the 'new' children's book, Geoffrey Trease. With another book to his credit recently, (*A Flight of Angels,*) he must surely have the longest unbroken career among children's writers. . . . After a spectacular debut in 1934 a steady flow of books has come from his resourceful and energetic pen. The present score, if my calculation is correct, is 105 books including plays and translations, of which 83 are for children; not a world record for productivity but, bearing in mind that he did not start until he was 25, evidence of phenomenal activity.

Trease began with a big bang. *Bows against the Barons* was a new kind of book from a new writer and from a publisher (Lawrence & Wishart) better known for political polemics than tales for young readers. Robin Hood, the hero of Trease's story, had a message for British readers in the hungry 'Thirties, and in delivering it the writer deliberately broke with the tired traditions of 'juvenile' fiction. *Bows against the Barons* was a landmark in fictional historical writing, and from it stem not only Trease's later and more sophisticated work but also that of every other writer in this area of fiction. This is not to say that it was an outstandingly good book. Black-and-white values were stated crudely, and the writing had no great stylistic distinction. Trease stood well to the Left politically—which of us didn't in those days?—and his eagerness to put over his point was much stronger than his sense of craftmanship. He was soon to make similar points with much greater subtlety, in *In the Land of the Mogul* (1938) and *Cue for Treason* (1940), in both of which he drew valid comparisons between the past and present ills.

The War then intervened, and Trease had other preoccupations, frankly and amusingly detailed in the second volume of his autobiography, *Laughter at the Door* (1974). After his return to civilian life his work widened in scope and strengthened in concentration. The late 'Forties represent perhaps the peak of his achievement, in books like *Trumpet in the West* (1947) which grimly contrasts the legalized brutality which followed Monmouth's Rebellion with the elegance and refinement represented by Purcell's music, and *The Hills of Varna* (1948), an adventure story of the Renaissance in which the action springs not from war and violence but from an intellectual quest, the search for a classical manuscript.

At the same time Trease, who earlier had experimented briefly and with no great success with a modern setting, turned to an overtly contemporary theme in *No Boats on Bannermere* (1949). He followed this with several other **'Black Banner'** stories pursuing the fortunes of the same group of young people at school and in their social lives. In these he challenged comparison with Ransome, even to the extent of trespassing in Ransome's own Lake District. Like Ransome's, his characters were not static but grew from book to book, and like Ransome he paid close attention to the mechanics of the stories. It would not be profitable to press the comparison further; Trease was no Ransome in style or in philosophy.

He returned, perhaps with relief, to historical themes. From a long list of books from the 'Fifties and 'Sixties one might single out the King Alfred story *Mist over Athelney* (1958) and a typical Treasean treatment of the outbreak of the French Revolution in *Thunder of Valmy* (1960). There followed two excellent accounts of Garibaldi's struggle for Italian independence, *Follow My Black Plume* (1963) and *A Thousand for Sicily* (1964). My personal favourite among the books of this period—perhaps my absolute favourite after *The Hills of Varna*—is *The Red Towers of Granada* (1966) which contains a sympathetic and convincing portrait of Edward I's Con-

sort, Queen Eleanor, and pays tribute to the scientific skills of the despised Moors in Spain.

At the height of his post-war creativity Trease wrote *Tales out of School* (1949), the first extended attempt in this country to set standards in the writing of children's fiction. In this small and influential book—later revised and expanded—he challenged all our preconceptions. The criteria which he here set out and argued with much vigour and humour are still valid, although they have been violated in much of Trease's own work as well as that of most of his contemporaries and successors. In *Tales out of School* Trease for the second time in his career set up a landmark. We have had an awful lot of words—I use the word 'awful' with care—on this subject since, and I for one look back with much affection and gratitude to this fresh and direct statement of basic values.

Trease's activities have not been exclusively literary. He is an excellent and popular speaker, and one with a rare gift for making contact with teenage audiences. He has been a powerful advocate of the rights of his fellow professionals, for many years a member of Council of their official body, the Society of Authors. Outstandingly he is the complete professional and master of his craft.

In 55 years of writing Trease has won no major literary award in this country. This has, I think, nothing to do with his occasional advocacy of unpopular causes. Rather it is that, while he has maintained over all those years a consistent standard of performance, he has rarely—perhaps never—risen above that standard. Looking through the long list of his publications one sees many familiar titles which call up pleasurable memories, none which possesses that elusive, indefinable but unmistakably quality of magic. Trease tells a good story skilfully, but his plots are seldom satisfactory. He seems consumed with the need to keep the pressure up, piling incident upon incident. Then, although he is most conscientious in developing his characters, ensuring that they react consistently to the pressure of circumstances and to their own natures, he has not, to my knowledge, created one entirely memorable character, one who continues to exercise the reader's imagination after the book has come to its appointed end. That, I suppose, is the ultimate test of a writer's achievement, that he has added to the International Gallery of Fiction an unforgettable portrait.

Still, if we were to press this criterion to its conclusion, the number of really great writers, for adults or children, would be small indeed. Geoffrey Trease has, over a long life, given much pleasure to readers of several generations, opening their eyes to past and present and enabling them to recognise relevant and important parallels between their situation and that of people long dead. We all, whether we are aware of it or not, see history through clearer, less prejudiced eyes because of his achievement. For this enlightenment, and for much joy gained through his exuberant story-telling, we say 'Thank you, and a very happy birthday, Geoffrey Trease'.

## Chris Powling

SOURCE: "Authorgraph No. 84," in *Books for Keeps,* No. 84, January, 1994, pp. 12–3.

Geoffrey Trease has never stuck to the rules. A 'strong awareness of his readers' says Margaret Meek in an early monograph 'has made him an innovator in ways that are often overlooked'.

From his very first book, *Bows against the Barons* (1934) with its portrayal of Robin Hood as a revolutionary figure, he challenged received opinion about historical fiction for children. Later books, *Cue for Treason* (1940) for instance, established another of his trademarks—strong female characters—long before the imperatives of Political Correctness. Similarly, his **'Bannermere'** books in the 1950s did much to transfer the school story from independent to state establishments. More recently, books like *Song for a Tattered Flag* (1991), a vivid account of the last days of Ceaucescu's Rumania, have reminded us that contemporary political events can provide appropriate material for children's fiction.

In short, the career of Geoffrey Trease so far—60 years long and 104 books wide—demonstrates that writing for children about public issues can be consistent with integrity, with artistry and with a willingness to allow young readers to think for themselves.

He can also paint a scene in swift, sharp strokes:

> 'All the way down to the bridge the river was dotted with lighters and wherries transporting fugitives and their chattels to safety. The houses built along the northern end of the bridge were burning. Much of Thames Street, along which Hugh had walked only a few hours before, was now on fire. But the wind had veered. The advance of the flames along the riverside seemed to be slowing down. The conflagration was wheeling away and roaring into the heart of the City.
>
> Conspicuous among the humbler craft was the royal barge, which came surging grandly past them on its way back to Whitehall. The tall figure of the King was unmistakable as he stood talking with his brother, pointing excitedly towards the bank.
>
> "Seeing for themselves—at a safe distance," said Grandfather tartly.'

Actually, even this latest book, *Fire on the Wind,* is something of a departure. At first, he wasn't much attracted by his publisher's suggestion of a book on the Fire of London. 'All my books are about human conflict. I'm never very interested in natural disasters—I'm sorry about them but you can't *do* anything, really. But I said I'd read around it and think . . . and eventually I saw how to do it in my own way. By focusing on the book trade, it became sympathetic to me and delighted her because she said "Even the reps will have to read this!"'

It's easy to see why this amuses someone who's lived on the earnings from his books all his professional life.

Professional, in fact, describes his approach to writing exactly. Since his much-loved wife Marian died in 1989, after 56 years of marriage, he's lived with his daughter Jocelyn in Bath—but in a separate apartment that allows him the conviviality and fun of family life, along with the privacy an author needs. His rooms are as neat and orderly as Geoffrey Trease himself and just as work-oriented: the sitting-room bookshelves offer row after row of titles in a variety of languages, but with only one name on the spine. It's a reminder that from his very first book, which sold 100,000 copies in Soviet Russia, his appeal has been international.

His workroom is where he looks most at home, though. Here, from the position of the typewriter (manual, his seventh in a working lifetime) to the reference volumes on diet, on costume and on a diversity of historical settings, everything is ergonomic—and already set up for this interview. The day-bed is spread with articles, documents and memorabilia. Whatever the occasion, Geoffrey Trease is always well-prepared and appreciates it if others are, too.

So where did it all begin? Was his childhood, as the third of three sons in the family of a Nottingham wine-merchant, especially bookish? 'Not really. I read what my elder brothers preferred and that was always adventure. I remember the Chatterbox volume of 1914 when I was barely five . . . and Ballantyne, Henty, and Gordon Stables. No fantasy, no nonsense. I never read the best things till later—Ainsworth instead of Scott, for instance.' What he loved was *stories*. 'I don't know where the itch to tell a story came from but the fact that I could not write shows how early it was. My father came home with a wine-and-spirit trade desk diary for the year, which he never used, and said "you have this, kipper, to scribble in" and scribble I did—I can see myself, still, sitting in the corner of the room scribbling away and muttering the narrative under my breath.'

Once he could write, his grasp of a strong opening sentence was immediate. Compare this, for example—

> 'Crash! The captain's head struck the deck.'
>
> (Geoffrey Trease, aged 7, starting the first story he can remember)

with this

> 'Crack! The long whip curled round his shoulders, burning the deck under his ragged tunic.'
>
> (Geoffrey Trease, aged 25, starting *Bows against the Barons*)

or this

> 'It was fun at first. The gnawing fear came later . . .'
>
> (Geoffrey Trease, aged 78, starting *Tomorrow is a Stranger*).

The storytelling itch was well established. By the age of 13 when, as a reward for his scholarship to Nottingham High School, he chose his first typewriter instead of the bike or cricket bat offered by his father. And it was certainly his desire 'to be a writer not a learned professor' which led to him giving up another scholarship, this time in Classics to Queen's College, Oxford, when he was 20.

Brief periods as a social worker, a journalist and a schoolmaster followed, till—newly married at 25 and occupying a rent-free flat in the basement of a friend's elegant town house in Bath—he sent off a proposal to a publisher for a book about the *real* Robin Hood. The response was immediate . . . and the rest, as they say, is history.

But not entirely historical novels. Only the intervention of Adolf Hitler, perhaps, blocked a promising career as a dramatist when *Colony,* his play for adults, was withdrawn from London's West End on the outbreak of war. Subsequently, he was called up to the Army Education Corps and service in India. Like the 16 other works he's written for adults (travel, autobiography and novels), it's a reminder of just how versatile Geoffrey Trease is—of his ability to write well in almost any form, including the scripts for radio and, later, television he wrote as occasion demanded when the war was over.

His approach to writing, in fact, is inherently dramatic as he acknowledges in one of his autobiographical pieces:

> 'In planning a play I had learned the value of deciding first upon the ending, that all important final curtain which sends the audience streaming out, satisfied and exhilarated, into the night . . . and so, backwards, step by step, to the beginning of the scene, and similarly backwards, scene by scene, act by act, to the beginning of the play itself. The method worked just as well with a novel, especially one with a strong storyline of adventure or mystery. I still plan my books like that, the closing chapter first, then backwards, episode by episode to the opening, until I have a firmly linked storyline of perhaps twenty chapters, most of them with their own dramatic climax (like the drop of a curtain ending the scene) to make the reader turn the page and hurry on to the next.'

Of course, the more successful an author is, so other demands on his time multiply. In Geoffrey's case, true to his principle of never writing about a country he doesn't know at first hand, there was much foreign travel. Also there were letters from readers to answer, his work on the Council of the Society of Authors and an increasing number of speaking engagements as a pioneer of what has come to be known as Writers-in-School. He enjoyed it all enormously but was always happy to return to The Croft, in the Malvern Hills, which was the family home for more than 30 years.

Then again, there was research to be done—with a fastidious readership to satisfy. When in *Mist over Athelney* (1958) he described a hermit settling down to a rabbit stew, a 10-year-old from Inverness wrote him an indignant letter protesting that there were no rabbits in En-

gland during the time of the Danish invasion. 'I sent him my apologies and a signed copy of the book. Since then I gather rabbit bones have turned up on Anglo-Saxon archaeological sites.' Mind you, he had his expert admirers, too. His description of the details of Queen Anne's obstetric history was queried by Sir Charles Trevelyan with his brother, G M Trevelyan, author of *The Age of Queen Anne.* From the Master's Lodge at Trinity College, Cambridge, came the reply 'Haven't the faintest idea . . . but, if Trease says so, he must be right'.

His commitment to historical fact remains as firm as ever. For all his sympathy with the Left, he refuses to doctor the evidence. 'I'm all in favour of race and gender equality . . . but I do object to any distortion of history. The fact that people in the past, even heroes, may have had views of which we disapprove strongly nowadays may lead you to tone something down . . . if you let your young hero treat animals, for instance, as he might easily have done 500 years ago, you'd immediately forfeit all sympathy on the part of the reader. But you can't *disavow* history or alter it as if these things had never been.'

So, having remained popular and celebrated throughout six decades of shifting taste and ideology, has he any advice for today's would-be writers for children? He ponders this for a while, then says, 'my general advice, which I'd have given at any time, is to make sure of an alternative career. Only when your part-time writing is doing so well that your salaried work is an intolerable interruption, should you give up the latter.'

Sound words . . . except, of course, they don't apply to Geoffrey Trease himself. When I pointed this out he smiled broadly and, with a maverick glint in his eye, said 'Ah yes . . . but I break all my own rules, you see'.

---

## TITLE COMMENTARY

### BOWS AGAINST THE BARONS (1934; revised edition, 1966)

**Geoffrey Trease**

SOURCE: "Bargain Basement," in *A Whiff of Burnt Boats,* Macmillan and Company Ltd., 1971, pp. 144–47.

While in London I had come across a book translated from the Russian, *Moscow Has a Plan,* in which a Soviet author brilliantly dramatised for young readers that first Five-year Plan which had already captured the imagination of the adult world. I did not want to write books like that, I could not, but Ilin's had planted a time-bomb in my mind which now suddenly exploded into questions and ideas. Why were all our own children's books still rooted in the pre-1914 assumptions which serious adult literature had abandoned? In the boys' adventure story especially there had been no development since my own childhood. Such stories still implied that war was glorious, that the British were superior to foreigners, that coloured 'natives' were 'loyal' if they sided with the invading white man and 'treacherous' if they used their wits to counterbalance his overwhelming armaments. In historical tales the Cavaliers and the French aristocrats were always in the right, no matter what the teachers explained at school, and the lower orders, like the lesser breeds, figured only in one of two possible roles, as bowling mobs or faithful retainers.

'Robin Hood', I wrote a few months later in a Co-operative Society magazine called *Dawn,* 'is about the only proletarian hero our children are permitted to admire.' My use of the word 'proletarian' reveals, incidentally, how slight was my acquaintance with Marxism. 'Yet even he', I continued indignantly, 'is not allowed to remain an ordinary working man! He has to be really Earl of Huntingdon. . . . '

It was in this spirit that I had approached a publishing firm whose sympathies were sufficiently indicated by its list, composed mainly of Marx, Engels, Lenin and contemporary Soviet novels with such alluring titles as *Cement.* Would the firm be interested in a Robin Hood story that would be revolutionary in more ways than one? The response was more than I had dreamed of. By return post the publishers informed me that they had been looking for someone to do this kind of book for a long time. Would I submit a synopsis and three chapters?

I set to work immediately. I had little notion in those days of what historical research was required. I had grown up in the Robin Hood country, nourished on the tradition. What more did I need to know? What, indeed? Some slight notion may be gained just from comparing the description of medieval Nottingham in that first story with the more accurate one I painstakingly built up in *The Red Towers of Granada,* thirty-two years later.

*Bows against the Barons* was, as Margaret Meek has fairly written, 'genuine black-and-white' and I would not quarrel now with the verdict in her Bodley Head Monograph: 'At this time Trease believed that it was his duty to be a propagandist of social and political realism in opposition to those writers who trafficked in improbability. We find his villains capitalist in utterance, and the heroes are the downtrodden proletariat of the thirties rather than twelfth-century peasants, but as an example of shaking up the mixture and telling a clear yarn it has still much to offer.'

The book was accepted on that sample material. Fifteen pounds advance on publication, and a straight ten per cent royalty. . . . I felt I had my foot on the ladder.

It was not on a rung I had expected. My becoming a children's writer was an accident, for it was in politics, not children, that I was then mainly interested. I wrote because there was something I wanted to say, a respectable motive when writing for adults but at that period suspect in a children's author, for we were suffering a reaction against the didactic pieties of the nursery bookshelf in the nineteenth century. I was too close to my own childhood to look back on it with sentimental nostalgia. I never have done since. Nor, while appreciating that children, like puppies and kittens, foals and fawns, possess certain unique attractions of freshness and vitality, have I ever shared the common English view that the young of any species is inherently more interesting and important than the mature. I was never concerned with children as a separate (and in many eyes enviable) race absorbed in a special and limited world of their own, so I could never have written stories for the youngest of all. The older they were, the more they appealed to me. I saw them as adults in the making, moving inexorably forward to a wider world that was, according to the way you looked at it, either their doom or their heritage. Being fundamentally an optimist, I saw it as a heritage, even though, like most inheritances, it brought its problems. I did not want to call to my readers, 'Stay in your magical childhood, you will never have it so good.' My impulse was to beckon them on and shout: 'There is a wider view from the next bend. Come along—it's dangerous, but it's worth it.'

It never occurred to me that I should study my readers' tastes and try to cater for them. With the arrogance of my own age I knew that what mattered was what I wanted to tell them, not what they wanted to hear. Many years later I came across a remark of Arthur Ransome's which showed that, utterly different as our books had been, we had this in common: we both wrote to please ourselves without much regard for the preferences of our public. Clearly such an attitude would not had been tenable if sufficient children were not prepared to take what we offered. But our stories were acceptable, I would guess, not because we studied childish tastes and put in the right ingredients but because some of those tastes had survived, deep down, in our own natures and came out spontaneously in our writing. Books, if they are any good, can be enjoyed on more than one level, and when children single out their reasons for specially loving a story they often pick things that disconcert and disappoint the author, at least until he has learnt to accept the experience as normal.

Thus, at one level, *Bows against the Barons* was written because I wanted to expose even to children the falsity of the romantic Merrie England image. But when I sent my hero stealing shadowlike through the bracken, creeping disguised into the villain's castle, or escaping perilously through the nightmare labyrinth of caves and passages which (I knew) underlay my native Nottingham, I was reliving the fantasies of my own boyhood and enjoying the work on this level, as much as the conscious fulfilment of my social purpose. I was certainly not deliberately sugaring a political pill.

**Margery Fisher**

SOURCE: A review of *Bows against the Barons,* in *Growing Point,* Vol. 5, No. 7, January, 1967, p. 834.

In 1934 Geoffrey Trease took a pioneering stride away from costume-fiction, to show history in the light of our own idiom and as honestly as might be. But though *Bows against the Barons* reacts against Lincoln-greenery, Robin Hood is still champion of poor against rich, peasant against oppressive squire—but in a more purposive, less absurdly romantic way than in many re-tellings for children. Trease's historical novels have changed in many ways in twenty years but they still and always reflect his concern for freedom—freedom to speak, to move about, to change. This is a revised edition of his first book but he has not made drastic alterations: as he says in a preface, he offers this as a youthful work. Simple and active, with his characteristic attention to concrete detail, it reads very well indeed. A village lad, with father away on a Crusade, is trying to support his mother, frustrated by cruel bailiff and grasping priest. Desperate with hunger, Dick kills a deer and has to leave his home. He joins Robin Hood's band and takes part in raids and exploits, sees the hero die, betrayed in the nunnery that took him in, and at last, with Little John, seeks freedom in the Derbyshire hills. A Trease novel nowadays would have less direct propaganda, greater control of plot perhaps, a fuller background, but the fire and conviction of the Garibaldi stories, for instance, are foreshadowed here.

**Ruth Hill Viguers**

SOURCE: A review of *Bows against the Barons,* in *The Horn Book Magazine,* Vol. XLIV, No. 1, February, 1968, pp. 67–8.

The author's first book, published in 1934 . . . , has been brought back into print with only a few minor changes, but with new illustrations [by C. Walter Hodges]. It tells the story of Dickon, a serf who, after killing one of the King's deer, fled to Sherwood Forest where he joined Robin Hood's band and played his part in a major rebellion against the nobles. This new story about Robin Hood, who was Mr. Trease's boyhood hero, attempts to give a truer picture than is gained from legendary accounts of the outlaws in Sherwood Forest. Full of skirmishes and great battles between nobles and serfs—the outlaws giving their support to the common people—the story ends with Robin Hood's death and the determination of his followers to continue working to make his dream of "an England without masters" come true. Although it lacks the skillful plotting and characterization of the author's later books, the story is, nevertheless, far from ordinary and may create a new demand for tales about Robin Hood.

**Margery Fisher**

SOURCE: "Landmarks: Geoffrey Trease *Bows against the Barons,*" in *Classics for Children & Young People,* Thimble Press, 1986, p. 63.

With direct prose and neutral dialogue Trease's narrative slips along easily in intended contrast to the ponderously detailed gadzookeries whose long domination he wanted to change. His first chapter title, 'Merrie England', shows his intention clearly. It opens with a youth suffering the bailiff's whip for a justifiable absence from work in the manorial fields. When Dickon shoots one of the deer plundering his mother's desperately needed cabbages, he takes refuge in Sherwood, becomes a member of Robin Hood's band and sees from the inside the struggle of peasants and poor townsfolk for freedom of speech and a fair reward for toil. He plays a boy's role of lurking and disguise as the castle of a local tyrant is captured and a more ambitious rising against Nottingham is defeated, with the betrayal and death of Robin as a sad ending. The view of Robin Hood as 'a man for the people, against their oppressors', with a vision of an England free from tithes and overlords, fitted the mood of the 1930s just as Trease's uncluttered narrative suited the new direction in writing for children. Trease wrote of this, his first book (for the revised edition of 1966), '. . . if I were writing it now I would write it rather differently', but there is still much virtue in a racy, well-planned tale presenting a legendary hero deduced and developed from the ballads but with a strongly historical bias, seen through the eyes of an idealistic lad. *Bows against the Barons* was truly a landmark in the development of historical stories for the young. Paradoxically its neutral style opened up the way for Rosemary Sutcliff's sensitive use of the heroic mode and Barbara Willard's dialectal speech patterns. Trease's first essay in the genre of historical fiction was a foretaste, and an important one, of the major and continuing contribution he has made over the years.

## COMRADES FOR THE CHARTER (1934)

**Geoffrey Trease**

SOURCE: "A Cottage in the Quantocks," in *A Whiff of Burnt Boats,* Macmillan and Company Ltd., 1971, p. 149.

Though my Robin Hood story would not be published for some months the publishers had encouraged me to begin a second, which they suggested might deal with the Chartist movement. This time, conscious of my own ignorance, I did a good deal of research, carrying armfuls of books from the public library and studying the age-yellowed pages of the *Bath Chronicle* for 1839. The Newport Rising of that year provided the dramatic climax I needed for a children's book, and for the main setting I used the Black Mountains which had so powerfully caught my imagination a few years earlier. Despite my research, however, *Comrades for the Charter* (as its title indicates) carried more than a flavour of twentieth-century politics. It was the easier to fall into anachronism since I had, from the start, set my face against the 'ye olde varlet' type of diction which deterred so many children from reading historical stories. My Sherwood outlaws and now my Chartists conversed in modern English. In this respect I was consciously following Naomi Mitchison, whose novel *The Conquered* I had read at school. My characters, unfortunately, lapsed occasionally into the phraseology of a Communist meeting.

### The Times Literary Supplement

SOURCE: "Fighting for Freedom," in *The Times Literary Supplement,* No. 3687, November 3, 1972, p. 1320.

Hester Burton's *Riders of the Storm* and Geoffrey Trease's *Comrades for the Charter* (the latter first appeared in 1934) share an interest in industrial relations and the rights of man. *Comrades for the Charter* suffers because the Chartist ideals do not blend well with the type of story. The kind of reader who will enjoy galloping over hilltops to intercept the spy will be too dispirited by the lack of success of the campaign. The author is not helped by the facts of history. . . .

### Victor E. Neuburg

SOURCE: A review of *Comrades for the Charter,* in *Children's Book Review,* Vol. II, No. 6, December, 1972, p. 187.

When, by happy chance, this book arrived I read it with nostalgia. As ever—a good story, strong characterisation, beautifully told. After the euphoria, however, slight doubts began to creep in. Was this really the same book as I had read with such pleasure as a boy? The author's note suddenly appeared ominous: 'a little shortening seemed desirable'. In whose interest? Then I recalled Geoffrey Trease, something over twenty-five years ago, speaking to me in rather deprecating terms. I think he was wrong to do so, and believe that his earliest work was his best. It could well have been re-issued without alteration.

Perhaps the whole matter will receive an airing when some future Ph.D. student undertakes one of those monumental studies in futility entitled 'Textual changes in the novels of . . .' In the meantime, such regrets as I have must give way before the sheer delight at seeing *Comrades for the Charter* in print again. A new generation of readers will, I hope, gain as much pleasure from it as I did.

### The School Librarian

SOURCE: A review of *Comrades for the Charter,* in *The School Librarian,* Vol. 20, No. 4, December, 1972, pp. 350, 353.

It is difficult to be objective about a book which one read and greatly enjoyed as a child thirty years ago. There is a simplicity and directness about Geoffrey Trease's early story of the chartist campaigns, which by some will be termed naivety. Moral blacks and whites, however, do not distort this tale of the growing struggle of the work-

ing people for basic human rights throughout Wales and England.

Trease's main strength, of course, is in telling a story—speed, excitement, mystery, all expertly measured out. Through it all comes a feeling for people being manipulated by and reacting against the forces of history.

Educationally the book serves the fundamental purpose of history by helping the reader to a better understanding of the present. Top juniors and younger secondary boys will simply enjoy it as we did.

### A. R. Williams

SOURCE: A review of *Comrades for the Charter,* in *The Junior Bookshelf,* Vol. 37, No. 1, February, 1973, pp. 56–7.

For a book originally published in 1934 *Comrades for the Charter* has certainly worn well if revision has been as slight as the author claims. The Chartist movement in Wales has always received attractive treatment at the hands of historians and authors of historical novels. Trease chooses to begin his story near Crickhowell on the southern fringe of Breconshire and begins the connection with Chartism by sending the 16-year-old Owen Griffiths south towards the pits when he walks out on his miserly farmer-master and runs into, first of all, the fugitive English apprentice Tom Stone, and, eventually, the peripatetic "chemist", John Tapper, undercover agent cum messenger for the Chartist movement. As his assistants the two boys see much of the dangers and disasters of industrial-political action in the South Wales coalfield and country-side. Perhaps the style and the content borrow or presage a touch of hokum from *How Green Was My Valley* and a hint of mannered grimness from *Rape of a Fair Country.* Interesting to reflect that Trease preceded both, the one by five, the other by twenty-five years. Though his novel omits the adult romance of the bigger ones it lays the foundations of intrigue and treachery later developed to the full. It was a good idea to revive the book.

### Peggy Heeks

SOURCE: A review of *Comrades for the Charter,* in *The Use of English,* Vol. 25, No. 1, Autumn, 1973, pp. 53–5.

History is a view of past events, not a card index of them and, just as each age needs to reinterpret the myths which help us to live, so each needs to rediscover its history. When authors set out on man's old search for the significance of the past, the answers they find depend on the questions their own age has inspired: to a large extent historical fiction reflects the period in which it was written more than the period with which it deals. Compare, for example, Rosemary Sutcliff's Civil War story, *Simon,* with Marryat's *Children of the New Forest,* Kingsley's

*Hereward the Wake* with Henry Treece's *Man with a Sword*, or read Geoffrey Trease's reissued **Comrades for the Charter,** written in 1934 when to many young Englishmen Russia seemed a likely saviour of the world. Trease found an ideal theme in the growth of the Chartist movement in Wales in the 1830's, interesting in itself and with obvious application to the days of unemployment and poverty one hundred years later. The opposing sides are overdrawn in a way reminiscent of old Tribune cartoons, where the rich always wore top hats, fat bellies and thick cigars, the workers, rags and bent backs, but the indignation against oppression blows so hot that it still carries the story, keeping us impatient for the next move. Associating past and present does add to the dimensions of the story, as Miller's *The Crucible* and Anouilh's *Antigone* showed, but writers can lead us astray if they search too closely for parallels with the present: the past's pattern never repeats exactly. One wonders if Trease's real concern was to recall nineteenth century freedom fighters or to alert children to the troubles of their own times. Would his story have been more effective set squarely in the depressed Wales of 1930, or would that have been unacceptable in those cushioned Ransome days when the furthest social indignation got was Eve Garnett's *A Family from One End Street,* now read as an amusing family story?

## CUE FOR TREASON (1940)

**Geoffrey Trease**

SOURCE: "The Waiting Time: Cue for Treason," in *Laughter at the Door: A Continued Autobiography,* St. Martin's Press, 1974, pp. 1–10.

One motive for writing juvenile books is to communicate your own enthusiasm. In [*Cue for Treason*] two loves combined to give it life, the Elizabethan theatre and the Cumbrian landscape. I knew Cumberland only from brief walking tours, but I was steeped in Shakespeare and Marlowe. I had acted in them at school, devoured them in print, and seen every possible production from the aged Benson on tour to the young Gielgud at the Old Vic. Of theatrical history, as of social history generally, I knew little. In those days I had none of the books on everyday life, costume, arms, architecture and other essential background knowledge that cram my shelves now. I found

*Trease working at his home in Abingdon, England, after World War II.*

one useful volume on the Elizabethan theatre in the library of the Oxford Union. I had a one-inch map of Cumberland and Bradley's *Highways and Byways,* in which I learned of the Cumbrian 'statesmen', or independent small farmers, with whose struggle against an enclosing landlord the tale begins. I was so ignorant that in the original edition I made him a baronet, twenty years before that rank was created.

Most readers are not, of course, pouncing pedants, though the observant child will detect such errors with immense glee. But, while there is no possible excuse for avoidable inaccuracy, vitality is far more important, and to the end of his days the author must be on his guard against losing it. The more research he does, the more he surrenders to the enchantment of authentic detail, the more he risks slowing down the action. When he finds himself thinking, 'This is marvellous, this is much too good to leave out!' it is time to ask himself, 'But where—*essentially*—does it fit in?' The writer's personal enthusiasm may be the motive power, but it must be controlled like any other engine.

It would be dull, and dangerous, to 'cater' deliberately for the children's own supposed tastes. These are hard to predict even in one's own country and impossible in a remote one. Many years after the writing of this Cumbrian story I met a publisher's representative newly back from west Africa. 'Do you know which of your books they all wanted?' she said. '*Cue for Treason.*' 'Oh,' I said, 'that'll be because I brought in Shakespeare— he's universal.' 'No,' she answered. 'It was because your first chapter has a riot over a land-boundary, and then your heroine runs away from a forced marriage. They said the book was about things that everybody was familiar with.'

I worked on this story in the bleak early months of 1940, and perhaps it gained gusto from the imaginative escape it offered me from the depressing atmosphere of the phoney war. It was much the best children's book I had so far written. Twenty years later Margaret Meek suggested, most generously, that 'with it a new era in the adventure story opened'. If so, the new era very nearly closed again, for by autumn the bombs had begun to fall in earnest. One delayed publication. Then, when I was just basking in the glow of excellent reviews, another destroyed the entire unbound stock in the warehouse. It was more than a year before Blackwell could reprint, but meanwhile the book was taken in America by Vanguard, and I knew its survival was assured.

## May Lamberton Becker

SOURCE: A review of *Cue for Treason,* in *New York Herald Tribune Books,* April 26, 1942, p. 8.

In the course of this rousing adventure story, older children can get an inside view of Shakespeare's own theatrical company in action, and a close-up of the Elizabethan stage in general. It all comes about naturally, in connection with an uprising in the North, one that so belongs to the times that it carries history into a young reader's consciousness.

There was a neighborhood revolt, in the picturesque Lake Country, against the enclosure of common lands by one Sir Philip Morton. When this surly newcomer built a wall, neighbors gathered by night and hurled it down in the accepted method of maintaining their rights. The only protestor recognized was the youth who tells the story: set as a scout to give warning, his green cap had been shot off by Morton's men and identified. Peter's first hideaway was in the midst of a company of strolling players, acting King Richard III in inn yards; he took refuge in the coffin that figures so prominently in that entertainment, and was carried first on to the stage and then by wagon over their route, where on discovery he met Kit, another runaway. This second fugitive was a success in girls parts for reasons Peter soon discovered; when the strollers disbanded the two went to London with a letter of introduction to Burbage and were befriended by Shakespeare himself. There they came upon evidence of a plot against the life of Queen Elizabeth; that brought Peter into the Secret Service and back to Cumberland to a series of sharp fights, till the foul Morton was headed for Tower Hill and the Queen's favor assured to Kit and Peter.

A hearty yarn, without gadzooks language but with excellent characterization, it makes Shakespeare entirely plausible, Burbage convincing, and the glimpse of Elizabeth quite authentic. It follows closely the accepted conventions of historical stories for boys, but girl readers are provided for by a device in disguises that has been popular ever since Shakespeare used it.

## Margery Fisher

SOURCE: A review of *Cue for Treason,* in *Growing Point,* Vol. 4, No. 1, May, 1965, pp. 516–19.

*Cue for Treason* . . . is one of Geoffrey Trease's best stories and I have never known it fail to please. Perhaps this is because he has a confident way of drawing characters we can understand who, all the same, fit properly into their period. This is the story of young Peter Brownrigg, who has to leave his Cumberland home after the village has come to odds with a local landlord who encloses a common grazing meadow. Peter's escape is aided, again, by a travelling acting company—with Trease, a most authentic body of people; and, indeed, the whole adventure that brings Peter on to the stage and gives him temporary employment as one of Cecil's spies is utterly convincing from start to finish. The tale is so well told, in such a rollicking style, that many children as young as eight or nine might take it as a first introduction to that popular branch of literature, the historical novel.

## Margery Fisher

SOURCE: A review of *Cue for Treason,* in *Growing Point,* Vol. 25, No. 3, September, 1986, pp. 4675–76.

Geoffrey Trease's influence on the style and approach of the historical novel is too well known to be more than mentioned here. *Cue for Treason,* first published in 1940, the fifth in what was to be a long line of historical-adventures, has the characteristics still to be found in the Mandeville tales of the 1970's and '80's, especially in the apt choice of period and circumstance. In this brisk, exciting tale of Elizabeth I's reign the author used contrasting scenes in Cumberland and London, Gloriana for pomp and dignity, Burleigh for undercover intrigue and Burbage's company for colour and to explain the contemporary situation of the stage. Young Peter Brownrigg, in hiding after a skirmish against a greedy landowner, and Kit Kirkstone, an heiress escaping from an unwelcome arranged marriage, find acting a refuge and a promising career, though for Kit it is one which public opinion will inevitably force to a conclusion. The triple bluff of a girl acting a boy actor acting female parts is one which Trease was to use more than once, outdoing Shakespeare himself in the twists and deceptions which the device could add to his stories, with the bonus of dramatic irony for the reader, enlightened before most of the characters to the truth.

This is an active, robust tale, with a very practical attention to such details of terrain, buildings and occasion as will make the action believable and easy for young readers of our time to translate from past to present. Peter climbs up to an upper room in one of those high Tudor riverside mansions in London to get back the script of Shakespeare's play of *Henry V* which, in his innocence, he had lent to a yellow-clad gallant in the street purporting to be an enthusiast of the theatre; he climbs by means of daggers inserted, like pietons, in the woodwork—and incidentally, is able to identify conspirators in a plot to assassinate Elizabeth (authentic, in fact, and one of several ways in which the theatre was involved in treason at the time). Later, the boy escapes from his enemies in a daring climb along the Striding Edge on Helvellyn, a fine piece of active description which could belong to any period. Historical novels are supposed in some measure to teach but this particular tale, direct enough in its open narrative style and neutral dialogue for readers as young as nine, conveys fact in a very simple way, using the unsophisticated attitudes of a lad and a girl to set the tone and only now and then indicating important historical issues (in Kit's plight as a marriageable heiress, for instance, or in the dismay they both feel when they realise that the magistrate whose help they have confidently sought is himself on the side of the conspirators). It is a method like that of Edith Nesbit in *House of Arden,* a way of giving the young a sense of period through concrete matters—like the precarious existence of travelling actors, money and food, modes of travel—with historical personages tactfully and sparingly introduced and with the central young hero and heroine left to settle into a tale of national issues which depends most of all on such attributes of youth as untapped courage, a penchant for stalking and hiding based on curiosity, an easy comradeship and uncomplicated loyalty, all of which have validity for any time and place. Parents who enjoyed this spanking tale in their

youth should give their children the chance to do the same.

## TRUMPETS IN THE WEST (1947)

### Virginia Kirkus' Bookshop Service

SOURCE: A review of *Trumpets in the West,* in *Virginia Kirkus' Bookshop Service,* Vol. XV, No. 18, September 15, 1947, p. 504.

A story of the conflict in the life of young Norwood between music, which he was studying with Purcell, and the struggle to maintain the rights of a free Englishman. In the 1680's, the period when this story took place, the struggle of Parliamentary government vs royal despotism, of Popism vs the English church, of Whig vs Tory—was at its decisive height. The Monmouth rebellion had been crushed. The other struggle continued—and nearly cost Jack his life. A well-told story, though the background never quite achieves the vitality it needs.

### Saturday Review of Literature

SOURCE: A review of *Trumpets in the West,* in *Saturday Review of Literature,* Vol. XXX, No. 46, November 15, 1947, p. 56.

In a day when earning a livelihood in music was practically impossible, except for an occasional genlus like Purcell, John Norwood left Somerset for London in the hope of making music his career. It was a turbulent time. James II was ruling as a dictator, but Englishmen did not accept his rule with grace. Factions were constantly struggling to maintain decent human freedom. Jack loved music, but hé loved freedom even more. Before very long he was not only recklessly expressing his political opinions but becoming deeply involved in Whig activities, even to the helping in the invasion of William of Orange.

This is a good, fast-moving tale—well characterized. There is the tense political setting and there is the interesting artistic background of London, with its growing interest in the theatre, with Purcell at the height of his fame and productiveness, and with Christopher Wrenn's genius becoming evident all over England.

### Nash K. Burger

SOURCE: A review of *Trumpets in the West,* in *The New York Times Book Review,* November 16, 1947, p. 5.

England at the time of the Glorious Revolution of 1688 is the background for this entertaining story of four teenagers who go up to London-town to seek a career. Jane to study music; her brother Hubert to be a great soldier in the King's army; Harry to study architecture under Sir Christopher Wren, and Jack to become a composer under the guidance of Henry Purcell. It is an exciting time in

England and these young people are witness to a number of stirring events that have profoundly affected English history. Jack is even a participant; he makes a trip to the Continent and has a part in the coming of William of Orange.

The simple life of English town and village is charmingly pictured, along with historical events and the individual adventures of the characters.

### The Horn Book Magazine

SOURCE: A review of *Trumpets in the West,* in *The Horn Book Magazine,* Vol. XXIV, No. 1, January-February, 1948, pp. 42–3.

Through the experiences of a young English musician in the time of Purcell and Sir Christopher Wren, Geoffrey Trease recreates the tumultuous years following Monmouth's rebellion when Parliamentarians were struggling against the tyranny of James II. Jack Norwood could not drop his right to think for himself at the command of Tory nobility, even when that right endangered his promising career in music. His story has significance for young people today, as it presents vividly certain dramatic scenes in the history of the Englishman's fight against dictatorship. A gripping story.

### THE HILLS OF VARNA (1948; U.S. edition as Shadow of the Hawk)

### Eleanor Graham

SOURCE: A review of *The Hills of Varna,* in *The Junior Bookshelf,* Vol. 12, No. 3, October, 1948, p. 142.

The period is 1509, and the opening scene is brilliantly laid in the Cambridge of that time, with a brawl in a tavern and a flight through the dark, snowy night. Erasmus—a great name to meet casually in such a setting—helps the young student to get away, sends him in search of an ancient Greek manuscript. Apt quotations from Erasmus himself stir the reader to great expectations. By daybreak the student is gone, to cross the Channel and travel right across Europe to rescue—no damsel in distress, but a book, from the monastery in the far-off Balkans.

Strange in 1948 to have such words as these of Erasmus brought back to us: "Why do such foolish names as English and French still exist to keep us separated? . . . The entire world is one common fatherland."

Thus far the book glows—but I came to wish that Mr. Trease had taken to himself the words he quotes from Socrates. "The difficulty, my friends, is not to avoid death, but to avoid unrighteousness: for that runs faster than death." The 'fight to avoid death,' everlasting fights, fisticuffs, intrigues, is what the author has used to whirl the reader onward, but at the cost of that earlier sense of

validity, which is quite lost. The atmosphere becomes twentieth century almost, and it is hard to keep in mind that Yorkshire lad of fifteen, covering the ground laboriously, as he would have to, in 1509, from Cambridge all the way to Albania and beyond. He got the manuscript—stole it—and lost it again; but he and the Italian girl who shares the last part of the journey with him, grew so familiar with the text during the time they had it in their hands, that they were able to recite it to Aldus of Venice, the great printer, so that he was satisfied with their version of it and remarks, "I shall go ahead; have the type set up . . . Then we can run off the edition without wasting any more time." Is it the machinery of today or the patient work of the craftsman of the past which young readers will see behind these words?

### R. C. A. Oates

SOURCE: A review of *The Hills of Varna,* in *The School Librarian and School Library Review,* Vol. 4, No. 4, March, 1949, pp. 229–31.

Morality is not the favourite subject of the modern didactic novelist; he is much more at home teaching us history or small-boat-navigation. Thus Mr. Trease, in *The Hills of Varna,* gives us a lesson on the Renaissance. . . .

Mr. Trease's problem is [that] boys are not predisposed in favour of the Revival of learning. Moreover he makes few concessions to boyish ignorance: he is determined to have Copernicus the subject of a tavern brawl on page 2, but he is careful to add, with an art which conceals its cunning, that Copernicus was a Pole and a new-fangled astronomer. It is likewise with Erasmus who is naturally built up as a Latin-speaking Dutchman of Rotterdam living in Cambridge. Mr. Trease either restrains or explains his history until the very last page when he lets loose a flood of Elizabethan notables. Sometimes his restraint (to the adult ear) creaks audibly: one waits, for example, for the word "palimpsest" on page 182, but it fails to arrive; and in reading of the man who first climbed a mountain for fun, the pedagogic pencil is itching to write "Petrarch" in the margin. The young reader of 13 will be more interested in the adventures of the 15-year-old hero in recovering a Greek manuscript from a remote monastery. The older reader will probably look for some "Test Questions" at the back of the book. Instead he will find a note revealing how much history and how much fiction have gone into the book.

### Virginia Kirkus' Bookshop Service

SOURCE: A review of *Shadow of the Hawk,* in *Virginia Kirkus' Bookshop Service,* Vol. XVII, No. 14, July 15, 1949, p. 362.

Again an action-centered, period-mounted story—this time of the Renaissance—which just brushes in the background and is chiefly concerned with the immediacy of the adventure at hand. Alan Drayton, a pupil of Erasmus and quick with his sword as well as with his wits, undertakes a mission from the master to bring back from a Balkan monastery a rare manuscript of a Greek play. In so doing he runs afoul of the Venetian Duke of Molfetta who wants the manuscript for his own collection, takes on—as a stow-away on the voyage from Venice to Greece—Angela, a young girl, sees their ship set fire by pirates, is attacked by Turks—and the Duke's agents, faces even grimmer experiences in the monastery, secures the manuscript only to lose it to the Duke . . . A good enough story which throws in a smattering of Renaissance learning and color.

### The Horn Book Magazine

SOURCE: A review of *Shadow of the Hawk,* in *The Horn Book Magazine,* Vol. XXV, No. 5, September-October, 1949, pp. 419–20.

The time of this well-developed historical story is the sixteenth century and the scene, opening in England at Cambridge University, moves swiftly to Venice and the Adriatic. The great Erasmus influences events and Aldus Manutius enters into the action. The plot revolves around the recovery of a lost Greek play from a monastery where it is about to be destroyed, and the struggle of two rival book-lovers to gain possession of it. Two young people, English and Italian, are engaged in the daring adventure this calls forth. Careful study has gone into the background of this exciting story.

### Anne Thaxter Eaton

SOURCE: A review of *Shadow of the Hawk,* in *The Christian Science Monitor,* October 27, 1949, p. 11.

*Shadow of the Hawk* is a story of the 16th century. Two young people, one English and one Italian, set out to recover the lost manuscript of a Greek play. Although they are aided and advised by Erasmus and Aldus Manutius, they nevertheless meet with enormous difficulties and dangers that call for quick wits, courage and endurance, before their quest in the face of many odds is successful. A swiftly moving tale, with well-drawn characters and a fascinating background that shows thorough knowledge of the period.

### Louise S. Bechtel

SOURCE: A review of *Shadow of the Hawk,* in *New York Herald Tribune Book Review,* October 30, 1949, p. 8.

This dramatic tale of Europe at the time of the Renaissance has swift action, a thrilling search, fights and hair-breadth escapes. At the same time, it has a background of learning, and offers an unusual introduction to the new thinking of the early sixteenth century through the mind of a young man. Opening in Cambridge with a tavern brawl over the beliefs of Copernicus, it takes the hero to talk with Erasmus, who sends him on a search for a Greek

manuscript. He stays with Aldus, the great printer in Venice, where the shadow of the jealousy of the Duke falls upon him as he starts on his perilous journey.

A disarming postscript tells how much is true in this exciting recreation of a book-world of old, written by a talented young Englishman. Few of its key people come into high-school lessons, but the tale illumines a period of European history which they study. The adventure is perhaps fantastic, but the intellectual background is fascinating.

### *NO BOATS ON BANNERMERE* (1949)

### Eleanor Graham

SOURCE: A review of *No Boats on Bannermere,* in *The Junior Bookshelf,* Vol. 13, No. 3, October, 1949, p. 161.

This is a slight affair, exciting, with a big blustering villain and four bright schoolchildren who bring him to justice. The scene is laid in the Lake District but the local colour is too thin to be very distinctive. There are some refreshing touches as, for instance, a more realistic relationship between Bill and his mother than usually gets into a children's story. There is an interesting picture of a headmaster, and Miss Florey is refreshing too, though not quite so credible, as the new headmistress, lately a distinguished archaeologist in Greece.

The story is told through the mouth of a 14-year old boy which certainly makes for speed and raciness in the telling. Bill himself is alive and vigorous—but then he speaks for himself. The other boy and the girls are less substantial, and Bill's sister bobs up when something is required of her with rather the effect of one of the lesser puppets in a Punch and Judy show. The plot is good as far as it goes but will not stand much probing. As the author could have made a much better book out of the material, I was left wondering what is good enough for children?

### The School Librarian

SOURCE: A review of *No Boats on Bannermere,* in *The School Librarian,* Vol. 5, No. 1, March, 1950, p. 60.

Adventure . . . we must have, and let us have lots of it, with the one proviso that like all true art it shall be, at least, so credible, that we swallow it hook, line and sinker, and like the fish, never realize we are caught till it is too late.

Certainly there are many authors to-day who can cast a prize-winning line. Geoffrey Trease has almost the neatest of any. His *No Boats on Bannermere* runs slickly off the reel and he is too much of an old hand to put everything in but the kitchen stove. So the mystery, graphically told by the young hero, is not too involved and yet keeps the reader guessing. The author could in fact—such is his power over his readers—dare to make his characters more subtle. As it is, the headmaster is eccentric but lovable; the headmistress, attractive and sporty but scholarly; the villain, ill-mannered; mamma, accommodating, and, in short, one has the feeling when reading about them of "I think we've met somewhere before."

### Virginia Kirkus' Service

SOURCE: A review of *No Boats on Bannermere*, in *Virginia Kirkus' Service*, Vol. XXXIII, No. 1, January 1, 1965, p. 9.

*No Boats on Bannermere* . . . is a very British trifle amusingly well-handled by this experienced author. The story is told in the first person by Bill Mellbury who has a talented eye for detail and a sharp pen for word pictures of the adults in his life. The Mellburys inherited a shore front cottage in the north of England. They arrived to find the local squire refusing them the use of the lake and generally behaving like a nay-saying 19th century villain. Bill and his younger sister Susan half teased themselves into believing the old boy was up to something awful and, by George!, if it doesn't turn out to be so. This is an expert variation on the buried treasure routine which has been made to render up some gold for recreational reading.

### Alberta Eiseman

SOURCE: A review of *No Boats on Bannermere*, in *The New York Times Book Review*, April 4, 1965, p. 22.

The British countryside, with its isolated homes, spacious estates and ancestral castles, is an irresistible setting for tales of adventure and mystery. *No Boats on Bannermere* takes place in the North of England, where Bill and Susan Melbury and their mother inherit a lake-shore cottage. The lake itself is off-limits to them: it belongs to the local squire, Sir Alfred, or so he claims. The children's suspicions are immediately aroused by this gentleman's boorish behavior. Bill and Susan track down Sir Alfred relentlessly, aided by two newly acquired friends—of all sleuths—the headmaster and headmistress of their respective schools. The story holds interest and provides some insights into British school life that should entertain American readers.

### Zena Sutherland

SOURCE: A review of *No Boats on Bennermere*, in *Bulletin of the Center for Children's Books*, Vol. XVIII, No. 9, May, 1965, pp. 137–38.

A cracking good story: written with style and humor, having a mystery that four children solve in credible fashion, and constructed with economy and craftsmanship, this tale of four children in an English village is a delight. The characterization is excellent, the portrayal of the headmaster being particularly felicitous. Bill and Susan,

whose mother has inherited a cottage in the village of Bannermere, are treated brusquely by the local squire, another newcomer. Bill is sure that Sir Alfred has a nefarious secret; although his secret isn't what Bill thinks, he has one and Bill and Susan and their friends ferret it out, with an utterly satisfactory ending in which all parties get their just desserts.

### WEB OF TRAITORS: AN ADVENTURE STORY OF ANCIENT ATHENS (1952; British edition as *The Crown of Violet*)

**Naomi Lewis**

SOURCE: "The Cavern and the Castle," in *The New Statesman & Nation*, Vol. XLIV, No. 1126, October 4, 1952, p. 388.

After the first two or three hearty pages, which I take to be a sop to the Philistine reader, I could not but admire *The Crown of Violet*, a rousing yet not insensitive tale set in Athens, about 400 B.C. "There's Xenophon," says our hero, Alexis. "He's a real sport. I don't think he's terribly intellectual though . . . And there's Plato. He's twenty. He's wonderful all-round person . . . etc." There is also Socrates, whose part in the story is more important. For Alexis is something of a rebel, questioning, for instance, the inequality of girls and women and other rigid Athenian assumptions. He is also of a literary turn (though he can ride and race) and sends in a play to the great Drama Festival. I find I have omitted to mention at least three mysteries in the plot, and much other circumstance. Skilful Mr. Trease! He is to be congratulated.

### Bulletin of the Children's Book Center

SOURCE: A review of *Web of Traitors*, in *Bulletin of the Children's Book Center*, Vol. VI, No. 3, November, 1952, p. 28.

A story of political intrigue in Athens during the time of Socrates and of a young boy who uses his ability as a dramatist to plead the cause of the philosopher. The author's use of modern idioms and slang is rather startling at first but since he is consistent in the usage it becomes less noticeable as the story unfolds. The action is swift-paced, the characters are realistically portrayed, and the book provides a good picture of the life of the period.

### Blanche Weber Shaffer

SOURCE: A review of *Web of Traitors*, in *Saturday Review*, Vol. XXXV, No. 46, November 15, 1952, p. 64.

Alexis, son of Leon, is just out of school and expects great things from his new freedom. Though brought up in the strict discipline of a prosperous home in fourth-century Athens, he is a natural rebel. His critical mind is stirred by his friendship with the alien girl Corinna and by listening to Socrates teaching in the market place. One of these meetings sets Alexis to writing a comedy ridiculing conceited and superstitious people but showing Socrates as he really is—full of humor and a defender of the truth.

Alexis is not only a lover of words and ideas, but a courageous young patriot who while writing a play discovers a plot to overthrow the Athenian democracy. A Spartan code message, a sinister stranger, a mysterious flute player, other unexpected people and happenings lead the reader from one excitement to another in this fascinating tale. It has a rich texture because two equally strong threads are constantly interwoven—the story of Alexis developing into a playwright and the liberation of his beloved Athens from the Spartan dictatorship. And what a setting! Athens, "the city of the violet crown," rises before the reader's eyes, with its theatre festivals, its torch races, and its glorious beauty. Alexis' family and friends come to life: his stern father and gentle mother, his cautious and proper friend Lucian, the unpredictable Corinna, and Uncle Paintbrush, a character who seems to come straight from a comedy of Aristophanes. Only a writer with a deep love of Athens could have produced a story in which the characters and the setting are so perfectly integrated. Because it is so true and so convincing and because the love of freedom is in the minds and hearts of all men today, this is a story for our time. Geoffrey Trease, a graduate of Oxford University, has written his book in the very spirit of Oxford.

### Learned T. Bulman

SOURCE: "Trouble in Athens," in *The New York Times Book Review,* Part II, November 16, 1952, p. 14.

With his usual lively style Geoffrey Trease brings Athens alive for young people much as he did the Elizabethan era in *Cue for Treason.* In this tale young Alexis' thirst for knowledge brings him to Socrates and his circle. To prove to his father that Socrates is a great thinker, Alexis writes a comedy and enters it in the Drama Festival. Inadvertently he also discovers a plot to overthrow Athens, but with the help of the mysterious girl Corinna, he is able to bring the conspirators to justice. A stepping stone to more adult material, *Web of Traitors* is a good mixture of information and excitement.

### *New York Herald Tribune Book Review, Part II*

SOURCE: "Villains in Varied Eras," in *New York Herald Tribune Book Review,* Part II, November 16, 1952, p. 18.

Mr. Trease, an English ex-teacher and soldier, is known here chiefly for a fine biography of Raleigh, and an excellent Elizabethan adventure story *Cue for Treason.* In England, he is also known for an interesting book on boys' reading. His new book is set in the Athens of 400 B.C. and will appeal to both boys and girls over twelve. It

is humorous, exciting, and cleverly informative about the era when the wars with Sparta were drawing to a close. The hero is a young playwright, a boy who has just put on the tunic of a man. He dictates his play in secret to an interesting girl who finally rescues him from the villains. The climax shows why the play had to be kept secret: it was the means of his managing the exit of the traitors from Athens.

Some young people who might not be easily lured into a book with this ancient setting will like it if they take one glimpse at the conversation, which is modeled on fairly colloquial, and very lively, boys' talk of our time.

### *MESSAGE TO HADRIAN* (1956; British edition as *Word to Caesar*)

### Pauline Winnick

SOURCE: A review of *Message to Hadrian,* in *Library Journal,* Vol. 81, No. 11, June 1, 1956, p. 1553.

Incident-packed, swiftly paced historical novel in which a young Roman orphan travels from Britain to Rome with a letter to the new emperor which can exonerate his exiled poet-friend of false charges framed by the powerful leader of Rome's underworld whose agents he must outwit and outrace to effect justice and settle his own future. Written in first person, with today's colloquialisms, this is recommended for junior high and also for slow high school readers.

### *The Junior Bookshelf*

SOURCE: A review of *Word to Caesar,* in *The Junior Bookshelf,* Vol. 20, No. 3, July, 1956, pp. 152–53.

Geoffrey Trease has made his considerable reputation as a writer for the young on a comparatively short list of books. *Word to Caesar* is his first "straight" story for some time, and it is possible at this stage to appreciate in a clearer way what his contribution is to the improvement discernible in children's historical novels over the last few years, an improvement with which his own name has been associated. The fact is, compared with the nearly incomparable Rosemary Sutcliff, Geoffrey Trease is no more than adequate. *Word to Caesar* happens to be set in Roman Europe at the time of the accession to the imperial throne of Hadrian; although equipped with an expertly applied veneer of special knowledge, it is just a straight adventure story; the young Paul, whose father commands a small Roman garrison in the Lake District, is the sole survivor of a barbarian assault upon the district. He escapes on a ship bound for Chester, and is taken up *en route* by an exiled Roman poet, Severus. The villain—double dyed—is Calvus, whose motives for stopping Paul from getting back to Hadrian with his message to the emperor which would remove the stain from Severus' reputation and rehabilitate him in Rome, are never very clearly stated. There are a lot of hairbreadth escapes, some swimming in the Rhône and elsewhere, and a number of overheard conversations. The story is told at a good pace, and compared with many established writers, Geoffrey Trease conveys a decently *adult* tone in the telling of it. But this is no more than entertainment for a wet afternoon, and it is unlikely to inspire the young with a vision of the past to sustain them in the present, as can Miss Sutcliff's recent books.

### Margaret Sherwood Libby

SOURCE: A review of *Message to Hadrian,* in *New York Herald Tribune Book Review,* July 8, 1956, p. 9.

Livelier reading than the very good **Silken Secret** and **Web of Traitors** and yet as excellent in local color, this book will attract and hold the interest of readers of eleven and twelve as well as the slow (and the good) older readers. If they like historical novels and have become fascinated by the puzzle of the "lost legion" by reading Rosemary Sutcliff's *Eagle of the Ninth* or a tale or two from *Puck of Pook's Hill,* so much the better. The plot is simple and exciting from the surprise assault and massacre at the border fort and young Paul's rescue by an exiled poet, Lucius Fabius Severus, through a merry chase as Paul crosses Gaul to Italy and the Sabine hills, threatened constantly by a dangerous conspirator who is determined to prevent the delivery of Severus' message to Hadrian. Paul relates his own adventures, some plausible, some a bit too lucky, but it all adds up to a good tale.

### Chad Walsh

SOURCE: "Road to Rome," in *The New York Times Book Review,* August 12, 1956, p. 24.

If its hero and narrator were not a youth in his mid-teens, this tale might pass for an adult novel. The characterizations, though not enmeshed with psychological subtleties, are crisp and clear; the plot deals with the adult world of war, chicanery and political intrigue. Mr. Trease compliments his readers by assuming that their eyes are turned toward the problems and passions of the big world.

The story begins in second-century Britain, a lightly Romanized land, always fearful of uprisings by the painted tribes. Paul, the narrator, is the son of an Army officer who is killed in one of those attacks. The wounded lad is befriended by a Roman poet who has been unjustly exiled and, in turn, Paul attempts to reach Rome and the ear of Hadrian to right the injustice. It is a long, eventful road he travels, encountering crooks, chariot racers and gladiators. The contrasting scenes of provincial Britian and imperial Rome are deftly done and the reader soon feels at home in a civilization often amazingly familiar to us of the twentieth century—with its gangsters and timid legalists. A smartly paced, solid, well-constructed novel.

### Olive Dean Hormel

SOURCE: "Little Davy Grows and a Cat Thinks of Tigerhood," in *The Christian Science Monitor,* September 6, 1956, p. 4.

Paulus is only sixteen when he loses his father in an uprising of Britain's native tribes against Caesar's legions, and real adventure begins for him as he seeks to escape. In the course of events he owes his life to the exiled poet Severus, and when word comes that the Emperor Trajan has been succeeded by Hadrian, who is a friend of Severus, the boy offers to carry letters to Rome begging permission for Severus to return.

Adventure follows upon adventure. But this is much more than a tale of adventure, for it presents the detailed life of a little-known period of actual history, combining social customs, architecture and engineering, geography and politics in a smoothly coordinated whole, giving a clear picture of the Roman Empire. One grows with the developing awareness of Paulus. Mr. Trease has written many fine historical novels, of which this is one of the best.

### Nance O'Neall

SOURCE: A review of *Message to Hadrian,* in *Saturday Review,* Vol. XXXIX, No. 46, November 17, 1956, p. 72.

Adventures fall thick and fast in this tale of a fifteen-year-old Briton who carries a plea for pardon from a Roman political exile, languishing in sunless England, to the new emperor, Hadrian, in imperial Rome. Though excitement is the order of the day, Geoffrey Trease, as usual, details his historical background accurately and without any loss of interest. The reader not only feels the magnitude of Rome's empire but also glimpses everyday customs and habits, ranging from Roman baths and chariot races to life on the Sabine farm which was once Horace's.

Boys from twelve to fifteen will not want to put this down. If they do, the girls will pick it up.

### 📖 THUNDER OF VALMY (1960; U.S. edition as Victory at Valmy)

#### The Junior Bookshelf

SOURCE: A review of *Thunder of Valmy,* in *The Junior Bookshelf,* Vol. 24, No. 5, November, 1960, p. 310.

Mr. Trease has a flair and aptitude for writing for the young, particularly in the realms of the historical story. He has amassed here another careful and very varied collection of facts and used them to build a story of the early years of the French Revolution. Mr. Trease peoples his facts with Pierre Mercier a peasant and artist, Madame de Vairmont his teacher and patron, and Pauline his first sister and niece of the unpleasant Marquis de Morsac. There is abundant liveliness, a myriad characters, continual movement, and a good picture and some atmosphere of the times. But Mr. Trease has become almost too clever. He is well practised but his familiarity with his medium appears to have made him a little blasé so that all trips along rather too neatly and slickly, making a story that is easy to read but not particularly easy to remember. It becomes only a brief memory and not a lasting impression, while his characters too, suffer from superficial and conventional treatment. A little more thought and a little more time spent with character and incident would deepen and enrich the very adequate framework, conception, and facts of the story.

### Virginia Kirkus' Service

SOURCE: A review of *Victory at Valmy,* in *Virginia Kirkus' Service,* Vol. XXVIII, No. 21, November 1, 1960, pp. 925–26.

Trease is a master of the historical adventure and here scores another victory. Set in the early days of the French Revolution, this is a tempestuous tale, tragic yet marvelous. The events are experienced through 17-year old Pierre, a peasant boy befriended by an aristocrat who has recognized his artistic talent. Through her he enters a world only glimpsed from outside, where he learns that class is not the sole basis for judging humanity. Madame de Vairmont, his patroness, is deeply concerned in eliminating the outrages levelled against the common people. A wealthy Marquis, on the other hand, cares nothing for people "below him". Trease tells his story against historical events shaded by the author's perceptive appreciation of real nobility, regardless of "breed", and by his handling of historical figures in human terms, not sensationalized. But for his growing and loyal following, Trease's chief characteristic lies in his being a master of suspense. Here credibility and understanding are brought to a period in history too often treated in documentary vein. First rate tale, authentic and sound.

### Ruth Hill Viguers

SOURCE: A review of *Victory at Valmy,* in *The Horn Book Magazine,* Vol. XXXVII, No. 1, February, 1961, p. 58.

Exceptionally real and exciting is the French Revolutionary background of this story. Pierre was one unimportant boy in France's starving masses until the successful artist Madame de Vairmont discovered him drawing pictures with charcoal on a whitewashed wall, took him into her home, and taught him all the art she could. Although Madame had lived among the nobility she had come up from the common poor and had many friends among those working for the good of the people. Pierre found himself in the thick of intrigue: among the nobility while he was painting the portrait of the niece of the

Marquis de Morsac, among the revolutionaries while in the home of his patroness; at one moment in the guardhouse waiting to be escorted to the Bastille, the next riding like a hero on the shoulders of the crowd. There is not a dull moment in this tale, and the characters are convincing even while they are very definitely out of the ordinary.

### R. Bradbury

SOURCE: A review of *Thunder of Valmy,* in *The School Librarian,* Vol. 10, No. 4, March, 1961, p. 362.

For a romantic novelist, the French Revolution has always been a popular period. This novel tells of the early days of the Revolution, seen through the eyes of Pierre Mercier, a young peasant with remarkable artistic talent. This brings him to the notice of Madame de Vairmont, an eccentric but lovable artist, who trains him and then obtains for him a commission from the Marquis de Morsac to paint his niece. Pauline de Morsac is a vivacious young lady, with a mind of her own, and she and Pierre have many exciting adventures. We see the idealists of the revolution, when,

> *'Bliss was it in that dawn to be alive,*
> *But to be young was very heaven.'*

Through young eyes we view the fateful meeting of the States-General, the Tennis Court Oath, the Fall of the Bastille, the sack of the Tuileries, and lastly the battle of Valmy.

The tale is exciting and fast-moving, but why should peasants from near Versailles speak in the homely accents of North country folk in modern England?

### Marion West Stoer

SOURCE: A review of *Victory at Valmy,* in *The Christian Science Monitor,* May 11, 1961, p. 7.

Writing of the Paris of 1791, Wordsworth said, "Bliss was it in that dawn to be alive, But to be young was very Heaven!" Geoffrey Trease, in his present book, shows why such a sentiment was appropriate. The early years of the French Revolution are here described in a swift-paced, suspenseful, bright-colored historical novel. Young Pierre Mercier, a gifted artist—but a commoner—is a protégé of the eccentric Madame de Vairmont. In her home he hears influential men of the day tell about the storm that is brewing, and he is in a position not only to witness but to take part in events as they develop, in Versailles, Paris, and the unquiet countryside. Mr. Trease has a gift for making history come alive, combining authenticity with three-dimensional characters who step briskly through the pages. Boys and girls alike will find entertainment here, and more besides, for the underlying theme shows that in time of conflict, guns are no match for an idea whose time has come.

## FOLLOW MY BLACK PLUME (1963)

### Margaret Sherwood Libby

SOURCE: "On Man's Search for His Past," in *The New York Herald Tribune Books,* New York, August 11, 1963, p. 9.

Courage and its development in man or boy are the theme of this excellent junior novel of an English boy and his tutor in Italy a hundred years ago. Mark Apperley, orphaned quite young, lived in awe and fear of his terrifying old grandmother who had brought him up. The tiny, determined woman dominated Mark's tutor, Mr. Bilibin, too—"a great pink clergyman," who towered over her. Sent on a trip to Italy together as part of Mrs. Apperley's plan to turn Mark into another "eminent, respectable and pompous Apperley" and also to keep him away from possible entanglements with girls, these two have most startling and overwhelming experiences.

Mrs. Apperley had brushed aside the notion that the revolutions in the Italian states could possibly interfere with their educational project. However, almost immediately after their arrival in Rome they found themselves actively involved in Garibaldi's defense of the Roman Republic in 1849, because of Mark's great friendship for an Italian boy and girl, Pietro and Tessa, both ardent patriots. Before Garibaldi's gallant campaign ended in disaster both were war-weary veterans. Mr. Bilibin realized that he was capable of a flaming enthusiasm for other things than ancient Roman monuments, and both he and Mark returned home to face the formidable grandmother certain that they would never be afraid again.

Mr. Trease's historical background (based on Trevelyan) is excellent and expertly handled, as usual. A fine historical tale, good reading for anyone and especially lively for boys in the early teens.

### Margery Fisher

SOURCE: A review of *Follow My Black Plume,* in *Growing Point,* Vol. 2, No. 4, October, 1963, pp. 214–15.

A picture in depth, one scene and many figures, or a panorama full of incident: action concentrated in a short space of time, or a chronicle covering many years. Which will you choose? Geoffrey Trease's new story is a magnificently crowded, compressed study of the year 1849 in Italy, when Mazzini and Garibaldi united in an effort to save the republic of Rome. The French attack on the city and Garibaldi's escape with his fighters are events enough for one story, and indeed the history of this period is intricate and unfamiliar enough to become confusing in hands less accomplished than those of Geoffrey Trease. As always, he emphasises the ideal behind historical event, and out of a bid for national unity he has woven one of his best stories. His hero is an English schoolboy, Mark Apperley, who is sent on the Continent with his tutor, the local curate, and one way and another manages to take part in the fighting—and, incidentally, to learn what it is all about. But it is the curate, Bilibin, who really steals the show, Bilibin who is a real nineteenth century churchman, odd to look at, absorbed in antiquities, shocked when he sees a girl campaigner put on trousers, but hiding under his fussy manner a real courage. Writing in a clear-cut, energetic style, the author selects just those practical details that will give authenticity without stiffness. The information that the reader must have is introduced easily, in the exuberant chat of the war-artist MacWhirter or in Mark's questions to his new friends, Pietro and Tessa, and, now and then, in pieces of straight information from the author. This excellent piece of historical writing is decorated with curious, evasive drawings [by Brian Wildsmith] which will puzzle some children but, to others, will suggest high adventure.

### The Junior Bookshelf

SOURCE: A review of *Follow My Black Plume,* in *The Junior Bookshelf,* Vol. 27, No. 5, November, 1963, p. 297.

Although at times the historical detail threatens to swamp the stirring tale of young Mark Apperley, Geoffrey Trease's skilful control never fails to balance fact and fiction into a satisfying and graceful equilibrium.

Mark, coddled and cosseted by a martinet of a grandmother, goes to Rome with his tutor to benefit his weak chest and study antiquities. Instead of a quiet holiday soaking in sun and admiring ruins, Mark lands in the middle of Garibaldi's ill-fated defence of Rome against the French. Mark is a lad of spirit and friendship with an Italian boy and girl urges him into joining the Student Corps. Soon he is hurled into battle: the sickening slaughter and crippling chaos of war are overtly reported by Mr. Trease and even the death of Pietro, Mark's friend, does not jar. Mark joins Garibaldi in his retreat northwards, an extension of the story which ensures plenty of excitement until the final page.

Apart from the young hero himself who grows in moral and physical stature as he faces crisis and challenge, Mr. Trease has a lively parade of characters: the worldly-wise and cynical artist-journalist, MacWhirter; the sober Bilibin, Mark's tutor, who reveals an unexpected bravado; Colonel Forbes, almost a caricature of the Englishman abroad, but courageous and intrepid in battle; the staunch Garibaldi, in conflict not only with the enemy but also with Mazzini.

### The Times Literary Supplement

SOURCE: "Dramas of Two Continents," in *The Times Literary Supplement,* No. 3222, November 28, 1963, p. 977.

Geoffrey Trease has always had a flair for the slightly unfamiliar theme or a fresh view of the familiar. In *Fol-*

low my Black Plume he takes a molly-coddled orphan boy to Italy to become a spectator, and later an actor, in the first tragic act of the War of Liberation. Garibaldi is a gift to the historical novelist. His courage, his gaiety, above all his panache, are perfect material. In the first clash with the French in Rome "He just laughed and said, 'You must follow my black plume'". One could hardly fail to make such a hero sympathetic and interesting, and Mr. Trease is too skilled in this field to fumble. He makes a good professional job of the mechanics of his story, dovetailing the invented theme of Mark's escape from his grandmother's tyranny with the facts of the defence of Rome and the great retreat most efficiently. In fact, if one is to criticize, one must admit that the book is just a little too slick, too calculated, too professional. One hankers, perhaps perversely, after a touch of inspired amateurism to spark this competent machine into life. Nevertheless this is Mr. Trease's best book for some time; it is moreover well within the range of readers of moderate ability, for whom the greater subtleties and beauty of Herr Bartos-Höppner's book [Save the Khan] are likely to remain hidden by reason of its formidable difficulty.

## THIS IS YOUR CENTURY (1965)

### Virginia Kirkus' Service

SOURCE: A review of This Is Your Century, in Virginia Kirkus' Service, Vol. XXXIII, No. 19, October 1, 1965, p. 1048.

Readable digest history is most difficult to write and the last, explosive half century tremendously difficult for either teachers or writers to bring into focus. The author has accomplished this with a flair seldom encountered in non-fiction prepared especially for younger readers. His descriptions are vivid. (Churchill: "A duke's grandson, he had no aristocracy of feature: according to mood; he resembled a dour bulldog, a cross baby or a mischievous cherub." Hitler: ". . . a tangle of psychological kinks . . .") And, the poets, novelists and artists of the last sixty years are also discussed as part of the total fabric of their times. The flavor of each decade is captured by various devices, as in this London children's chant from the mid '30's— "Hark the herald angels sing!/Mrs. Simpson pinched our King!" WW I, the rise of the dictators, the democracies, the communists, the Spanish Civil War, WW II, Korea and the Cold War are treated to essay chapters which represent an enormous amount of research in both special and popular sources. Handsomely illustrated with contemporary photographs, cartoons and special maps, the margins are wide and often include cropped photographs next to the paragraph they illustrate. There is a list of key dates and an analytical index.

### The Junior Bookshelf

SOURCE: A review of This Is Your Century, in The Junior Bookshelf, Vol. 29, No. 6, December, 1965, pp. 376–77.

It is never so easy to record the history of our own times as it is that of more distant ones; we are too close to the trees to expect to get a clear view of the wood. Mr. Trease is, therefore, to be congratulated on attempting this formidable task, and even more on the considerable measure of success he achieves.

This is a straightforward narrative account of the events of the past sixty-five years, profusely illustrated with telling photographs. It is essentially a political history, social and economic affairs generally being mentioned only so far as they influence events and the photographs often revealing more than the text; and there is little attempt to cover cultural trends or scientific and technical development. Within these limits, however, it is good. Although the author tries to cover the whole world in his survey, he manages to reduce events to an easily assimilated form, and, except for an almost total silence on Central and South America, there seem to be no important omissions, though I felt that he dealt with the Commonwealth too summarily and, in particular, that the sections concerning India and Pakistan were too sketchy. The events of the twenty years since the end of the second World War are given insufficient space in two chapters, which also lack the clarity that is such a good feature of the rest of the book.

It is, I suppose, inevitable that the author is less partial when describing distant events than recent ones, and is more dispassionate in analysing the causes of the first World War than those of the second. What does come out strongly is his hatred of war altogether as he repeatedly points out not only its barbarity but its futility; indeed, he takes the liberal and humane view of events in general.

I like the survey, with which the book opens, of the world at the time of Queen Victoria's death, and its emphasis on the personalities who are to dominate the first half of the century. Its picture of life in a horse-drawn radio-free world is likely to engage the reader's interest from the start. If this flags from time to time as the book goes on, it is less the fault of the author than of his material, which cannot always be presented in terms of personalities or exciting events. There are a number of examples of facts being introduced without sufficient explanation, and such phrases as "If we remember all the Arab countries then subject to the Sultan of Turkey" presuppose a greater knowledge than most readers will probably possess. It is, also, not always easy to compare maps on different pages, but on the credit side is an excellent index.

### The Times Literary Supplement

SOURCE: "Life in the World Today," in The Times Literary Supplement, No. 3328, December 9, 1965, p. 1151.

This is your Century sets out to give British teenagers knowledge of their own times, a pride in their national heritage and a sense of responsibility for the future, and it should be very successful. The narrative is well sustained and exciting, the international scene is skilfully drawn and the thumbnail sketches of the main historical figures are full of life and vigour. The political and economic conditions in the various countries are brought into focus by means of trends and events which young people can grasp. Geoffrey Trease has in his postscript armed himself against middle-aged carpers by predicting their criticism. He himself uses a number of queries to maintain interest. Two more might perhaps be posed: is it correct to say of Gandhi that in any country but India he would have been dismissed as a crank; and did Mountbatten really "impose" independence on India and Pakistan?

## Margery Fisher

SOURCE: A review of *This Is Your Century,* in *Growing Point,* Vol. 4, No. 8, March, 1966, p. 666.

A cavalcade of world history from 1900, emphasising the interdependence of the countries of the world and the complex relationship of social, economic and political event. A boy or girl of twelve and upwards who wants to get an idea of how the modern pattern of life came about can start with this compendious but extremely readable book and pass on to more specialised study. He will learn nothing misleading here, for this is an admirable clear analysis of a complex period, and Geoffrey Trease is just the person, with his thorough and energetic mind, to make such an analysis. His flair for the *arrangement* of fact makes it possible for him to relate people, causes and events without losing sight of the continuity of history or bothering the reader with irrelevancies. As for sheer good writing, the opening description of Victoria's death, or the account of the rise of China, are two examples of many where generalisation and fact are admirably combined.

## THE RED TOWERS OF GRANADA (1966)

### Margery Fisher

SOURCE: A review of *The Red Towers of Granada,* in *Growing Point,* Vol. 5, No. 5, November, 1966, p. 804.

In the reign of Edward I, a boy is driven from his village as a leper, and on his miserable way to Nottingham he helps an elderly Jew attacked by thieves. Solomon is a doctor, who diagnoses Robin's leprosy as a harmless skin disease and takes him into his family—a family well-born but living in ghetto conditions. The Queen falls ill and Solomon is asked to travel to Spain to find a remedy once successful for her complaint. The ensuing adventures are vigorously narrated in a story boldly original in content and most professional in the managing of historical detail.

### The Junior Bookshelf

SOURCE: A review of *The Red Towers of Granada,* in *The Junior Bookshelf,* Vol. 30, No. 6, December, 1966, p. 392.

Geoffrey Trease takes Edward I's expulsion of the Jews from England as the background for his latest novel. The hero, as a suspected leper, is also an outcast and throws in his lot with a Jewish doctor and his family who go to Spain in search of a medicine that will cure Queen Eleanor of her fatal illness. He has many swashbuckling adventures and falls in love before returning to England, too late, with the potion. As is to be expected with this author, the story moves along at a spanking pace and the interest is never allowed to flag. The historical background is sound but unobtrusive, and the problem of racialism lightly touched upon. Charles Keeping's illustrations are as stimulating as ever.

### Kirkus Service

SOURCE: A review of *The Red Towers of Granada,* in *Kirkus Service,* Vol. XXV, No. 4, February 15, 1967, p. 213.

It is 1290, the time of the Expulsion of the Jews from England by King Edward I. One Jewish family, selected for a special mission by the Queen, makes its exile in Spain to find the Golden Essence which she believes can cure her illness. Robin is the devout Catholic who accompanies them, exiled from his own people by the ignorance of a priest who judged him a leper. The villain is Pierre, the Jewish physician's unscrupulous servant who overhears a fragment of conversation and, believing that the doctor is searching for the Elixir of Life, sets two Spanish hoodlums on his trail. Robin's tolerance of religions other than his own grows (somewhat too obviously) as the quest leads him, the family, and several "infidel" friends into danger. The wiliness and money sense of the Jews who have lived for centuries by their wits is one stereotype which casts doubt on how deeply the tolerance has penetrated, and the labelling of all Moors as "infidels" (Robin's choice of a wife, though half-Moorish, is a blue-eyed Christian) is another. The ultimate failure of the quest—the Queen dies in the interim—echoes the failure of the author to convince us either of Robin's change or of the plausibility of the servant's plot. Despite the vividly drawn medieval backdrop and some fast-paced suspense, mangled motives strain conviction.

### Ethel L. Heins

SOURCE: A review of *The Red Towers of Granada,* in *The Horn Book Magazine,* Vol. XLIII, No. 4, August, 1967, p. 477.

In a striking opening scene, set in the year 1290, Robin, a young scholar of Oxford, assumed to be a leper, is officially cast out of church, family, and society. Befriended by Solomon, a learned Jewish physician, Robin soon learns that his "disease" is but a mild skin ailment; he gladly attaches himself to Solomon's household in the Nottingham ghetto and is warmly received by the old physician's lively son and daughter. When the Jews are expelled from England, Solomon, bound for Spain, is summoned secretly to the ailing Queen and asked to obtain for her a rare medicine from a noted Moorish doctor. Slowly the family journeys southward by land and sea to Toledo, then on to Cordova, and finally to Granada. The quest for the elusive Moor and his elixir has many of the elements of a conventional cloak-and-dagger tale, for it is filled with well-engineered adventure, intrigue, and narrow escapes. But the characters are particularly warm and alive, and the story—which moves from the bleak background of medieval England to the high civilization of Spain, with its Moorish, Jewish, and Christian cultures—is told with spirit and brilliance.

## Val Randall

SOURCE: A review of *The Red Towers of Granada*, in *Books for Keeps*, No. 76, September, 1992, p. 11.

A swashbuckling adventure with the bonus of powerfully distinctive illustrative work. In this 1966 re-release, Trease evokes the flavour of thirteenth-century life in England and Spain with this usual meticulous attention to historical detail. Robin of Westood is exiled from his village, wrongly believed to be suffering from leprosy. He falls in with Solomon of Stamford—a Jewish doctor—and his family. When Solomon is summoned by the dying Queen Eleanor to seek the Golden Essence which may save her life, their journey to Spain begins. They are pursued by ruthless villains, compelled to fight for their lives, sheltered by Jewish and Moslem communities. Tension and reader interest are maintained throughout and the two female characters are, refreshingly, more than the mere ciphers too often encountered in this genre.

📖 **THE PHOENIX AND THE FLAME: D. H. LAWRENCE, A BIOGRAPHY (1973; British edition as *D. H. Lawrence: The Phoenix and the Flame, a Biography*)**

### The Times Literary Supplement

SOURCE: "Clear Outline Portrait," in *The Times Literary Supplement*, No. 3719, June 15, 1973, p. 677.

More than forty years ago, young Geoffrey Trease wrote for his old school magazine a brief obituary notice of an old boy who had just died. "To most members of the school his name is probably unknown or at best a byword when censorship is discussed. Lawrence's work is not likely to interest the average boy. . . . Nevertheless . . . the school will be proud of her rebellious son long after those more conventionally honoured are forgotten." With the rebellious son now firmly established as one of the most important writers of the century, the average boy finds himself studying as a set book for O-levels the novel William Heinemann turned down in 1912 as "one of the dirtiest books he had ever read". Far from being uninterested, the boy (or girl) is very often strongly attracted to this writer with his intense belief in the life of the flesh, his distrust of industrialization and intellectuality. Films

of his books have extended this attraction to many who have never read him.

Now Mr Trease, following his excellent life of Byron, has written Lawrence's life for the young. Richard Aldington once recorded the fact that "more books of personal reminiscence were published about [Lawrence] than about any other English author since Lord Byron". Everyone who knew him seems to have written about him, or passed on knowledge and feelings to those who have. Lawrence's own numerous letters have been called "the best of our century". There is a wealth of fascinating material. Any adult who has read at all widely about Lawrence is bound to feel (as people do reading an anthology) the omissions. Mr Trease has left out this strong incident, that revealing episode, even ones with particular appeal to the young. He has, for instance, quoted "The Best of School" but not "Last Lesson of the Afternoon", or the fact that for years after he left teaching Lawrence was haunted by a dream "that I've clean forgotten to mark the register and the class have gone home".

Mr Trease gives some impression of the fearful sadness and problems and jealousies involving the Weekley children, but leaves out the appalling incident when Frieda tracked them down to a house in Chiswick "and crept in by the back door and came up the stairs and came into the nursery" where the girls were with their grandmother and aunts. The grandmother and aunts stormed at her, "and unfortunately the children joined in and told her to go", one of them recalled years later. Of course the book is Lawrence's story, and the incident happened to Frieda; but the whole business of her children was enormously relevant to their relationship, and this small example of ostracism and persecution is central to their experience together. Too often Lawrence had to "stand firm and keep his eyes open", not let go and lose himself as he believed an artist should.

The contradictions and complexities and richnesses are inevitably reduced in a narrative of only 165 pages. But what is left is a memorable chronological account, full of authentic dialogue and telling comment. Perhaps for the first time, freed from cluttering detail and controversy, the bare bones of Lawrence's life stand clearly revealed. "Life itself is the reason for living", Lawrence wrote. Geoffrey Trease's careful delineation of his life can be thoroughly recommended to the young, and to anyone else who has not the stamina for a full-length biography. If the skilful digest whets appetites for something more substantial, so much the better.

### Margery Fisher

SOURCE: A review of *D. H. Lawrence: The Phoenix and the Flame*, in *Growing Point*, Vol. 12, No. 3, September, 1973, pp. 2213–15.

Geoffrey Trease has almost given us a double biography in **The Phoenix and the flame,** for Lawrence and his wife Frieda both stand out large and bold in the pages of his book. This is proper biography. Character, action and creative work are linked with confidence and with no false assumptions. The fact that Geoffrey Trease is a Nottingham man himself gives him material for a brilliant and intuitive reconstruction of Lawrence's childhood, the environment from which novels like *Sons and lovers* and *The white peacock* emerged, the people who serve as models for so many of his characters. With Lawrence one can safely accept identifications and these first chapters in particular send one straight back to the novels, to relive Nottingham at the beginning of the century, to glimpse the man who wrote them through the place that bred him:

". . . Lawrence was a 'scholarship boy' among the sons of professional and business men. The gulf between the classes was wide. A scholarship had a smack of charity about it. The snobbery was not universal—not all boys showed it, and some only because their parents put it into their heads—but he was made aware of it. Once another boy invited him home to tea, discovered that his father was a miner, and then said that it was impossible for them to be friends. Lawrence, however, was sensitive and touchy, and probably did not make the most of what opportunities he had. He merely recalled, in later years, that he had 'made a couple of bourgeois friendships, but they were odd fishes'."

In the latter part of the book the relating of political and national events to private life is skilful but Geoffrey Trease never makes the mistake of overloading the background of his portrait, even if it is a period that seems pretty remote to the present generation. The 'twenties are seen from the point of view of Lawrence's writings and his own influence on our social outlook today is clearly traced, without being over-stated. There is nothing evasive about this biography nor any touch of sensation-mongering. It is a straightforward, sensitive, lucidly written junior biography of a novelist who is making a very direct appeal to young readers today. If they read this book they will see more in the novels than the theories and situations which seem immediately to concern them.

## Kirkus Reviews

SOURCE: A review of *The Phoenix and the Flame: D. H. Lawrence,* in *Kirkus Reviews,* Vol. XLI, No. 21, November 1, 1973, p. 1218.

Trease is so unobtrusively successful in projecting Lawrence and his life that one tends to underestimate his accomplishment—doesn't he have the intense, minutely recalled memoirs of Jessie Chambers (the Miriam of *Sons and Lovers*) and Frieda to draw on, not to mention the recollections of numberless other articulate friends? But this is no patchwork of quotes and synopses. Trease handles the relationship between Lawrence's early life and his fiction with skill and sense, the man's powerful impact on everyone he was involved with (and especially the women) is seen through the beholders' (victims?) eyes, and from his meeting with Frieda to his early death readers too will be caught up and carried along by the fasci-

nation. Trease's commentary on the author's writing is neither rigorous (or textbookishly balanced) criticism nor the kind of plodding summary that prevails in YA author biographies, but just the sort of appreciation that can give youngsters a handle for approaching the works. There is perhaps (for better or worse) less turbulence and pasion than the subject might be expected to inspire and less emphasis on his mystical-romantic exaltation of sex. Trease does however acknowledge the prominence of sex in Lawrence's fiction and philosophy (and its role in his personal relationships), presenting this as a corrective balance to the repression and hypocrisy of the time; he also refers, though almost in passing, to the later misanthropy, the easy tiring of people and places, the identification with Christ. In all, a sound approach to an important writer and compelling figure who has, as Trease points out in his annotated bibliography, inspired much nonsense.

## Paul Heins

SOURCE: A review of *The Phoenix and the Flame: D. H. Lawrence,* in *The Horn Book Magazine,* Vol. L, No. 1, February, 1974, pp. 60–1.

In an introductory note, the author states that although he never met D. H. Lawrence, he "walked the same streets of that English Midland city and the same school corridors, . . . faced some of the same teachers in the same old classrooms." And with quiet sympathy he has told the story of a rebellious but extremely significant twentieth-century novelist who flouted conventions and was—at least, in part—responsible for the current acceptance of an uncensored vocabulary in literature. There is nothing overtly sensational in the presentation of the facts of the novelist's life, although the telling is enhanced by "the authentic word-by-word dialogue all based on the first-hand recollections of people present at the time." Central to the biography is the theme of conflict: between Lawrence's refined Victorian mother and his lusty coal-mining father; between Lawrence and his father; between Lawrence and his mother in relationship to his personal love life; between the ancient world of nature, which Lawrence loved, and the modern world of industrial exploitation, which he hated; and even between Lawrence's respect for marriage and his elopement with another man's wife—Frieda Weekley. The novels and the poetry are not, on the whole, subjected to critical analyses, but are correlated to the events of Lawrence's life; for, at their best, they are not inventions, but embodiments of his feelings as well as of his experiences. As for his ideas, they may have "shocked the world but have now in many respects become part of our everyday lives."

## Margaret Meek

SOURCE: A review of *D. H. Lawrence: The Phoenix and the Flame,* in *The School Librarian,* Vol. 22, No. 1, March, 1974, pp. 58–9.

In the accepted canons of literature Lawrence's reputation stands high with the young even when they know little of the period that produced him and would have cared little for the people that surrounded him. His story is a tangled web of events, ideas, creative power and what Mr Trease calls 'hysterical nonsense'. To pick one's way through it all needs just this astringent sympathy and appraisal. Here we have the passionate warmth of the man. With clarity and restraint we are given those parts of a picaresque life which most illumine the books. The events which shocked the bourgeois system are not evaded nor is the childishness excused. The writer emerges to be better understood. As with Byron and his verse, Geoffrey Trease has given the young a credible hero and fuller awareness of a great novelist.

## POPINJAY STAIRS: A HISTORICAL ADVENTURE ABOUT SAMUEL PEPYS (1973)

### The Times Literary Supplement

SOURCE: "Gunpowder, Treason and Plot," in *The Times Literary Supplement,* No. 3734, September 28, 1973, p. 1117.

At the beginning of *Popinjay Stairs* Denzil Swift, a naval officer paid off for the winter, comes to the aid of Samuel Pepys, Dr Fane and his niece Deborah when they are attacked by highwaymen. Important naval papers are stolen, and Pepys employs Denzil to find them. One highwayman is discovered—dead. Denzil goes on a wild-goose chase after a mysterious playwright, who turns out to be Deb in disguise. Blackmailers approach Pepys and, failing in their purpose, abduct Deb. Denzil rescues both Deb and the papers and we leave him with prospects of promotion and the promise of a wife. Geoffrey Trease skilfully combines plot and sub-plot in this neatly written story, which moves along at a good speed and without skimping authentic detail.

### Judith Aldridge

SOURCE: A review of *Popinjay Stairs,* in *Children's Book Review,* Vol. III, No. 5, October, 1973, pp. 147–8.

Geoffrey Trease is a master of the swift-moving adventure story with an enticing opening and a taut plot which sweeps the reader on to an entirely satisfactory ending. Characters are not developed in depth but are vigorous and credible. Though evocation of the past is not the main purpose, there is sufficient feeling for the period and accuracy of detail for the reader to accept the setting without a sense of 'fancy dress'.

*Popinjay Stairs* goes further into its period, Restoration England, than some historical adventures by involving in a central position an actual person, Samuel Pepys. With the help of Denzil, a paid-off second lieutenant, an old scientist friend Dr. Fane and his handsome daughter Deb, Pepys pursues an adventurer who has stolen important naval documents with which to make his fortune and

discredit Pepys. The incident is not historical but feasible in the light of known events in Pepys life, and the man who appears in Trease's pages is acceptable as the writer of the diary and the reformer of the Navy. Interwoven with this plot is the story of Deb's involvement with the theatre.

Together they make a colourful, exciting story moving from the dark, smelly streets of London's underworld to the very different worlds of the theatre and the river. The narrative is economical and generally effective with an occasional infelicitous cliché—'A pistol barked, spat fire'—which only attracts attention because it is unusual.

Lively weekend and holiday reading.

### Margery Fisher

SOURCE: A review of *Popinjay Stairs,* in *Growing Point,* Vol. 12, No. 6, December, 1973, pp. 2283–86.

[A] light but accomplished adventure in which Pepys is the central figure and the author with casual erudition airs such subjects as Admiralty organisation, the theatre, the Royal Society and the danger of entering the thieves' sanctuary, Alsatia. In a book as good-humoured and swift as this one the reader has neither time nor inclination to notice that he is being taught a good deal about Restoration politics in general and in particular the difficulties of keeping the Navy in good heart. Though the particular plot against Pepys is fictional, it has plenty of basis in fact, and the involvement of a young Naval lieutenant and a red-haired crypto-playwright, niece of a scientist, is plausibly contrived. Geoffrey Trease has written plenty of stories like this but he is such a good storyteller, he mixes talk and action with such a skilful and generous hand, that I hope it will be a long time before he gives up his particular strategy for capturing young readers.

### Marcus Crouch

SOURCE: A review of *Popinjay Stairs,* in *The Junior Bookshelf,* Vol. 37, No. 6, December, 1973, pp. 415–16.

Geoffrey Trease is the best near-misser in the business. All his books are conscientious in research, very adequately written, full of neat character-sketches, thoroughly readable. Yet they never quite take the reader by storm, giving him that revelation of a living past as the very best historical novels do. Perhaps it is because he is too good a theorist. He has worked out what are the ideal contents of a book for children, and puts them into his stories as if he were making a mosaic rather than a novel. His are perhaps the best of formula-stories, but the formula shows up just a little too clearly for the reader's comfort.

Having said this, it must be added that *Popinjay Stairs* is as lively a story as he has given us for a long time. The scene is London after the Great Fire, with spy-mania in the air after the Dutch victory in the Medway and Mr.

Pepys pulling the navy together. A dishonest contractor tries to blackmail Mr. Secretary into giving up his efforts to root out corruption in the Admiral's Office and is suitably frustrated. A lively young feminist has a pseudonymous success in the theatre. There is dirty work in the back streets and on the Thames. Young love is rewarded. The plot is worked out admirably. And yet . . . Is it that Mr. Trease, who was one of the pioneers of the New Literature for children, has lost some of his old faith in his audience? He seems to pull some of his punches in this entertaining but not quite adequate story.

## SONG FOR A TATTERED FLAG (1992)

### Peter Hollindale

SOURCE: A review of *Song for a Tattered Flag,* in *The Times Educational Supplement,* No. 3976, September 11, 1992, p. 9.

In the Author's Note to his novel about the 1989 Romanian uprising, Geoffrey Trease acknowledges his debt to John Simpson's book. *Dispatches from the Barricades.* Many people's memories of two major world events of recent years, first Romania and then the Gulf War, will be shaped by Simpson's brilliant reporting from Bucharest and Baghdad, and by his extraordinary gift for conveying the human reality behind the propaganda and the saturation television coverage. In one memorable broadcast from Romania, Simpson even found a moment of improbable compassion for the fallen Ceausescu.

No such indulgence to the broken Romanian tyranny is offered in Trease's book, but his objective . . . [is] to penetrate beyond the television blandness of so much reporting which falls short of Simpson's remarkable standard, and to give a sense of immediate first-hand experience. The question [the] book asks is "What was it like to be young, and to be there?" . . .

In a television programme about his life's work, Trease declared his intention always of inviting his young readers into the adult world, which may be scary in prospect but is exciting and worthwhile. In book after book he has shown young heroes and heroines, ancient and modern, suddenly caught up in political intrigue and crisis, and finding that they have a meaningful adult part to play. This is so with Greg Byrne, half Romanian though brought up in England, when he visits his mother's native country in December 1989, as a violinist in a youth orchestra. When the orchestra leaves he finds a pretext to stay behind for a few days, in order to seek out the girl cousin he has never met. Trease's ingenious plotting ensures that Greg is in the right place at the right time for the revolution's key events, first in the northern city of Timisoara where the revolution began, and then in Bucharest for its climax.

The novel is partly documentary, an account of one of modern history's great moments, but the vivid sense it gives of history on the turn, of the localised confusion which is then and there redrawing world political maps, comes from Greg's nerve and determination and observant eye for detail, and from our awareness of the many-faceted nature of his life. In the midst of crisis he is still a violinist, still an adolescent falling for his attractive cousin Nadia. Even when threatened by Securitate menace, life has a richer texture than politics alone can give it.

### Marcus Crouch

SOURCE: A review of *Song of a Tattered Flag,* in *The Junior Bookshelf,* Vol. 56, No. 5, October, 1992, pp. 212–13.

Geoffrey Trease was always quick to see contemporary parallels in an episode of history, and here he is writing an historical novel about near-enough present-day events. Greg, whose mother is Romanian, goes on tour with his youth orchestra—he shares a modest desk among the second fiddles—and finds himself playing the final concert in Bucharest before Ceausescu and the top hierarchy of the Communist Party. Here is a chance, he sees, to look up the cousin who had made a cautious approach to his mother. In the next few days he witnesses, and involuntarily takes part in, a revolution. Without pushing credibility too far Mr. Trease makes his young hero see the major events of these thrilling and dangerous times and he reports them clearly and intelligently. At the same time Greg gets to know and admire Nadia, the cousin he has discovered, and through her discovers something of domestic life under a dictatorship. The portrait of Josef, the middle-of-the-road worker who wants no trouble, is particularly convincing. The story ends with the execution of the Ceausescus and the opening-up of Romania to the world. It would have been good to see Greg reacting to reconstruction and Nadia playing her part in rebuilding her country, but Mr. Trease is of course right to finish on a high note. A sequel would not be out of place.

Mr. Trease has always told a good story. His narrative technique is immaculate, and he demonstrates here his mastery of timing. The balance between great events and personal ones is well maintained. Most of all he shows involvement in his theme, and takes the reader with him into the perilous streets and squares of a city at breaking point. This seems to me his best book in recent years, with all the old political commitment directed with a deeper understanding and restraint.

### Adrian Jackson

SOURCE: A review of *Song for a Tattered Flag,* in *Books for Keeps,* No. 77, November, 1992, p. 27.

Even such recent history as this may not be part of young readers' memories, but the images of the overthrow of the Ceausescus in Romania are still vivid in my mind and Trease skilfully shows the way fiction can get inside documentary fact in a way that gives it powerful new life. The brooding sense of fear, the enormous bravery of people resisting that fear and then the bullets, is very well conveyed. There's a marvellous sense of relief and release as the Ceausescus are removed from power. Hindsight makes the happy ending of fiction seem shallow, but it's an excellent book.

**Sue Rogers**

SOURCE: A review of *Song for a Tattered Flag,* in *The School Librarian,* Vol. 40, No. 4, November, 1992, p. 160.

A recent political event comes vividly alive as Geoffrey Trease brilliantly captures the tension, emotion and turbulence of the Romanian Uprising of December 1989. The story is a fast-moving and dramatic adventure featuring Greg and Nadia as the main characters. Greg is an eighteen-year-old British musician on a tour of Eastern Europe with his youth orchestra. At the last concert in Bucharest he meets Ceausescu and is overwhelmed by the fear the Dictator and his Securitate inspire in the people. Nadia, who is Romanian, is a distant cousin of Greg's and he stays on with her after the orchestra has departed. Tension builds as Greg and Nadia are involved in the first uprising in Timisoara and the book concludes with the dramatic scenes of the final overthrow of Ceausescu in Bucharest.

Twelve-to sixteen-year-olds and many adults will enjoy this wonderful novel.

**Val Randall**

SOURCE: A review of *Song for a Tattered Flag,* in *Books for Keeps,* No. 84, January, 1994, p. 10.

Another good value, high-quality offering from Walker Books and the vintage pen of Geoffrey Trease. Nick, visiting Bucharest with his youth orchestra, contacts a long-lost cousin and becomes involved in the events leading to the downfall of Nicolae Ceausescu.

Trease communicates the tension and fear generated in ordinary people by Ceausescu's rule and, though his prose is occasionally rather old-fashioned, he recreates the people's revolution in an utterly believable way.

Both sexes would enjoy this, since hero and heroine play equal parts. . . .

[Many collections] would benefit from the inclusion of such a fascinating and finely detailed novel.

---

Additional coverage of Trease's life and career is contained in the following sources published by Gale Research: *Contemporary Authors New Revision Series,* Vol. 38, *Major Authors and Illustrators for Children and Young Adults, Something about the Author,* Vols. 2, 60, and *Something about the Author Autobiography Series,* Vol. 6.

# CUMULATIVE INDEXES

# How to Use This Index

## The main reference

Baum, L(yman) Frank
1856-1919 ............................. **15**

lists all author entries in this and previous volumes of *Children's Literature Review.*

## The cross-references

See also CA 103; 108; DLB 22; JRDA;
MAICYA; MTCW; SATA 18; TCLC 7

list all author entries in the following Gale biographical and literary sources:

*AAYA* = *Authors & Artists for Young Adults*
*AITN* = *Authors in the News*
*BLC* = *Black Literature Criticism*
*BW* = *Black Writers*
*CA* = *Contemporary Authors*
*CAAS* = *Contemporary Authors Autobiography Series*
*CABS* = *Contemporary Authors Bibliographical Series*
*CANR* = *Contemporary Authors New Revision Series*
*CAP* = *Contemporary Authors Permanent Series*
*CDALB* = *Concise Dictionary of American Literary Biography*
*CLC* = *Contemporary Literary Criticism*
*CLR* = *Children's Literature Review*
*CMLC* = *Classical and Medieval Literature Criticism*
*DAB* = *DISCovering Authors: British*
*DAC* = *DISCovering Authors: Canadian*
*DAM* = *DISCovering Authors Modules*
    *DRAM: dramatists module*
    *MST: most-studied authors module*
    *MULT: multicultural authors module*
    *NOV: novelists module*
    *POET: poets module*
    *POP: popular/genre writers module*

*DC* = *Drama Criticism*
*DLB* = *Dictionary of Literary Biography*
*DLBD* = *Dictionary of Literary Biography Documentary Series*
*DLBY* = *Dictionary of Literary Biography Yearbook*
*HW* = *Hispanic Writers*
*JRDA* = *Junior DISCovering Authors*
*LC* = *Literature Criticism from 1400 to 1800*
*MAICYA* = *Major Authors and Illustrators for Children and Young Adults*
*MTCW* = *Major 20th-Century Writers*
*NCLC* = *Nineteenth-Century Literature Criticism*
*PC* = *Poetry Criticism*
*SAAS* = *Something about the Author Autobiography Series*
*SATA* = *Something about the Author*
*SSC* = *Short Story Criticism*
*TCLC* = *Twentieth-Century Literary Criticism*
*WLC* = *World Literature Criticism, 1500 to the Present*
*YABC* = *Yesterday's Authors of Books for Children*

# CUMULATIVE INDEX TO AUTHORS

# CUMULATIVE INDEX TO NATIONALITIES

# CUMULATIVE INDEX TO TITLES

Title Index

Title Index

Title Index

Title Index

Title Index

**Title Index**